The Real World of Democratic Theory

The Real World
of Democratic Theory

Ian Shapiro

PRINCETON UNIVERSITY PRESS

PRINCETON AND OXFORD

Copyright © 2011 by Princeton University Press

Published by Princeton University Press, 41 William Street, Princeton, New Jersey 08540
In the United Kingdom: Princeton University Press, 6 Oxford Street, Woodstock, Oxford-
shire OX20 1TW

press.princeton.edu

Library of Congress Cataloging-in-Publication Data
The real world of democratic theory / Ian Shapiro ... [et al.].
    p. cm.
    "Sequel and complement to an earlier volume, Democracy's Place, which was first
published in 1996."
    Includes bibliographical references and index.
    ISBN 978-0-691-09000-9 (hardcover : alk. paper) — ISBN 978-0-691-09001-6
(pbk. : alk. paper) 1. Democracy. I. Shapiro, Ian.
JC423.R325 2011
    321.8—dc22

    2010007999

British Library Cataloging-in-Publication Data is available
This book has been composed in Sabon & Gill Sans
Printed on acid-free paper.
Printed in the United States of America
10 9 8 7 6 5 4 3 2 1

For Douglas Rae

Contents

Preface

THIS BOOK is conceived as a sequel and complement to an earlier volume, *Democracy's Place*, which was first published in 1996. As with the earlier collection, its chapters were originally written as freestanding essays over the preceding decade, and they range from theoretical arguments to concrete applications. I have added an extended introduction in which the essays are located in the changing, not to say tumultuous, global political climate since 1996—during which democracy's fortunes have ebbed and flowed in dramatically unforeseeable ways. I also spell out the connections among the essays, and their relations to my larger ongoing endeavor to develop an appealing democratic account of justice. The volume is intended to stand on its own as an integrated whole, but it is also, therefore, an interim report on what Isaiah Berlin might have described as the journey of an aspiring hedgehog.

If the reader concludes that I am chasing my shadow, or that the journey is for some other reason hopeless or ill-conceived, this should not reflect adversely on the many people who have tried to help me along the way. Foremost among these are my coauthors of chapters 3, 4, and 6: Courtney Jung, Ellen Lust, Mayling Birney, and Michael Graetz. They gave generously of their time in the revising of our joint contributions. Needless to say, none of them is implicated in the chapters of which they are not coauthors or in my larger enterprise—of which they might not approve.

I will not try to list the many people who have commented helpfully on the particular essays in forums too numerous to recall. You know who you are. I should, however, mention those who have read part or all of the present manuscript and offered much good advice, some of which has been heeded. These are Lisa Ellis, David Mayhew, Nicoli Nattrass, Andrzej Rapaczynski, Frances Rosenbluth, David Runciman, and Sue Stokes. Their help is thankfully acknowledged, and where their advice has been ignored the usual caveats apply. Thanks are also due to Ian Malcolm, who continues to do his best to keep the hedgehog on its path. I owe an enormous debt of gratitude to Ana Arjona, who is the Platonic form of a research assistant. She has worked tirelessly on this project with amazing efficiency, dedication, and good cheer while teaching, writing her dissertation, and raising her twins—not to mention responding swiftly to a host of other research tasks on my behalf. The funds to employ her were provided by Yale University, whose support is noted with appreciation. These acknowledgments would be incomplete if I did not take due account of Lauren Lepow's skill, unsurpassed, in my experience, as a manuscript editor.

The chapters that follow found their way into the present volume by various routes. Chapters 4 and 5 are previously unpublished in English, though an earlier version of chapter 5 has appeared in Spanish as "Contención y cosmopolitismo democrático," in *Foro Internacional* 193, vol. 48, no. 3 (2008). The other chapters have all been published in English in some form, though most have been substantially revised for the present purpose. Chapter 1 originally appeared in an edition of Locke's *Two Treatises of Government* and *A Letter Concerning Toleration* that I edited for the Yale University Press series Rethinking the Western Tradition in 2003. Chapter 2 builds from a review essay on recent work in democratic theory that first appeared in *Government and Opposition* 43, no. 3 (Summer 2008). An earlier version of chapter 3 appeared in *Politics and Society* 33, no. 2 (June 2005). It has been revised and updated; changes include the addition of a new afterword dealing with developments in South Africa, the Middle East, and Northern Ireland over the past five years. A shorter version of chapter 6 first appeared in the *National Tax Journal* 59, no. 3 (September 2006), and was expanded into something close to its present form in *Divide and Deal: The Politics of Distribution in Democracies,* edited by Ian Shapiro, Peter Swenson, and Daniela Donno (New York: New York University Press, 2008). Chapter 7 is adapted, updated, and expanded from my introduction to *Abortion: The Supreme Court Decisions*, 3rd ed. (Indianapolis: Hackett, 2007). It has not appeared in English in its present form, though a similar version appeared in Spanish as "El derecho constitucional del aborto en los Estados Unidos," in *Doxa* 31 (2008). Chapter 8 combines and builds from replies to critics of *Democratic Justice* and *The State of Democratic Theory* that appeared, respectively, in *The Good Society* 11, no. 2 (June 2006), and *Critical Review of International Social and Political Philosophy* 8, no. 1 (March 2005). Copyright material has been reprinted with appropriate permission.

The Real World of Democratic Theory

Revisiting *Democracy's Place*

DEMOCRACY IN 1996

Democracy's Place appeared in 1996, a heady moment for democracy's partisans in many parts of the world.[1] Five years had passed since the Soviet Union's collapse, long enough for people to believe that it was real. The Russian disenchantment with the West that would follow NATO's bombing of Kosovo and subsequent expansion lay in the future, as did the creeping revival of Russian authoritarianism that we have witnessed in recent years. It was not yet clear that most of the Asiatic republics of the former Soviet Union would fail to replicate the comparatively easy Eastern European transitions to democracy. Russia was still giddy in the wake of the dramatic transition from Gorbachev to Yeltsin, and much of its population remained in the magnetic thrall of Western consumerism. China might not yet be showing signs of a political transition, but there, too, central planning was giving way to market capitalism—fostering much speculation that democratization might not be far behind. Democracy seemed to be on the march in the former communist world.

No less striking than the largely bloodless transitions in the former Soviet bloc were developments in southern Africa. Against all predictions, in 1990 F. W. de Klerk's apartheid government had freed all political prisoners, unbanned the African National Congress, and agreed to the elections that installed Nelson Mandela as president in April of 1994. Close observers of South Africa's spiraling economic and political decline during the 1980s would have given heavy odds against any such outcome—had it occurred to anyone to ask. By December of 1996 the provisional constitution had been replaced by a permanent one that was widely recognized as one of the most progressive constitutions in the world, though not before it had been sent back to Parliament for a variety of changes by the new Constitutional Court. This procedural probity suggested that the new democratic South Africa would be respectful of the rule of law. To the north, the appalling

[1] Ian Shapiro, *Democracy's Place* (Ithaca: Cornell University Press, 1996).

Rwandan genocide that had killed more than 800,000 people had subsided. Robert Mugabe, who had just been reelected president of Zimbabwe, was yet to atrophy into the corrupt dictator he would become. South African deputy president Thabo Mbeki declared that an African Renaissance was in the offing.[2]

If democracy and the rule of law were entrenching themselves in the postcommunist world and South Africa, the picture elsewhere was more mixed. In the Middle East, promising negotiations between Israel and the PLO that had produced the Oslo Accords on a two-state solution in August of 1993 had been blown apart by Yitzhak Rabin's assassination at the hands of a disgruntled right-winger in November of 1995. In 1996 it was not yet clear how big the missed opportunity was, or how badly the conflict would deteriorate into a second major intifada five years later and massive escalations of conflicts with Hezbollah in Lebanon and Hamas in Gaza and the West Bank after that. The huge loss of American prestige across the region that would follow George W. Bush's invasion of Iraq in March of 2003 had not yet occurred, making it still plausible that, with a bit of luck, the United States might yet broker a settlement.

Latin America also presented a mixed picture for democrats in 1996. The breakdown of democracy across the region in the 1960s and 1970s had been followed by an era of redemocratization, despite the "lost decade" of economic crises in the 1980s. There had been democratic transitions in several Southern Cone countries as well as El Salvador, yet authoritarian legacies had not been entirely dispatched. Augusto Pinochet, the architect of Chile's 1973 coup and then its authoritarian dictator, was still commander-in-chief of the army—a position he would retain until retiring to the Senate in 1998. In 1992 Peruvian president Alberto Fujimori had shut down Congress, suspended the constitution, and purged the judiciary. Fujimori had nonetheless been comfortably reelected with almost two-thirds of the vote in 1995—a less than prepossessing development for those who see fidelity to the rule of law as integral to democracy's health in the longer run. There was cause for cautious optimism in Venezuela. Hugo Chavez's coup attempt had failed in 1992, and his election as president lay in the future. In Mexico, fragile democratic institutions had survived the 1994 peso crisis, suggesting that Mexican democracy might be more deeply rooted than many had thought. This supposition would turn out to be correct in the 2000 election. Outgoing President

---

[2] Thabo Mbeki, "I Am an African," speech on the adoption of the South African Constitution Bill, May 8, 1996, http://www.polity.org.za/article/mbeki-i-am-an-african-adoption-of-sa-constitution-bill-1996-08051996-2004-01-01 [07-22-2009].

Zedillo conceded his Institutional Revolutionary Party's defeat, leading the PRI voluntarily to relinquish power after more than seven decades in office.

Democratic political competition seemed to be alive and kicking in many older democracies in 1996. Italy and Japan had recently instituted major electoral reforms, replacing systems that had been widely seen as fostering corruption with mixed systems combining proportional representation and single-member districts. New Zealand had adopted a similar system, with an eye to producing governments that better reflect voters' preferences.[3] In the United States two years earlier the Democrats had lost control of both houses of Congress for the first time in a generation, yet Bill Clinton comfortably defeated Bob Dole in 1996 and returned to the White House. In Britain, the corrupt and dispirited Tories whom John Major had inherited from Margaret Thatcher were on their last legs, and a charismatic new leader of a reinvented Labour Party was waiting in the wings. Long-dominant monolithic parties had lost their political monopolies in Japan and India. It seemed that political scientists might soon be able to dispense with the rather awkward category of "single-party dominant democracies" that had been invented to accommodate them. For those who saw political competition and alternation in power as a vital ingredient of democratic politics, this was poignant—if anecdotal—evidence of democratic vitality.

More systematic data were also encouraging. By 1996 there were 81 democracies in the world, up from 59 at the start of the decade—a number that had itself represented a substantial recent increase. From 1960 through the mid-1980s democracies in the world had numbered in the 30s. Though this was close to a doubling of the 19 democracies that existed at the end of World War II, the number of democracies in the world seemed to have plateaued. In 1984 Samuel Huntington expressed the conventional wisdom in asserting that it was unlikely that many more democracies would come into being.[4] By 1996 events had proved Huntington clearly wrong. Not only had the number of democracies doubled; for the first time democracies outstripped nondemocracies. In 1974, when there were 36 democracies, 100 countries were nondemocracies. The number of nondemocracies had fallen to 85 by 1990, whereas democracies had risen to 59. The balance had shifted by 1996 to 79 nondemocracies as against 81 democracies. Most of the world's population continued

---

[3] See Takayuki Sakamoto, "Explaining Electoral Reform: Japan versus Italy and New Zealand," *Party Politics* 5, no. 4 (1999): 419–38.

[4] Samuel Huntington "Will More Countries Become Democratic?" *Political Science Quarterly* 99, no. 2 (1984): 193–218.

to live under nondemocratic regimes, but for the first time most political systems were democracies.[5]

Pyrrhic Victory?

Despite democracy's recent triumphs and what plausibly seemed to be encouraging trends, democracy's partisans had cause for concern in 1996. It was far from clear how much difference democracy actually made in people's lives. Notably more consequential than democracy seemed to be the growing pressure on governments, of whatever stripe, to embrace an emerging economic orthodoxy known as neoliberalism. Implementing neoliberal policies involved granting unprecedented authority to technically well-schooled economic elites who promised to liberate their economies from stultifying regulators and open them to the widely touted benefits of free trade. With communism off the table everywhere except in such vestigial outposts as Cuba and North Korea (and somewhat ambiguously in China), it was becoming virtually impossible for governments to resist the pro-market, antiregulatory, and antiredistributive policies that traveled under the neoliberal banner. Poverty, inequality, and the inherited injustices that so often motivate people to demand democracy would be tackled, on this view, but improvements in these areas would be by-products of the rising tide that neoliberal policies promised.

Technocratic faith in the prevailing market wisdom was ascendant. Political economists and prognosticators of many ideological stripes were voluble about the virtues of "shock therapy" in the transition from communism to capitalism, despite its manifest human costs.[6] Indeed, one

[5] These data are taken from "Polity IV Project: Political Regime Characteristics and Transitions, 1800–2007," http://www.systemicpeace.org/polity/polity4.htm [06-02-2009]. Following convention here, a country is considered a democracy if it has a score of 6 or higher on the Polity scale.

[6] Jeffrey Sachs and Wing Thye Woo, "Structural Factors in the Economic Reforms of China, Eastern Europe, and the Former Soviet Union," *Economic Policy* 9, no. 18 (April 1994): 102–45; Jeffrey Sachs, "Privatization in Russia: Some Lessons from Eastern Europe," *American Economic Review* 82, no. 2 (1992): 43–48; David Lipton and Jeffrey Sachs, "Creating a Market Economy in Eastern Europe: The Case of Poland," *Brookings Papers on Economic Activity* 1 (1990): 75–133; Juan Antonio Morales and Jeffrey Sachs, "Bolivia's Economic Crisis," in *Developing Country Debt and Economic Performance*, ed. Jeffrey Sachs, vol. 2 (Chicago: University of Chicago Press, 1990), pp. 159–266; and Janos Kornai, *The Road to a Free Economy* (New York: W. W. Norton, 1990). For a discussion of other neoliberal economists of the period, see Ganez Venelin, "The 'Triumph of Neoliberalism' Reconsidered: Critical Remarks on Ideas-Centered Analyses of Political and Economic Change in Post-Communism," *East European Politics and Societies* 19, no. 3 (2005): 343–78.

influential commentator from the political left had argued that market reforms should be rammed through before democratization, lest those harmed by the reforms deploy their newfound political strength to block them.[7] This was at a time when the widely touted "East Asian miracles" had occurred either in authoritarian countries like Hong Kong, Singapore, South Korea, Indonesia, Thailand, and Taiwan, in the partial democracy in Malaysia, or in the dubiously democratic Japan that had been continuously governed by the Liberal Democratic Party since its founding in 1955. True, these economies had often been protectionist, and they were managed by activist states whose decisions bred major market distortions. But the costly dimensions of these choices would not become evident until the Asian bubble burst later in the decade.[8] In 1996, the name of the game was economic growth, to which democracy was widely seen as at best irrelevant and quite possibly an irritant.

Developing country governments, keen to elide local opposition to the policies that might attract international investors, went so far as to ask the IMF and World Bank to tie their hands with even more draconian austerity packages than were deemed necessary by those institutions.[9] The new ANC government in South Africa began distancing itself from its frankly redistributive Reconstruction and Redevelopment Programme (RDP) almost as soon as it took office in 1994. By 1996, RDP had been unceremoniously dumped in favor of GEAR. The order of the nouns in its title made GEAR's neoliberal priorities clear. *Growth, Employment, and Redistribution* meant reversing RDP's logic (which had been couched in a pastiche of post-Marxist and Keynesian rhetoric) in favor of pro-growth incentives for market actors. These, it was said, would produce employment that would in turn generate redistribution.[10]

By the mid-1990s a comparable dynamic had been observed in Latin American country after Latin American country. Pro-labor and populist governments had come into office in the late 1980s in Argentina, Mexico, and Venezuela. Once in power, they quickly reversed their protectionist and interventionist policies, opened their economies internationally, and

[7] Adam Przeworski, *Democracy and the Market* (Cambridge: Cambridge University Press, 1991), pp. 136–87.

[8] They were, for example, entirely opaque to Joseph Stiglitz at the time. See his "Some Lessons from the East Asian Miracle," *World Bank Research Observer* 11, no. 2 (August 1996): 151–77, http://wbro.oxfordjournals.org/cgi/reprint/11/2/151 [06-09-2009].

[9] See James R. Vreeland, *The IMF and Economic Development* (Cambridge: Cambridge University Press, 2003).

[10] Asghar Adelzadeh, "From RDP to GEAR: The Gradual Embracing of Neo-Liberalism in Economic Policy," *Transformation* 31 (1996): 66–95. As Nicoli Nattrass has pointed out to me, GEAR was never fully implemented.

reduced state intervention.[11] True, there had been some resistance to the wave of neoliberal policies. Venezuela's Carlos Andrés Pérez had faced two coup attempts in 1992 before being impeached the following year. In Ecuador, President Abdalá Bucaram's austerity measures led to street riots that forced him from office in 1996. There was considerable social unrest in parts of Argentina. But for the most part the reversals had been accepted as necessary. Indeed, many of the leftist governments that engaged in radical policy-switches to implement them were subsequently reelected.[12]

Nor was the ascendant faith in neoliberalism limited to the postcommunist and developing worlds. In Britain and the United States, "New" Labour and the Democratic Leadership Council (DLC) had reinvented their respective parties to an extent that would have been unimaginable a decade earlier. The Labour Party debate had centered on whether Clause IV of its constitution calling for nationalization of the means of production, drafted by Sidney Webb in 1917 and adopted by the party the following year, should be abolished. For the New Labourites, Clause IV was an antediluvian albatross. They saw it as emblematic of everything that had rendered James Callaghan's government vulnerable to defeat by Margaret Thatcher in 1979 and kept Labour, first under Michael Foot's left-wing leadership and then amid the timid tinkerings of Neil Kinnock and John Smith, in the political wilderness ever since. When Tony Blair ascended to the Labour leadership in 1994, it was clear that Clause IV, which he had long opposed, was on the way out.

On the western side of the Atlantic, the Democrats' historic drubbing in the 1994 congressional elections had empowered the DLC, which Bill Clinton had led for the two years prior to his election as president in 1992. Any doubts about where the New Democrats were heading ideologically were put to rest by their majority support for the Personal Responsibility and Work Opportunity Reconciliation Act of 1996, which had been designed, as President Clinton said in his 1996 reelection campaign, to "end welfare as we know it."[13] Aid to Families with Dependent Children, a stalwart of the New Deal enacted in 1935, was abolished. The idea of welfare as an entitlement was replaced by time-limited programs linked

---

[11] See Victoria Murillo, *Labor Unions, Partisan Coalitions and Market Reforms in Latin America* (Cambridge: Cambridge University Press, 2001).

[12] See Susan C. Stokes, *Mandates and Democracy: Neoliberalism by Surprise in Latin America* (Cambridge: Cambridge University Press, 2001).

[13] House Democrats voted for the final bill by a majority of 98 to 97, with two not voting. In the Senate the Democrats divided 25 to 21 with one not voting. Since all Senate Republicans and all but five House Republicans voted for it, the bill passed in a landslide. See "Vote Tallies: 1996 Welfare Amendments," http://www.ssa.gov/history/tally1996.html [06-08-2009].

to work and with a two-year lifetime cap. The market reigned supreme; henceforth people would have to sink or swim in it. The toothless rage that erupted on the left of the Democratic Party confirmed, to the New Democrats, that they were on the right track.[14]

In politics few things beat success, or at least the appearance of success. It was far from clear in 1996 what tangible results, if any, would stem from the attempts by New Labour and the New Democrats to reinvent themselves. Tony Blair's electoral ascendancy lay in the future, and the Democrats would be kept at bay on Capitol Hill for the next dozen years. But it was testimony to the perceived success of the emerging neoliberal orthodoxy that Blair and Clinton had thrown their lots in with it. On coming into office President Clinton had created a new National Economic Council to direct economic policy out of the White House under the supervision of Robert Rubin, a man who had spent the preceding twenty-six years rising through the ranks at Goldman Sachs. First at the NEC and then as treasury secretary, Rubin partnered with Federal Reserve chairman Alan Greenspan (whom Clinton had inherited from Ronald Reagan and reappointed) to reduce deficits, regulation, and trade barriers. The Greenspan-Rubin approach gained credibility as the deficits that had called forth doomsday scenarios from groups like the Concord Coalition in the early 1990s began trending downward—from above 4.5 percent of GDP in 1992 to below 1.5 percent by 1996, and a projected surplus (which did, indeed, eventuate) two years later.[15] Market deregulation was a general motif on the legislative front during the Clinton years. NAFTA passed in 1993 and was signed into law in the face of opposition by majorities of Democrats in both houses of Congress.[16] Telecommunications deregulation followed three years later[17]

[14] See Barbara Vobejda and Dan Balz, "President Seeks Balm for Anger over Welfare Bill," *Washington Post*, August 22, 1996, p. A1, http://www.washingtonpost.com/wp-srv/politics/special/welfare/stories/wf082296.htm [06-08-2009].

[15] See usgovernmentspending.com, http://www.usgovernmentspending.com/federal_deficit_chart.html [06-08-2009].

[16] The House of Representatives approved NAFTA on November 17, 1993, by a vote of 234 to 200. Democrats opposed the bill with 156 votes in favor and 102 against it. http://clerk.house.gov/evs/1993/roll575.xml [12-22-2009]. The Senate approved the bill a few days later, with 61 to 38 votes. Democrats cast 28 votes against it and 27 supporting it. http://www.senate.gov/legislative/LIS/roll_call_lists/roll_call_vote_cfm.cfm?congress=103&session=1&vote=00395 [12-22-2009].

[17] The Telecommunications Act was approved in 1996 in the House of Representatives by a vote of 414 to 16, and in the Senate by a vote of 91 to 5. "The Fallout from the Telecommunications Act of 1996: Unintended Consequences and Lessons Learned," *Common Cause Education Fund Report*, May 9, 2005, http://www.commoncause.org/atf/cf/%7B8A2D1D15-C65A-46D4-8CBB-2073440751B5%7D/FALLOUT_FROM_THE_TELECOMM_ACT_5-9-05.PDF [12-22-2009].

and banking deregulation three years after that—both with bipartisan backing.[18]

By 1996 the Clinton administration was also taking bold steps to advance neoliberal policies internationally. Its strong support for replacing the half-century-old General Agreement on Tariffs and Trade with the World Trade Organization (dedicated to promoting growth through free trade) in 1995 made clear that the U.S. agenda to liberalize world trade went well beyond regional agreements like NAFTA. The administration's management of the Mexican currency crisis cemented its reputation for deft handling of the global macroeconomy. Contrary to the apocalyptic predictions of Republicans who had fought the $20 billion in cash and loan guarantees the United States offered as part of a $50 billion international plan to forestall a contagious collapse of the peso, Mexico's Zedillo government repaid the United States three years ahead of schedule.[19] The stock of the neoliberals at the helm was high, along with the Dow Jones Industrial Average—which had more than doubled during Clinton's first term.[20]

The United States and the world were in the midst, and under the spell, of the biggest economic boom in history. Parties, and even political institutions, seemed increasingly irrelevant to the policies that would be adopted to ensure stable growth and full employment. So long as smart pragmatic hands were on the tiller, crises could be managed, if not averted, and prosperity guaranteed. In his 1992 election campaign candidate Bill Clinton had lambasted then president Bush for "coddling aging rulers with undisguised contempt for democracy." Exhibit A was China, from which Clinton insisted that all trade privileges would be withdrawn, if he were elected, pending significant improvements in their human rights record.[21] Yet within four months of taking office President Clinton had unilaterally reversed himself. The administration renewed China's coveted Most Favored Nation (MFN) trading status with the assertion that "we are hopeful that China's process of development and economic reform will be accompanied by greater political freedom." But Clinton left no doubt that China's size and importance for the world

---

[18] The Senate passed the law with 90 to 8 votes. David Leonhart, "Washington's Invisible Hand," *New York Times*, September 26, 2008, http://www.nytimes.com/2008/09/28/magazine/28wwln-reconsider.html [12-22-2009].

[19] David Sanger, "Mexico Repays Bailout by U.S. Ahead of Time," *New York Times*, January 16, 1997, http://www.nytimes.com/1997/01/16/business/mexico-repays-bailout-by-us-ahead-of-time.html?pagewanted=all [06-08-2009].

[20] "Dow Jones Industrial Average (DJIA) History," http://www.nyse.tv/dow-jones-industrial-average-history-djia.htm [06-09-2009].

[21] Jacob Weisberg, "Republicans, Democrats, and China: On Human Rights, Both Parties Talk the Talk but Don't Wok the Wok," *Slate*, June 13, 1998, http://www.slate.com/id/2318/ [06-09-2009].

economy made this move imperative regardless of any domestic political changes.[22] It was almost as if Frederick Engels had been right, after all, that a time would come when politics would be displaced by administration; he just got the mode of production wrong—confusing socialism with capitalism.[23]

If many who had expected democracy to foster meaningful political competition were disappointed in 1996, so were many others who thought democracy would be an instrument for reducing inequality and promoting social justice. The idea that majority rule will lead to egalitarian redistribution has a venerable history. Nineteenth-century elites resisted expansion of the franchise because they feared that widespread democracy would produce exactly that result. Socialists who endorsed the "parliamentary road to socialism" (including Karl Marx toward the end of his life) agreed, hoping that the workers would do through the ballot box what they had not done at the barricades. The intuition both groups shared was that if majority rule is imposed on a massively unequal status quo, then most voters should be expected to favor taxing the rich and transferring the proceeds downward. With their collective action problem solved, the poor would soak the rich. This was formalized in political science via the median voter theorem, which predicts majority support for downward redistribution, given a distributive status quo like that in the advanced capitalist democracies.

Yet one of the great puzzles of modern democracy has been the lack of any systematic relationship between expanding the franchise and downward redistribution. Democracies often redistribute income and wealth, but they do so in a bewildering variety of directions. The generalization, if there is one to be had, seems to be that although democracies spend somewhat more on the poor than do nondemocracies, this spending has little, if any, ameliorative effect on inequality, and it leaves significant proportions of their populations in poverty.[24] This was dramatically the case with the sharp rise in inequality in the United States between the early 1970s and the mid-1990s, even though the Voting Rights Act was passed in 1965 and the voting age was reduced to eighteen in 1971. Real incomes of many toward the lower end of the income distribution fell during this period (or were sustained only through the replacement of

[22] *Weekly Compilation of Presidential Documents* 29, no. 21 (Monday, May 31, 1993): 981–82, U.S. Government Printing Office, http://www.gpo.gov/fdsys/pkg/WCPD-1993-05-31/html/WCPD-1993-05-31-Pg981.htm [05-09-2009].

[23] Engels famously described socialism as a condition in which "the government of persons is replaced by the administration of things," in *Socialism: Utopian and Scientific* (Broadway, NSW, Australia:Resistance Marxist Library, 1999), p. 92.

[24] See David Nickerson, "Do Autocracies Obey Wagner's Law?" (mimeo, Yale University, 2000).

single-earner with two-earner households), and the gap between the poor and the wealthy widened substantially.[25] By 1996 it was clear that the United States had entered a second Gilded Age. Similar, if less extreme, distributive patterns could be observed in other advanced industrial democracies. In much of the developing world, as I have noted, left-wing governments, once in office, were often quick to junk redistributive agendas under the joint pressures of skittish capital markets and neoliberal orthodoxy. Democracy's spread was impressive in 1996, but its impact was questionable.

The Academic Assault on Democracy

Surprising as the absence of downward redistribution might have been to many citizens and activists, it raised few eyebrows in the academy. Scholars of varying ideological stripes had for decades been questioning democracy's capacity to produce rational—or even coherent—decisions, as well as its value in promoting social justice. John Roemer expressed the prevailing academic wisdom when he warned against idealizing democracy by defining it "to consist of all good things" in the same way that, during the 1960s, many on the left had idealized socialism.[26] Rather than encourage people to harbor unrealizable expectations of democracy's benefits, better to get them to alter their expectations. Thus Giuseppe Di Palma insisted that the democratic ideal should be disengaged "from the idea of social progress" if it is to endure, and Huntington advised political leaders to avoid linking their attempts to consolidate democracy to their constituents' demands for social justice.[27]

[25] Andrew Winnick, *Toward Two Societies: The Changing Distribution of Income and Wealth in the United States since 1960* (New York: Praeger, 1989); Carole Shammas, "A New Look at Long-Term Trends in Wealth Inequality in the United States," *American Historical Review* 98, no. 2 (1993): 412–31; and Edward Wolff, "Trends in Household Wealth in the United States," *Review of Income and Wealth* 40, no. 2 (1994): 143–74. For data on the changing absolute and relative shares of income and wealth for the bottom quintile of the population in the United States over the past half century, see Lawrence Mishel, Jared Bernstein, and John Schmitt, *The State of Working America 1998–9* (Ithaca: Economic Policy Institute/Cornell University Press, 2000), pp. 48–51, 261–64.

[26] John Roemer, "Does Democracy Engender Justice?" in *Democracy's Value*, ed. Ian Shapiro and Casiano Hacker-Cordón (Cambridge: Cambridge University Press, 1999), p. 56. See also John Mueller, *Capitalism, Democracy, and Ralph's Pretty Good Grocery Store* (Princeton: Princeton University Press, 2001), which argues that despite democracy's virtues it should not be expected to constrain private markets or reduce inequality.

[27] Guuiseppe Di Palma, *To Craft Democracies: An Essay on Democratic Transitions* (Berkeley and Los Angeles: University of California Press, 1990), p. 23, and Samuel P. Huntington, *The Third Wave: Democratization in the Late Twentieth Century* (Norman: University of Oklahoma Press, 1991), pp. 165–69.

I dissented from this consensus in *Democracy's Place*, arguing instead that democratic legitimacy depends on the possibility democracy holds out of reducing domination. If people who were oppressed under apartheid or communism experience no improvement in their lives brought by the successor democratic regimes, then their allegiance to democracy should be expected to atrophy. And if disadvantaged groups in established democracies find that no government ameliorates their oppression, then they, too, face increasing incentives to defect. The better course for democrats, I argued, is to design and then work to promote variants of democracy that can reduce domination. To be sure, not every form of democracy will achieve that. But some will do better than others. The creative challenge is to discover which they are, and how to move things in their direction. That was the agenda I sketched in the last chapter of *Democracy's Place* and developed more fully in *Democratic Justice*, published in 1999.

My central focus in *Democratic Justice* was on civil institutions; political institutions were dealt with only incidentally. The present volume takes them up directly. Its chapters detail elements of a comprehensive democratic account of public institutions. They deal with its philosophical foundations; its implications for competing theories; how democracies are best created, sustained, and defended in the post–Cold War world; the nature of public opinion and its role in democratic politics; and the relations between majoritarian and nonmajoritarian institutions in democratic systems. As a prelude to describing its contents more fully, I revisit the attacks on democracy that have been put forward by the partisans of reason and justice. The attacks might have seemed increasingly moot, along with democracy itself, in the years of neoliberal ascendency. But the global financial collapse of 2008–9 has called neoliberalism more radically into question than most people could have imagined possible before it happened. This moves democracy—and, a fortiori, democracy's critics—back to center stage.

The friends of reason mounted a double attack on democracy. Most fundamentally, they denied that democratic procedures can be counted on to reflect voters' preferences, insisting that apparent majorities are often the chimerical artifacts of decision rules. They pointed out that deft agenda-setters can manipulate outcomes by taking advantage of features of majority rule first noticed by Condorcet in the late eighteenth century. Even when outcomes are not consciously manipulated, the argument went, they are often arbitrary: had options been considered in a different order, a different outcome could have prevailed as the majority winner. Why, then, accord legitimacy to the results that majority rule actually generates?[28]

---

[28] For standard statements of this view, see William H. Riker, *Liberalism against Populism: A Confrontation between the Theory of Democracy and the Theory of Social Choice*

The alleged lack of legitimacy attending democratic decisions was buttressed by a second assault in the name of reason, to wit, that democracy subverts, undermines, or distorts "normal" outcomes that would occur but for democracy's meddlesome interference. Arbitrary coalitions, masquerading as agents—if not embodiments—of the general will, were only part of the story. Other commonly adduced culprits were powerful lobbies that work their wills through the political process, millionaires and billionaires who fund their own political campaigns and then enjoy disproportionate political influence, campaign contributors who buy influence with checkbooks and credible threats to fund opponents when their agendas are thwarted, "rents" extracted from activists and contributors by venal politicians, uncontrollable bureaucrats with agendas of their own—the list was long.

The "normal" counterfactual—how things would be but for the odious political interference in question—was often specified implicitly, if at all. Usually it was some kind of market shadowing idea: what markets would have produced had they been left to their own devices. This view naturally lent itself to the notion that majority rule should be limited, whether by constitutional courts, independent banks, or other agencies that can be insulated from the insidious influences of electoral politics. The academic agenda to constrain majority rule in the name of rationality thus provided ideological ballast to neoliberalism in the real world. Powerfully ascendant as this orthodoxy had seemed in 1996, it had a long way to run.

AFTER 1996: NEOLIBERALISM VERSUS DEMOCRACY

An important signal and symbol of neoliberalism's accelerating momentum came from Tony Blair's New Labour government the following year. Five days after his landslide victory, Blair declared that the Bank of England would be granted independent authority over interest rates. This was a dramatic move even for a post–Clause IV Labour Party—an early indicator that Blair and his chancellor Gordon Brown would outdo Margaret Thatcher's pro-market orientation of the 1980s. No less remarkable was Parliament's ready acquiescence in the emasculation of its institutional authority. Expecting developing countries to accept technocratic medicine as a condition for IMF loans was one thing. For the mother of all parliaments to cede even operational authority over interest

---

(San Francisco: W. H. Freeman, 1982); and William H. Riker and Barry R. Weingast, "Constitutional Regulation of Legislative Choice: The Political Consequences of Judicial Deference to Legislatures." *Virginia Law Review* 74 (1988): 373–401.

rates was quite another. The Tories flirted with advocating reversal of Labour's move from time to time,[29] but never proposed it in either of their vain attempts—in 2001 and 2005—to unseat Blair's government.

The reason was plain. The American model that combined aggressive deregulation with trade openness and technocratic control of monetary policy seemed unbeatable. Encouraging as things had looked from this point of view in 1996, the major economies took off like rockets for the next dozen years. There were setbacks, to be sure—most notably the bursting of the technology bubble in 2000 and the dislocations resulting from 9/11 the following year. But the global economic juggernaut shrugged them off. In 2003 the U.S. stock market began what would turn out to be the biggest bull market in its history. The Dow peaked comfortably above 14,000 in October of 2007 with worldwide stocks following suit.[30] Economic growth rates were more modest (which should, perhaps, have been recognized as a warning that a colossal new equities bubble was in the making), but strongly robust for almost all the advanced economies.[31] Some countries performed less well, but this was often blamed on their not adopting the full neoliberal diet. For instance, many Western European countries protected wages from the downward pressures wrought by increased capital mobility, and they had to endure higher unemployment rates as a result. But the general trends were impressive by almost any measure. They were dramatized by notable anecdotal cases, with countries like Ireland and Iceland often touted as exemplifying the benefits of heeding the neoliberal consensus.[32]

Nor was economic success limited to the advanced industrial democracies. The late 1990s had been a difficult time in Latin America. Following

[29] See, for example, Andrew Grice and Philip Thornton, "Tory Heading for U-turn on Bank, " *The Independent*, July 27, 1999, http://www.independent.co.uk/news/tory-heading-for-uturn-on-bank-1108930.html [06-24-2009].

[30] Dow Jones Indexes, http://www.djindexes.com/DJIA110/learning-center/ [07-04-2009].

[31] In the United States, GDP growth was above 3 percent per year for six of the dozen years after 1996 and above 4 percent for three of them. It fell below 2 percent only in the 2001–2 recession and in 2008. Comparable statistics could be cited for most of the advanced industrial democracies. (Statistics taken from the U.S. Department of Agriculture—which combines data from the World Bank's World Development Indicators, the IMF's International Financial Statistics, Global Insight, and Oxford Economic Forecasting—and the Economic Research Service.) http://www.ers.usda.gov/Data/Macroeconomics/#HistoricalMacroTables [07-28-2009].

[32] See "Lessons from the Irish Miracle," *Economist*, October 14, 2004, http://www.economist.com/opinion/displaystory.cfm?story_id=E1_PNRGVPG [07-03-2009]; "Tiger, Tiger, Burning Bright," *Economist*, October 14, 2004, http://www.economist.com/surveys/displaystory.cfm?story_id=E1_PNGTDQS [07-03-2009]; and Hannes Gissurarson, "Miracle on Iceland," *Wall Street Journal*, January 29, 2004, http://courses.wcupa.edu/rbove/eco343/040Compecon/Scand/Iceland/040129prosper.htm [07-03-2009].

the Mexican crisis, there had been protracted financial crises in Colombia and Brazil, and a major financial and concomitant political crisis rocked Argentina between 2001 and 2002. But for the most part in the new century Latin American economies benefited from the growth and stability in the world economy. They played ball with the new global orthodoxy, opening up to world trade and shrinking their public sectors. A resurgence of left parties (which would control the presidencies of eleven out of eighteen countries in the region by 2008) brought modest growth in public spending, but no retreat from the world economy.[33]

Thabo Mbeki's prediction of an African Renaissance moved into the realm of the thinkable. Growth rates accelerated to 6 percent a year between 2004 and 2008, placing Africa on an unprecedented par with Latin America. Africa's foreign trade increased dramatically, as did direct foreign investment in the continent. Stock markets began proliferating across sub-Saharan Africa, their capitalization rising from virtually nothing in 1990 to $245 billion by 2009 (excluding South Africa, which has long had a developed stock market).[34] Recovery in most of East Asia was also rapid, Japan being the exception that proved the rule. A decade after the East Asian collapse the World Bank was crowing about a regional renaissance there.[35] East Asia became the global direct foreign investor's destination of choice, achieving annual growth rates in the 9 percent range and lifting hundreds of millions out of poverty. This is to say nothing of the rapid economic advances in India, which provided additional ballast, were it needed, for the perceived wisdom of the new economic model.[36]

It is scarcely surprising that those who raised skeptical questions about the rationalist assault on democracy drew little attention outside the academy in the years following 1996. We were shouting at the wind. The likes of Adam Przeworski and Jeffrey Sachs might have backed away from their earlier flirtations with shock therapy in the face of mount-

---

[33] See Susan Stokes, "Globalization and the Rise of the Left in Latin America" (mimeo, Yale University 2008).

[34] Ethan B. Kapstein, "Africa's Capitalist Revolution," *Foreign Affairs* 88, no. 4 (July/August 2009): 119–20.

[35] Indermit Singh Gill and Deepak Bhattasali, *An East Asian Renaissance* (Washington, DC: The World Bank, 2007), http://books.google.com/books?hl=en&lr=&id=yLPfJx5PEZ4C&oi=fnd&pg=PA43&dq=east+asia+recovery+financial+crisis&ots=_Rt3UV_93A&sig=SU7Kv1bNzgE3APSEPGHO3ZLbtcE [07-23-2009].

[36] According to the World Bank, "China and India have emerged in recent years as drivers of global economic growth, accounting for 2.9 percentage points of the five per cent growth in global output in 2007." "India, China Drivers of Global Economic Growth: World Bank," *Times of India*, April 23, 2009, http://timesofindia.indiatimes.com/NEWS/Business/International-Business/India-China-drivers-of-global-economic-growth-World-Bank/articleshow/4437799.cms [07-28-2009].

ing evidence that its economic benefits were ambiguous at best—scarcely justifying its collateral social costs. But the mainstream of political and economic opinion was in the grip of what seemed increasingly to be the One True Model of the Only Viable Economy. There were no plausible competitors in the world, and none even on the horizon.

The new preoccupation with militant Islam after 9/11 did nothing to change that. Just how much militant Islam had replaced communism as a political threat to the West after the Cold War was hotly debated between Samuel Huntington and the critics of his "clash of civilizations" hypothesis.[37] But it was abundantly clear to anyone who cared to look that, like communism, Islamic fundamentalism lacked a viable political economy. Where Islamic fundamentalists had come to power, in Afghanistan and Iran, the economic results had been disastrous. To the extent that Islamic fundamentalism had a socioeconomic model at all, it was focused on the fourteenth century, not the twenty-first. For all practical purposes, democratic capitalism had won the day, and those with what seemed to be the demonstrated capacity to run it had the bit between their teeth and the wind at their backs.

And the emphasis, increasingly, was on capitalism rather than on democracy. The chattering classes in the West were agog at China's double-digit growth rates—especially when compared with Russia's manifestly corrupt and sputtering transformation.[38] Annual renewals of MFN had

[37] Huntington's *Foreign Affairs* article appeared in 1993, "The Clash of Civilizations?" *Foreign Affairs* 72, no. 3 (Summer 1993): 22–49, and the book in 1998, *The Clash of Civilizations and the Remaking of World Order* (New York: Simon and Schuster, 1998). The debate accelerated after 9/11 and especially after the invasion of Iraq. As one indirect measure of this within academia, by 1996 there had been a combined total of 8 citations of Huntington's work on the ISI Web of Science citation index. This increased to 37 citations for 1997; 75 for 1998; 84 for 1999; 111 for 2000; 86 for 2001; 124 for 2002; 138 for 2003; 142 for 2004; 130 for 2005; 127 for 2006; 121 for 2007; and 142 for 2008. Computed from the ISI citation Web site at http://apps.isiknowledge.com/WOS_GeneralSearch_input .do?highlighted_tab=WOS&product=WOS&last_prod=WOS&SID=1E6B6eKefGPL8P aH24L&search_mode=GeneralSearch [06-26-2009]. Google Scholar, which (unlike the ISI index) captures many nonacademic citations as well, showed a cumulative citation of 3,468 for the article and 4,955 for the book by July 2009. http://scholar.google .com/scholar?hl=en&q=huntington%20clash%20of%20civilizations&rlz=1R2SKPB_ enUS332&um=1&ie=UTF-8&sa=N&tab=ws [06-26-2009]. On the response to Huntington, see then president Mohammed Khatami's advocacy of a dialogue among civilizations in his address to the UN in September 2000. http://www.unesco.org/dialogue/en/khatami.htm [07-28-2009]. See also Edward Said, "The Clash of Ignorance," *Nation*, October 4, 2001, http://www.thenation.com/doc/20011022/said [07-28-2009]; "The Myth of 'The Clash of Civilizations,'" http://video.google.com/videoplay?docid=-6705627964658699201&hl=en [07-28-2009].

[38] China's GDP growth rates as reported by its National Bureau of Statistics were as follows: 10 percent in 2003, 10.1 percent in 2004, 10.4 percent in 2005, 11.6 percent in 2006, and 11.9 percent in 2007. "China Profile," Economist Intelligence Unit (2009).

been obviated by the enactment of Permanent Normal Trading Relations with China, despite the objections of House Democrats.[39] Democracy might be slow to arrive and often precarious when it did, but the dynamism and resilience of the expanding capitalist world order seemed beyond question. The fiscal crises early in the new century had been deftly managed without systemic breakdown. This fed the perception that those who had their act together in the global economy were on an endless up escalator, and that, to stay on it, countries had simply to shape up and hew to the new orthodoxy. It did not much matter how they managed the domestic political fallout of implementing the troika of trade openness, deregulation, and technocratic management of macroeconomic policy; the important thing was to Get It Done.

REVISITING DEMOCRACY'S PLACE

Not that democracy was in full retreat in the years after 1996. To be sure, the authoritarian tendencies in Russia troubled many democrats, as did the dearth of democracy in much of Asia. Democracy suffered major setbacks in Pakistan and Zimbabwe, and elections in the Congo in 2006 did little to increase the country's governability or stem continuing conflicts in Ituri and Kivu. Arab kingdoms that had long been impervious to democracy's pull were no less so following the disastrous American attempt to impose democracy in Iraq. The neoconservative domino theory—that democracy would quickly flourish there and then spread across the region—turned out to be as inaccurate as an earlier and opposite domino theory that had predicted an unstoppable communist advance if South Vietnam were allowed to fall to the Viet Cong.[40] The debacle surrounding Iran's 2009 election showed democratic and constitutionalist forces to be losing much of the ground they had gained in the early years of the decade, with Mahmoud Ahmadinejad and the Republican Guard ascen-

---

[39] On September 20, 2000, the U.S. Senate voted 83 to 15 to extend permanent normal trade relations to China. Thirty-seven Democrats and forty-six Republicans voted yes. Seven Democrats and eight Republicans voted no. http://www.international.ucla.edu/eas/documents/senatevote.htm [12-21-2009].

[40] The fear of a domino effect in Southeast Asia, commonly associated with Henry Kissinger, was first proposed by William Bullit, a former ambassador to Moscow. See Gearóid Ó Tuathail, Simon Dalby, and Paul Routledge, *The Geopolitics Reader* (London: Routledge: 1998), p. 69. On the George W. Bush administration's democratic domino theory for the Middle East, see Greg Miller, "Democracy Domino Theory 'Not Credible,'" *Los Angeles Times*, March 14, 2003, http://articles.latimes.com/2003/mar/14/world/fg-domino14 [07-28-2009].

dant.[41] Democracy faced rough sledding in Thailand, where allegations of electoral fraud produced a series of crises including a military coup in 2006.[42] Democracy also seemed less secure in parts of Latin America, with both left- and right-wing populist strongmen revamping constitutions in Venezuela, Colombia, Ecuador, Bolivia, and Nicaragua to run for additional terms in office. President Zelaya's plan to do the same in Honduras threw the country into a crisis in late 2009.[43] Democracy was creaking in Argentina in the new century, as the government became increasingly cavalier about using its power over the legislature to enact laws without submitting them to public debate—often blatantly buying off the opposition with money and favors.[44] The recently reestablished democracy in Turkey came under increasing Islamist pressure that threatened to undermine it after 2007.[45]

Yet despite these setbacks, the overall trend toward democracy had continued. By 2007 democracies in the world outnumbered nondemocracies by 95 to 67, another sharp increase in the tally of democracies over the previous decade.[46] And there was heartening anecdotal evidence to accompany the trend. The peaceful inauguration of opposition leader John Atta Mills as Ghana's president in January of 2009 following a razor-thin upset victory over the incumbent Nana Akufo-Addo in the 2008 election revealed Africans to be at least as adept as Mexicans and

[41] See Ali Alfoneh, "Ahmadinejad versus the Technocrats," *Middle Eastern Outlook*, no. 4 (May 2008). In his second term, it is estimated that former Guards or Basij commanders occupy eight cabinet posts, as well as constituting one-third of parliament. See Kambiz Foroohar and Henry Meyer, "Iran Revolutionary Guards Amass Power While Backing Ahmadinejad," *Bloomberg*, June 29, 2009, http://www.bloomberg.com/apps/news?pid=20 601087&sid=a6btiOq7DxNY [12-22-2009].

[42] See "Explainer: Thailand's Ongoing Political Crisis," *CNN International*, April 13, 2009, http://edition.cnn.com/2009/WORLD/asiapcf/04/13/thailand.backgrounder/index. html [12-21-2009].

[43] Sara Miller Llana and Tim Rogers, "Nicaragua Is Latest in Latin America to Reject Term Limits," *Christian Science Monitor*, November 19, 2009, http://www.csmonitor. com/World/Americas/2009/1119/p10s01-woam.html?utm_source=feedburner&utm_ medium=feed&utm_campaign=Feed%253A+WhatsNewInPd+(What's+New+in+Public+ Diplomacy) [12-21-2009].

[44] See Roberto Gargarella, "Democracia de elites," *La Nación*, December 21, 2009, http://www.lanacion.com.ar/nota.asp?nota_id=1208405 [12-21-2009].

[45] See Ayaan Hirsi Ali, "Can Secular Turkey Survive Democracy?" *Los Angeles Times*, May 9, 2007, and "Slipping in Turkey: An Islamist Government's Commitment to Democratic Principles Is Looking Shaky" (editorial), *Washington Post*, November 23, 2009.

[46] These data are taken from "Polity IV Project: Political Regime Characteristics and Transitions, 1800–2007," http://www.systemicpeace.org/polity/polity4.htm [06-02-2009]. Following convention here, a country is considered a democracy if it has a score of 6 or higher on the Polity scale.

Americans at coping with political transitions following knife-edge elections.[47] South Africa's survival of the leadership crisis that led to Mbeki's orderly replacement by Kgalema Motlanthe and then Jacob Zuma was another potential train wreck averted by a fledgling democracy.[48] Brazil's massive, if fragile, democracy remained stable, even though it continued to be something of a "racial democracy," with the black population—around half the country's 160 million—substantially excluded from government, the judiciary, and the higher ranks of the civil service and military.[49] Luiz Inácio Lula da Silva was elected president in 2002 and reelected in 2006, but he resisted the temptation to change the constitution so that he could run for another term.[50] The year 1999 saw a remarkable democratic success in the world's largest Muslim-majority nation, Indonesia, following popular protests that had toppled Soeharto the previous year after more than three decades in power.[51] Subsequent elections in 2004 and 2009 proceeded without major obstacles.[52] In short, democracy remained an important—and growing—force in the world, even as it took a backseat to the economic demands of globalization.

An important truth underscored by the most serious financial collapse since the Great Depression is that experts often know less than they are willing to admit—even to themselves. The sheer complexity of the financial crisis has forced governments to continue working with many of the architects of the system that failed, and, partly for that reason, pressure has mounted to subject them to new regimes of accountability. As governments have scrambled to pick up the pieces, questions concerning by whose authority they act and for what purpose are thrown into sharp relief. If technocrats are to be subservient, once again, to democratic control, we need to know what that means, why it is justified, how it is estab-

[47] Mills won the runoff by 50.23 to 49.77 percent. Michelle Sieff, "Ghana's Democracy Continues to Mature," *World Politics Review*, January 13, 2009, http://www.worldpolitics review.com/Article.aspx?id=3156 [07-11-2009].

[48] See Ian Shapiro and Kahreen Tebeau, eds., *After Apartheid: The Second Decade* (Charlottesville: University of Virginia Press, 2010).

[49] Jan Rocha, "Analysis: Brazil's Racial Democracy," *BBC News*, April 19, 2000, http://news.bbc.co.uk/2/hi/americas/719134.stm [12-21-2009].

[50] "Lula Rejects Proposed Law to Allow Him to Seek a Third Term," *Bloomberg*, May 15, 2009, http://www.bloomberg.com/apps/news?pid=20601086&sid=aUg3DG3AHZsc& refer=latin_america [12-21-2009].

[51] Eric Thompson, "Indonesia in Transition: The 1999 Presidential Elections," *NBR Briefing, Policy Report*, no. 9 (December 9, 1999).

[52] See Hannah Beech, "Indonesia Elections: A Win for Democracy," *Time*, July 8, 2009, http://www.time.com/time/world/article/0,8599,1909198,00.html [12-21-2009]. See also "Advancing Democracy in Indonesia: The Second Democratic Legislative Elections since the Transition," National Democratic Institute for International Affairs (June 2004), http://www.ndi.org/files/1728_id_legelections_063004.pdf [12-21-2009].

lished and maintained, and how it can work in the face of contemporary challenges. With the technocrats on the defensive, democrats might have the upper hand—at least for a while. This makes it all the more incumbent on them to rethink democracy from the ground up, doing what they can to help it rise to the occasion. That is my agenda here.

Chapter 1 is concerned with the bedrock justification for majority rule, the presumptive decision rule of choice—on my account—for large-scale politics. Most contemporary discussions of democracy start from Rousseau's framing of the problem, but I make the case that, for pluralist societies, Locke offers more serviceable conceptual tools. Americans have long associated Locke with the robust defense of individual rights. However, they typically miss the fact that his account of political rights is embedded in—and in the end depends on—majority rule as the trumping font of political legitimacy. Locke's account has the added advantage of not requiring the possibility of anything akin to Rousseau's general will, or what modern social choice theorists, following Kenneth Arrow, have referred to as a social welfare function. Locke's reasoning casts the alleged irrationality of majority rule in a decidedly different light. It rests on more realistic assumptions about politics than does the neo-Rousseauist literature, and it appeals to something close to what John Rawls has described as a political, rather than a metaphysical, view of ultimate justification in politics.[53]

If individual rights depend, ultimately, on the power of the majority for their recognition and enforcement, as Locke contended, this still leaves open the question whether majoritarian politics is more desirable than the alternatives before a society, in extremis, crosses that threshold marked by what he described as "a long train of abuses" of the people by the sovereign. That is my concern in chapter 2. Locke, who was a theorist of democratic legitimacy on my account but not of democratic procedures, had little of interest to say on the organization of everyday politics.[54] Modern discussions of this subject are traced, instead, to the late eighteenth-century preoccupations of the American founders. They sought to create what James Madison described as a "non-tyrannical republic" rather than a pure democracy, owing to their fear that a "majority faction" might invade the rights of the minority. Madison was convinced that factions, whose causes are "sown in the nature of man,"

[53] John Rawls, "Justice as Fairness: Political, not Metaphysical," *Philosophy and Public Affairs* 14, no. 3 (Summer 1985): 223–51.

[54] Locke held the conventional view that different institutional arrangements made sense for different types of polity, but he never explored any of them in any depth. See John Locke, *Two Treatises of Government and A Letter Concerning Toleration* (1681), ed. Ian Shapiro (New Haven: Yale University Press, 2003), pp. 157–58.

cannot be eliminated. Instead the answer was to multiply factions by expanding the republic.[55]

Like Locke, but in a different way, Madison saw more deeply into democracy than do our contemporary friends of reason who attack its alleged irrationality. Whereas they object to voting cycles as indicating the lack of a rational social ordering of voters' preferences, Madison saw the potential for fluid and changing majorities as forestalling the potential for one group to tyrannize over others. This would subsequently become known as the pluralist theory of democracy, for which crosscutting divisions and unpredictable outcomes are necessary. If cleavages of race, class, religion, and ethnicity are all mutually reinforcing, then minorities know that they will always lose. They might as well go to war if they think they can win, or turn to crime if they cannot. If, by contrast, cleavages are crosscutting, then majorities will vary from issue to issue as coalitions form and re-form—holding out the possibility that today's losers might become tomorrow's winners. In my view Madison was right that political competition, motivated by institutionalized uncertainty over outcomes, is the best guarantee against domination of some groups by others. As is underscored by my survey in chapter 2 of recent literature on democracy and domination, it has done better over time than any going alternative.

In chapter 3 my focus shifts to the project of creating national democracy, and particularly the extent to which it can, or must, be imposed from above. It is often observed that democracy is not adept at providing public goods, a view I endorsed in *Democracy's Place*.[56] At least since Jeremy Bentham's time, political economists have been aware that the impossibility of preventing anyone from enjoying the benefits of public goods creates perverse incentives for people to avoid paying for them. As a result, coercion is conventionally judged to be necessary in the provision of public goods.[57] Coercion is seldom appealing, but it is especially vexing if the public good in question is a democratic constitutional order. This is partly because those doing the coercing might have questionable motives, and partly because consent of the governed is democracy's legitimating ideal.

[55] "Extend the sphere, and you take in a greater variety of parties and interests; you make it less probable that a majority of the whole will have a common motive to invade the rights of other citizens; or if such a common motive exists, it will be more difficult for all who feel it to discover their own strength, and to act in unison with each other." James Madison, *Federalist* No. 10, in Alexander Hamilton, James Madison, and John Jay, *The Federalist Papers*, ed. Ian Shapiro (New Haven: Yale University Press, 2009), pp. 47–58.

[56] See *Democracy's Place*, pp. 251–54.

[57] See my discussion in *The Moral Foundations of Politics* (New Haven: Yale University Press, 2003), pp. 22–23.

In chapter 7 of *Democracy's Place* Courtney Jung and I had argued that during the South African transition it was unsurprising that attempts to find a democratic path to democracy through roundtable negotiations in 1991 and 1992 broke down. Giving all stakeholders a seat at the table meant including groups such as the far-right white elements and the ethnic Zulu Inkatha Freedom Party, neither of whom wanted to see a transition to majority rule. They torpedoed the negotiations, and were eventually excluded from the secret talks between the National Party government and the ANC which led to an agreement that was for all practical purposes imposed on the society. The Far Right's attempt to derail the agreement by starting an insurrection in Bophuthatswana in March 1994 was put down by force, and Inkatha finally abandoned its boycott two weeks before the first democratic elections the following month—when it became clear that they could not be stopped. Much of the world cheered as this happened because few doubted that a public good was being provided.

Viewed in retrospect, our discussion of democratic imposition was too simple. Closer examination of the successful South African transition, the failures in the Middle East, and the ambiguous results in Northern Ireland over the past three decades reveals the importance of combining decisive leadership from above with building vital support from below. Writing now also with Ellen Lust, Jung and I explore the dynamics of these three cases in chapter 3. We argue that the combination of violent conflict and imperfect democracy brings about particular challenges and opportunities for negotiating settlements that are often overlooked. We show how, like the American Federalists, Nelson Mandela and F. W. de Klerk understood the importance of building constituencies for the new dispensation they sought to create, and then taking advantage of that support to solve essential commitment problems at key junctures of the negotiations over the creation of the new democratic order. It is true that leadership, understood in this context as the capacity and willingness to take unusually great personal political risks in order to achieve political settlements, is vital at junctures when decisive steps have to be taken. If it is lacking when it is needed, as it was following Yitzhak Rabin's assassination in November of 1995, then transition negotiations fail.

But while necessary, leadership is not sufficient. The Clinton administration's failure to understand this prevented their seeing why a two-state solution to the Israel-Palestine conflict eluded them at Camp David in the summer of 2000. Five years earlier the reality had been quite different. The same two-state solution that was rejected at Camp David had been agreed to in Oslo in August 1993, after which Rabin and Yasir Arafat worked hard—and effectively—to build support for it in their communities. By the summer of 2000 Arafat, who had by then been humiliated for years by successive Israeli governments, lacked the popular support to deliver anything like that agreement. His manifestly corrupt PLO had lost ground to Hamas, whose support would thenceforth be essential to an agreement. Israeli and American administrations since that time have been unwilling to deal with Hamas, despite its unambiguous victories in elections in Gaza and the West Bank in 2006. So long as that remains the case and Hamas retains its support on the ground, there will be no chance of a settlement.

This raises the question when to negotiate with adversaries in the quest for democratic settlements, a subject Lust and I explore further in chapter 4 via a consideration of the options facing the Obama administration in the Middle East. Part of the reason why democracy has, partly, to be imposed, is that political parties and movements involved in negotiations are not monolithic. Typically they are divided over whether to negotiate settlements, and those who stand to lose if democracy is instituted will stop it if they can. As a result, it is in the interest of those who are bargaining to create a new democratic order—reformers within the ancien régime and the moderates in the opposition—to do what they can to help their negotiating partners to convince, co-opt, or marginalize the potential spoilers on the other side. Transition negotiations thus present a complex challenge in which each side has an interest in maximizing what it will get from the eventual settlement, while ensuring that their adversaries can satisfice—do well enough that the spoilers on their flanks cannot derail the process.

An undernoticed corollary of this mutual dependence of government reformers and opposition moderates concerns the role of preconditions in negotiations. Most transition negotiations are complicated by the impulse of various players to insist on conditions that the other side must meet for talks to start or to keep going. Requirements to end violence, decommission arms, accept certain "nonnegotiable" features of an eventual settlement, or exclude particular groups as beyond the pale are often insisted upon—partly to placate standpatters and revolutionaries on the negotiators' flanks. But when those flankers are spoilers, as they often are, they have every incentive to violate whatever preconditions the other side has established—to weaken the hands of the negotiators on their side and reduce the likelihood of a settlement. Lust and I note that it was vital to the success of South Africa's negotiations that both sides resolutely avoided establishing preconditions. We explore the implications of this for the Middle East, explaining why it should lead to a different approach from that adopted by the Clinton, Bush, and early Obama administrations.

If democracy is the best system of government and negotiations to produce it are so fragile, perhaps the better course for democrats is to be less squeamish about imposing it from the outside when they can. This is my subject in chapter 5. Addressing it in today's world puts a larger question on the table. If democracy is the best system of government, perhaps the whole world should be a single democracy. After all, the division of the world into sovereign nation-states is morally arbitrary. This division underwrites massive global inequalities via a scheme of global apartheid that is euphemistically known as the Westphalian system. Evolving technologies of force make military power increasingly global in its reach. Climate change renders poor countries "price-takers" in the global system,[58] as the developing countries pointed out in the unsuccessful climate summit in Copenhagen in 2009.[59] Economic integration renders decisions taken in one part of the world hugely consequential elsewhere, as the 2008 banking crisis and attendant financial meltdown made patently clear. If we are to be cosmopolitan democrats, as I argue that we should, then should we not favor the creation of a democratic world state?

Some eyes will, understandably, glaze over at the posing of such questions. They call to mind the lost traveler who approached a farmer in Donegal to ask for directions to Dublin and got the answer: "Well, I wouldn't start out from here." But understanding why pressing for world government should be judged undesirable, for cosmopolitan democrats, even if it were feasible, is useful to illuminate their best stance toward the project of exporting democracy. World government, I argue, would not solve the problems that lead cosmopolitan democrats to support it. There is no good reason to suppose that world government would diminish worldwide conflict or injustice, or even bring decision making into closer conformity with the democratic principle of affected interest than is currently the case. World government's proponents commit the fallacy of comparing the reality of the nation-state system with the ideal of world government, not with what it would be like in practice. We should favor delinking rights to participate in decision making from national citizenship, but this should be done decision by decision. Sometimes it means devolving authority downward to subnational units, sometimes upward to regional units such as the European Union, and sometimes to international entities like the United Nations. We should also favor the creation of institutions to buttress the international rule of law. But this is a far cry from abolishing national government in favor of the creation of a world state.

[58] See Nicholas Stern, "The Economics of Climate Change," Richard T. Ely Lecture, *American Economic Review: Papers & Proceedings* 98, no. 2 (2008): 1–37, esp. p. 28.
[59] John Broder, "Many Goals Remain Unmet in 5 Nations' Climate Deal," *New York Times*, December 18, 2009, http://www.nytimes.com/2009/12/19/science/earth/19climate.html [12-23-2009].

With democratic world government off the table, more pertinent questions arise: how much international proselytizing should democrats do, and what policies, if any, should they support to assist democracy's spread? One potential answer is that they should be isolationists. If democracy depends vitally for its legitimacy on support of the governed, then arguably the stance toward other countries should be to let them create their own democracy if the support exists—and otherwise ignore them unless they attack us. Against this view, I argue that democrats should indeed be committed to opposing domination in the world and reducing it where possible. With respect to the internal politics of other countries, this means supporting viable democratic oppositions if they seek our support and if we can provide it without jeopardizing democracy at home.

Opposing tyrannical regimes in order to resist the spread of domination and reduce it where possible is a worthy goal for democrats, but best viewed through the prism of containment. I have argued elsewhere that this doctrine, first developed by George Kennan to face down the Soviet threat in the 1940s, provides the best available basis for confronting threats to democracy and encouraging its global diffusion.[60] Some critics of my view took me to be defending U.S. national security policy during the Cold War. In fact my argument was that during the Cold War the United States was least successful when it abandoned containment. In the 1952 election Dwight Eisenhower and his future secretary of state John Foster Dulles attacked containment, vilifying it as appeasement and advocating "rollback" of the Soviets instead. Ironically, once in office the Eisenhower administration abandoned rollback in favor of containment in Eastern Europe. In Iran, by contrast, in 1953 they toppled the democratically elected government, replacing it with the hugely unpopular shah. Subsequently the United States fought a failed war of choice in Vietnam, again abandoning containment—much to Kennan's chagrin. Ironically, today Eastern Europe is democratic, whereas the sites where we were more aggressively interventionist are not.[61]

Containment's critics leveled many of the same attacks in the post–Cold War era that the advocates of rollback pushed in the 1950s. I respond to these arguments in chapter 5, explaining why containment is not appeasement now any more than it was then, but why, during the post–Cold War era, containment nonetheless stands in need of a new kind of authorization and implementation that involves both international institutions and cooperation among regional powers. I also explore, more fully than I did in the book, containment's foundations in democratic

[60] Ian Shapiro, *Containment: Rebuilding a Strategy against Global Terror* (Princeton: Princeton University Press, 2007).

[61] An exception is South Korea, which finally achieved a democratic turnover of government in 1997.

theory. Whereas Kennan's defense of containment was strategic all the way down, I make a normative case for its desirability that is rooted in containment's elective affinities with the ideal of nondomination. This account does not require agreement on basic values or worldviews, or even on an expectation that there can be such agreement. Rather, it takes deep pluralism of values and worldviews for granted. We do not need others to accept, or even understand, our beliefs or practices. Nor do we need to accept or understand theirs. We need only insist that we will not allow adversaries to impose their ways of life on us, or on others, so long as we are in a position to stop them.

Some will doubt that containment can provide a sufficiently robust basis for the international engagement that may be called for if one is serious about preventing, or at least limiting, domination. My claim is not that containment exhausts our international obligations; there may be reasons for humanitarian intervention, when it is feasible, to prevent extreme suffering and vulnerability due to human or natural catastrophe. But calls for humanitarian intervention differ from calls to undertake democratic regime change. The former typically arise in response to episodic events—such as eruptions of genocide or natural disasters. The possibilities for working with indigenous or regional governments will often be problematic in such circumstances, and the urgency of the situation might justify intervening by reference to the maxim that sometimes it is wiser to seek sanctification—if not forgiveness—afterward than to ask for permission before the fact. This should not be done lightly. If it is bungled, or if the ex post justifications turn out not to be widely accepted, this will undermine the intervening power's legitimacy.

Intervening to achieve regime change to democracy differs from humanitarian intervention for a second reason. By its terms democracy stands in need of legitimation from below. Those over whom power will be exercised must authorize it. It is always possible that the forces of the intervening power "will be greeted in the streets as liberators," as some predicted would be the case in Iraq in 2003, but I argue in chapter 5 that this is almost always an unwise bet that democrats should be leery of taking. However, these considerations do not arise in the case of humanitarian intervention, where the goal is to prevent or mitigate an immediate or impending catastrophe—not to create a democratic regime.

Democracy against Justice?

In chapter 6 my focus shifts to the tensions between democracy and justice. The advent of neoliberalism was well under way by 1996, as we have seen, but the extent of its eventual impact on the distribution of income and wealth had yet to be fully appreciated or, indeed, experienced. Between the 1970s and the mid-1990s the world saw a significant overall reduction in poverty, though its distribution was uneven. High growth rates in China and India dragged tens of millions out of poverty, but there were few improvements in Africa and Latin America after the 1970s. The advanced countries enjoyed comparatively low poverty rates, but these have been increasing since the mid-1970s.[62]

More striking have been the increases in inequality. There had been some reductions in inequality when measured worldwide in the 1970s and 1980s, related principally to the above-average income growth in China and South Asia.[63] But this tailed off in the 1990s. Inequality between rich and poor countries increased sharply, as did inequalities within many countries—including the world's wealthiest democracies.[64] The evaporation of significant amounts of wealth in the global real-estate and stock-market crashes of 2008–9 has reduced the portfolios of many of the very wealthy.[65] The resulting impact on employment, commodity prices, international aid, and trade will be reverberating for years, so that the overall impact of the collapse on poverty and inequality will not be known for some time. It is hard to conjure up plausible scenarios in which this will not be regressive.

Some of the most unequal countries are democracies, a fact that throws the tension between democracy and justice into sharp relief. In South Africa, for instance, the ANC won reelection by well over 60 percent of the vote in 1999, 2004, and 2009, even though the great bulk of the redistribution forecast to trickle down as a result of GEAR has not taken place. A small black wealthy class has developed, and there has been a modicum of redistribution from whites to blacks. But overall inequality has not decreased. Indeed it increased in the decade following the transition, and poverty deepened.[66] South Africa still has one of the highest Gini coefficients in the world. It has one of the highest rates of HIV infection, partly because of the Mbeki government's recalcitrance in ac-

[62] See Xavier Sala-i-Martin, "The World Distribution of Income (Estimated from Individual Country Distributions)," NBER Working Paper 8933 (2002), and "Growing Unequal? Income Distribution and Poverty in OECD Countries," OECD Summaries (2008), http://www.oecd.org/dataoecd/45/42/41527936.pdf [07-27-2009].

[63] See Glen Firebauch and Brian Goesling, "Accounting for the Recent Decline in Global Inequality," *American Journal of Sociology* 110, no. 2 (September 2004): 283–312.

[64] "Growing Unequal?" and Almas Heshmati, "The World Distribution of Income and Income Inequality," IZA Discussion Paper no. 1267 (2004).

[65] "Under Attack: A Special Report on the Rise and Fall of the Wealthy," *Economist*, April 4–10, 2009), pp. 4–16.

[66] Jeremy Seekings and Nicoli Nattrass, *Class, Race, and Inequality in South Africa* (New Haven: Yale University Press, 2005), pp. 300–375.

knowledging its causes and distributing retroviral drugs.[67] Land reform since the transition has been negligible. At least a third of the population remains unemployed.[68] Yet the ANC continues winning easy reelection even though it parries or ducks most pressures to redistribute income, wealth, and other resources.[69] Indeed the top marginal tax rate, which had been set at 60 percent by the apartheid government in 1979, was reduced to 42 percent in 2000 and further to 40 percent in 2003.[70]

That democracies can engage in regressive redistribution is a truth not only about developing countries that are "price-takers" in edgy international capital markets. Substantial increases in inequality in many of the advanced democracies have been aided and abetted by neoliberal policies. It is, to be sure, often difficult to know to what extent changes in inequality in a country result from government policies. As Robert Nozick noted long ago, endogenous changes in the economy are a constant source of new inequalities that should be expected often to operate at cross-purposes with the redistributive policies of governments.[71] There have, nonetheless, been notable instances of democracies enacting tax changes, sometimes with widespread popular support, that were predictably regressive in their distributive effects. Perhaps the most dramatic of these in recent years was the repeal of the federal estate tax in the United States in 2001, which shifted some $40 billion a year in taxation from America's wealthiest taxpayers to those lower down the income scale. On the books since 1916, the federal estate tax had been the most progressive measure in the tax code. All of it was paid by the wealthiest 2 percent of taxpayers, and more than half of it was paid by the wealthiest 0.5 percent. In *Death by a Thousand Cuts* (published in 2005) Michael Graetz and I sought to explain why it was repealed.[72]

The estate tax repeal presents a profound puzzle because it defied the standard accounts of why democracies fail to engage in the downward

---

[67] See Nicoli Nattrass, *The Moral Economy of AIDS in South Africa* (Cambridge: Cambridge University Press, 2004), and *Mortal Combat: AIDS Denialism and the Struggle for Antiretrovirals in South Africa* (Scottsville, South Africe: University of Kwazulu-Natal Press, 2007).

[68] *South Africa Human Development Report 2003*, United Nations Development Programme (Cape Town: Oxford University Press, 2003); Shapiro and Tebeau, *After Apartheid*.

[69] Shapiro and Tebeau, *After Apartheid*.

[70] Nicoli Nattrass, Jeremy Wakeford, and Samson Muradzikwa, *Macroeconomics: Theory and Policy in South Africa*, 3rd ed. (Cape Town: David Philip, 2003), p. 289.

[71] Robert Nozick, *Anarchy, State and Utopia* (New York: Basic Books, 1974), pp. 160–64.

[72] Michael J. Graetz and Ian Shapiro, *Death by a Thousand Cuts: The Fight over Taxing Inherited Wealth* (Princeton: Princeton University Press, 2005).

redistribution that the median voter theorem predicts. For instance, John Roemer, among others, has suggested that the presence of issues other than distribution that voters care about—such as race or abortion—explains why politicians in search of the median voter do not favor more downward redistribution.[73] But we found that public support for estate tax repeal is robust regardless of other issues. Indeed, in surveys people favored repeal by *larger* margins when they considered it in isolation from other issues than when they did not. Moreover, stand-alone bills (that were neither parts of any log roll nor bundled with other legislation) calling for estate tax repeal repeatedly passed both houses of Congress with significant bipartisan support. The puzzle about it arises from distributive concerns alone; it does not depend on the existence of other dimensions of politics.

An implication of our study is that, for some distributive issues at least, the logic of dividing a dollar by majority rule might supply better theoretical intuitions than does the median voter theorem—however modified through the addition of other dimensions. If three voters must divide a dollar by majority rule, there is no distribution that is not in principle vulnerable to upset by some majority coalition. If A and B agree on a 50/50 division, giving C nothing, then C will propose a 60/40 division to A in his favor, excluding B, and so on ad infinitum. There is no division that avoids this potential instability. This suggests that a good deal of the politics of distributive conflict in democracies involves coalition busting, coalition building, and sustaining coalitions that others have incentives to destroy. The story of the estate tax repeal was a story of building a coalition of unlikely bedfellows that included representatives of the ultrarich, but also small business, environmental activists, the Congressional Black Caucus, lobbyists for gay rights, farmers, and newspaper owners, among others. Their success depended on great political creativity in building the repeal coalition, holding it together in the face of forces that threatened to smash it, and using it to splinter the coalition that had kept the status quo on estate taxes in place for decades. It is a story that suggests that we might get a better grip on the dynamics of distributive politics in democracies, and new possibilities for downward redistribution, by studying other unlikely distributive coalitions in history. The coalition to abolish the slave trade, the coalition to enact the Civil Rights Act, and the coalition to pass the Americans with Disabilities Act come to mind as suggestive possibilities. They all involved the creation of broad innova-

[73] Roemer, "Does Democracy Engender Justice?" pp. 56–68, and John Roemer, Woojin Lee, and Karine Van der Straeten, *Racism, Xenophobia, and Distribution: Multi-Issue Politics in Advanced Democracies* (New York: Russell Sage Foundation; Cambridge, MA: Harvard University Press, 2007).

tive coalitions to produce substantial distributive changes that benefited previously disadvantaged minorities. These examples suggest that there might be other opportunities for dispossessed minorities to develop unexpected alliances that will be instrumental in redressing specific grievances. Indeed, the search for such focused coalitions might well pay better dividends than would generalized appeals for egalitarian provision of welfare, income, wealth, or other resources through government redistribution.

The battle over estate tax repeal illuminates dimensions of the interaction between public opinion and distributive politics that Graetz and I did not explore as fully as we might have done. Writing now also with Mayling Birney, we note in chapter 6 that the intensity of public opinion has a significant effect on the ways in which distributive politics play themselves out. A little-known fact is that American mass preferences about tax questions (as distinct from the preferences of tax activists) are not particularly intense. Mass preferences about the estate tax are especially lacking in intensity. It is easy to get as many as 70 percent of Americans to say that they favor estate tax repeal when this is polled as a stand-alone issue, but the support quickly dissipates when people are asked either to rank estate tax repeal with other possible tax cuts or when repeal is linked to cuts in popular programs. The great bulk of the polling that was done in the run-up to the 2001 repeal posed as a stand-alone issue the question about repealing the estate tax. It was done by groups working for the repeal who knew in advance what the results would be. Their aim was to create momentum by wide dissemination of the results, and to convince politicians that they would not pay an electoral cost for supporting repeal. Once the politicians were convinced of this, the battle became one of organized coalitions that actually had little to do with public opinion. Beliefs about the estate tax turn out to be comparable to many issues in the "culture wars," such as gay rights, abortion, and gun control. As Morris Fiorina and his coauthors have shown, although activists are intensely split about them, they do not sharply polarize mass opinion.[74]

The George W. Bush administration followed its 2001 individual tax cuts with business-oriented tax cuts the following year. Incumbent administrations usually lose seats in midterm elections, but the Republicans made gains in both the House and the Senate in 2002, underscoring—had there been any doubt—that their tax-cutting agenda involved no electoral cost. The following year Congress passed additional tax cuts, this time in capital gains and dividend rates. In 2004, President Bush won

[74] See Morris Fiorina, Samuel Abrams and Jeremy Pope, *Culture War? The Myth of Polarized America* (New York: Pearson Longman, 2005).

the election by some 2.5 percent, or 3 million votes, over John Kerry, even though the Iraq war had by then manifestly begun to sour.[75] The Democrats, still reeling from their loss of control of Capitol Hill a decade earlier, were indisputably on the ropes.

Yet when the newly legitimated President Bush, backed by an even further strengthened Republican Congress, made privatizing social security his first order of business in his second term, he ran into a brick wall. The same tactics that had been so effective with the estate tax repeal were all deployed. Conservative think tanks funded media campaigns. Studies and plans promoting privatization were aired on Capitol Hill. Huge quantities of presidential time and political capital were expended, with George W. Bush spending almost two months on the road promoting privatization in 2005. None of it was to any avail, however. Public opinion remained overwhelmingly opposed to privatization, and, in sharp contrast to the battle over the estate tax, senators and congressmen learned in overwhelming numbers from their constituents that any attempt to enact it would come at a massive electoral cost.[76] Hopeless as the median voter model is for understanding estate tax repeal, it thus supplies a pretty good account of the politics of social security privatization.

An implication of this contrast is that the politics of distributive conflict play out exceedingly differently depending on just how intense mass preferences about it turn out to be. Consider another example. Bill and Hillary Clinton believed that they had a winning issue in universal health care in the 1992 campaign, but the rug was pulled out remarkably quickly once the opponents got to work. Unlike the failed crusade to alter public opinion about social security privatization, the campaign to destroy public support for President Clinton's health-care reform with the infamous "Harry and Louise" commercials in 1993 seems to have been remarkably effective.[77] Public support for publicly funded health insurance turns out to be notably less tensile than many Democratic activists, for whom its merits are all but self-evident, have hoped. This is a lesson the Obama administration was forced to relearn in 2009–10. Perhaps it is not surprising that most middle- and upper-income U.S. taxpayers are as disinclined to

[75] See Shapiro, *Containment*, chap. 1.

[76] Jill Zuckman, "Bush Finds Congress Is No Pushover," *Chicago Tribune*, May 31, 2005, http://www.encyclopedia.com/doc/1G1-132874430.html [07-28-2009].

[77] Raymond L. Goldsteen et al., "Harry and Louise and Health Care Reform: Romancing Public Opinion," *Journal of Health Politics, Policy and Law* 26, no. 6 (2001): 1325–52, http://muse.jhu.edu/journals/journal_of_health_politics_policy_and_law/v026/26.6goldsteen.html [09-07-2009].

fund health insurance for tens of millions of low-income Americans as they are to fund welfare.

It is hard to guess about these matters with much confidence, because we lack a developed body of knowledge—or even informed theoretical speculation—about what determines the intensity of public opinion about distributive questions. From the haphazard ways in which politicians tackle these issues, it seems that their consultants and pollsters are flailing in the dark as well. We know little, if anything, about why media campaigns and "push polling" succeed in altering opinion on some issues and not others. We do not even have systematic data on the intensity of mass preferences over a range of distributive issues or on how this has evolved over time. There have been isolated studies showing that mass preferences for public goods are more price inelastic than are those for private goods,[78] and that people are more inclined to pay for public goods if they expect to derive personal benefits from them[79] or they believe the goods in question cannot be provided privately.[80] But the systematic study of these issues is in its infancy in the United States, and it seems even less developed elsewhere.

The tension between democracy and justice is not exhausted by the subject of distributive politics, meager as our understanding of it might be. At least since Plato wrote the *Republic*, democracy's skeptics have worried that majority rule can foster domination. The authors of *The Federalist* were greatly concerned about the power of majority factions, as we have seen. Commentators from Alexis de Tocqueville (who coined the phrase "tyranny of the majority") and John Stuart Mill through contemporary defenders of constitutionalism all share the view that the crosscutting cleavages constituting a pluralist society are insufficient to protect against majority tyranny. In their view, institutional checks and balances, geared to frustrating—or at least slowing—majoritarian politics are also needed. There are many ways to do this. Supermajority requirements, bicameral legislatures, overrepresentation of particular groups, staggered elections, and federalism are all features of the U.S. institutional scheme that throw sand in the wheels of majoritarian politics. But what has garnered the most attention is the separation-of-powers system in which enumerated powers are allocated to the legislature, the executive, and the judiciary—a modern incarnation of the Aristotelian

[78] Donald P. Green, "The Price Elasticity of Mass Preferences," *American Political Science Review* 86, no. 1 (1992): 128–48.

[79] Donald P. Green and Irene Blair, "Framing and the Price Elasticity of Private and Public Goods," *Journal of Consumer Psychology* 4, no. 1 (1995): 1–32.

[80] Daniel Kahneman and J. Knetsch, "Valuing Public Goods: The Purchase of Moral Satisfaction," *Journal of Environmental Economics and Management* 22 (1992): 57–70.

polity in which the best regime is a composite of government by the one, the few, and the many.[81]

The American founders were convinced that such a system would contribute both to political stability and to limiting tyranny. Because "power is of an encroaching nature," as Madison put it in *Federalist* No. 48, it "ought to be effectually restrained from passing the limits assigned to it."[82] Just how this was supposed to happen was, however, less than clear. Unlike the role played by crosscutting cleavages, where people's interests can be counted on to get them to form and re-form coalitions rather than try to take over the country, the separation-of-powers scheme relies on everyone's accepting its legitimacy. Neither Congress nor the courts command armies that can be deployed against the president. Indeed his authority as a civilian commander-in-chief depends on the military's continuing acceptance of his legitimate role.

Madison was one of the first to acknowledge that "a mere demarcation on parchment of the constitutional limits of the several departments is not a sufficient guard against those encroachments which lead to a tyrannical concentration of all the powers of government in the same hands."[83] But he did not describe the system of incentives by which "ambition" would in fact be made, as he insisted in *Federalist* No. 51 that it should be made, to "counteract ambition."[84] Sometimes institutional branches do indeed constrain one another's behavior, as when the Supreme Court insisted on the release of Nixon's tapes,[85] and Congress investigated the White House and passed the Budget and Impoundment Act of 1974 following the Watergate scandal.[86] How much of this is the result of institutional jealousy is difficult to tell. When popular support to limit presidential authority is lacking, as with the George W. Bush administration's concentration of power under color of the unitary theory of the executive following 9/11, Congress and the judiciary often show little appetite for trying.[87]

Indeed, it may well be that parliamentary supremacy is a better check on executive power than is institutional separation of powers—at least

---

[81] See J.G.A. Pocock, *The Machiavellian Moment: Florentine Political Thought and the Atlantic Republican Tradition* (Princeton: Princeton University Press, 1974).

[82] *The Federalist Papers*, p. 251.

[83] Ibid., p. 255.

[84] Ibid., p. 264.

[85] *United States v. Nixon*, 418 U.S. 683 (1974).

[86] Budget and Impoundment Act of 1974, http://www.polisci.ccsu.edu/trieb/Budtlfrm .htm [12-21-2009].

[87] For the view that there is an equilibrium in the U.S. separation of powers, see Bernard Manin, "Checks, Balances, and Boundaries: The Constitutional Debate of 1787," in *The Invention of the Modern Republic*, ed. Biancamara Fontana (Cambridge: Cambridge University Press, 1994), pp. 27–62.

with respect to competition for power between the legislature and the executive. Modern experience in Latin America and elsewhere suggests that presidential systems, in which chief executives enjoy independent electoral mandates and authority, are less stable and more coup prone than are parliamentary systems.[88] Perhaps legislatures are better able to constrain executives when legislatures are institutionally strong, as in the United States and Costa Rica, as Matthew Shugart and John Carey have suggested,[89] but even then they are seldom likely to act without popular support to stiffen their backs, and even less likely to do so in the face of popular opposition.[90]

Most of the attention garnered by discussions of the separation of powers has focused on the role of courts in interpreting constitutions and bills of rights. The U.S. Supreme Court's powers are laid out in Article III of the Constitution, but it was not clear that this included the power to strike down legislation until Chief Justice John Marshall did just that in 1803, declaring in *Marbury v. Madison* that it is "emphatically the province and duty of the Judicial Department to say what the law is."[91] The question remains, however, whether bills of rights, and independent courts whose job it is to guard them, actually make any difference to the protection of rights on the ground. Many constitutional lawyers, particularly those who came of age during the heyday of the Warren Court in the 1950s and 1960s, believe that they do.[92] If the third wave of democratiza-

---

[88] See Juan Linz, *The Breakdown of Democratic Regimes: Crises, Breakdown and Re-equilibration* (Baltimore: Johns Hopkins University Press, 1978), and "Presidential or Parliamentary Democracy: Does It Make a Difference?" in *The Failure of Presidential Democracy,* ed. Juan J. Linz and Arturo Valenzuela (Baltimore: Johns Hopkins University Press, 1994), pp. 3–90. Presidentialism's instability seems to be mitigated somewhat when the president's party has a majority in the legislature, when there are favorable conditions for coalition politics in the legislature, and when there is centralized executive authority in the government. See Joe Foweraker, "Institutional Design, Party Systems and Governability—Differentiating the Presidential Regimes of Latin America," *British Journal of Political Science.* 28 (1998): 651–76; and José Cheibub and Fernando Limongi, "Democratic Institutions and Regime Survival: Parliamentarism and Presidentialism Reconsidered," *Annual Review of Political Science* 5 (2002): 151–79. For additional discussion, see my *The State of Democratic Theory* (Princeton: Princeton University Press, 2005), pp. 86–100.

[89] See Matthew S. Shugart and John M. Carey, *Presidents and Assemblies: Constitutional Design and Electoral Dynamics* (Cambridge: Cambridge University Press, 1992), chaps. 7–8, especially pp. 154–58, 165.

[90] These issues will be taken up more fully in volume 3 of *Democratic Justice,* currently in preparation.

[91] *Marbury v. Madison,* 5 U.S. (Cranch 1) 137 (1803), at 177–78.

[92] Prominent among these is Ronald Dworkin. See his *Law's Empire* (Cambridge, MA: Harvard University Press, 1986) and *A Bill of Rights for Britain: Why British Liberty Needs Protection* (London: Chatto & Windus, 1991). For other classic statements, see John Hart Ely, *Democracy and Distrust: A Theory of Judicial Review* (Cambridge, MA: Harvard University Press, 1980), and Alexander Bickel, *The Least Dangerous Branch: The*

tions in the world that began in 1974 is anything to go by, their belief has won the day.[93] As Donald Horowitz has pointed out, whereas the American taste for federalism and independently elected presidents has not proved popular, bills of rights and independent courts have become near universal in new democracies—especially those created since 1989.[94]

This is curious in view of how hard it is to show that judicial review matters for the prevention of tyranny. Countries like Britain, Sweden, Norway, and until recently the Netherlands, which have shown little appetite for judicial review, have not done any less well at protecting human rights than has the United States. There have been periods in the United States when the federal judiciary has successfully championed individual rights and civil liberties against the legislative branch of government, that of the Warren Court being the best known.[95] But there have also been eras when the Court has legitimated racial oppression, denial of civil liberties, and concentration of power in the executive branch.[96] The behavior of the White, Taft, Taney, Burger, Rehnquist, and Roberts Courts suggest that the Warren Court might well have been an historical anomaly. Certainly the Supreme Court's tepid response to the incursions on civil liberties in the Patriot Act[97] and the behavior of the executive branch since 9/11 does not suggest that it is much of a bulwark for their protection.[98]

Supreme Court at the Bar of Politics (New Haven: Yale University Press, 1986). For a contrarian view from a lawyer, see Mark Tushnet, *Taking the Constitution Away from the Courts* (Princeton: Princeton University Press, 2000) and *Weak Courts, Strong Rights: Judicial Review and Social Welfare Rights in Comparative Constitutional Law* (Princeton: Princeton University Press, 2007).

[93] "Third wave" is Samuel Huntington's term, deployed to distinguish the wave of democratization that began in 1974 (and is presumably still ongoing) from the two previous waves that took place between 1828 and 1926, and 1943 and 1962. Huntington, *The Third Wave.*

[94] Donald L. Horowitz, "*The Federalist* Abroad in the World," in *The Federalist Papers,* ed. Shapiro, pp. 502–32.

[95] There are terminological issues at stake here on which substantive issues turn. For instance, in the *Lochner* era the Supreme Court struck down much legislation in the name of protecting individual freedoms, but the legislation in question was aimed at increasing social and economic guarantees—promoting civil rights at the expense of social rights. See *Lochner v. New York* 198 U.S. 45 (1905). For discussion of the *Lochner* era, and for a general discussion of the evolution of American constitutional law through the years of the Warren Court (1953–69), see Lawrence H. Tribe, *American Constitutional Law* (New York: Foundation Press, 1978).

[96] See Rogers M. Smith, *Civic Ideals: Conflict Visions of Citizenship in U.S. History* (New Haven: Yale University Press, 1997), pp. 165–409.

[97] The USA PATRIOT Act was passed in October 2001 and renewed in March 2006. Public Law 107-56, 107th Congress, http://www.gpo.gov/fdsys/pkg/PLAW-107publ56/html/PLAW-107publ56.htm [07-23-2009].

[98] See Frederick Schwarz and Aziz Huq, *Unchecked and Unbalanced: Presidential Power in a Time of Terror* (New York: New Press, 2008).

Yet the question remains: if there *is* a constitutional court, what role should it play in a democratic constitutional order? I take this question up in chapter 7 via a consideration of the U.S. Supreme Court's involvement with abortion rights. The Court's abortion jurisprudence has evolved considerably in the three-and-a-half-plus decades since the justices identified a woman's constitutionally protected right to abortion in *Roe v. Wade*.[99] This evolution partly reflects changes in the court's personnel, all of whom have been replaced since Justice Harry Blackmun penned his majority opinion in January of 1973. But the evolution also reflects ongoing struggles between the Court and state legislatures, and, more recently, the U.S. Congress. These struggles, in turn, reflect larger political currents. The National Organization for Women, founded in 1966, quickly grew into the largest women's organization in the country. Securing and protecting a woman's right to abortion has always been central to NOW's agenda, included as part of their proposed Equal Rights Amendment that was first introduced into Congress in 1982. Cultural conservatives have been mobilizing against them since 1970s. The Moral Majority, founded in 1979, and the Christian Coalition, created eight years later, have worked relentlessly to reverse *Roe* through political action, litigation, and attempts to influence appointments of federal judges. These campaigns and countercampaigns have fueled controversy over why the Court intervened in the abortion conflict by recognizing a woman's right to abortion as part of a constitutionally guaranteed right to privacy that is nowhere specified in the Constitution.

I explore this debate here for the light it sheds on a conception of democracy that is geared toward minimizing domination. One helpful way to think about judicial review from this perspective takes off from our understanding, in the wake of Arrow, that there are no perfect democratic decision rules—no mechanisms of collective decision that do not create losers with legitimate grievances. In *Democracy's Place* I rejected the libertarian response to this conundrum: that collective action should be minimized. What libertarians think of as the private sphere of noncollective action turns out on inspection to be sustained by a particular collective action regime that is imposed on those who would prefer some alternative. In light of the governmental response to banks and businesses that were judged "too big to fail" in 2008 and 2009, it is hard to see how anyone could conclude otherwise. The real choice is never over whether-or-not collective action; rather, it is over what sort of collective action.

Granting that collective action is inescapable does not, however, undermine the observation that all mechanisms of collective decision

---

[99] *Roe et al. v. Wade*, District Attorney of Dallas County 410 U.S. 113 (1973).

are problematic. Recognizing this means seeing that it is misguided to fetishize any particular collective decision as the final word in democratic politics. Even when they result from procedurally proper decisions, all collective outcomes are better thought of as provisional and open to revision—as their costs to those who are disadvantaged by them come into view and possibilities for mitigating those costs materialize. Courts play a constructive role in this process not when they usurp legislative functions, but rather when they get legislatures to revisit their collective decisions—revising them so as to minimize domination. I illustrate this contention via an examination of the Court's evolving abortion jurisprudence. I explain why the imperialistic character of Justice Blackmun's decision in *Roe* undermined the Court's legitimacy, but how it has developed a more defensible and effective stance since the late 1980s. This involves restricting itself to a reactive role in which the Court strikes down legislative decisions that foster avoidable domination, but invites further legislative action that can vindicate the legislature's goals in a less oppressive way. The search for accommodation can succeed only up to a point, but the history of the abortion controversy reminds us that necessity can be the mother of invention. There is often more scope for accommodation than people realize before they have to try to find it.

Even when the possibilities for accommodation have been exhausted, courts that adopt the reactive and iterative posture I recommend offer advantages from the perspective of minimizing domination. They provide forums in which divisive conflicts can be played out incrementally and at the margin, rather than as winner-take-all conflicts in which losers have no incentive to continue working within the system. Here the "cases and controversies" requirement of Article III of the U.S. Constitution offers decided advantages. It prohibits courts from supplying advisory opinions to the other branches on the constitutionality of proposed legislation, and it limits them to deciding only those issues that are actually litigated in particular cases. This means that there are always gaps in time, and often gaps in predictability, as to just what will transpire between the enactment of a statute and its being tested in the courts. These gaps can help blunt zero-sum conflicts even if they do not contribute to their resolution. Defending judicial review on these grounds parallels my neo-Lockean defense of majority rule. In both cases the aim is to arrive at collective decisions that minimize domination rather than those that converge on "the right" answer.

This, too, is well illuminated by the conflict over abortion in the United States. In 1992, in his opinion in *Planned Parenthood v. Casey*, Justice Antonin Scalia took issue with the majority's embrace of a standard that allows states to regulate abortions so long as they do not place an "undue burden" on women. Scalia denounced this as "amorphous," and bound to invite litigation because it is "inherently manipulable and will prove hopelessly unworkable in practice."[100] Subsequent litigation revealed Scalia's claim about the unworkability of the undue burden standard to be at least partly wrong, as my discussion in chapter 7 reveals, but his objection that the standard invites litigation misses the benefits this can offer in managing conflict over deeply divisive issues in pluralist societies. In 1835 Tocqueville remarked that "there is hardly a political question in the United States which does not sooner or later turn into a judicial one."[101] This is not to be sniffed at when the alternative is an unambiguous resolution that leaves losers with the incentive to reach for their guns.

In the final chapter of *Democracy's Place* I sketched a democratic conception of justice that built partly on this intuition that mechanisms for the pursuit of loyal opposition are important in forestalling disloyal opposition. The rationale underlying that argument is that much of what draws people to demand democracy is the desire to escape domination. Joseph Schumpeter was the first in a long line of self-styled political realists, as we have seen, to insist that it is wrongheaded to expect democracy to diminish injustice on any definition, and that it is dangerous to democracy's health to foster expectations that it might.[102] The contrarian case that I sketched in *Democracy's Place* and developed more fully in *Democratic Justice* was incomplete. I explored democracy's implications for the governance of civil institutions over the course of the human life cycle, reserving the subjects of distribution and public institutions for subsequent volumes that are now in preparation and for which the material published here serves as a prolegomenon. *Democratic Justice* has attracted its share of critical discussion over the past decade, much of which has been helpful to me in refining my account.

Some of those criticisms are addressed in chapter 8, in the course of which I explain the rationale for my approach to political theory more fully than I have done hitherto. I also elaborate on earlier accounts of rights and basic interests, the challenges of inequality, the limits of deliberation, and my—admittedly still rudimentary—treatment of public institutions. I hope that these responses forestall misunderstandings of

[100] *Planned Parenthood of Southeastern Pennsylvania et al. v. Casey et al.*, 505 U.S. 833 (1992), at 986.

[101] Alexis de Tocqueville, *Democracy in America* (1835), vol. 1, trans. George Lawrence, ed. J. P. Mayer (New York: Harper Perennial, 1969), p. 270.

[102] Joseph Schumpeter, *Capitalism, Socialism and Democracy* (New York: Harper, 1942), pp. 250–83.

my views and supply greater substance to the ideal of nondomination on which my democratic theory of justice rests. It was a commitment to an ideal of this kind, I think, that motivated Locke's mature writings about politics and gave them their enduring illumination and political appeal. Making that case persuasive is the task that I turn to next.

CHAPTER ONE

John Locke's Democratic Theory

INTRODUCTION

THE DEMOCRATIC tradition has ancient origins, but contemporary formulations are generally traced to Jean-Jacques Rousseau's discussion
of the general will in *The Social Contract*, published in 1762. Joseph
Schumpeter went so far as to characterize Rousseau's account as the
"classical" theory of democracy, even though his was really a neoclassical view—an eighteenth-century adaptation of the ancient Greek theory
in which democracy had meant ruling and being ruled in turn.[1] Many
commentators have followed Schumpeter's lead in treating Rousseau as
the father of modern democratic theory, yet it is my argument here that
John Locke merits the distinction. He developed the elements of an account of democracy that is more realistic, far-reaching, and appealing
than is Rousseau's, and it has greater continuing relevance than does
Rousseau's to contemporary democratic thinking. Locke conceived of the
relationship between people and ruler as one of authorship at a more
fundamental level than did Rousseau, placing the authorizing people,
acting collectively, at the center of his account of political legitimacy. Yet,
unlike Rousseau, he did not reify collective action or the general will in
ways that have since been debunked by social choice theorists. Moreover,
Locke's democratic theory had other dimensions as well, ranging over
accounts of the moral equality of persons, what we might today describe
as a political rather than a metaphysical approach to moral and political
disagreement, and a strong defense of majority rule as the wellspring of
institutional legitimacy.

   Some will find my suggestion jarring not so much for the invidious comparison with Rousseau as for the fact that Locke is typically portrayed
as a theorist of individual rights rather than of democracy. In the debate
over the ideological origins of the American Revolution, for instance, the
Lockean view is contrasted, as a rights-centric one, with a civic republican interpretation of the founders' self-understandings. There has been
no suggestion by protagonists on either side of that debate that Locke's

---

[1] See Joseph Schumpeter, *Capitalism, Socialism, and Democracy* (New York: Harper,
1942), pp. 250–68.

view was democratic.[2] Add to this the fact that Locke spent almost no time discussing political participation or representative institutions, and the prima facie case for him as a democratic theorist seems decidedly bleak. It is my contention, however, that the deep structure of Locke's account of politics is profoundly democratic. His understanding of the moral equality of persons lends itself better to democratic than to liberal thinking, even if his is not the "strong democracy" characteristic of the participatory and deliberative democratic traditions.[3] Moreover, as an institutional matter his defense of individual rights is nested in, and subordinate to, majority rule—casting his historical role as a proto–liberal rights theorist in a dubious light. This last contention is not new. As long ago as 1940 Willmoore Kendall noted that Locke's partiality to majority rule lived in tension with his account of individual rights.[4] Kendall saw this as a deficiency of Locke's theory, whereas on my account his defense of majority rule is part of a more sophisticated view of institutional legitimacy than Kendall was able to grasp. Another way to put this is that although Locke was no theorist of democratic participation, he was an innovative theorist of democratic legitimacy.

Does this mean the historical Locke was a democrat? Up to a point, albeit a debated one.[5] The gravamen of my claim here has more to do with the logic of his argument than with his intentions, but I mean to show that even they exhibited a democratic hue that has not been fully appreciated. As a matter of personal biography we know that Locke evolved over the course of his life: a fairly conservative, or, at any rate, apolitical person in his early adult years—one who gave unreflective endorsement to authoritarian political arrangements—he became a political insurrec-

[2] For a discussion of this debate, see my "J.G.A. Pocock's Republicanism and Political Theory: A Critique and Reinterpretation," *Critical Review* 4, no. 3 (Spring 1990): 433–71.

[3] Benjamin Barber, *Strong Democracy* (Berkeley and Los Angeles: University of California Press, 1984); James Fishkin, *Democracy and Deliberation: New Directions for Democratic Reform* (New Haven: Yale University Press, 1993); and Amy Gutmann and Dennis Thompson, *Democracy and Disagreement* (Cambridge, MA: Harvard University Press, 1998).

[4] Willmoore Kendall, *John Locke and the Doctrine of Majority Rule* (1940) (Urbana: University of Illinois Press, 1965).

[5] See Richard Ashcraft, *Revolutionary Politics and Locke's Two Treatises of Government* (Princeton: Princeton University Press, 1986); Mark Goldie, "John Locke's Circle and James II," *Historical Journal* 35, no. 3 (1992): 557–86; Ellen Wood, "Locke against Democracy: Consent, Representation and Suffrage in the *Two Treatises*," *History of Political Thought* 13, no. 4 (Winter 1992): 657–89; Ashcraft, "The Radical Dimensions of Locke's Political Thought: A Dialogic Essay on Some Problems of Interpretation," *History of Political Thought* 13, no. 4 (Winter 1992): 703–71; and Wood, "Radicalism, Capitalism, and Historical Contexts: Not Only a Reply to Richard Ashcraft on John Locke," *History of Political Thought* 15, no. 3 (Autumn 1994): 324–72.

tionist in Shaftesbury's circle in the 1670s and after. His political outlook expressed itself mainly in terms of the great issue of the day: whether there is a legitimate right to resist an illegitimate monarch to the point of removing him by force. Locke famously concluded that there is indeed such a right. This argument might be thought to have little consequence for democratic politics, dealing, as it does, with the legitimacy of revolution. Moreover, it seems clear that in some respects even the Locke of the 1680s and after distanced himself from the most radical political movements of his day. Without delving deeply into these historical controversies, I will argue that Locke's account of the conditions under which revolution is legitimate is nonetheless decidedly democratic in its assumptions, and that the ever-present possibility of legitimate revolution has significant democratic consequences for thinking about day-to-day politics.

I begin with an exploration of Locke's account of three dimensions of human moral equality, where I show that his inclusive view of all human beings as equally God's property, as intrinsically rational, and as the "authors" of the state was advanced for his day and, moreover, exhibited a fundamentally democratic egalitarian outlook. This is followed by a discussion of Locke's views on toleration and dissent, where I show that, in addition to embracing a comparatively capacious view of toleration for his own day, Locke's justification for the limits on toleration that he advocated was in some respects akin to the mature John Rawls in his "political, not metaphysical" mode, though Locke's political, not metaphysical stance turns out on close inspection to be more thoroughly political (and less problematic) than does Rawls's. This leads to a discussion of Locke's account of the relations between majority rule and institutional legitimacy, where I argue that Locke's embrace of majority rule was less starry-eyed than that of subsequent democratic theorists, but that it was by the same token more attractive given the realities of politics in pluralist societies.

HUMAN MORAL EQUALITY

The first and most basic sense in which we are equal, for Locke, is as God's property. Here we need to elucidate both the senses in which we are equal and those in which we are God's property, since both turn out to be relevant to subsequent democratic understandings.

Starting with the latter, Locke's view of humans as God's property is a special case of his workmanship theory by reference to which authority, ownership, and even authentic knowledge are all rooted in acts of creative making. This theory was developed as a consequence of Locke's position on the nature and meaning of natural law. If one took the view, common among natural law theorists of his day, that natural law is eternal and unchanging, this threatened another notion many thought compelling: that God is omnipotent. By definition, an all-powerful God could not be bound by natural law. Yet if God is conceded to have the capacity to change natural law, then we cannot declare it to be timeless. Locke wrestled with this tension without ever resolving it to his own satisfaction, but in his moral and political writings he came down decisively in the voluntarist, or will-centered, camp.[6] He could not relinquish the proposition that for something to have the status of a law, it must be the product of a will. By adopting this voluntarist view, Locke aligned himself with other will-centered theorists of the early Enlightenment, notably the German natural law theorist Samuel von Pufendorf.[7]

We find similar reasoning in Locke's *Essays on the Law of Nature*, delivered as lectures at Christ Church in 1663–64. Here, Locke's treatment of human capacities was linked to his theology in a different way; it rested on his categorial distinction between natural right and natural law, which explained human autonomy. Rejecting the traditional Christian correlativities between right and law, Locke insisted instead that natural law "ought to be distinguished from natural right: for right is grounded in the fact that we have the free use of a thing, whereas law is what enjoins or forbids the doing of a thing."[8] What humans perceive as natural law is in fact God's natural right; an expression of his will. In this sense right is prior to law in Locke's analytical scheme.[9] Locke's theory of own-

---

[6] John Locke, *Two Treatises of Government*, ed. Ian Shapiro (New Haven: Yale University Press, 2003), pp. 123–24, 160. All italics in subsequent quotations from Locke appear in the original work. For further discussion, see Patrick Riley, *Will and Political Legitimacy* (Cambridge, MA: Harvard University Press), pp. 61–97. See also Ian Shapiro, *The Evolution of Rights in Liberal Theory* (New York: Cambridge University Press, 1986), pp. 100–118.

[7] See T. J. Hochstrasser, *Natural Law Theories in the Early Enlightenment* (Cambridge: Cambridge University Press, 2001); Ian Hunter, *Rival Enlightenments: Civil and Metaphysical Philosophy in Early Modern Germany* (Cambridge: Cambridge University Press, 2001); and James Tully, *A Discourse on Property: John Locke and His Adversaries* (Cambridge: Cambridge University Press, 1980).

[8] John Locke, *Essays on the Law of Nature* (1663–64), ed. W. Von Leiden (Oxford: Clarendon Press, 1958), p. 111.

[9] By following Hobbes and Pufendorf in this formulation of the distinction, Locke was embracing an important departure from the Thomist tradition, rooted in Grotius's revival of the Roman law conception of a right as one's *suum*, a kind of moral power or *facultas* that every man has, and which has its conceptual roots, as Quentin Skinner has established, in the writings of Suarez and ultimately Gerson and the conciliarist tradition. *The Foundations of Modern Political Thought* (Cambridge: Cambridge University Press, 1978), 2:117, 176–78. See also Richard Tuck, *Natural Rights Theories* (Cambridge: Cambridge University Press, 1979), and John Finnis, *Natural Law and Natural Right* (Oxford: Clarendon Press, 1980) pp. 207–8.

ership flows naturally out of this scheme, transforming the workmanship model of knowledge into a normative theory of right. It is through autonomous acts of making that rights over what is created come into being. Making entails ownership, so that natural law is at bottom God's natural right over his creation.[10] Locke's frequent appeals to metaphors of workmanship and watchmaking in the *Two Treatises* and elsewhere underscore that for him men are obliged to God because of his purposes in making them. Men are "the Workmanship of one Omnipotent, and infinitely wise Maker. . . . They are his Property, whose Workmanship they are, made to last during his, not one anothers pleasure."[11]

Why does this account of natural law and God's workmanship matter for the moral equality of persons? Two reasons. First, because we are all God's creatures, on Locke's account, we were all protected from being owned by one another. It might ring strange to the contemporary ear that Locke felt the need to deny that people can be one another's property, but his central preoccupation in the *First Treatise* was to refute defenses of absolutism that appealed to Adam's "Right of Dominion over his Children."[12] Conventional defenders of absolutism, notoriously Sir Robert Filmer, had contended "that Fathers, by begetting them, come to an Absolute power over their children."[13] Locke insisted, by contrast, that God makes children and uses their parents for that purpose. Parents are "but occasions for [children's] being, and when they design and wish to beget them, do little more towards their making, than *Ducalion* and his Wife in the Fable did towards the making of Mankind, by throwing Pebbles over their Heads."[14] Were parents givers of life, Locke conceded, they might have some sort of quasi-ownership claim, but they are not. Even in this hypothetical eventuality, Locke resists the absolutist case by arguing that "every one who gives another any thing, has not always thereby a Right to take it away again,"[15] and he insists that because the woman "hath an equal share, if not greater," in nourishing a child, the creationist theory in any case does not justify paternal absolutism. It is "so hard to imagine the rational Soul should presently Inhabit the yet unformed Embrio, as soon as the Father has done his part in the Act of Generation, that if it must be supposed to derive any thing from the Parents, it must certainly owe most to the Mother."[16]

---

[10] Locke, *Essays on the Law of Nature*, pp. 111, 187.

[11] Locke, *Two Treatises*, II, § 6, p. 102. For further discussion see Tully, *A Discourse on Property*, pp. 35–38, and John Dunn, *The Political Thought of John Locke* (London: Cambridge University Press, 1969) p. 95.

[12] Locke, *Two Treatises*, I, § 50, p. 34.

[13] Ibid., I, § 52, pp. 35–36.

[14] Ibid., I, § 54, p. 37

[15] Ibid., I, § 52, pp. 35–36.

[16] Ibid., I, § 55, p. 37. See also II, § 52–53, p. 122.

Regardless of these calculations, Locke is unequivocal that Filmer's case fails for the more fundamental reason that to give life "is to frame and make a living Creature, fashion the parts, and mold and suit them to their uses, and having proportion'd and fitted them together, to put into them a living Soul."[17] Parents do not fashion the child and, most commonly, do not even intend to create it; they do so as a by-product of the instinctive desires God has placed in them. "They who say the *Father* gives Life to his Children, are so dazzled with the thoughts of Monarchy, that they do not, as they ought, remember God, who is the *Author and Giver of Life*."[18] Parents have fiduciary responsibility for their children on Locke's account, but it expires upon their maturity. Parents are obliged to provide for their children "not as their own Workmanship, but the Workmanship of their own Maker."[19]

This is why Locke insists that children are not born *in* a "state of *Equality*, though they are born to it." Adults have "a sort of Rule and Jurisdiction over them when they come into the World, and for some time after, but 'tis a temporary one." The bonds of children's subjection "are like the Swadling Cloths they are wrapt up in, and supported by, in the weakness of their Infancy." Developing age and reason loosen these bonds, "till at length they drop quite off, and leave a Man at his own free Disposal."[20] The power to command "ends with nonage." Thereafter, although "*honour* and respect, support and defense, and whatsoever gratitude can oblige a Man to the highest benefits he is naturally capable of, be always due from a Son to his Parents; yet all this puts no Scepter into the Father's hand, no Sovereign Power of Commanding."[21] The only legitimate sanction at the parent's disposal is the power to withhold inheritance, or "to bestow it with a more sparing or liberal hand, according as the Behavior of this or that Child hath comported with his Will and Humor."[22] Parents are to "inform the Mind, and govern the Actions of their yet ignorant Nonage, till Reason shall take its place and ease them of that Trouble."[23] This treatment of children reflects an inclusive view of the right to make decisions for oneself: the only justifiable basis for paternalism is incapacity.

One reason that Locke's view of moral equality has had staying power since he wrote is that the obvious secular analogue of his claim that we are all God's property is that we are nobody's property. The workman-

---

[17] Ibid., I, § 53, p. 36.
[18] Ibid., I, § 52, pp. 35–36.
[19] Ibid., II, § 56, p. 123.
[20] Ibid., II, § 55, p. 123.
[21] Ibid., II, § 69, pp. 129.
[22] Ibid., II, § 72, p. 130.
[23] Ibid., II, § 52–58, pp. 122–24.

ship model persisted in the Western intellectual consciousness long after it was cut loose from its Lockean theological moorings. If we abandon the theology yet still embrace the workmanship ideal, as most in the Enlightenment tradition since Locke—be they conservatives, liberals, or radicals—have done, the logic of his argument against Filmer continues to hold. Indeed, it can be extended: parents cannot own children because they do not make them, but by the same token nor can anyone else own them. In this way the egalitarian logic of his argument against Filmer extends beyond their theological disagreements.[24]

A comparably inclusive view is reflected in Locke's discussion of women. Feminist commentators on the history of political theory note correctly that there were limits to Locke's embrace of gender equality.[25] In the *First Treatise* he describes women as the "weaker Sex," and, although he insists there is no biblical authority for men's dominion over women, that it is a matter of human law, he says "there is, I grant, a Foundation in Nature for it."[26] Moreover, in the *Second Treatise*, he says that its "being necessary, that the last Determination, i.e. the Rule, should be placed somewhere, it naturally falls to the Man's share, as the abler and the stronger."[27] Yet, taken in context, in both cases these statements were concessions to considerably more paternalistic views that Locke was challenging, and it should be noted that the bulk of his discussion is concerned with hemming in what Locke took to be the husband's inevitable power.

We have already seen that Locke resisted patriarchalism with respect to children partly on the ground that if children were seen as human creations, women's ownership claim would outweigh that of men. Beyond this, Filmer had contended that "God at the Creation gave the Sovereignty to the Man over the Woman, as being the Nobler and Principal Agent in Generation,"[28] a belief that Locke maintained is utterly inconsistent with a biblical teaching, "for God in the Scripture says, *his Father and his Mother that begot him*."[29] Locke is equally dismissive of Filmer's claim that "*Monarchical Power of Government [is] settled and*

[24] For discussion of the evolution of secular variants of the workmanship ideal since the seventeenth century, see my *Democracy's Place* (Ithaca: Cornell University Press, 1996), chap. 3.

[25] Carole Pateman, *The Sexual Contract* (Stanford: Stanford University Press, 1988), pp. 38, 41, 54, 94. Susan Moller Okin, *Women in Western Political Thought* (Princeton: Princeton University Press, 1979), p. 199.

[26] Locke, *Two Treatises*, I § 47, pp. 32–33.

[27] Ibid., II § 82, p. 135.

[28] Sir Robert Filmer, *Patriarcha and Other Political Writings of Sir Robert Filmer, Edited from the Original Sources*, ed. Peter Laslett (Oxford: Blackwell's Political Texts, 1949), p. 245.

[29] Locke, *Two Treatises*, I, § 55, p. 37.

fixed by the Commandment, Honour thy Father and thy Mother," since as Locke observes, "no Body will say a Child may withhold Honour from his Mother, or, as the Scripture terms it, *set light by her*, though his Father should command him to do so, no more than the Mother could dispense with him, for neglecting to *Honour* his Father, whereby 'tis plain, that this Command of God, gives the Father no Sovereignty, no Supremacy."[30]

Perhaps more remarkably, Locke treated marriage as an egalitarian contract, grounded in the idea of mutual consent: "*Conjugal Society* is made by a voluntary Compact between Man and Woman: and tho' it consist chiefly in such a Communion and Right in one anothers Bodies as is necessary to its chief End, Procreation; yet it draws with it mutual Support, and Assistance, and a Communion of Interests too."[31] The husband prevails in situations of unavoidable conflict, but this nonetheless "leaves the Wife in the full and free possession of what by Contract is her peculiar Right, and gives the Husband no more power over her Life, than she has over his." Indeed, the power of the husband "being so far from that of an absolute Monarch, that the *Wife* has, in many cases, a Liberty to *separate* from him; where natural Right, or their Contract allows it, whether that Contract be made by themselves in the state of Nature, or by the Customs or Laws of the Countrey they live in; and the Children, upon such Separation fall to the Father or Mother's lot as such Contract does determine."[32] In short, Locke was remarkably ahead of his time with respect to women's equality, and, as Carole Pateman and Rogers Smith have noted, the egalitarian logic of his argument is subversive of all authority relations, including those arising in marriage.[33]

Likewise in his discussion of slavery in the *Second Treatise*, Locke insists that "The *Natural Liberty* of Man is to be free from any Superior Power on Earth, and not to be under the Will or Legislative Authority of Man, but to have only the Law of Nature for his Rule."[34] Human beings may not sell themselves into slavery because they are God's property. "No body can give more Power than he have himself; and he cannot take away his own Life, cannot give another power over it."[35] Slaves may be taken as a result of legitimate victory in war on Locke's account, but only because the defeated enemy has forfeited his right to life "by some Act that deserves Death," and the victor "to whom he has forfeited it, may

---

[30] Ibid., I, § 62, p. 41.

[31] Ibid., I, § 78, p. 52.

[32] Ibid., I, § 82, pp. 54–55.

[33] Rogers Smith, "Beyond Tocqueville, Myrdal, and Hartz: The Multiple Traditions in America," *American Political Science Review* 87, no. 3 (September 1993): 556; Pateman, *The Sexual Contract*, pp. 38, 41, 54, 94.

[34] Locke, *Two Treatises*, II, § 22, p. 19.

[35] Ibid., II, § 23, p. 19.

(when he has him in his power) delay to take it, and make use of him to his own Service, and he does him no injury by it."[36] Legitimate slavery is, in effect, nothing more than the continuation of a state of war between the lawful victor and the captive, who never, strictly, becomes his master's property.[37] There can be no master-slave relationship among members of a legitimate political association, which has to be based on consent. We are all equally immune from being owned by other humans, and by the same token bound to recognize that we cannot own others.[38]

In addition to our all being equally God's property, Locke argued that "*all men by Nature are equal*"[39] owing to God's decision. On Filmer's account, God had given the world to Adam and his heirs. Existing property rights and the system of political authority had allegedly passed to current owners and European monarchs in this way through primogeniture. Locke insisted, by contrast, that God gave the world to mankind in common—subject to the provisos that it not be wasted, and that "enough, and as good" remain available to others to use in common.[40] To this moral theory Locke added two dubious empirical claims that combined to get him from the theory of inclusive use-rights to the common to something like the view of property that contemporary libertarians embrace—often without realizing how it depends on these contingencies. The first was that with the introduction of money the injunction against waste, although not in principle transcended, for practical purposes became obsolete.[41] Second, Locke was convinced that the productivity effects of enclosing

---

[36] Ibid.

[37] As a result, if the slave concludes that "the hardship of his Slavery out-weigh the value of his Life, 'tis in his Power, by resisting the Will of his Master, to draw on himself the Death he desires." Ibid.

[38] Numerous Locke scholars have puzzled over how, if at all, Locke's views about slavery can be reconciled with the fact that he supported and even profited from the African slave trade and slavery in America—not least because African slaves were not captured in war and women and children were enslaved, which was expressly prohibited on the just war theory. The most comprehensive treatment of this subject is James Farr's "'So vile and miserable an estate': The Problem of Slavery in Locke's Political Thought," *Political Theory* 14, no. 2 (May 1986): 263–89. Farr makes a convincing case that the two really cannot be reconciled, and that Locke simply avoided the contradiction. This is in line with Dunn's earlier conclusion that "what we confront here is not an example of bland but deliberate moral rationalization on Locke's part but merely one of immoral evasion." Dunn, *The Political Thought of John Locke*, p. 175n. Of course the fact that Locke never publicly embraced authorship of the *Two Treatises* in his lifetime meant that he was not forced to account for the contradiction publicly or to confront the charges of hypocrisy that his enemies might otherwise have leveled at him. See also James Farr, "Locke, Natural Law, and New World Slavery," *Political Theory* 36, no. 4 (2008): 495–522.

[39] Locke, *Two Treatises*, II, § 54, pp. 122–23.

[40] Ibid., II, § 27, pp. 111–12.

[41] Locke believed that as well as not being subject to physical decay itself, money made possible the comparatively more productive use of natural resources through trade and

common land would be so great that the "enough, and as good" proviso could in practice also be dispensed with—thereby legitimating private ownership. For "he who appropriates land to himself by his labour, does not lessen but increase the common stock of mankind."[42]

Although Locke's theory permitted substantial inequalities to develop, it nonetheless provided the basis for an egalitarian collective constraint on them: if either of his empirical claims turns out not to be true, the provisos kick in with all the force of natural law behind them. In short, Locke was not a believer in equality of result, nor was he a mere proponent of equality of opportunity, or what Ronald Dworkin has described as starting-gate equality.[43] Use-rights to the common are universal and inextinguishable on Locke's account. Although he does not say this, it would thus be reasonable to infer that anyone who is deprived of access to the common owing to private ownership thus has a legitimate claim to at least what he would have been able to earn from unenclosed land. If this does not "trickle down" as a by-product of the productivity effects of enclosure, then the natural law guarantee is activated.[44]

God's decision to treat humans as one another's peers extends beyond these natural law protections, for Locke; it is built into the nature of human agency. We are all miniature gods on his account in that, provided we do not violate natural law, we stand in the same relation to the objects we create as God stands to us. We own them just as he owns us.[45] Natural law, or God's natural right, sets the outer boundaries to a field within which humans have divine authorization to act as little gods, creating rights and obligations of their own. And although Locke denies that parents create children, for reasons already discussed, he insists that God has endowed humans with great creative power. He minimizes the independent contribution of common resources to the value of what people produce by arguing that the world which has been given us in common is God's "waste," and insisting that "labour makes the far greater part"

productive work. See Richard Ashcraft, *Locke's Two Treatises of Government* (London: Allen and Unwin, 1987), pp. 123–50, and *Revolutionary Politics and Locke's Two Treatises of Government*, pp. 270–85, and, for the view (which Ashcraft criticizes) that Locke thought the proviso transcended with the introduction of money, C. B. Macpherson, *The Political Theory of Possessive Individualism* (Oxford University Press, 1962), pp. 203–21.

[42] Locke, *Two Treatises*, II, § 37, pp. 115–16.

[43] Ronald Dworkin, "What Is Equality? Part I: Equality of Welfare," *Philosophy and Public Affairs*. 10, no. 3 (Summer 1981): 185–246, and "What Is Equality? Part II: Equality of Resources," *Philosophy and Public Affairs* 10, no. 4 (Fall 1981): 283–345.

[44] For additional discussion of this point, see Shapiro, *The Evolution of Rights in Liberal Theory*, pp. 89–100.

[45] See John Locke, *An Essay Concerning Human Understanding* (1690), ed. Peter Nidditch (Oxford: Clarendon Press, 1975), bk. 2, chap. 27, and bk. 1, chap. 30. See also Tully, *A Discourse on Property*, pp. 108–10, 121.

of its value.[46] This is why Locke was so confident of the productivity effects of enclosure. The goods produced on an acre of enclosed land are at least ten—more like a hundred—times more than those "yielded by an acre of Land, of an equal richnesse, lyeing wast in common." As a result, someone who encloses ten acres "may truly be said, to give ninety acres to Mankind," at least.[47]

Locke applied his workmanship model to political arrangements no less than to property. Whereas for Filmer political rulers received their authority from God, on Locke's account political institutions are the property of the human beings who create them through a social contract. Indeed, in what might seem quaint by today's criteria for knowledge, Locke held that the study of ethics and politics is superior to that of the physical world because it concerns products of the human will to which we have privileged access through introspection. He distinguished "ectype" from "archetype" ideas, the former being general ideas of substances, the latter constructed by man. This generated a radical disjunction between natural and conventional knowledge, underpinned by a further distinction between "nominal" and "real" essences. In substances that depend on the external world for their existence (such as trees or animals), only nominal essences can be known to man. The real essence is available only to the maker of the substance, God. In the case of archetypes, however, nominal and real essences are synonymous, so that real essences can by definition be known by man. Because the social world is a function of archetype ideas, it follows that real social essences can be known by man. We know what we make. Man can thus have incontrovertible knowledge of his creations—most importantly, for our purposes, of his political arrangements and institutions.[48]

We know what we make just as we own what we make, be it property created through individual work or a commonwealth created by collective

---

[46] Locke, *Two Treatises*, II, § 25–51, pp. 111–21.

[47] Ibid., II, § 37, pp. 115–16.

[48] See Locke, *An Essay Concerning Human Understanding*, bk. 2, chaps. 31–32, bk. 3, chaps. 3, 6. In this he was following Hobbes, who had distinguished knowledge that depends on the human will from knowledge that is independent of it. As Hobbes put it, the pure, or "mathematical," sciences can be known a priori, but the "mixed mathematics" such as physics depend on "the causes of natural things [which are] not in our power." Hobbes, *De Homine* (1658) (New York: Anchor, 1972), p. 42. So he likened study of politics to that of mathematics on the grounds that "civil philosophy is demonstrable, because we make the commonwealth ourselves." As far as the natural world is concerned, we can only speculate, because we "know not the construction, but seek it from effects." See his Epistle Dedicatory to his *Six lessons to the Professors of Mathematics*, in *The English Works of Thomas Hobbes* (London: John Bohn, 1966), 7:183–84. For further discussion of this issue, see Tully, *A Discourse on Property*, pp. 9–27, and Shapiro, *The Evolution of Rights in Liberal Theory*, pp. 109–10.

agreement. God makes man, we are told in the *First Treatise*, "*in his own Image after his own Likeness*, makes him an intellectual Creature and so capable of *Dominion*."[49] Human beings are equal to one another in these endeavors because their capacity for creativity, their status as miniature gods, is both universal and God-given. It may not legitimately be given, taken away, or otherwise compromised by other human beings. Indeed, natural law requires that each person preserve himself, and that "when his own Preservation comes not in competition," each person ought "as much as he can, *to preserve the rest of Mankind*, and may not unless it be to do Justice on an Offender, take away, or impair the life, or what tends to the Preservation of the Life, the Liberty, Health, Limb or Goods of another."[50] Locke was adamant that "the *State of Nature* has a Law of Nature to govern it, which obliges every one: And Reason, which is that Law, teaches all Mankind, who will but consult it, that being all equal and independent, no one ought to harm another in his Life, Health, Liberty, or Possessions."[51]

Reason, then, is equally available to all. Locke was quick to defuse arguments from authority by appealing to man's natural and unencumbered reasoning capacities, a view that informs his discussion in the *Essay Concerning Human Understanding* as well as *A Letter Concerning Toleration*. So he insists in the *Essay* that it is not only those trained in logic who are capable of reason. "He that will look into many parts of Asia and America, will find men reason there perhaps as acutely as himself, yet who never heard of a syllogism, nor can reduce any one argument to those forms."[52] God, Locke insists,

has not been so sparing to men to make them barely two-legged creatures, leaving it to Aristotle to make them rational. . . . He has given them a mind that can reason, without being instructed in methods of syllogizing: the understanding is not taught to reason by these rules; it has a native faculty to perceive the coherence or incoherence of its ideas, and can range them right, without any such perplexing repetitions.[53]

Rank does not supply privileged access to reason any more than education does. Locke insists in the *Letter Concerning Toleration* that although princes are born superior to other men in power, "in nature" they are equal. "Neither the right nor the art of ruling does necessarily carry along

[49] Locke, *Two Treatises*, I, § 30, pp. 22–23.

[50] Ibid., II, § 6, p. 102.

[51] Ibid.

[52] Locke, *An Essay Concerning Human Understanding* (New York: Dover, 1959), vol. 2, bk. 4, p. 389.

[53] Ibid., p. 391.

with it the certain knowledge of other things."[54] And we have seen that in the *Second Treatise*, Locke avers that the laws of nature are more easily intelligible than positive laws, and in his discussion of parental authority the whole basis of his attack on Filmer is that this is limited to their "ignorant nonage." For Locke, adults are all assumed to be equally capable of rational behavior. He thus thought human moral equality was manifest in the scriptures, but that it can also be seen in our rational capacities and through observation of our place in nature.[55]

TOLERATION AND DISSENT

Human beings enjoy liberty to act as miniature gods within the constraints of natural law, for Locke, but they do not have license to violate the constraints themselves. This inevitably raises the question: what happens when people disagree about their obligations to one another, about what respecting one another's autonomy as God's creatures requires, or about whether natural law is otherwise being compromised by actions people are taking or contemplating? That which humans comprehend as reason is in part God's law, as I have just noted, but Locke realized that he had to confront the possibility—indeed, the strong likelihood—that people would disagree over the meaning of the scriptures or what reason otherwise requires. One way in which he responded was by embracing a capacious doctrine of toleration.

Locke went out of his way to make toleration in general not contingent on the truth or falsity of the belief to be tolerated. We are all subject to "the duties of peace and goodwill . . . as well towards the erroneous as the orthodox."[56] In *A Letter Concerning Toleration*, he insisted that the state may not force religious conformity on anyone, for "every church is orthodox to itself; [and] to others, erroneous or heretical." A church must therefore be a voluntary association of individuals that the magistrate both safeguards and limits, but may not regulate internally. "[T]he care of souls is not committed to the civil magistrate." His power consists

---

[54] Locke, *Two Treatises*, p. 230.

[55] Locke's characteristic mode of argument is to insist that nature, reason, and scripture all converge on the proposition he seeks to defend. For further discussion, see Shapiro, *The Evolution of Rights in Liberal Theory*, pp. 80–149.

[56] Ibid., p. 227. This exceptionally broad theory of religious toleration, and Locke's view that the ends of civil society are purely secular, are additional reasons for questioning the interpretation of Locke as a conservative Thomist. For further discussion of Locke's religious radicalism in his later writings, see Ashcraft, *Locke's Two Treatises of Government*, chaps. 1 and 2.

in "outward force," but "true and saving religion consists in the inward persuasion of the mind."[57]

Locke was well aware that an unqualified principle of toleration can generate paradoxes, conflicting injunctions, and self-defeating conclusions. He therefore imposed three kinds of limits on toleration. The first concerns toleration of practices inimical to the principle of toleration itself; that is, actions which, if tolerated, result in people's being forced to do things they would not otherwise do. "For all force, as has often been said, belongs only to the magistrate, nor ought any private persons at any time use force unless it be in self-defense against unjust violence."[58] "Unjust violence" seems to mean direct violation of another's will, a refusal to tolerate another's private actions. Toleration requires intolerance of antitolerant acts: "[F]or who could be free when every other Man's Humor might domineer over him?"[59]

Next, Locke is unequivocal in the *First Treatise* that, because all people are bound by the laws of nature, they have liberty to act freely but not license to do as they please. Thus children are under the authority of parents until they are old enough to understand that law, and thus practices like cannibalism, sale of children, adultery, incest, and sodomy, all of which "cross the main intention of Nature,"[60] cannot be tolerated. We leave aside, for now, how Locke expects us to know what is and is not against the main intention of nature; what is clear is that he expects that the civil law will uphold this law and will not tolerate transgressions of it.

Finally, actions should not be tolerated if they are prejudicial to the existence of the political order. Thus atheists ought to be suppressed not because Locke disagrees with their beliefs (though he does), but because those beliefs threaten the commonwealth. "Promises, covenants, and oaths, which are the bonds of human society, can have no hold upon an atheist."[61] Analogous considerations lead Locke to the conclusion that Papists and "Mahometans" ought not to be tolerated because they owe allegiance to alien civil powers. "That church can have no right to be tolerated by the magistrate which is constituted upon such a bottom that

[57] Locke, *Treatise of Civil Government and A Letter Concerning Toleration*, pp. 225, 218, 219.

[58] Ibid., p. 223.

[59] Locke, *Two Treatises*, II, § 57, p. 123–24.

[60] Ibid., I, § 59, p. 39.

[61] Ibid., 246. For an extended account of Locke's views on promising and trust, and their political applications, see John Dunn, "The Concept of 'Trust' in the Politics of John Locke," in *Philosophy in History: Essays on the Historiography of Philosophy*, ed. R. Rorty, J. B. Schneewind, and Q. Skinner (Cambridge: Cambridge University Press, 1984), pp. 279–301.

all those who enter into it do thereby *ipso facto* deliver themselves up to the protection and service of another prince."[62]

It is difficult to know to what extent such beliefs were sincerely held by any writer in the political climate of Restoration and revolutionary England. On the subject of atheism, Locke regarded questions about the existence of God as separate from questions about alternative religions. It is clear from the *Essay* that he was convinced by versions of the cosmological proof and the argument from design.[63] In *A Letter Concerning Toleration*, he seems to follow Hooker in invoking a version of the argument from common consent.[64] For whatever reason, Locke regarded the existence of God as self-evident. But his decisive *political* reason for denying toleration to atheists, Catholics, and Muslims rested on his worry about their incentives for fidelity to the commonwealth. In this he was an early proponent of a view akin to John Rawls's "political, not metaphysical" outlook concerning political legitimacy. True and saving religion might consist of inward persuasion of the mind, but if the mind of an Englishman becomes persuaded of the veracity of Catholicism or Islam, or, indeed, unpersuaded of God's existence, then he is out of luck. In short, the acceptability of a belief turns on its compatibility with the legitimate political order, not on whether its veracity is demonstrable by Locke's criteria.[65]

These considerations notwithstanding, Locke's view of toleration was a variant of the conventional Whig one in the 1680s. Since the Restoration, Charles and James had been attempting to expand toleration for Catholics and nonconformists to undermine the religious and political power of the Anglican clergy. Charles's embrace of toleration in 1662 and his declaration for indulgence a decade later met with insurmountable political opposition, but James had considerably more success with his similar declaration in 1687. James's uneasy alliance with both Catholic and Protestant nonconformists was broken at the Revolution as a result of Anglican promises to tolerate nonconformists in the general interests of Protestantism. This was realized to some extent in the

[62] Locke, *Two Treatises*, p. 245.

[63] See Locke, *An Essay Concerning Human Understanding* (Dover edition), bk. 2, pp. 306–24. For commentary, see Tully, *A Discourse On Property*, pp. 38–43.

[64] "All men know and acknowledge that God ought to be publicly worshipped; why otherwise do they compel one another unto the public assemblies? Men, therefore, constituted in this liberty are to enter into some religious society." Locke, *Two Treatises*, p. 232.

[65] Rawls defines his "political, not metaphysical" approach by reference to an "overlapping consensus" on principles that are likely to "persist over generations and to gain a sizable body of adherents in a more or less just constitutional regime, a regime in which the criterion of justice is that political conception itself." Rawls, *Political Liberalism* (New York: Columbia University Press, 1993), p. 15.

Toleration Act of 1689, even if that law did little more than exempt some narrowly defined groups of dissenters from some specific penalties. The act achieved its purposes, however. It split Protestant from Catholic dissenters, the latter being excluded from toleration legislation. Henceforth, Catholicism could be regarded as treasonable, as it was in the Act against Popery of 1700, aimed at "preventing the further growth of popery and of such treasonable, and execrable designs and conspiracies against his Majesty's person and government."[66] Locke's view was thus in the mainstream of Whig thinking on toleration that triumphed at the Revolution, even if he advocated tolerating a wider array of dissenting groups than would most.

Locke's account of toleration was buttressed by an antiauthoritarian theory of biblical hermeneutics. Underlying his rejection of Filmer's patriarchalism was a challenge to Filmer's reading of the scriptures, and particularly to the inherently hierarchical worldview that emanates from Filmer's contention that God gave the world to Adam and his heirs. Underlying *that* rejection, as Richard Ashcraft has noted, was Locke's radical claim that where the scriptures admit of more than one interpretation, no earthly authority may declare one reading to be authoritative.[67] Our prejudices and opinions "cannot Authorize us to understand the Scripture contrary to the direct and plain meaning of the Words," but where there is silence or ambiguity, the reader must judge how "*it may best be understood.*"[68] In the course of rejecting Filmer's claim that scriptural warrant for Adam's sovereignty over Eve can generate a justification for absolute monarchical authority, Locke insists that the burden lies with whoever is advancing an interpretation to give reasons that the reader will find plausible.[69]

Locke insisted that each reader is sovereign over what counts for him as a convincing interpretation of a text. As Locke argued in the *Letter on Toleration*, those things "that every man ought sincerely to inquire into himself, and by meditation, study, search, and in his own endeavours attain the knowledge of, cannot be looked upon as the peculiar possession of any one sort of men."[70] When people disagree over the meaning of the scriptures, they have to weigh the evidence for themselves. God speaks directly to every individual through the text, so that no human authority is entitled to declare one interpretation authoritative in the face of a

[66] The acts referred to in this paragraph are reprinted in A. Browning, ed., *English Historical Documents 1660–1714*, vol. 8 (London: Eyre & Spottiswoode, 1953), pp. 359–410.

[67] Ashcraft, *Locke's Two Treatises of Government*, pp. 65–68.

[68] Locke, *Two Treatises*, I, § 36, p. 26.

[69] Ibid., I, § 49, pp. 33–34.

[70] Ibid, p. 229.

conflicting one.[71] This freedom to comprehend natural law by one's own lights supplied the basis for Locke's right to resist that could be invoked against the sovereign, and to which he himself appealed in opposing the English crown during the 1680s. Ashcraft captures Locke's interpretive radicalism well when he notes that it was "designed to undermine the authoritative weight of an interpretation of the Bible advanced by any individual or group of individuals as an interpretative guide to the meaning of that work."[72]

This is not to say that Locke believed every interpretation of the scriptures to be equally valid. On the contrary, he thought that there is a correct interpretation on which reasonable people will usually agree, and he seemed confident that he could convince people that his reading of the scriptures was consistent with their commonsense interpretations. Although God speaks with more truth and certainty than do men, "when he vouchsafes to speak to Men [through the scriptures], I do not think, he speaks differently from them in crossing the Rules of language in use amongst them. This would not be to condescend to their Capacities, when he humbles himself to speak to them, but to lose his design in speaking, what thus spoken, they could not understand."[73] Commonsense readings of the scriptures must, therefore, reveal their true meaning. We have to countenance the possibility that people will continue to disagree, and we must protect their right to do so, but Locke did not doubt that most of the time people could be brought to agree.

I will have more to say about Locke's treatment of political disagreement anon. For now it is worth noting that there is a certain circularity to his view, parallel to that which attends Rawls in his "political, not metaphysical" mode. Rawls seeks a "political" conception of justice that "can gain the support of an overlapping consensus of reasonable religious, philosophical, and moral doctrines in a society regulated by it." He regards this as essential for people who disagree profoundly on religious, philosophical, and moral matters to "maintain a just and stable democratic society."[74] It is not entirely clear on Rawls's account whether, in order for a religious, philosophical, or moral doctrine to be judged reasonable it must meet independently derived criteria, as he sometimes claims, or whether it must be compatible with political arrangements that can be endorsed by adherents to any of the other doctrines that happen

---

[71] Locke, *Two Treatises*, I, § 46, p. 32. For an extended discussion of Locke's hermeneutical and methodological critique of Filmer's reading of the scriptures, see Ashcraft, *Locke's Two Treatises of Government*, chap. 3.

[72] Ashcraft, *Locke's Two Treatises of Government*, p. 67.

[73] Locke, *Two Treatises*, I, § 46, p. 32.

[74] Rawls, *Political Liberalism*, p. 10.

to prevail in the society—whether overlapping consensus is derived from reasonableness or the reverse.[75]

To be sure, expansive as it was for his day, Locke's view of toleration is more restrictive than is Rawls's. Yet it seems to exhibit an analogous ambiguity in that it is difficult to pin down whether he ultimately thinks commonsense interpretations of the scriptures should be thought commonsensical because they are compatible with political arrangements that those with different readings can endorse, or rather for some independent reason. And, as with Rawls, difficulties attend both views. If there is to be an independent criterion, the question arises as to where it comes from and what is to be said to those who are unpersuaded of its basis in reason or common sense. If, on the other hand, we adopt the contingent view, there is the danger that there might not be an overlapping consensus. There might not be enough common ground between competing interpretations—say Locke's and Filmer's—to sustain any political order. After all, considerations of this kind were presumably partly what was at issue for Locke in the 1680s. In some moods at least Rawls seems to want to square the relevant circle by claiming that his proposed principles are compatible with the most diverse possible array of doctrines while still being able to sustain a stable political order. The reasons Locke gives for limiting toleration as he does suggest that analogous considerations played into his thinking, but we will see that when push comes to shove he moves in a more decidedly democratic direction than does Rawls.

Democratic Foundations

At this point it might reasonably be asked whether Locke's view is not more liberal than democratic. After all, we have seen that it is the traditional liberal value of toleration, buttressed by a strongly individualist view of scriptural interpretation, that lies at the core of his political doctrine—a far cry from the conventional democratic commitment to participation. This is true; indeed as Kendall notes, given his doctrine, Locke is surprisingly thin on mechanisms of popular consultation.[76] Moreover, as Ruth Grant has convincingly argued, Locke did not think of day-to-day participation as a basic category of political legitimation.[77] Closer examination reveals, however, that his underlying conception of legitimacy is democratic more than liberal, particularly once we focus on his

[75] For further discussion, see Ian Shapiro, *The Moral Foundations of Politics* (New Haven: Yale University Press, 2003), chap. 5.

[76] Kendall, *John Locke and the Doctrine of Majority Rule*, p. 34.

[77] Ruth W. Grant, "John Locke on Women and the Family," in Locke, *Two Treatises*, pp. 286–308.

discussion of the practical implications of disagreement over the meaning of natural law and the right to resist.

Locke's assumption that people can typically be brought to agree on fundamental moral and political questions was obviously at variance with his own political experience. He acknowledged this in the most Hobbesian of terms: "For though the Law of Nature be plain and intelligible to all rational Creatures," he tells us in his discussion of the aims of political society in the *Second Treatise*, "yet Men being biased by their Interest, as well as ignorant for want of study of it, are not apt to allow of it as a Law binding on them. . . . Men being partial to themselves, Passion and Revenge is very apt to carry them too far, and with too much heat, in their own Cases."[78] For Hobbes, this view could generate a command theory of law to force men to be rational; for Rousseau it would generate a Lawgiver to manipulate men to be "genuinely" free. Locke, however, takes the idea of consent of the governed too seriously to make an analogous move. Like the young Rawls of *A Theory of Justice*, he seems to want to reason about the legitimacy of political institutions in a way that pays homage to considerable diversity of belief yet shields it from self-interest. As is well known, Rawls deployed a "veil of ignorance" to get at this: people are assumed to be choosing institutions knowing that there is a plurality of worldviews and conceptions of the good but not what their particular one is.[79] Locke, who conceived of the social contract as an actual agreement, would not have been much interested in hypothetical speculation of this kind. For him, reconciling disagreement with the view that political legitimacy is based on consent is an inescapable political problem. Whereas Rawls's "political, not metaphysical" move retains a rationalist component, Locke's is political all the way down. This is because Rawls restricts the range of acceptable views based on where they come from, whereas for Locke the decisive criterion is what they should be expected to lead to.

For Rawls, acceptable political arguments appeal only to public reason rooted in the overlapping consensus among the different views in society, not to the comprehensive religious and metaphysical doctrines to which people may be committed. This creates difficulties for him in thinking about the legitimacy of movements for political reform such as the civil rights movement. Such reform endeavors were often avowedly religious in inspiration, manifestly rooted in the comprehensive doctrines of their adherents. Of their leaders he says that "they did not go against the ideal of public reason; or rather, they did not provided they thought, or on

---

[78] Locke, *Two Treatises*, II, § 124–25, p. 155.
[79] See John Rawls, *A Theory of Justice*, 2nd ed. (Cambridge, MA: Harvard University Press, 1999), p. 11.

reflection would have thought (as they certainly could have thought), that the comprehensive reasons they appealed to were required to give sufficient strength to the political conception to be subsequently realized."[80] The obvious question to ask Rawls is what he would say to the pro-segregationist who believed his views, though right because dictated by God, were compatible with what public reason should endorse. Because Locke focused exclusively on the political effects of beliefs in determining what should be tolerated, he did not need to indulge in such conceptual gymnastics to adjudicate among comprehensive doctrines while trying to appear not to be so doing. This consequentialist understanding of "political, not metaphysical" places him closer to Jürgen Habermas than to Rawls in the contemporary debate.[81]

The right of resistance defended in the *Second Treatise* was intensely charged politically. Locke placed himself at odds with the Whig establishment in 1689 by embracing the Lawsonian view that, when James had been compelled to leave the throne, an entire dissolution of government had resulted. In violating the terms of the social contract James had, in Locke's view, gone into a direct state of war with the people. Accordingly, they had the right to resist him and to remove him as king.[82] Locke's view entailed not only that the king had been removed from office justly, but also that the rule of law and the legal authority of Parliament had ended, necessitating a return of power to the general community. As a general matter, this means that, once the right to resist potentially comes into play, the political stakes cannot be higher. It also makes all the more consequential the issue of what to do in the face of disagreement concerning how and by whom resistance is to be deemed legitimate.

In the course of arguing against both mixed and limited monarchy, Filmer had noted that in either case there is no final and authoritative judge within the constitution. Neither Parliament nor any court could resolve a charge of tyranny against the king. Locke tacitly accepted this position, as Franklin notes,[83] yet he never answered Filmer's charge that this would be an open invitation for continual resistance and even attempted revolution by anarchic individuals and groups disaffected by the actions of the king or Parliament. It was exactly this type of conflict that the Whigs wanted to avoid. Locke tried to downplay these radical implications of his view by holding that not every illegal act by the king justi-

---

[80] Rawls, *Political Liberalism*, p. 251.

[81] See Jürgen Habermas, "Reconcilliation through the Public Use of Reason: Remarks on John Rawls's *Political Liberalism*," *Journal of Philosophy* 92 (March 1995): 109–31.

[82] For an excellent discussion of Tory and Whig attitudes toward resistance, and how they differed from Locke's view, see J .H. Franklin, *John Locke and the Theory of Sovereignty* (Cambridge: Cambridge University Press, 1978), pp. 98–123.

[83] Ibid., pp. 94–95.

fied revolution, "[I]t being safer for the Body, that some few private Men should be sometimes in danger to suffer, than that the head of the Republick should be easily, and upon slight occasions exposed." Unless a ruler actively places himself "into a State of War with his People, dissolve the Government, and leave them to that defense, which belongs to everyone in the State of Nature," he may not legitimately be resisted.[84] Indeed, in the chapter on prerogative power, Locke went so far as to maintain that the independence of the ruler is such that there may be circumstances in which he may act where there is no law, and even in some cases "against the direct Letter of the Law"[85] provided this is for the public good. Wise and good princes will use this power well; others will misuse it.

This is only to push the matter back an additional step, however. Even in extreme cases—arguably especially in such cases—disagreement over whether the ruler has placed himself at war with his people has to be anticipated. Locke's instructive answer is that the "People have no other remedy in this, as in all other cases when they have no Judge on Earth, but to *appeal to Heaven*."[86] This appeal to heaven implies a resort to force. It might seem to bring Locke uncomfortably close to the Hobbesian position that although a person cannot be blamed in certain circumstances for resisting legitimate authority, such resistance is not itself legitimate—all he can do is hope that it will be recognized as valid in the life to come.[87]

MAJORITY RULE

But Locke's view differs from Hobbes's. Locke clearly supposes that genuine cases of a government's violation of its trust will be obvious, because he expects those who are not biased by interest, a group he assumes—perhaps heroically—will comprise most people, to converge on commonsense conclusions. The operational test of this is majoritarian for him: the right to resist does not lay "a perpetual foundation for Disorder" because it "operates not, till Inconvenience is so great, that the Majority feel it, and are weary of it, and find a necessity to have it amended."[88] There is no protection for minority perceptions of violations of the social contract or natural law in this scheme, or any provision to protect minorities from majority perceptions that the social contract or natural law have been

---

[84] Locke, *Two Treatises*, II, § 205, pp. 190–91. See also Franklin, *John Locke and the Theory of Sovereignty*, p. 95.

[85] Locke, *Two Treatises*, II, § 164, pp. 173–74.

[86] Ibid., II, § 168, p. 175.

[87] Thomas Hobbes, *Leviathan* (1651) (London: Pelican Books, 1968), pp. 268–70.

[88] Locke, *Two Treatises*, II, § 168, p. 175.

violated. Given the importance Locke famously attaches to personal consent as the final legitimating mark of all political action and institutions, it might seem remarkable that at the end of the day majority rule is its only guarantor.[89] Locke *predicts* that in reality people will be slow to resist, that the right to resist—even in circumstances of manifestly tyrannous acts—will frequently not be exercised.

> For if it reach no farther than some private Mens Cases, though they have a right to defend themselves, and to recover by force, what by unlawful force is taken from them; yet the Right to do so, will not easily ingage them in a Contest, wherein they are sure to perish; it being as impossible for one or a few oppressed Men to *disturb the Government*, where the Body of the People do not think themselves concerned in it, as for a raving mad Man, or heady Male-content to overturn a well-settled State; the People being as little apt to follow the one, as the other.[90]

In short, unless and until "a long train of Abuses, Prevarications, and Artifices, all tending the same way," trigger the right to revolution, people must accept the decisions emanating from the prevailing political order.[91] Until that threshold is crossed for a great many, even perceived violations of natural law must for all practical purposes be endured. On entering civil society, people give up the individual right to self-enforcement, and they can reassert it only at the risk of being executed for treason. On the other hand, if a long train of abuses, etc., *does* convince the great majority to revolt, there is no legitimate earthly power to stop them. In these respects, Locke's account recognizes the priority of politics to disagreements about rights and laws, so that Kendall is right to insist that those who appeal to Locke as a conventional defender of rights-based liberalism are misguided.[92]

If this were all Locke had to say on the subject of majority rule, the case for him as an early theorist of democracy would be flimsy indeed. In fact, however, he is quite explicit about the majoritarian foundations of political legitimacy. In the state of nature, "*every one has the Executive Power* of the Law of Nature," but this right is given up at the formation of civil society.[93] Thereafter, "it being necessary to that which is one body to move one way; it is necessary the Body should move that way whither the greatest force carries it, which is the *consent of the majority*: or else it

[89] For a useful discussion of the weaknesses in Locke's account of majority rule as a mechanism for representing personal consent, see Riley, *Will and Political Legitimacy*, pp. 93–97.

[90] Locke, *Two Treatises*, II, § 208, p. 192.

[91] Ibid., II, § 225, p. 199. See also § 226–33, pp. 199–204.

[92] Kendall, *John Locke and the Doctrine of Majority Rule*, pp. 63–74.

[93] Locke, *Two Treatises*, II, § 13, pp. 105–6.

is impossible it should act or continue one Body, *one Community*, which the consent of every individual that united into it, agreed that it should; and so everyone is bound by that to be concluded by the *majority*."[94] This leads Locke to defend a default presumption in favor of majority rule "in Assemblies impowered to act by positive Laws where no number is set by that positive Law that empowers them." Majority rule thus has "by the Law of Nature and Reason, the power of the whole."[95]

Locke recognizes the fact that the public assembly will be characterized by a "variety of Opinions, and contrariety of Interests, which unavoidably happen in all Collections of Men," and therefore, unanimity is unlikely.[96] For Rousseau, this reality would necessitate a Lawgiver to guide and enlighten the public as to the general will. But for Locke, the determination of the majority is sufficient, "for where the *majority* of the community cannot conclude the rest, there they cannot act as one Body, and consequently will be immediately dissolved again."[97] It is "the consent of any number of Freemen capable of a majority to unite and incorporate into such a society" that provides the "*beginning* to any *lawful Government* in the World."[98] It may be true, as Ellen Wood has emphasized, that Locke never advocated expansion of the franchise (which was unusually wide in seventeenth-century England).[99] But the more salient point for the longer term is that his argument provides no basis for limiting the franchise. His egalitarian commitments discussed in the first half of this essay press inexorably in the direction of universal inclusion—the only legitimate grounds for excluding people from decision making that affects them being incapacity.

For Locke, it is majoritarian rather than individual consent that authorizes institutional arrangements. The majority may choose to retain all powers of government, thereby creating a "perfect" democracy. Alternatively, it may delegate some or all of its powers, creating various "forms of commonwealth," such as oligarchies or elective or hereditary monarchies. As Ashcraft notes, "formally, Locke is committed to the view that the majority of the community may dispose of their political power as they see fit, and this includes, of course, their power to constitute a democracy," which is the "form of government that remains closest to the institution of the political community itself."[100] Whatever form of

[94] Ibid., II, § 96, p. 142.

[95] Ibid.

[96] Ibid., II, § 98, pp. 142–43.

[97] Ibid.

[98] Ibid., II, § 99, p. 143.

[99] Wood, "Locke against Democracy," pp. 660–63.

[100] Ashcraft, *Locke's Two Treatises of Government*, p. 183. Ashcraft is quick to point out, however, that this does not necessarily mean that Locke is advocating democracy as the most desirable form of day-to-day government.

government is chosen, it rests ultimately on conditional delegation from the majority. The majority never relinquishes its "Supream Power," which comes into play when delegated power either expires or is abused.[101] Unless a substantial majority comes to agree that abuse has occurred, the opposition of the individual will have no practical effect.[102] Opposition may otherwise be legitimate, but even when it is undertaken against an action that is life threatening, an individual or minority might have to wait for vindication until the next life, as we have seen.[103] In practice, in this world, natural law constrains the actions of governments only to the extent that a majority discerns it and acts on it.

But why *majority* rule? Liberal writers for whom consent supplies the basis of political legitimacy typically appeal to unanimity, not majority rule, particularly on significant questions—effectively granting a veto to all individuals who might wish to withhold their consent. For instance, James Buchanan and Gordon Tullock argue in *The Calculus of Consent* that people would insist on unanimity rule before collective action could be taken concerning the issues they regard as most important. Only on less consequential matters would they see the sense of accepting majority rule, or perhaps even delegation to an administrator, when they trade off the costs of participating in decision making against the likelihood that an adverse decision will be made.[104] Buchanan and Tullock do not supply us with criteria for distinguishing more from less consequential decisions, but it seems safe to assume that Locke's right to resist would be at or close to the top of the list. Yet, as we have seen, he protects it with majority rule only. Why?

The answer is that Locke had a more realistic view of politics than did the hypothetical contract theorists of the second half of the twentieth century. As Patrick Riley has noted, "the social contract, for Locke, is necessitated by natural law's inability to be literally 'sovereign' on earth, by its incapacity to produce 'one society.'"[105] Theorists like Buchanan and Tullock, Rawls, and Robert Nozick are often criticized for writing as if the institutions of civil association—private property, contracts, rules of inheritance—can exist independently of collective action.[106] Locke made no such assumption, and he would surely have recognized its infeasibil-

[101] Locke, *Two Treatises*, II, § 132, p. 157.

[102] Ibid., II, § 208–9, p. 192.

[103] Ibid., II, § 202–10, p. 189–93.

[104] James Buchanan and Gordon Tullock, *The Calculus of Consent: Logical Foundations of Constitutional Democracy* (Ann Arbor: University of Michigan Press, 1962), pp. 172–262.

[105] Riley, *Will and Political Legitimacy*, p. 64

[106] See *Democracy's Place*, chap. 2, and Stephen Holmes and Cass Sunstein, *The Costs of Rights* (New York: W. W. Norton, 1999).

ity—after all, in his lifetime every enclosure of land required an act of Parliament. Once we recognize that collective action is ubiquitous to civil association, then it makes little sense to assume that regimes in which change is difficult are those in which important individual freedoms will be best protected. As Locke was acutely aware, the status quo can be the source of political oppression. When this is so, obstacles to collective action will sustain that oppression. In the real world of ongoing politics, Brian Barry and Douglas Rae have shown that majority rule, or something close to it, is the logical rule to prefer if one assumes that one is as likely to oppose a given outcome as to support it regardless of whether it is the status quo.[107] From this perspective the libertarian constitutional scheme is a collective action regime maintained by the state, and disproportionately financed by implicit taxes on those who would prefer an alternative regime. Locke recognized, as Laslett put it, that "it is the power that men have over others, not the power that they have over themselves, which gives rise to political authority."[108]

In short, Locke's institutional theory differs from that of modern libertarians because he operates with a different underlying theory of power—as ubiquitous to human interaction rather than as a by-product of collective action. As a result, unequivocal as he was that consent is the wellspring of political legitimacy, he saw majority rule as its best available institutional guarantor. Hence his concluding insistence that the *"Power that every individual gave the Society,* when he entered into it, can never revert to the Individuals again, so long as the Society lasts, but will always remain in the Community; because without this, there can be no Community."[109] And the judgment whether or not the government is at war with the community must reside with the people: "If a Controversie arises betwixt a Prince and some of the People, in a matter where the law is silent, or doubtful, and the thing be of great Consequence, I should think the proper *Umpire,* in such a Case, should be the Body of the *People.*"[110] Common misconceptions to the contrary notwithstanding, the relation between the people and the government is not a contract. Rather, it is one of trust. Should a question arise as to whether that trust has been violated by a prince or legislature, *"The People shall be Judge;* for who shall be *Judge* whether his Trustee or Deputy acts well, and according to the trust reposed in him, but he who deputes him, and must,

[107] Brian Barry, *Political Argument* (1965), 2nd ed. (Herefordshire: Harvester Wheatsheaf, 1990); Douglas Rae, "The Limits of Consensual Decision," *American Political Science Review* 69 (1975): 1270–94.

[108] Peter Laslett, "Introduction," in John Locke, *Two Treatises*, p. 111.

[109] Locke, *Two Treatises*, II, § 243, pp. 208–9.

[110] Ibid., § 242, p. 208.

by having deputed him still have a Power to discard him, when he fails in his Trust."[111] And the people act by majority rule.

Locke understood that the fundamental political question for human beings is not whether-or-not collective action. Rather, it is what sort of collective action. His presumption in favor of the supremacy of legislative authority reflects this. Legislatures are legitimate just because they embody majority rule, which, in the end, is the best available guarantor of the freedoms people seek to protect through the creation of government. Although Locke perceived advantages to a separation of powers involving an independent executive and "federative" (geared to foreign affairs and to relations with those in the state of nature), he was unequivocal that these are subordinate to the legislative power because it alone embodies the consent of the governed through majority rule.[112] Even in the case of a dissolution of government there need not be a return to a state of nature. Rather, power can devolve to the people who "may constitute themselves as a *new Legislative*, as they think best, being in full liberty to resist the force of those, who without Authority would impose any thing on them."[113] The people, acting as a body by majority rule, have greater legitimacy than the alternative: individuals or arbitrary powers acting unilaterally.[114]

Locke's recognition that power is inevitably exercised in collective life perhaps also accounts for why his discussion of tacit consent seems so cavalier, at least in comparison to that of a theorist like Nozick (who engages in a tortured, and ultimately unsuccessful, argument for forcibly incorporating "independents" who refuse to join the society in a manner that can be said not to undermine their consent).[115] Locke insists that "every Man, that hath any Possession, or Enjoyment, of any part of the Dominions of any Government, doeth thereby give his *tacit Consent*, and is far forth obliged to Obedience to the Laws of that Government, during such enjoyment, as any one under it."[116] His claim that their tacit

[111] Ibid., § 240, p. 208.

[112] Ibid., §§ 149–58, pp. 166–71.

[113] Ibid., § 212, p. 194.

[114] Radical as this indissoluble link between consent and majority rule might seem, John Marshall makes a compelling case that part of Locke's motive was conservative: he was attempting to convince the gentry, yeomanry, and merchants that a rare and limited right of resistance to the monarch could be endorsed "which would not threaten the social hierarchy and lay the foundations for anarchy or for frequent challenge of the political establishment and which was perfectly compatible with the re-establishment of a mixed monarchy with different personnel." John Marshall, *John Locke: Resistance, Religion and Responsibility* (Cambridge: Cambridge University Press, 1994), pp. xvi–xvii, 205–91.

[115] For consideration of the difficulties attending Nozick's discussion of compensating independents who are forced to become members, see Shapiro, *The Evolution of Rights in Liberal Theory*, pp. 169–78.

[116] Locke, *Two Treatises* II, § 119, pp. 152–53.

consent is reasonably taken for granted because they are free to leave is obviously belied by most people's circumstances.[117] Yet if one takes the view that even those who have given express consent must inevitably expect often to be at odds with actions of the government, then this seems less troubling. Only from the unrealistic perspective of someone who thinks it possible to live in a form of political association with others in which one's consent is never violated does it seem troubling that one's only protection is majority rule. No other decision rule provides better protection.[118]

It is sometimes said that this is why constitutional courts and bills of rights are needed to protect individuals and minorities from the vicissitudes of democratic politics. At least since Mill's and Tocqueville's time, it has been characteristic for liberal constitutionalists to worry about majority tyranny, but as I discuss in the next chapter, history has revealed these worries to have been misplaced. It seems that Locke's underlying institutional commitment to majority rule was indeed more farsighted than critics such as Kendall appreciated.

That said, it might nonetheless be objected that Locke's insistence that majority rule is the best available institutional guarantor of the entitlements human beings create for themselves, the agreements human beings make with one another, and the natural law constraints on all their actions, it is an ultimate guarantor with few—if any—implications for day-to-day politics. This is partly what Kendall had in mind when complaining that Locke's commitment to majoritarianism is not buttressed by any mechanism of popular consultation. There is truth to this, but two points should be noted in mitigation. First, Locke's account looks a good deal more plausible if we think of the reality of democratic systems rather than democratic ideals. Actual democratic systems involve a mix of decision-making mechanisms and considerable delegation to administrative agencies; many empower courts to conduct judicial review. But these different mechanisms are all subservient to majoritarian political

[117] Ibid., § 121, pp. 153–54. Taken in context, it was a more radical claim than it might seem to us, since the king's subjects were not generally free to renounce that status—regardless of whether they had given express consent. In our own time the examples of the USSR and Iraq should remind us that even a right not to have exit legally proscribed is by no means without value. A useful discussion of Locke on tacit consent is Paul Russell, "Locke on Express and Tacit Consent: Misinterpretations and Inconsistencies," *Political Theory* 14, no. 2 (May 1986): 291–306.

[118] Indeed, from this perspective Locke's remark that in a marriage the husband prevails in situations of unavoidable conflict could be interpreted as a claim about what Locke expected would happen as an empirical matter rather than something he would choose to defend. The man prevails because someone must and the bulk of the force is on his side, but not because it is otherwise desirable that he should. And as I noted, Locke sought to limit this power to their common endeavors and to preserve the wife's right of exit.

decision making in various ways, whether through systems of appointment, control of funding and jurisdiction, oversight, or some combination of these. Constitutional systems sometimes limit democracy's range, to be sure, particularly in separation-of-powers systems such as the United States. But constitutions generally contain entrenched guarantees of democratic government as well. Moreover, they are themselves revisable at constitutional conventions or via amendment procedures whose legitimacy is popularly authorized. Even liberal constitutionalists like Bruce Ackerman agree that critical moments of constitutional founding and change require popular democratic validation if they are to be seen as legitimate over time.[119] In short, the practice in modern democracies is consistent with Locke's picture of various institutional arrangements—some more participatory than others—existing against a backdrop of popular sovereignty.

There is a second and more specific sense in which Locke might be seen as being more prescient about democracy than Kendall gave him credit for having been, linked to the reality that mechanisms of popular consultation turn out to be fraught with difficulty. Modern social choice theory has taught us that it is doubtful that there can be any such thing as a Rousseauian general will in even minimally diverse societies. As a result, we should think of democracy as a way of ensuring that, however inclusive decision making can be made to be, the possibility of opposition from those whose interests might be harmed by the exercise of power is an important discipline. Majority rule is less a system of representation from this point of view than one of "flexing muscles," as Adam Przeworski puts it; "a reading of the chances in the eventual war."[120] Though he did not intend it thus, it would be difficult to conjure up a more apposite expression of the sentiment behind the discussion of majority rule in chapter 19 of the *Second Treatise*. It calls to mind Machiavelli's argument that elites are best disciplined by the lurking danger of ferocious populism.[121] It is this strand of democratic thinking that would come to be neglected as democratic theorists became consumed with the Rousseau-inspired quest to identify a general will.

That Locke fails to provide for mechanisms of popular consultation looks less worrisome, from this perspective, as does the objection that his right to resist issues in a theory of revolution more than one of govern-

---

[119] Bruce Ackerman, *We The People: Foundations* (Cambridge, MA: Harvard University Press, 1993).

[120] Adam Przeworski, "Minimalist Conception of Democracy: A Defense," in *Democracy's Value*, ed. Ian Shapiro and Casiano Hacker-Cordón (Cambridge University Press, 1999), p. 48.

[121] See John McCormick, "Machiavellian Democracy: Controlling Elites with Ferocious Populism," *American Political Science Review* 95, no. 2 (June 2001): 297–313.

ment. All governments live in the shadow of possible revolution, as Iran's political elites were sharply reminded at the end of 2009.[122] The way for them to avoid it is to be responsive to the interests of the majority, who might otherwise conclude that their trust has been violated. This may be a more sober view of democratic politics than those that have enthralled many theorists since Locke's time. At the same time, however, his has done better over the long run—and with good reason.

[122] Robin Wright, "Latest Iran Protests Show a Resilient Opposition," *Time*, December 7, 2009, http://www.time.com/time/world/article/0,8599,1946038,00.html [12-09-2009].

CHAPTER TWO

Tyranny and Democracy: Reflections on Some Recent Literature

> If majority governments . . . be the worst of Governments those who think and say so cannot be within the pale of republican faith. They must either join the avowed disciples of aristocracy, oligarchy or monarchy, or look for a Utopia exhibiting a perfect homogeneousness of interests, opinions and feelings nowhere yet found in civilized communities.
> —James Madison, "Memorandum on 'Majority Government'" (1833)

LOCKE SAW majority rule as the ultimate check on political tyranny, but, at least since Plato wrote the *Republic*, people have worried that it has the potential actually to facilitate tyranny. A recurring response to this troublesome possibility has been to limit the power of untrammeled majorities. Two main tacks have been taken in the literature. One is to embellish democratic procedures by building in such institutional safeguards as supermajority requirements and bills of rights. The other main tack has been to resist the identification of democracy with majority rule, or indeed with any decision rule that is evaluated without reference to whether the outcomes it generates facilitate tyranny. Proponents of various "substantive" conceptions of democracy hold that achieving true democracy involves a commitment to "nondomination," to "equal concern and respect," to protecting the interests of "discrete and insular minorities," or some other substantive or quasi-substantive constraint.

The need for institutional constraints was perhaps taken most seriously by the American founders—most notably by James Madison, who insisted in *Federalist* No. 10 that the new American polity should be a nontyrannical republic rather than a "pure democracy."[1] Madison's view has always had its critics, the most trenchant of whom in the twentieth century was Robert Dahl. As early as 1956 Dahl registered skepticism that democracies with constitutional courts respect individual freedoms more than do democracies without judicial review, a view he developed

---

[1] Alexander Hamilton, James Madison, and John Jay, *The Federalist Papers*, ed. Clinton Rossiter (New York: Mentor, 1961), p. 81.

more fully in a seminal article the following year.[2] Subsequent scholarship has shown Dahl's skepticism to have been well-founded.[3] Indeed, there are reasons to suspect that the popularity of independent courts in new democracies might have more in common with the popularity of independent banks than with the protection of individual freedoms. They can operate as devices to signal foreign investors and international economic institutions that the capacity of elected officials to engage in redistributive policies will be limited.[4]

This suggests a more general query: do the architects of democratic transitions put too much stock in constitutions as instruments of democratic stability? As Dahl said of the United States, "to assume that this country has remained democratic because of its Constitution, seems to me an obvious reversal of the relation; it is much more plausible to suppose that the Constitution has remained because our society is essentially democratic."[5] Other scholarship supports Dahl's contention. One strand of research, reaching from Tocqueville to Robert Putnam, emphasizes the role of civic traditions and associations in underwriting well-functioning democracy.[6] Another strand, from Seymour Martin Lipset and Barrington Moore to Adam Przeworski, suggests that economic factors are more consequential.[7] It seems clear that social and economic factors outweigh

---

[2] Robert Dahl, *A Preface to Democratic Theory* (Chicago: University of Chicago Press, 1956), pp. 105–12; and "Decision-Making in a Democracy: The Supreme Court as National Policymaker," *Journal of Public Law* 6 (1957): 279–95.

[3] Robert Dahl, *Democracy and Its Critics* (New Haven: Yale University Press, 1989), pp. 188–92; Gerald Rosenberg, *The Hollow Hope: Can Courts Bring About Social Change?* (Chicago: University of Chicago Press, 1993); Ran Hirschl, *Towards Juristocracy: The Origins and Consequences of the New Constitutionalism* (Cambridge, MA: Harvard University Press, 1999); and Jeremy Waldron, *Law and Disagreement* (Oxford: Oxford University Press, 2001).

[4] See Ran Hirschl, "The Political Origins of Judicial Empowerment through Constitutionalization: Four Lessons from Four Constitutional Revolutions," *Law and Social Inquiry* 25 (2000): 91–147.

[5] Dahl, *Preface*, p. 143.

[6] Alexis de Tocqueville, *Democracy in America* (1835), vol. 1, trans. George Lawrence, ed. J. P. Mayer (New York: Harper Perennial, 1969), pp. 50–58, 277–315; Robert Putnam, *Making Democracy Work: Civic Traditions in Modern Italy* (Princeton: Princeton University Press, 1993) and *Bowling Alone: The Collapse and Revival of American Community* (New York: Simon and Schuster, 2000). For criticism, see Margaret Levi, "Social and Unsocial Capital: A Review Essay of Robert Putnam's *Making Democracy Work*," *Politics and Society* 24, no. 1 (1996): 45–46.

[7] Seymour Martin Lipset, "Some Social Requisites of Democracy: Economic Development and Political Legitimacy," *American Political Science Review* 53, no. 1 (1959): 61–105; Barrington Moore, *The Social Origins of Dictatorship and Democracy: Lord and Peasant in the Makings of the Modern World* (Boston: Beacon Press, 1966); Adam Przeworski, Michael Alvarez, José Cheibub, and Fernando Limongi, *Democracy and Development: Political Institutions and Well-Being in the World, 1950–1990* (Cambridge: Cambridge University Press, 2000).

constitutional arrangements in accounting for the health of democracies, and, as I discuss in relation to Charles Tilly below, other processes connected to the control of violence and the political impact of inequality are likely to be important as well.

It is scarcely surprising, however, that the American founders focused intensively on institutional arrangements, just as the architects of the transitions to democracy elsewhere have done. Politicians have to work with the civic traditions and social structures they inherit. Their capacity to create propitious economic conditions, assuming they know what these are, is severely limited. In any case it takes a long time. But at moments of founding or transition, choices about foundational institutions must nonetheless be made—after which they will likely be difficult and costly to change. Constitutional arrangements might account for a small proportion of the variance in democratic viability, but when they are up for grabs it is natural to focus on them and try to get them right.

In a new edition of *A Preface to Democratic Theory*, published in 2006, Dahl notes that Madison's views evolved considerably over the course of his lifetime.[8] In 1787 Madison was a young man of thirty-six, with the great bulk of his political life ahead of him. As he himself wrote to Thomas Jefferson two years later, "We are in a wilderness, without a single footstep to guide us."[9] It would be remarkable indeed if his twenty-four years in the rough-and-tumble of government and high office (he served for eight years each as a member of Congress, as secretary of state, and as the fourth president of the United States) had left his views about politics unaltered. For one thing, his role, starting in 1792, in founding and then shaping the early evolution of the Republican Party (which was soon renamed the Democratic-Republican Party, and eventually, under Andrew Jackson, the Democratic Party) helped Madison shed his fear of political parties. These were, to be sure, more like elite networks than the mass membership parties of today, but they were nonetheless institutional expressions of his once-dreaded "factions."

Madison's embrace, along with Thomas Jefferson's, of political parties was partly occasioned by their rival Alexander Hamilton's political success in turning the Federalist Party into the engine for a political agenda that differed starkly from theirs. Even though Madison and Jefferson were largely unsuccessful in their attempts to derail Hamilton's nationalist and industrial agenda, the effort had a lasting legacy of which they were perhaps barely cognizant: it helped institutionalize electoral competition over policy and for office as the sine qua non of democratic politics.

[8] Dahl, "Reevaluating Madisonian Democracy," afterword to the expanded edition of *A Preface to Democratic Theory* (Chicago: University of Chicago Press, 2006), pp. 152–72.

[9] James Madison, letter to Thomas Jefferson, June 30, 1789, quoted in Ron Chernow, *Alexander Hamilton* (New York: Penguin Press, 2004), p. 280.

Much of the discussion of political parties and elections in *The Federalist* gives the impression of people trying to learn how to swim by walking up and down beside a lake while debating the theory of swimming. By diving in and battling for their views in electoral politics after 1792, the politicians of America's founding generation learned how to compete, and, more important, they began manufacturing a culture of democratic competition.

It was in light of this experience that Madison's views about the danger of "majority factions" would eventually change. His battles against Hamilton led him to view the tyranny of the minority as a more serious problem to be guarded against than the tyranny of majority factions. This led Madison to favor expanding the suffrage to those whites without landed property. It was a radical move for Madison, somewhat grudgingly made—but made nonetheless. Perhaps it was rendered easier by his recognition that westward expansion would be accompanied by widely dispersed ownership of land, but Dahl points out that in 1821 Madison wrote a note in which he was unequivocal that a universal suffrage would be preferable even if this were not the case.[10] Madison also became more sanguine about political parties, which he described as "a natural offspring of freedom." For the mature Madison, competition among parties was freedom's best guarantor. By the end of his life Madison had thus come to a view that is considerably closer to Dahl's than it is to the view for which he had proselytized so eloquently in *The Federalist* as a young man.[11]

Modern social choice theorists have held that the problem is worse than these eighteenth-century authors realized in that majority rule can lead to arbitrary outcomes and even to minority tyranny. Extending an old insight of the marquis de Condorcet, in 1951 Kenneth Arrow showed that under some exceedingly weak assumptions, majority rule leads to outcomes that are opposed by a majority of the population. For instance, if voter I's ranked preferences are A>B>C, voter II's are C>A>B and voter III's are B>C>A, then there is a majority for A over B (voters I and II), a majority for B over C (voters I and III), and a majority for C over A (voters II and III).[12] This outcome, known as a voting cycle, violates the principle of transitivity—generally taken to be an essential feature of rationality. It permits a self-contradictory ranking of societal preferences. Moreover, it opens up the possibility that whoever controls the order of voting can determine the outcome, provided she knows the preferences of the voters. At a minimum we have to live with the possibility that a given

[10] Dahl, "Reevaluating Madisonian Democracy," p. 166.
[11] Ibid., pp. 160–67.
[12] Kenneth Arrow, *Social Choice and Individual Values* (New York: Wiley, 1951).

collective outcome is arbitrary in that, had voting occurred in a different order, a different result might have prevailed.

Nicholas Miller has noted the existence of a tension between the concept of stability implicit in the public choice literature since Arrow, much of which has been consumed with how to prevent cycling, and the pluralist idea of stability that turns on the presence of crosscutting cleavages of interest in the population.[13] The periodic turnover of governments is facilitated by just the kind of heterogeneous preferences that create the possibility of cycling. It is the institutionalized uncertainty about the future that gives losers an incentive to stay with the process in hopes of winning next time. This is one reason that Dahl has long held that political competition under majority rule is a better guarantor of minority interests than are constitutional or other institutional constraints. The multiplication of factions and their representation through parties in the political system, as Madison eventually came to see, is what makes democracy work. Analogous reasoning sometimes leads students of comparative politics to contend that competitive democracy does not work when heterogeneous preferences are lacking. If the preference-cleavages in the population are not sufficiently crosscutting to produce this result, they propose alternative institutional arrangements, such as Arend Lijphart's "consociational democracy," which includes entrenched minority vetoes and forces elites representing different groups to govern by consensus as a cartel, avoiding political competition.[14]

Sidestepping the theoretical debate on how troubled, if at all, we should be at the possibility of cycles, we do well to consider their likelihood.[15] It has long been known that various constraints on the structure and diversity of preferences will rule cycles out.[16] At least one theoretical result suggests that cycles are comparatively unlikely in large populations even when preferences are heterogeneous.[17] An exhaustive empirical study by Gerry Mackie has revealed almost every alleged "irrational" cycle that

---

[13] Nicholas Miller, "Pluralism and Social Choice," *American Political Science Review* 77 (1983): 735–43.

[14] See Arend Lijphart, "Consociational Democracy," *World Politics* 21 (1969): 207–25, and *Democracy in Plural Societies* (New Haven: Yale University Press, 1977). I leave to one side the great empirical difficulties associated with determining whether preferences in a population are mutually reinforcing or crosscutting, and how, if at all, they can be transformed from the former to the latter. See my *Democracy's Place* (Ithaca: Cornell University Press, 1996), pp. 177–80, 216–18.

[15] For an argument that the importance of cycles has been exaggerated, see my *The State of Democratic Theory* (Princeton: Princeton University Press, 2003), pp . 10–16.

[16] Dennis Mueller, *Public Choice II* (Cambridge: Cambridge University Press, 1989), pp. 63–66, 81–82.

[17] A. S. Tangian, "Unlikelihood of Condorcet's Paradox in a Large Society," *Social Choice and Welfare* 17 (2000): 337–65.

has been identified in the social choice literature to be based on faulty data or otherwise spurious.[18] The threat to democracy posed by Arrow and his progeny seems, in practice, to be comparatively small. The possibility of cycles might help keep people committed to democratic systems, but the relative rarity of cycles makes democracies a good deal more stable than Arrow's theorem would lead us to expect. In the area of tax policy, for instance, there is undoubtedly a potential coalition to upset every conceivable status quo, as we can see by reflecting on a society of three voting to divide a dollar by majority rule: whatever the distribution, a majority will have an interest in changing it. Yet tax policy remains remarkably stable over time.[19]

Let us turn from institutional constraints to substantive considerations. Charles Tilly has recently suggested that we think of democratization as "a dynamic process that always remains incomplete and perpetually runs the risk of reversal—of de-democratization."[20] Tilly insists that whether a country is a democracy is a question of degree, not of either/or. Whether the focus is on institutional arrangements, substantive outcomes, procedures, or even processes, most people define democracy in static ways. Tilly likes the last best, especially in Dahl's formulation, but it, too, rests on a static checklist approach. Instead, Tilly proposes that we "compare regimes with regard to how democratic they are," and "follow individual regimes through time, observing when and how they become more or less democratic."[21] Particularly given the erosion of civil liberties in the advanced democracies in the wake of the U.S.-led "war on terror," this is a refreshingly realistic approach.

A regime is democratic, for Tilly, "to the degree that political relations between the state and its citizens feature broad, equal, protected and mutually binding consultation." This depends on three processes, which he describes as "increasing integration of trust networks into public politics, increasing insulation of public politics from categorical inequality, and decreasing autonomy of major power centers from public politics."[22]

Tilly's discussion of trust networks calls to mind the social capital literature developed by Putnam and others, but Tilly's view is distinctive. Whereas Putnam focuses on trust within and among civic associations, Tilly thinks the vital question is whether or not trust networks are integrated into the state. Trust, for Tilly, "consists of placing valued out-

[18] Gerry Mackie, *Democracy Defended* (Cambridge: Cambridge University Press, 2000).

[19] See John Witte, *The Politics and Development of the Federal Income Tax* (Madison: University of Wisconsin Press, 1985).

[20] Charles Tilly, *Democracy* (Cambridge University Press, 2007), p. 10.

[21] Ibid.

[22] Ibid., pp. 13–14, 23.

comes at risk to others' malfeasance, mistakes, or failures." Trust relationships are those "in which people regularly take such risks." To the
degree that people integrate their trust networks into politics, he argues,
"they come to rely on governmental performance for maintenance of
those networks." But at the same time this empowers them because they
gain beneficial connections with government.[23]

This might seem to bring Tilly disconcertingly close to endorsing a cli-
entelist view of democracy, in which trafficking in personal favors and re-
warding private interests displaces public contestation over policy, a view
that has been powerfully criticized by Matthew Cleary and Susan Stokes
in their recent work on Latin America.[24] But Tilly argues by reference to
the nineteenth-century U.S. experience that the integration of trust networks into public politics both increased overall political participation
and encouraged the formation of political clubs and other institutions
that pulled people into the public realm. On Tilly's account, integrating
trust networks into public politics gives people a stake in the successful
functioning of the state. "They acquire an unbreakable interest in the
performance of government. The political stakes matter. Paying taxes,
buying governmental securities, yielding private information to officials,
depending on government for benefits, and releasing network members
for military service cement that interest and promote active bargaining
over the terms of its fulfillment."[25]

Tilly's discussion of inequality is reminiscent of Michael Walzer's argument in *Spheres of Justice*, and in particular Walzer's claim that it is not
inequality as such that is objectionable but rather the translatability of
inequality in one realm of social life into the capacity to exercise power
and influence in other realms.[26] In Tilly's formulation "Democracy works
better, and democratization is more likely to occur, when political processes reduce translation of everyday categorical inequalities into public
policies." By "categorical inequality" Tilly means the "organized differences in advantage by gender, race, nationality, ethnicity, religion, community, and similar classification systems." For Tilly, democracy is more
likely to advance when there is a degree of equalization across realms,
but, more important, where there is a "buffering of public politics from
categorical inequality."[27] Thus he follows the recent work of Jeremy
Seekings and Nicoli Nattrass on South African inequality in recognizing

[23] Ibid., p. 81.

[24] Matthew Cleary and Susan Stokes, *Democracy and the Culture of Skepticism: Political Trust in Argentina and Mexico* (New York: Russell Sage, 2006).

[25] Tilly, *Democracy*, p. 95.

[26] Michael Walzer, *Spheres of Justice: A Defense of Pluralism and Equality* (New York:
Basic Books, 1984).

[27] Tilly, *Democracy*, p. 111.

little reduction in overall inequality since the 1994 transition,[28] yet he is nonetheless heartened by the relative buffering of South African politics from inequality when compared with the apartheid years—even though it "goes without saying" that South African democratization "remains incomplete."[29]

Tilly's third dimension of democratization and de-democratization concerns power centers other than the state, which have to be domesticated or neutralized for democracy to work. The key is to reduce "autonomous power clusters within the regime's operating territory, especially clusters that dispose of their own concentrated coercive means."[30] Contra Daron Acemoglu and James Robinson,[31] Tilly holds that "elite assent is not a precondition for democratization." Indeed, democratization can occur as a by-product of attempts by elites to maintain power. Thus he says that although Vladimir Putin's regime spent much of the time expanding state capacity in ways that were inimical to democracy, Putin also promoted longer-term changes that might "eventually facilitate Russian democratization." In particular, despite his "permitting the Russian military dangerously broad autonomy in the Caucasus," he also subordinated capitalists who had acquired substantial independence from state control after 1991. "Putin's anti-democratic smashing of oligarchs to reestablish state control over energy supplies helped eliminate rival centers of coercive power within the Russian regime."[32] This is reminiscent of David Held's argument about the first wave of democratization, to wit, that democratization *followed* the centralization of power into what we today think of as Weberian states that exercise monopoly of legitimate coercive force.[33] There had to be commanding heights for democrats to seize.

Tilly intends his book to be a guide for action. If he is right, he concludes that "those of us who hope to see democracy's benefits spread across the undemocratic world will not waste our time focusing on preaching democratic virtues, designing constitutions, forming non-governmental organizations, and identifying pockets of democratic sentiment within undemocratic regimes. We will, in contrast, spend a great deal of effort

---

[28] Jeremy Seekings and Nicoli Nattrass, *Class, Race, and Inequality in South Africa* (New Haven: Yale University Press, 2005).

[29] Tilly, *Democracy*, p. 131.

[30] Ibid., p. 137.

[31] Daron Acemoglu and James Robinson, *Economic Origins of Dictatorship and Democracy* (Cambridge: Cambridge University Press, 2006).

[32] Tilly, *Democracy*, p. 139.

[33] David Held, *Democracy and the Global Order: From the Modern State to Cosmopolitan Governance* (Cambridge: Polity Press, 1995) and "The Transformation of Political Community: Rethinking Democracy in the Context of Globalization," in *Democracy's Edges*, ed. Ian Shapiro and Casiano Hacker-Cordón (Cambridge: Cambridge University Press, 1999), pp. 84–111.

promoting the integration of trust networks into public politics, helping to shield public politics from categorical inequality, and working against the autonomy of coercive power centers."[34]

There is much that is plausible and attractive in Tilly's account, not least his alerting us to the ways in which democracy is fragile and can quickly atrophy—if not collapse. He points out that de-democratization often goes faster than democratization because elites can often defect quite easily. "The already rich and powerful can much more easily withdraw their trust networks, install inequalities, and create autonomous power centers," whereas democratization requires "integrating large numbers of ordinary people" into trust relationships.[35] This is a sobering observation (though it lives in some tension with his earlier claim that elite acquiescence is unnecessary for democratization). During the period between the Depression and the collapse of the USSR, economic elites in the capitalist democracies had reason to worry that capitalism might collapse, and that socialist and communist ideologies might seduce the disadvantaged populations in their own countries. This gave them prudential reasons to be concerned about the people at the bottom. In an era when the idea that capitalism might collapse is no longer taken seriously by economic elites and there is no competitor ideology that could vie for the allegiance of the poor, these prudential reasons inevitably wane. It becomes that much easier to adopt a Malthusian attitude toward the poor—to move to the suburbs and build more prisons.[36] Comparable considerations should raise grave concerns about the erosion of civil liberties in countries like the United Kingdom and the United States as by-products of the Global War on Terror.[37] Hard-won freedoms might be a good deal more difficult to restore than they have been to destroy.

But one wonders whether aspects of Tilly's argument do not sometimes operate at cross-purposes with one another. For instance, integrating trust networks into public politics might have the consequence not of strengthening democracy but rather of making the power of the state available for repression within civil institutions. Sarah Song alerts us to this danger in her recent discussion of arguments about the political risks

[34] Tilly, *Democracy*, p. 205.

[35] Ibid., p. 195.

[36] It might be said that Islamic fundamentalism has replaced communism as the main ideology that defines itself against, and as an alternative to, democratic capitalism, and that it could begin to command the allegiance of the dispossessed in the advanced countries. There is some truth to this, but Islamic fundamentalism differs from communism in that it lacks a political economy and is not, therefore, at bottom a competitor to capitalism. For further discussion, see my *Containment: Rebuilding a Strategy against Global Terror* (Princeton: Princeton University Press, 2007).

[37] Ibid, p. xiv.

of multicultural accommodation.[38] When groups like the Mormons and the Santa Clara Pueblo win exemptions from proscriptions of their traditional practices that would otherwise violate the law, and when criminal defendants win acquittal by offering "cultural defenses" as accommodations of their minority values, they are integrating their trust networks into public politics in Tilly's sense. But Song makes a compelling case that such protections bring with them the potential for domination of particular groups—often women—within those subcultures. She also shows that deference to minority cultural practices often rests on, and reinforces, gender stereotypes about those subcultures that are taken for granted in the dominant culture.

Unlike Brian Barry, for whom such considerations weigh against virtually all forms of cultural accommodation,[39] Song makes the case that cultural accommodation might sometimes be warranted—so long as it is accompanied by additional mechanisms for the protection of vulnerable groups within the protected minorities. But there's the rub. It will typically be the leaders of the minority groups who press the case for cultural accommodation, and they will not likely be sensitive to the concerns of marginalized groups within their subcultures. Song cites the case of the 1998 legislation accommodating polygamy in South Africa, which included economic protections for existing wives when new ones are added to a polygamous household. Assuming that these protections will be enforced on the ground (something that is not obvious), one wonders whether it is in any case the exception that proves the rule. For one thing, the existing status quo there was an established polygamous system that was enshrined in tribal law, and the question was to what extent the egalitarian provisions in the new constitution could limit its reach. For another, the debate on South Africa's marital law took place in the glare of national and international publicity in the aftermath of the country's recent and remarkable democratic transition. This is a notably different context from everyday politics in democratic systems, where political entrepreneurs and local "leaders" often go unchallenged when they claim to speak for communities and "their" traditions. This is not to mention the cultural stereotypes that so often pervade "cultural defenses" in American criminal courts that Song so ably documents.[40]

A different worry about Tilly's argument is that integrating trust networks into public politics might weaken state capacities in undesirable

---

[38] Sarah Song, *Justice, Gender, and the Politics of Multiculturalism* (Cambridge: Cambridge University Press, 2007).

[39] Brian Barry, *Culture and Equality: An Egalitarian Critique of Multiculturalism* (Cambridge, MA: Harvard University Press, 2001).

[40] Song, *Justice, Gender, and the Politics of Multiculturalism*, pp. 87–100.

ways. Consider President George W. Bush's 2001 "Faith-Based Initiative," which committed $8 billion in tax credits to religious and other charitable groups that would be authorized to deliver public services. It seems made to order from the point of view of Tilly's first criterion, in that it gives charitable groups a direct interest in, and dependence on, government. But critics reasonably wondered whether the real agenda behind the Faith-Based Initiative was actually to destroy the state's capacity to deliver the services in question. President Bush might not have been disingenuous, or at least not entirely so, when he said in its defense that "Government cannot be replaced by charities," but that "it should welcome them as partners rather than resenting them as rivals."[41] But the worry was that replacing, or at least diminishing, government might be the result. If welfare and other programs providing services to the poor are turned over to charities, who would monitor their activities or pick up the slack if they failed to deliver? Who would even know that they were failing to deliver?

Even where Tilly's processes are not perversely self-defeating, they might operate at cross-purposes with one another. It is true as he says, for instance, that white South African elites have acquiesced in the "buffering" of politics from economic inequality—at least by comparison with the apartheid era. But what if, as seems a reasonable inference from the reality on the ground, the implicit quid for the quo has been that the government lets them maintain their lifestyles in gated communities protected by private security companies? Tax rates remain low, and wealthy whites insulate themselves from danger in what Douglas Rae has described in the U.S. context as a "segmented democracy."[42] This, in turn, contributes to the weakness of the South African state, marked by limited capacity to deliver basic services or to control gang violence in the townships. And, as Tilly notes, weak states have limited capacities to democratize. A weak state "fails to suppress or subordinate autonomous power centers, allows citizens to insulate their trust networks from public politics, and tolerates or even encourages the insertion of categorical inequalities into public politics." Weak states "endure a high proportion of conflicts, often violent, in which the state is no more than peripherally involved." They have "less capacity to check defections, protect minorities, and enforce decisions arrived at through mutual contestation."[43]

---

[41] David Kuo and John DiIulio, "The Faith to Outlast Politics," *New York Times*, January 29, 2008, p. A25.

[42] Douglas Rae, "Democratic Liberty and Tyrannies of Place," in *Democracy's Edges*, ed. Ian Shapiro and Casiano Hacker-Cordón (Cambridge: Cambridge University Press, 1999), pp. 165–92.

[43] Tilly, *Democracy*, pp. 164, 175.

Tilly is right to underscore that democratic accountability involves "mutually binding consultation" of the citizenry and the state.[44] For democracy to work, those affected by collective decisions must have a say in them, and they must feel bound by the outcomes of collective decisions as well. Tilly is also right that this generally involves reducing the autonomy of power centers that are outside the state and can threaten its authority. Sometimes, but not always, this can be aided through the integration of trust networks into politics and the insulation of government from social and economic inequalities. What should be as clear to us today as it was to the mature Madison of the early 1830s is that democratic competition under conditions of majority rule remains the bedrock of democratic accountability. Its alleged pathologies have often been oversold, and the alternatives to it have often been overhyped. It is, to be sure, a minimal democratic requirement. But minimal is not negligible, as the billions who continue to be governed without it know all too well.

[44] Ibid., pp. 13–14.

CHAPTER THREE

Problems and Prospects for Democratic Settlements: South Africa as a Model for the Middle East and Northern Ireland?

Courtney Jung, Ellen Lust-Okar, and Ian Shapiro

IF MAJORITARIAN democracy is the worst system of government, as Churchill said, "except for all those other forms that have been tried from time to time,"[1] the question arises how it is created and sustained. Almost no one thinks this can be done always and everywhere, yet sometimes democracy has been achieved in the most improbable settings. In the 1970s, the political conflicts in South Africa, Northern Ireland, and the Middle East were often grouped together as among the world's most intractable, highly unlikely to result in enduring democratic resolutions. They exhibited profound racial and ethnic animosities, reinforced by linguistic, cultural, economic and religious differences, and solidified by decades of more or less violent confrontation. They were often identified as paradigms of "divided" societies, and there seemed little chance of transitions to peaceful, let alone fully democratic, arrangements in any of them. Whether one focused on the players contending for power, the histories of the conflicts, or the capacities of outsiders to influence events, the prospects for negotiated settlements seemed dim.

The conflicts have diverged remarkably in subsequent decades. South Africa, often depicted in the grim 1970s as the most intractable of intractables, moved through a comparatively peaceful four-year transition to majority rule in a unitary state. Subsequent democratic elections put the African National Congress (ANC) securely in power without civil war, economic collapse, or catastrophic white exodus. To be sure, the continuing economic and social challenges are enormous, with a third of the population unemployed and one in nine infected with HIV, but by most measures South Africa has weathered the transition well. Democ-

---

An earlier version of this chapter was originally published as an article in June 2005. The present version includes an afterword, bringing it up to date five years later.

[1] Winston Churchill, speech in the House of Commons, November 11, 1947, in *Churchill by Himself: The Definitive Collection of Quotations* (New York: Public Affairs, 2008), p. 574.

racy may not yet be entrenched in South African politics, but it seems at least to have a fighting chance.

Northern Ireland has also made important advances since negotiations began in earnest in 1996. Both Republicans and Loyalists committed to cease-fires that have held, and most serious violence has abated sufficiently that people have started to think enduring peace a realistic possibility. The two sides signed an agreement in 1998 that majorities of both Catholics and Protestants supported. Yet the future of that 1998 Good Friday Agreement remains precarious. The failure of the power-sharing government to work had led to its repeated suspension by Westminster, including the reimposition of direct rule from Westminster between 2002 and 2007. As recently as March 2009 there were reasons to fear that a new round of sectarian violence might be in the offing.[2]

Establishing peace between the Palestinians and the Israelis has been even more elusive. There have been some major turning points in the Arab-Israeli conflict and periods of great optimism, most notably following the negotiation of the Camp David Accords and subsequent signing of the Israeli-Egyptian peace treaty in 1979, and the Palestinian-Israeli negotiation of the Oslo Accords in 1993. There have also been numerous less dramatic "openings" from one side or another. PLO acceptance of a two-state solution in 1988, Syria's decision to support the multilateral Madrid Conference in 1991, and Israel's decision to negotiate directly with the PLO all provided windows of opportunity for their negotiating partners. However, the principals have often been either unable or unwilling to seize the opportunities that emerge when one side makes concessions. For instance, in 1998 Benjamin Netanyahu rendered Yasir Arafat's concessions in the Wye Accords useless by unilaterally suspending their implementation, and Arafat refused Ehud Barak's concessions at Camp David II in 2000.

Backtracking and disappointing failure have been so frequent that the peace process often seems ritualistic and pointless. Different leaders participate more or less grudgingly at different times, almost always under intense American pressure. This was manifest in President George W. Bush's "road map" for peace in the summer of 2003. Israeli prime minister Ariel Sharon was induced to use the word "occupation" for the first time in relation to the conflict, but his insistence that this referred to people and population centers, not to the West Bank as such, made the seeming concession nearly meaningless. The concessionary speech

---

[2] See Tom Rivers, "New Wave of Violence Grips Northern Ireland," VOANews.com (March 10, 2009), http://www.voanews.com/english/archive/2009-03/2009-03-10-voa30 .cfm?CFID=274777920&CFTOKEN=24037997&jsessionid=88305b4554002437e7596e 4b8205d196d3f4 [08-22-2009].

delivered by Palestinian prime minister Mahmoud Abbas at the Aqaba summit, widely reported to have been drafted by the Bush White House, led Hamas to break off talks with the Palestinian Authority on ending the violence, and to further depletion in his already negligible approval ratings among Palestinians.[3] It was unsurprising that the unilaterally declared "truce" by Hamas and other militant groups quickly collapsed in light of the vast differences that remained over territory, settlements, "the right of return," disarmament, prisoners, and the dearth of popular support on both sides for politicians showing any inclination to bridge these gulfs. The Middle East peace process continues to vindicate the 1970s diagnosis by going nowhere—if often by Byzantine routes at enormous human and economic cost.

Whence these divergent outcomes? We argue here that there are lessons to be drawn from South Africa's comparative success that can illuminate the ongoing dynamics in Northern Ireland and the Middle East—both why they have not yet succeeded and whether and how they might succeed in the future. We label these conflicts with the compound acronym SAMENI, to signal that ours is an inductive effort based on the South African experience and a close examination of how similar dynamics have played out in the Middle East and Northern Ireland. In making this case, we agree with others that the three conflicts exhibit important similarities, but we believe that they have been misconstrued.[4] Scholars have focused on the putatively "divided" character of the societies—suggesting that conflicts engendered by ethnic, racial, and religious divisions preclude reconciliation. Hence the dire predictions about South Africa in the 1970s and 1980s. In our account, negotiations in these settings are best

---

[3] See "Sharon Backtracks on Israeli 'Occupation,'" Newsmax.com Wires (May 28, 2003), http://www.newsmax.com/archives/articles/2003/5/28/100340.shtml [06-13-2003], and James Bennett, "Hamas Breaks off Talks on Stopping Attacks on Israel," *New York Times*, June 11, 2003, pp. A1, A7.

[4] See Colin Knox and Paul Quirk, eds., *Peace Building in Northern Ireland, Israel and South Africa: Transition, Transformation and Reconciliation* (Basingstoke, UK: Palgrave, 2000); Ian Lustick, "Necessary Risks: Lessons for the Israeli-Palestinian Peace Process from Ireland and Algeria," *Middle East Policy* 3, no. 3 (1994): 41–59, and *Unsettled States, Disputed Lands: Britain and Ireland, France and Algeria, Israel and the West Bank-Gaza* (Ithaca: Cornell University Press, 1993); Donald Akenson, *God's Peoples: Covenant and Land in South Africa, Israel, and Ulster* (Ithaca: Cornell University Press, 1992); Heribert Adam, ed., Comparing Israel and South Africa: Prospects for Conflict Resolution in Ethnic States (Colorado: University Press of Colorado, 1990); Hermann Giliomee and J. Gagiano, eds., The Elusive Search for Peace: South Africa, Israel, Northern Ireland (Cape Town: Oxford University Press, 1990);]]] Benjamin Gidron, Stanley Nider Katz, and Yeheskel Hasenfeld, eds., *Mobilizing for Peace: Conflict Resolution in Northern Ireland, Israel/Palestine, and South Africa* (New York: Oxford University Press, 2002).

seen as a distinctive class of transplacements or negotiated settlements.[5] Their distinctiveness resides not in their "divided" character, but rather in their being imperfect democracies—subject to electoral constraints and dependent on democratic norms, which they violate, for legitimation. The ancién regime is a flawed democracy, not a conventional authoritarian system. No doubt all democracies are flawed to some degree, but in these situations the unusually large gulf between the democratic ideal the government claims to embrace and the reality on the ground produces dissonance both for those advantaged by the system and for those excluded from the government. The government's lack of legitimacy provides the impetus for regime change in these circumstances. It shapes the negotiations in distinctive ways and structures the available settlements. Success depends not on the key players' finding the Holy Grail, but rather on their converging on a solution that their constituents will accept as legitimate.

We identify the conditions under which negotiations are more likely to take off and succeed in circumstances of imperfect democracy, and we illustrate how they were successfully exploited or misused in the SAMENI cases. Leaders have been more able to commit to negotiating when violence is escalating, when they can overcome internal divisions in their movements, and when they can build support for the new dispensation as it comes into popular view. Once leaders make commitments, they are most likely to be able to keep them when their visible dependence on players from the other side means that there is no going back, when final disposition of contentious issues remains shrouded in uncertainty, and when the leaders enjoy enough popular support to enable them to convince, co-opt, or marginalize potential spoilers.

It will be clear from this claim that ours is not a deterministic argument. Individual players make decisions that could be made differently, often with consequential results. Moreover, many contingencies affect the outcomes of negotiations. Had F. W. de Klerk been shot by a disgruntled

[5] So, for example, we rely on the work of Samuel Huntington, *The Third Wave: Democratization in the Late Twentieth Century* (Norman: University of Oklahoma Press, 1991); Guillermo O'Donnell and Philippe Schmitter, *Transitions from Authoritarian Rule: Comparative Perspectives* (Baltimore: Johns Hopkins University Press, 1986); and Adam Przeworski, *Democracy and the Market* (Cambridge: Cambridge University Press, 1991) to think through the logic of SAMENI conflict resolution. These three negotiations have rarely been analyzed in the transplacement literature. One notable exception is Timothy D. Sisk, *Democratization in South Africa: The Elusive Social Contract* (Princeton: Princeton University Press, 1995). We also used the transplacement model to think through the dynamics of negotiation in South Africa, in Courtney Jung and Ian Shapiro, "South Africa's Negotiated Transition: Democracy, Opposition, and the New Constitutional Order," *Politics and Society* 23, no. 3 (1995): 269–308.

right-winger before the 1992 referendum, the South African transition might well have fallen apart. Had Yitzhak Rabin not been shot in 1995, a successful agreement between Israelis and Palestinians might have been concluded and implemented. We would then be trying to explain Middle East success in contrast to South African failure.[6] This is not to say that resolution is exclusively dependent on luck and contingencies of leadership—defying the possibility of useful theory. Contingencies do make it impossible to predict success in any given instance, but this does not exhaust the theoretical agenda. For one thing, on our account it is possible in many situations to predict failure, and, perhaps more important, to say something about how those situations would have to change for success to become a possibility. For another, when success is possible, we can and do develop accounts of the conditions that make it more or less likely.

Our procedure is as follows. We begin, in part 1, by explaining why the conditions that gave rise to these negotiations can usefully be classed together. In part 2 we then elaborate on the ways in which SAMENI negotiations constitute a distinctive class of negotiated settlements. In parts 3 and 4 we explore the conditions that facilitate the initiation, negotiation, and consummation of SAMENI agreements, explaining how circumstances coincided to allow South Africa to overcome the barriers to democratic legitimation, moving through all three stages with comparative ease, while negotiations in the Middle East and Northern Ireland have continually snagged. This leads to a discussion, in parts 5 and 6, of how negotiations could have succeeded in the Middle East and Northern Ireland, the conditions under which they might do so in the future, and some lessons for the future study of such conflicts.

---

[6] Counterfactual speculation is inherently difficult, though we adduce considerable evidence in support of these claims below. With respect to South Africa it merits reporting that F. W. de Klerk believes that had he been assassinated after the March 1992 referendum, the negotiations would likely have been concluded successfully, but that this is much more doubtful had it occurred before the referendum when the government was losing by-elections to conservatives. De Klerk reports that the decision to call the referendum was the only unilateral decision of his presidency. He consulted no one in the cabinet or the National Party leadership because he knew they would oppose it. Even if a new leader wanted to call a referendum, he doubts that either of the likely contenders (Pik Botha and Roelf Meyer) would have been able to do so, given the need to establish themselves in the party leadership. At the very least the process would have been significantly delayed (interview with author, December 9, 2003). Given our discussion of the importance of timing below, this might well have been sufficient to derail it permanently.

If de Klerk had been killed, the only conceivable replacement who might have been able to carry the NP and the military through negotiations was Roelf Meyer. But Meyer was a very junior minister, without much standing in the party. It seems more likely that Pik Botha would have assumed leadership and resorted to reforming apartheid.

1. Comparability of SAMENI Negotiations

The white South African, Israeli, and Northern Irish regimes have all depended heavily on appeals to democratic legitimacy to which they conspicuously failed to live up. The National Party (NP) government in South Africa was first elected in 1948 on a platform of "separate development" that would guarantee democratic representation for every race in its "own" territory. The maldistribution of land and other resources at the core of this plan, not to mention the forced removals of tens of thousands from their homes that began in the 1950s, meant that it was always hopelessly illegitimate in the eyes of nonwhite South Africans and much of the rest of the world. Israel, too, was conceived of as a democratic state from the beginning. If the presence of Israeli Arabs as second-class citizens made this problematic from the start, it was nothing compared with the legitimacy problems that would pile up in the decades following the occupation of the West Bank and Gaza in 1967. In both cases, the introduction of partial democratic reforms failed to remove the stain of exclusion.

The democratic legitimacy of Northern Ireland was also undermined by the gerrymandered origins of the state. From the beginning, Catholics rejected British rule as imperialist. The great majority of them saw the partition in 1921 as a cynical ploy to create an artificial Protestant majority, and they resisted it—often violently. As a result, the partition could be sustained only through repression. The British repeatedly resorted to special powers legislation and "proscription," with results similar to the emergency regulations that would become semipermanent features of apartheid South Africa and Israel's occupied territories.[7] In all three cases the government faced inescapable tension between its need for democratic legitimacy and its undemocratic practices. This supplied impetus for reform.

Even imperfect democracy constrains the players, however. Unlike authoritarian leaders engaged in negotiating transitions, as in Spain, govern-

[7] Under the Special Powers Act (1922) the minister for home affairs could, among other things, "arrest without charge or warrant, intern without trial, prohibit the holding of coroners' inquests, flog, execute, use depositions of witnesses as 'evidence' without requiring them to be present for cross-examination or rebuttal, destroy buildings, requisition land or property, ban any organization, be it political, social, or trade; prohibit meetings, publications, and even gramophone records." John McGuffin, *Internment!* (Tralee, Ire.: Anvil Books, 1973), p. 22. Proscription is the power to outlaw organizations, enshrined in the 1887 Criminal Law and Proceedings (Ireland) Act. "Proscription in its contemporary guise is located in Section 21 of the Northern Ireland (Emergency Provisions) Act 1978." "A person is guilty of an offense if he belongs or professes to belong to a proscribed organization." Clive Walker, "Political Violence and Democracy in Northern Ireland," *Modern Law Review*. 51, no. 5 (September 1988): 612.

ments in flawed democracies can be voted out of office. This is consequential, because it means that both sides must keep an eye on their constituents as well as their opponents. Not only must they protect their positions vis-à-vis the opposition until negotiations have been concluded, but they must also persuade, co-opt, or outflank opponents on their own side and build constituencies in support of the new dispensation. This means that elites' abilities to maneuver through the vicissitudes of public opinion are vital for success. The realities of flawed democracy play important roles in pushing negotiators to the table, but they also affect whether the elites can stay there and what they can achieve when they do.

Some might still object to our classification on other grounds that the three conflicts are not relevantly alike. The issues, stakes, and constraints may seem to have been so different that each situation has arguably followed a distinctive logic. After all, South Africa achieved a transition to majority rule within a unitary state, whereas in both the Middle East and Northern Ireland negotiations have focused on creating or maintaining partitions. But this gets the cart before the horse. In fact, stakeholders in all three conflicts have entertained variations on each of these solutions at different times, and, if our argument is correct, different solutions might have been negotiated in any of them. Indeed, and ironically, partition might reasonably have been judged more likely in South Africa, ex ante, than in the other two conflicts—if only for demographic reasons. The basic question is not: what is the right outcome? Rather, it is: is there an outcome on which elites can converge while maintaining their popular support, and, if so, will they in fact converge on it and remain there for long enough to implement it?

One might concede this yet still wonder about Northern Ireland's fitting the transplacement logic, given the roles of multiple players in several countries. It is true that political leaders in Great Britain and the Republic of Ireland have influenced the conflict and attempts to resolve it. But what matters is not the geographic location of the participants. Rather, it is the ways in which the existence of a flawed democracy both exacerbates the regime's legitimacy crisis and permits grassroots constituencies to constrain negotiators' attempts to arrive at solutions. By the time the most recent round of negotiations began in the mid-1990s, Northern Ireland had been under direct rule from Westminster for twenty-five years. Continuing sectarian violence against British rule undermined the government's claim to democratic legitimacy, and, in particular as the EU began to develop European standards for the treatment of minorities, Prime Ministers John Major, and then Tony Blair, grew impatient to resolve the conflict. In fact, as we will see, many of the negotiating dynamics that shaped the South African transition evolved similarly in

Northern Ireland—notwithstanding their transnational character. As a result, it meets the test for all fruitful comparative research: that the cases be sufficiently similar to make comparison possible and sufficiently different to make it illuminating.

Perhaps more powerful challenges to our comparison are related to the Middle East. Some will contend that the conflict there is fundamentally different from that in Northern Ireland or South Africa on the grounds that the stakes for the actors—both Israelis seeking to defend a Jewish state and Palestinians invested in regaining their homeland—are inherently zero-sum. The great lesson of the wars of religion of the seventeenth century is often taken to be that when national sovereignty becomes bound up with collective religious identities, the result is perpetual war. The standard solution has long been thought to lie in the de-emphasis of such exclusionary grounds for citizenship via such mechanisms as religious disestablishment. Most players in, and commentators on, the Middle East operate on the assumption that this is not possible there. It is said to be too threatening to the Zionist self-understanding, and to its mirror image: that the Palestinian people have an inalienable right to national self-determination.

But consider a South African perspective on this objection. Apartheid was self-consciously exclusionary, built on an ascriptive basis that left no room for assimilation. Moreover, the racial ideology of apartheid was underpinned by a religious mission; its architects were doctrinaire Calvinists who saw themselves as one of the last outposts of Christian civilization—defending it from communism in the East and a corrupt and degenerate West. As recently as 1985, had anyone seriously suggested that white South Africans would endorse a multiracial state—let alone under a majority-rule, black government—they would have been laughed out of town or locked up. Nor should we forget that, whereas five million Jews face a similar number of Palestinians in Israel, Gaza, and the West Bank, in South Africa five million whites faced twenty-five million blacks. Demography alone might lead one to believe that the zero-sum character of the South African conflict in the mid-1980s looked less tractable than is the case in the Middle East. The magnitude of the unexpected South African transformation suggests that analogous changes in beliefs about religion and ethnicity might indeed be possible in the Middle East.[8]

[8] In this connection it is perhaps heartening that at a conference on democratic transitions and consolidation consisting of some 100 academic experts from 36 countries plus 33 heads and former heads of state held in Madrid in October/November 2001, a final report was adopted in which it was agreed that "rights of citizenship should apply equally to all citizens," and that the majority "must avoid all temptation to define the nation in ethnic

A different lack-of-comparability objection focuses less on the stakes involved in the conflict and more on the proposed solution. Some might claim that in the Middle East no two-state solution will ever be perceived as legitimate. Manifest disparities of wealth, status, and power, combined with the partial character of most proposed variants of the Palestinian state, call its sustainability into question—particularly as Jewish settlements in the West Bank have multiplied. It is doubtless true that any two-state solution would confront legitimation problems reminiscent of "separate but equal" in the American South. But this does not mean that it could not endure for a long time; indeed, the American example suggests that it could. It simply suggests that in the longer term it may be a way station en route to a different destination. Living with a settlement can change what people can live with. *Brown v. Board of Education* would not have been possible in 1896.

A comparable objection is that the two-state solution that became the underpinnings of the Oslo process would have been unenforceable. Any future Israeli government would remain free to roll tanks into the West Bank or Gaza if it became unhappy with the settlement. In contrast, this reasoning goes, in South Africa the enforcement problem was dealt with by a fundamental shift in power to the ANC. However, as we argue in part 3, the enforcement difficulties associated with SAMENI negotiations should not be judged by standards that are not met in most political circumstances. Switzerland and Costa Rica are substantially demilitarized states that could be invaded by neighbors but are not. Moreover, it is not obvious that the enforcement problem was solved by the ANC's triumph in South Africa. The army might have defected at various points—as indeed it still could. In short, the similarities underlying these conflicts should not be missed because they have evolved differently since the 1970s, because of the location of the parties as insiders and outsiders, or because of other alleged sui generis features of one situation or another.

2. The Character of SAMENI Negotiations

SAMENI negotiations resemble other transplacements in three ways. First, like other transplacements, SAMENI negotiations occur in a power stalemate in which no one can impose change. Neither the regime nor

---

terms in the constitutional text or its political practice." See Diego Hidalgo, ed., *Conference on Democratic Transitions and Consolidation* (Madrid: Siddharth Mehta Ediciones, 2002), p. 34. See also Ari Shavit, "Cry, the Beloved Two State Solution," *Haaretz*, August 7, 2003, http://www.jfjfp.org/BackgroundQ/two-states_aug03.htm [08-22-2009].

its opponents can dictate a solution, yet there is a potential coalition of government reformers and opposition moderates who may be able to negotiate an agreement both prefer to the status quo.[9] For transplacements to succeed, the innovative coalition must remain sufficiently strong that, should an agreement be reached, its members can carry their constituencies along and impose the settlement on government hard-liners and opposition radicals who resist it. Because multiple factors must come together in the right sequences, there are many more ways for all negotiated settlements to fall apart than for them to succeed.

Second, SAMENI negotiations resemble other transplacements in that, because they concern political fundamentals, the stakes are inevitably high. Questions of sovereignty, involving regime type, territorial boundaries, or both, are at issue. If an agreement is reached and implemented, it will lead to irreversible changes in a major part of political reality. The negotiations involve intertwined issues of personal security, economic survival, and collective destiny that have been politicized by decades of conflict. Even if negotiations fail, or the agreement is not implemented, the power balance is likely to change, making return to the status quo ante difficult or impossible. Political futures are on the line for the principals, giving them large and increasing stakes in the outcomes. In short, like other transplacements, SAMENI negotiations exhibit the life-or-death quality of politics that is about the basic rules of the game.

This is partly why transplacement negotiations are so fragile. Government reformers and opposition moderates must work together. Yet they are still, in most ways, adversaries who must constantly judge one another's agendas and abilities, as well as reassess their own. They can signal to each other their intention to continue in the process, but to do so they must take decisive steps in facing down opposition within their own ranks even before it is clear that an enforceable agreement will be reached. As a result, although the principals know that success may write them into the history books, the risks are huge. At critical junctures they must be willing to confront historical allies on their own flanks to gain a prize that will be theirs only if their negotiating adversaries can do the same thing. Moreover, they have little reason to trust those with whom they are dealing. It is, in short, one thing for there to be a potential coalition in favor of a negotiated settlement; quite another for it to form and sustain itself long enough to get the job done. Because this requires splintering existing coali-

---

[9] The language of hard-liners and reformers, moderates and radicals, is used in the literature on democratic transitions. See in particular Przeworski, *Democracy and the Market*, pp. 67–70, and Huntington, *The Third Wave*, pp. 151–64. The terms *reformers* and *moderates* do not refer to the content of political ideologies. Rather, they denote players who are willing to entertain outcomes that differ from their political ideals in search of a mutually acceptable solution.

tions and fending off attacks from historical allies who feel threatened or even betrayed, it takes creative ingenuity, courage, and luck.

A third way in which SAMENI negotiations resemble other transplacements often goes unnoticed owing to the widespread proclivity to hive them off as "divided societies." Viewed in that way the conflicts seem to involve particularly intractable forms of political violence. It is true that there have been periods of considerable violence in South Africa, the Middle East, and Northern Ireland, but this scarcely differentiates them from other transplacements—as in Chile in the 1970s or El Salvador in the 1980s, for example. Yet it is not so much the amount of violence that commentators focus on as the type, and in particular the fact that it occurs among groups that define themselves by reference to such categories as race, religion, or ethnicity. The common assumption that these categories are ascriptive, if not primordial, leads people to misidentify the conflicts as inherently zero-sum, and to miss the possibilities for unanticipated alliances and the redefinition of political identities as negotiations evolve. That there was a non-Solomonic settlement in South Africa surprised many people. If our analysis is correct, they should not have been surprised, and those who continue to insist on the sui generis character of the violence in the Middle East and Northern Ireland should not make the same error.

Yet on our account SAMENI transplacements are nonetheless distinctive because they are both motivated and complicated by conditions of imperfect democracy. Unlike standard transplacements in countries like Spain, Poland, and Chile, the government is elected. Yet, as we have noted, they are imperfectly democratic because large populations under the government's control are disenfranchised or partly enfranchised in ways that are widely seen as unjust. This reality creates inescapable legitimacy problems for the regime, which must claim to be democratic when obviously it is not. By entering negotiations, reformers acknowledge, however implicitly, this deficiency in their system. This means that they are usually on the defensive—arguing about the terms and pace of change rather than its necessity. This in turn means that no settlement can succeed unless there is broad agreement that the democratic deficit that gave impetus to negotiations has been substantially attenuated, if not abolished. Once parties to a conflict appeal to democracy as their source of legitimation, widely accepted democratic norms rule out racial oligarchies, and in today's world they even make religious and ethnic oligarchies suspect. Moshe Halbertal explained this imperative well following the collapse of the July 2000 Palestinian-Israeli Washington summit: "Between the Mediterranean and the Jordan there are roughly five million Jews and five million Palestinian Arabs. You cannot have a Jewish and democratic state without dividing this land, and those who oppose that are dooming Israel to an apartheid state, which might have secure borders, but might not be worth securing."[10]

The opposition in SAMENI conflicts often emanates from a liberation movement (the ANC, the PLO, and the IRA, in these cases) and is not, as such, democratically elected, but it gains significant leverage from the fact that the government lacks democratic legitimacy. By entering negotiations, the opposition inevitably becomes democratically constrained as well. Its leaders must be able to claim plausibly that they represent a major constituency, if not the majority, and to move toward a settlement that will be popularly validated. In short, although the regime and its opponents may both be imperfectly democratic, they claim to be democrats and depend on popular support in a more robust sense than do the players in other transplacements. The need for democratic legitimation greatly complicates negotiations, defying attempts to reduce them to stylized elite games. We are thus sympathetic to Elisabeth Wood's contention that the transitions literature has been overly focused on elite interactions, with insufficient attention to the larger political contexts within which they occur.[11] But where Wood contends that such negotiations are driven from below, we take a more interactive view. Negotiators are constrained by popular opinion, but to succeed elites must make the right choices at critical junctures—including choices about how to respond to popular opinion and when to try to shape it. One of the trickiest problems arises from the reality that negotiating a settlement usually involves concessions that force the principals to move away from their mandates. The challenge then becomes finding ways to avoid alienating constituencies whose endorsement is essential to the settlement's legitimacy.

The central question in all transplacements is this: can the reformers and moderates agree on a settlement and successfully face down the hardliners and radicals on their flanks? However, SAMENI transplacements are distinctive in that the parties must also maintain enough grassroots support that backers of the ancién regime continue to see the settlement as legitimate while partisans of the new dispensation regard it as repairing the democratic deficit. Quite simply, negotiators must be able to hold onto power until a settlement has been concluded, and this, in the presence of uneven progress and the attendant fluctuations in public opinion, is exceedingly difficult. The potential to disrupt negotiations by using democratic institutions to pressure the opponent, ironically, provides new opportunities and sources of power to those who seek to scuttle agreements, as spikes in suicide bombings in Israel have often demonstrated.

[10] Moshe Halbertal, as quoted by Thomas Friedman, "Yasir Arafat's Moment," *New York Times*, July 28, 2000, p. A21.

[11] Elisabeth Wood, *Forging Democracy from Below: Negotiated Transitions in El Salvador and South Africa* (Cambridge: Cambridge University Press, 2000).

Moreover, the dynamics of negotiations will be affected by democratic turnovers in power. If the negotiating government loses an election, as has often been the case in Israel, new players must then establish their credentials as bona fide reformers who are determined to conclude an agreement. As well as constantly reassessing their own interests in proceeding, each side must thus worry about whether the other can maintain enough support among their core constituencies to carry through their own side of the bargain. They must also worry about how concessions they might make threaten to alienate their own supporters. Ehud Barak's willingness to put sovereignty over parts of Jerusalem on the table for the first time in the failed 2000 Washington negotiations is a case in point. His subsequent loss of popularity at home was partly linked to the realization that it would be difficult, if not impossible, for any Israeli leader to declare Jerusalem off-limits in future negotiations.[12]

3. Onset of SAMENI Negotiations

Catalysts for SAMENI negotiations can take the form of sticks, carrots, or—more likely—both. The main stick for government reformers will likely be a deteriorating, and increasingly costly, status quo that depletes their political capital and increases their willingness to negotiate. This may be because of internal developments such as terrorist bombings or an ungovernability campaign. Alternatively, it could result from external factors such as sanctions, or pressure from international human rights groups or a powerful ally. Changing structural, global, or popular constraints may render the status quo less viable, and alternatives more readily imaginable. Evolving ideological paradigms can also shift perceptions of the viability or meaning of persisting in conflict. The fall of communism, the increasing bankruptcy of race as an organizing principle of political and social life, or the development of international norms regarding minority rights might highlight the democratic deficit and undercut the grounds that have hitherto justified coercion by the regime. As Guillermo O'Donnell and Philippe Schmitter have noted, since World War II it has been difficult either for governments, or for those who benefit from authoritarian rule, to justify nondemocratic governance as a

[12] A poll conducted by the Palestinian Center for Policy and Survey Research (PCPSR) in Ramallah and the Harry S. Truman Research Institute for the Advancement of Peace at the Hebrew University, Jerusalem, found that 55.7 percent of Israelis surveyed believed that "Israel made too much of a compromise" at the Camp David Summit. PCPSR, "Results of Israeli Public Opinion Poll: July 27–31, 2000," www.pcpsr.org/survey/polls/2002/p1israelipoll.html [06-07-2003].

permanent condition. Democracy's near universal status as the only legitimate form of government is buttressed by domestic demands for democratization, with the result that repression can be defended only as a temporary interregnum on the way to a "real" democratic regime.[13] As for carrots, these might include the prospect of peace, an end to pariah status in world opinion, a variety of economic incentives, or a desire to do the right thing and go down in history as a statesman.[14]

Comparable considerations apply to the opposition. Sticks could include the inability to sustain grassroots support for a costly and unwinnable guerrilla war, international pressure, depleted weapons, or dissension within the liberation movement. Among the carrots may be the legitimation afforded by recognition and talks with the government, the allure of power, access to international players, promises of economic support from third parties, or the advantages of peace and prosperity. In all three cases under discussion, the combination of sticks and carrots ushered in unprecedented negotiations that held out the hope of ending decades of intractable conflict.

3.1. How the Unthinkable Became Thinkable in South Africa

Throughout the 1980s the South African government faced a deteriorating status quo. The ungovernability campaign mounted by the United Democratic Front (UDF) massively raised the costs of keeping order in the townships by organizing a generation of young black activists with a more militant opposition style than their parents'.[15] The currency collapse that followed South Africa's inability to meet international debt obligations in 1985 sent the economy into a tailspin, and the relentless chorus of outside political and economic pressure began to be matched by attacks on apartheid from growing numbers of Afrikaner intellectu-

---

[13] Guillermo O'Donnell and Philippe C. Schmitter, *Transitions from Authoritarian Rule: Tentative Conclusions about Uncertain Democracies* (Baltimore: John Hopkins University Press, 1986), p. 15.

[14] Some incentives are long-standing. For example, most observers argue that business elites in South Africa, Northern Ireland, and Israel have long favored a peace settlement, and we have found striking evidence of this in Israel, where eighteen out of twenty-five top business executives we surveyed in 2003 favored an Oslo-style solution and only two opposed it (see appendix to chap. 3). However, there is no evidence in any of these cases that the pressure from the business community was responsible for either the initiation or the continuation of negotiations.

[15] The UDF was the backbone of internal opposition to apartheid in the 1980s, and widely considered the internal wing of the then banned ANC. Jeremy Seekings, *The UDF: The United Democratic Front in South Africa, 1983–1991* (Athens: Ohio University Press, 2000).

als.[16] By the second half of the 1980s, polls revealed that most whites believed that apartheid threatened the country's future. For elected officials this dramatically decreased the costs of entering negotiations.[17] NP confidence in the medium-term viability of the apartheid state was particularly shaken by the escalation of violence following the collapse of the second phase of CODESA roundtable negotiations in May 1992.[18]

The two most important carrots had to do with the collapsing Soviet empire after the mid-1980s. Because the leaderships of the ANC and the South African Communist Party (SACP) overlapped substantially, white fear of majority rule had been inescapably intertwined with fear of communism. After 1989 a communist government in South Africa was no longer a serious threat, and white elites began to realize that majority rule need not mean the destruction of capitalism or the expropriation of private property.[19] The political corollary of this development was a more flexible and pragmatic ANC leadership with whom serious negotiations, if not yet partnership, could be imagined. That this would also mean an end to pariah status, the possibility of economic revival, unfettered overseas travel, and countless other benefits of normalization no doubt also helped. Once white South Africans began thinking the unthinkable, it could start looking attractive. Brazil, rather than Cuba, could be their model.

NP carrots were ANC sticks. In the early 1980s a strapped USSR had stopped ANC and SACP financial backing and military training on the grounds that South Africa was not in a revolutionary situation.[20] This was a closely held secret within the ANC leadership, but it was only a matter of time until the government would know it as well. Overtures to China led nowhere, forcing the ANC-in-exile to rethink its military strategy and start building up internal opposition. The UDF was formed

[16] An antiapartheid Afrikaner intellectual movement had its foundation in the late 1960s. Herbert Adam and Hermann Giliomee, *Ethnic Power Mobilized: Can South Africa Change?* (New Haven: Yale University Press, 1979).

[17] Suzanne Booysen, "The Legacy of Ideological Control: The Afrikaner Youth's Manipulated Political Consciousness," *Politikon* 16, no. 1 (1989): 7–25.

[18] The acronym stands for Conference on a Democratic South Africa. These were part of the "prenegotiations" in that the government insisted on involving over twenty interests, including those who held no brief for a democratic transition, such as the extreme white Right and the Inkatha Freedom Party. Predictably they went nowhere. See Jung and Shapiro, "South Africa's Negotiated Transition," pp. 285–86.

[19] In fact white economic elites realized this before the politicians did, and began secret talks with the ANC as early as 1986, in Lusaka and Dakar. See Sisk, *Democratization in South Africa*, p. 78.

[20] "Statement of the National Executive Committee of the African National Congress on the Question of Negotiations," Lusaka, October 9, 1987, cited in Steven Friedman, *The Long Journey: South Africa's Quest for a Negotiated Settlement* (Johannesburg: Raven Press, 1993), pp. 10–11.

in 1983 in opposition to Tricameral Parliament elections that had offered limited representation to "Coloured" and other disenfranchised racial minorities. This ushered in a new era of populist opposition with a massive ungovernability campaign in the townships.[21] Widespread internal unrest raised the stakes for the NP government at the same time as it marginalized the Pan Africanist Congress (PAC) and Inkatha forces within the liberation movement. But the government's ferocious repression of the opposition, particularly after 1986, as well as its huge reserves of military and paramilitary power (South Africa had—and has—by far the most powerful and best equipped army in Africa), made it plain that the Soviets were right about the low odds of successful revolution.

The most important carrot in getting the ANC leadership to the bargaining table was the prospect of power. The low odds of military success meant that the de Klerk government's willingness to negotiate had to be taken seriously. Even if the ANC had to accept the prospect of power sharing in an interim government at least, this was surely better than nothing. Moreover, it opened up the possibility of a new status quo that could subsequently develop into full majority rule—as turned out to be the case.

3.2. Shifting Constraints and Possibilities in the Middle East

The Israeli decision to enter negotiations mirrored the South African one in several ways. Maintaining the status quo had became more expensive with the eruption of the first intifada. The anger of Palestinian youth, and organizational efforts by the Unified National Leadership of the Uprising (UNLU), took a toll on Israeli public support for the occupation. Israelis returned increasingly to their pre-1967 beliefs that occupation of the West Bank and Gaza was neither feasible nor desirable.[22] No doubt a drop-off in world support for Israel, caused by vivid nightly depictions on CNN

---

[21] The Tricameral Parliament was a last-ditch attempt by the NP to refashion the tatters of apartheid's divide-and-rule strategy by creating separate houses of Parliament for Coloureds and Indians (though none for Blacks).

[22] Israeli support for talks with the PLO consequently increased. A *New York Times* poll in April 1987 found that only 42 percent of respondents favored such talks. In contrast, a *New York Times* poll conducted in March 1989 found that 58 percent of Israelis supported negotiations with the PLO if it recognized Israel and ceased terrorist activity. A poll by *Yediot Aharonot* found similar results the following month, with 59 percent of respondents supporting talks with the PLO. Mark Tessler, *A History of the Israeli-Palestinian Conflict* (Bloomington: Indiana University Press, 1994), 724–25. An independent poll conducted for PM Rabin on the eve of the Oslo Agreement also confirmed that the public would support an agreement, even if Arafat was involved. David Makovsky, *Making Peace with the PLO: The Rabin Government's Road to the Oslo Accord* (Washington, DC: Washington Institute for Near East Policy, 1996), p. 62.

of the confrontation between stone-throwing youth and well-armed Israeli soldiers, reinforced this. By the early 1990s, the Israeli economy
was also suffering from the rapid influx of Soviet Jews,[23] which added an
economic dimension to the political malaise and prodded the leadership
in the direction of negotiations. Shifting public opinion meant conditions
were ripe for a solution that could not only create peace and order, but
also restore the democratic legitimacy of the Israeli state.

By 1991, there were increasing pressures within Israel for an agreement
with the Palestinians. After the Gulf War, which neutralized Syria and
moved moderate Arab states into closer alliance with the United States,
the Bush administration decided that the time for negotiations was ripe—
adding to both the pressure and the sense of opportunity for Israel.[24] There
was also a growing domestic constituency supporting an agreement with
the Palestinians. Frustrated by the intifada and alarmed by the noticeable
decrease in U.S. government support, army generals, the business community, and a large segment of the Israeli political Left called for a peace
process.[25] Rabin capitalized on this frustration when he ran successfully
against Shamir, promising an "autonomy agreement" with the Palestinians and restoration of U.S.-Israeli relations.[26] In 1993, Rabin decided
for the first time to talk to the PLO and Arafat, then the most powerful
Palestinian leader who would be essential to any deal.[27]

At the same time, the costs of entering negotiations were falling for
Arafat. He had weathered the internal criticism for acknowledging the
State of Israel in 1988 and, with the help of political platforms set forth
during the intifada, gained general Palestinian acceptance for a two-state
solution.[28] He also faced less opposition from Arab leaders to entering

---

[23] During the 1990s, 900,000 former Soviet immigrants arrived, the largest immigration
to Israel since the mid-1950s. More than 330,000 of these arrived in 1990 and 1991. Nurit
Yaffee and Dorith Tal, "Immigration to Israel from the Former Soviet Union" (2000), p. 4
http://www.cbs.gov.il/engprfl.htm [06-18-2003].

[24] James A. Baker III (with Thomas DeFrank), *The Politics of Diplomacy: Revolution,
War and Peace, 1989–1992* (New York: Putnam's Sons, 1995), p. 422.

[25] On the development of business community support for agreement/continuing peace
process, see "In the Middle East: 'Peace is now irreversible,'" *Business Week*, November
20, 1995, pp. 62–64. A survey we conducted showed that twenty-two of twenty-five business executives believed the peace agreement would have a positive impact on their businesses, and twenty of twenty-four believed that it was of major importance. See appendix
to chap. 3.

[26] Makovsky, *Making Peace with the PLO*, p. 12.

[27] Rabin continued to oppose direct deals with the PLO until mid-1993, and only after
August approved the draft Oslo Accords. Avi Shlaim, "The Oslo Accord," *Journal of Palestine Studies* 91 (Spring 1994): 32.

[28] Pamphlets distributed during the intifada, as well as a coordinated demonstration
of Palestinian, Israeli, and international actors in 1990, called for "Two States for Two

negotiations, with Egypt's move toward peace in 1979, King Hussein's relinquishing of the West Bank in 1988, and Syria's willingness to participate in the multilateral Madrid Conference in 1991. His perception of Israel's strength might not have changed, but the domestic and regional costs of negotiating seemed notably lower after 1991 than at any previous time.

The intifada had strengthened the Palestinians by putting pressure on Israel to negotiate, but the PLO also faced mounting pressure to enter negotiations. It had become increasingly isolated since the early 1980s—abandoned by Egypt in the 1979 Camp David agreement and thrown out of Lebanon in 1982. Yet these challenges paled by comparison with the events of 1990–91. The fall of the Soviet Union and Eastern Bloc diminished military and financial support. Then Arafat took the wild, and ultimately disastrous, gamble of supporting Iraq during the first Gulf War—leading the PLO to the edge of financial and political bankruptcy.[29] Dismayed Gulf States withdrew financial support, and Kuwait threw Palestinian workers out of the country. Defeated Iraq was in no position to help. The PLO could not pay monthly salaries, let alone support its functions.[30] Finally, Syria had seized the opportunity of the Gulf War to move closer to the United States, first agreeing to join in the U.S.-led coalition and then accepting an invitation to the Madrid Conference. So it is not surprising that, following the failed USSR coup attempt in August and the Syrian acceptance of the Madrid Conference, the PLO authorized a Palestinian delegation, led by Haider Abdul Shafi, to start negotiations. As Farouq Qaddumi explained, it was time for the PLO to join the peace process or exit history.[31]

Both the intifada and the presence of a non-PLO negotiating team at Madrid were creating an alternative Palestinian leadership. Much as Arafat welcomed the new legitimacy for the idea of a Palestinian state, it was becoming alarmingly possible for Palestinians and others to imagine this

---

Peoples," a marked contrast to earlier calls for the elimination of Israel. Hanan Ashrawi, *This Side of Peace* (New York: Touchstone, 1995).

[29] PLO coziness with Iraq was not new. In the late 1980s, Iraq had promised it that it would commit fifty-four army divisions against Israel after the end of the Iran-Iraq war, and Arafat had described Iraq as the defender of the "eastern gate" of the Arab nation. Similarly, in December 1989, Arafat praised the unveiling of a new Iraqi ballistic missile as a "gift to the *intifadah*." Yazid Sayigh, *Armed Struggle and the Search for State: The Palestinian National Movement* (Oxford: Clarendon Press, 1997), pp. 640–41.

[30] Approximately 400,000 Palestinians were thrown out of the Gulf countries, and the PLO lost an estimated $10 billion between 1991 and 1993. Graham Usher, *Palestine in Crisis: The Struggle for Peace and Political Independence after Oslo* (London: Pluto Press, 1995), pp. 1–2.

[31] Sayigh, *Armed Struggle and the Search for State*, p. 660.

state without a role for him and the PLO. Negotiating at Oslo was a way to preserve their role, though this came at a price. Negotiations involve concessions, and, until an agreement is actually consummated, making concessions increases the leadership's vulnerability to a flank attack. Fear of losing his grip on the Palestinian leadership propelled Arafat to accept concessions, and it also forced him to confront the possibility of an endgame rather than an endless peace process. Time and momentum were on his side, but if things dragged on for long enough without an agreement, they would turn against him.

3.3. Opportunities to End Stalemate in Northern Ireland

Negotiations in Northern Ireland resulted from a different mix of sticks and carrots. Neither Britain nor the Irish Republic had suffered unsustainable damage from the conflict, and the contending parties within Northern Ireland had ample popular legitimacy and access to the limited type of military equipment needed to continue the conflict. The Northern Ireland economy was depressed, but economic problems were not generally blamed on the Troubles, and budget transfers from Britain ensured that Northern Ireland was able to spend beyond its means.[32] Nonetheless, most relevant parties were engaged in talks to end the conflict for much of the 1990s. Why?

Solving this puzzle requires attention to the unusual combinations of participants in the Northern Ireland conflict. The transplacement model of hard-liners, reformers, moderates, and radicals, which captures the principal dynamics of negotiations in South Africa and the Middle East, was complicated there by the fact that in recent decades there had been four sets of major players, each with its own moderate and hard-line factions powerful enough to scuttle an agreement: Great Britain, the Irish Republic, the Ulster Unionist Party (UUP), and the Social Democratic and Labour Party (SDLP) and Sinn Fein together on the Nationalist side. Once the "external" players (Britain and Ireland) decided to work toward settlement, the participation of the "internal" players was gradually achieved through a combination of political sticks and carrots, guarantees, and pressure.

The 1985 Anglo-Irish Agreement marked the start of a new peace process. When Irish taoiseach Garrett FitzGerald came to power in 1982, he immediately began to shift relations with both Britain and the North. The agreement between the British and Irish governments regularized co-

---

[32] The difference between what Northern Ireland collects in revenue and what it receives in transfers from London is the subvention. Northern Ireland's is higher than Scotland's or Wales's. Interview with Dr. Esmond Birnie, former MLA, UUP July 29, 2003.

operation on conflict resolution between the two governments and would eventually set the terms of the accord.[33] It required that the constitutional status of Northern Ireland would not be changed without majority consent. This guaranteed the status of Northern Ireland as part of the United Kingdom in the short run, but it opened the door to the possibility that its status could be changed in the future. And it did more than that. The very fact that the British government agreed to this possibility underscored their acknowledgment of Northern Ireland's questionable democratic legitimacy. Imagine their signing on to something similar about Surrey.

Albert Reynolds was elected Irish taoiseach in 1992. He pushed "talks about talks" forward by starting parallel dialogues with John Major's government in Britain and with the SDLP and Sinn Fein in Northern Ireland. In 1993 Major and Reynolds announced the Downing Street Declaration as the starting point of a peace process. The British government reiterated that it had "no selfish strategic or economic interest in Northern Ireland," and went on to acknowledge that the possibility of a united Ireland was in the hands of the Irish people alone.[34] By signaling that it would not guarantee the Unionist position indefinitely, Britain raised the cost of recalcitrance to Unionists and ceded the contestability—if not illegitimacy—of the status quo. The Irish Republic in turn promised that a settlement would include amending the Irish Constitution to remove the claim that the Irish Parliament had in principle the right to incorporate and govern Northern Ireland. The declaration thus moved further toward establishing the framework within which both sides would pursue their aspirations.[35] It also made clear that any future settlement would have to come to grips with Northern Ireland as a distinct entity, at least for the foreseeable future.

The Downing Street Declaration stated that negotiations would be limited to those parties not engaged in paramilitary violence. In response, the IRA announced a complete cessation of all military activity in August 1994, forcing Loyalists to parry with a cease-fire. Within six months, the British and Irish governments issued a Frameworks for the Future policy document, aimed at translating the Joint Declaration into concrete terms.

[33] See Brendan O'Leary and John McGarry, *The Politics of Antagonism: Understanding Northern Ireland* (London: Athlone Press, 1996), p. 226; John Darby, *Scorpions in a Bottle* (London: Minority Rights Group, 1997); and Eamonn Mallie and David McCittrick, *The Fight for Peace: The Secret Story behind the Irish Peace Process* (London: Heinemann, 1996).

[34] John Darby, "Northern Ireland: The Background to the Peace Process," CAIN Web Service (June 5, 2003), http://cain.ulst.ac.uk/events/peace/darby03.htm [06-17-2003].

[35] We are grateful to Brendan O'Leary for suggesting this interpretation of the effect of the declaration on aspirations. See his "Afterword: What Is Framed in the Framework Documents?" *Ethnic and Racial Studies* 18 (1995): 862–72.

The guidelines for a final settlement included the structure of interrelations among Ireland, Britain, and Northern Ireland, and the composition of a devolved government within Northern Ireland. As in South Africa and the Middle East, then, negotiations over a settlement in Northern Ireland were seriously under way by the early 1990s. Understanding why the outcomes diverged as they did concerns us next.

4. Theory and Practice of Commitment

If negotiations are to lead to viable agreements, the adversaries must rely on one another. A potential obstacle is the classic commitment problem described by Thomas Schelling: if each side knows that the other might subsequently defect, why should either agree?[36] In theory, commitment problems are ubiquitous in democratic politics, given the lack of third-party enforcement. Despite numerous attempts to show that compliance with democratic outcomes can be in the interests of all, no theoretical account has been developed that shows why electoral losers with the power to defect so often do not do so.[37] It would be unthinkable for an American president who lost an election to order tanks down Pennsylvania Avenue, even if he had no realistic hope of ever regaining power through the ballot box. The same could be said of politicians in many other democracies who routinely accept results that consign them to political oblivion. We must therefore take care not to judge potential settlements in the transition context by a standard that predicts perpetual civil war throughout the democratic world.[38]

That said, there are reasons to expect commitment problems surrounding transplacements to be particularly acute. Following decades of sometimes-violent conflict, they are marriages of convenience among parties with few reasons for mutual trust. As Rabin put it in 1993: "Peace is not made with friends. Peace is made with enemies, some of whom—and I won't name names—I loathe very much."[39] Even if reformers and moderates are willing to move toward agreement, they are bound to be skeptical of one another's motives and good faith.

---

[36] Thomas C. Schelling, *The Strategy of Conflict* (Cambridge, MA: Harvard University Press, 1960).

[37] See Przeworski, *Democracy and the Market*, chap. 1, and "Minimalist Conception of Democracy: A Defense," in *Democracy's Value*, ed. Ian Shapiro and Casiano Hacker-Cordón (Cambridge: Cambridge University Press, 1999), pp. 23–55.

[38] For elaboration, see Ian Shapiro, *The State of Democratic Theory* (Princeton: Princeton University Press, 2003), pp. 88–93.

[39] "From Setbacks to Living Together," *New York Times*, September 5, 1993, p. 10.

This is further complicated in the quasi-democratic settings characteristic of SAMENI transplacements because the negotiating partners must be responsive to public opinion. Indeed, it might be possible for opponents of negotiations to use public opinion to undermine reformers or even to remove them from power. Unless the reformers and moderates build support for the idea of an agreement among the grassroots constituencies they depend on, the rug can be pulled out from under them. Yet by the same token negotiators can also employ the constraints of democratic legitimation to signal their commitment to a settlement. By making concessions public, political elites tie themselves to positions they will not easily be able to abandon without damaging their future electoral prospects. In so doing they burn bridges to existing sources of legitimation, forcing them to look for new ones. In this sense the quasi-democratic character of SAMENI negotiations may offer possibilities for dealing with commitment problems that are not available in other transplacements.

Reformers and moderates have incentives to do what they can to help strengthen one another to deal with hostile flanks, but these incentives are mixed. On the one hand they need to strengthen their adversaries. Because negotiated transitions occur only when government reformers and opposition moderates are too weak to achieve unilateral change but strong enough to achieve it if they cooperate, they must have adversaries who can stay in power long enough to deliver. Yet, on the other hand, they must not strengthen their adversaries too much. Both sides will want to extract the best possible terms for their supporters so far as the content of an agreement is concerned, and they have no reason to make this task more difficult than necessary. Moreover, in many cases the protagonists will expect to compete for political support in the new order, if it arrives, and a stronger adversary is more difficult to compete with than a weaker one. Even if the eventual settlement is expected to be a partition, other considerations create similar pressures. Strengthening your adversary will turn out to have been costly if there is no agreement and the situation reverts to one of open conflict. While each side thus has incentives to optimize its own political strength vis-à-vis conservative and revolutionary flanks, it is best for them if their adversary merely satisfices: becomes just strong enough to deliver an agreement from which potential spoilers can be marginalized if they cannot be co-opted.[40]

The capacity to demonstrate commitment is shaped by how bad things are likely to get should the negotiations fail. If the principals believe that withdrawing from negotiations is either unlikely or exceedingly costly for them, this will stiffen their backs to stay the course when the going gets

[40] See Jung and Shapiro, "South Africa's Negotiated Transition," pp. 280–82.

rough. More important, passing a costly or unacceptable reversion point helps them signal to their negotiating adversaries that they are serious about achieving a successful agreement. This is why things sometimes have to get worse before they can get better. An unpalatable reversion point for either or both parties by no means guarantees agreement—there are other possibilities, such as civil war or military coup. But if your adversary knows that the status quo ante is decreasingly tenable for you, it becomes easier for him to believe that you are serious about looking for an accommodation.

Both sides must be concerned not only with their adversary's desire to reach an agreement, but also with their capacity to deliver. As a result, the credibility of negotiating commitments is unavoidably dependent on how successful reformers and moderates are at co-opting or marginalizing flank attacks. You have little reason to trust even an adversary you believe to be sincere if you think that the ground may be cut from under him. This possibility can be forestalled in various ways. One is to actually be the flanking force. This Nixon-to-China logic suggests that the closer negotiators are to the ideological extremes in their parties, the more credible their commitments will be. An alternative is to face down the flanking opposition at critical junctures, or visibly to burn bridges with it while retaining the support of the military. One way or another, the negotiating principals must ensure that their adversaries have good reasons to believe that they can deliver down the stretch.

4.1. South African Success

These commitment problems were managed in three ways in South Africa. First, the situation on the ground became decreasingly attractive to the NP and eventually to the ANC as well. The combination of economic malaise, a sustained national uprising, and international opprobrium took an increasing toll on white South Africans. The September 1992 Bisho massacre made graphic the possibility that escalating violence could spiral out of control. It gave both sides a sobering view into the abyss, motivating them to resume negotiations that had been abandoned with the breakdown of CODESA II—this time in secret.[41] Second, potential flank attacks were effectively neutralized. De Klerk's history as an orthodox Afrikaner and conservative member of the NP initially strengthened his hand within his own party. Similarly, on entering the negotiations Mandela enjoyed substantial political capital that stemmed from his personal legitimacy. In contrast to Inkatha leader Mangosuthu Buthelezi, who was compromised by his dealings with the apartheid regime in the 1980s,

---

[41] Ibid., p. 288.

Mandela, having refused to renounce violence as a condition for release from twenty-seven years in prison, had become unassailable within the ANC. A radical flank did emerge during negotiations, but Mandela's legendary status and position as founder of the ANC's military wing made his authority impossible to challenge.

Third, and perhaps decisively, decisions made by Mandela and de Klerk early in the negotiations helped diminish their commitment problems. De Klerk's bold steps in 1992 showed how bridge burning enhances credibility, and how even flawed democracy can be used to move negotiations forward. In 1990 and 1991 he lost a series of by-elections while he was negotiating with the ANC, emboldening right-wing attacks on him. He called their bluff, however, by holding a snap referendum in March 1992 that he won by a two-thirds majority among the white electorate with absolute majorities in every region of the country. He insisted throughout the referendum campaign that the critical issue of power sharing (the political equivalent of sovereignty over Jerusalem for Israelis or policing and IRA decommissioning for Protestants in Northern Ireland) was nonnegotiable. In fact he was forced to moderate this demand later in the negotiations, but even then this was obscured by the fact that the ANC, which had steadfastly rejected all compromise on majority rule, gave de Klerk the wiggle room he needed by agreeing to a constitutionally mandated interim government of national unity. The ANC nonetheless refused to commit to a permanent government of national unity. They kept constitutionally mandated power sharing out of the statement of entrenched principles the Constitutional Court would eventually use to judge the acceptability of the final constitution. By the time the final constitution, which dropped power sharing, was negotiated in 1995, the NP was no longer in a position to insist on anything.

This was one of several respects in which the ANC played its cards perfectly during the negotiations. At the time of the referendum, no one knew how long an interim settlement would last or what the final agreement was going to look like. In many places interim settlements have been known to drag on for decades, and some may reasonably have expected this in South Africa. Once de Klerk had made his move, the ANC helped him satisfice by compromising on the power-sharing issue in the interim constitution. This was essential for him to retain his grassroots support. By then he had burned his bridges with the Far Right and legitimated the negotiated transition among the white electorate, even though—fortuitously, as we argue later—it was not entirely clear where it would lead.

Governments have an initial advantage in transition negotiations because they control the military and hence the possibility of a return to authoritarianism should negotiations fail. However, that advantage diminishes for a leader who alienates the conservative flank (which often has its own links to the military hierarchy) and moves toward the position of his adversary during negotiations. Facing down the hard right magnified de Klerk's personal political investment in achieving the successful negotiated settlement. Failure would have been immensely costly for him, possibly not survivable. It would likely have been followed by a massive escalation in violence for which he would have been held responsible by the whites who had trusted him, opening the way for an authoritarian leader or the army to seize the initiative. We cannot be sure de Klerk had passed a point of no return by the time of the referendum, but clearly he was well into his Rubicon, treading in deep water. He would have been in dire straits had he found himself there alone.

The ANC pooh-poohed the referendum at the time as one more illegitimate "whites only" vote, but once it was over, they had de Klerk exactly where they wanted him. He could no longer point to constraints coming from the Right as a way of limiting the concessions he could make. By the time of the final agreement in 1993 it was the government that had made the decisive power-sharing concession, and by then there was no going back for de Klerk.

The compromise over power sharing also illustrates how the opposition can manage potentially hostile flanks within its own ranks. During negotiations, the initiative was not most seriously in danger of shifting to more radical organizations outside the ANC (which by this point were hopelessly weak), but rather of shifting to a radical flank of youth within the ANC mobilized by Winnie Mandela, Peter Mokaba, and Chris Hani. Conceding power sharing for an interim settlement only enabled the ANC leadership to keep critics on board at the decisive meeting of February 1993.[42] The ANC leadership could plausibly (and correctly, as it turned out) make the case that time was on their side, and that once the reality had changed on the ground, they would be negotiating over the final settlement from a position of much greater strength.

To be sure, they were helped by a variety of factors: the ANC's good organization compared with that of potential opposition interlopers, Mandela's legendary status, and the assassination of Chris Hani in April 1993, which removed the most popular radical leader from the scene and reinforced the commitment of both sides to a settlement. Hani's murder might have unraveled the peace process altogether as millions of African youth emptied into the streets to mourn and seek revenge. As it happened, however, de Klerk and Mandela moved quickly, and with a united front, to forestall such an outcome. But the main reason the

---

[42] Ibid., pp. 290–91.

ANC coalition stayed together was that the moderate leadership, which included tough-minded and pragmatic negotiators like Cyril Ramaphosa with unassailable antiapartheid credentials, could make a plausible case that by conceding power sharing in the interim arrangement, they had not conceded anything of importance. It meant that within four years the ANC would have achieved an outcome through negotiations—majority rule democracy with themselves in decisive control—that they lacked the military capacity to impose on the government at any time before the transition.

If the ANC played its cards perfectly in the 1992 settlement, does this mean that they got the better of de Klerk in the negotiations? Making that case would require establishing that the ANC leadership could both have remained intact and continued as the principal protagonist on the opposition side while agreeing to a permanent power-sharing arrangement. This is doubtful, not only because of the internal conflict it would have provoked in the ANC, but also because any such deal would have empowered Buthelezi's Inkatha as an important opposition player with a share in power. Inkatha was the third-largest party in South Africa and the best bet for the NP to dilute ANC power and support. The NP, which had long courted Inkatha as a moderate alternative to the ANC, would have insisted on maximizing the strength of all minority parties with an eye to weakening the ANC.[43] Having successfully marginalized Buthelezi, the ANC had no reason to travel down that path. "Ordinary democracy" rather than power sharing was thus their reservation price for the permanent constitution, making their optimizing and satisficing strategies identical. Agreeing to interim power sharing was needed to move de Klerk toward, if not past, his point of no return; resisting anything more was essential to maintaining their own position. For this reason it seems clear that although de Klerk could have scuttled the negotiations, paying whatever political price that entailed, he could not have negotiated better terms for the NP.

Notice, however, that massive though the concession was to give away constitutionally mandated power sharing in the final constitution, the outcome could have been worse for the NP. This is not a negligible list of what they achieved: entrenched democratic principles with a constitutional court to interpret them; a two-thirds majority requirement to alter the constitution; entrenched protections of property rights and civil freedoms; absence of high representation thresholds that would disenfranchise minor parties; the guarantee of an amnesty process and protection

---

[43] Inkatha played an important role in the government of national unity in the decade after the transition, but on sufferance from the ANC, which found it expedient to co-opt Buthelezi by keeping him in the cabinet.

of civil service jobs for at least five years; and a powerful party whip system that the NP believed would strengthen its leverage in Parliament. Four general elections later, ANC hegemony still means that there is little meaningful national political competition.[44] If and when the ANC begins to fracture, leading to a more fluid political environment, then the entrenched democratic guarantees will be important devices in giving minority parties the chance to become more consequential political players.[45] Accordingly, it would be a mistake to say that de Klerk was giving away the store by failing to secure constitutionally mandated power sharing for the long run. Arguably the NP made some unnecessary minor concessions and to that extent did not get the ANC merely to satisfice in areas where it might have done.[46] But on the major constitutional questions of democratic politics, commitments were extracted from the ANC that might not have been, and indeed have not been in other transitional contexts.

This is not to say other outcomes are unimaginable. A more astute NP leadership in the 1980s might have made a deal with Buthelezi to partition the country before the UDF had consolidated itself as the principal opposition player. Had that happened, the South African conflict today might more closely resemble the Middle East, with disputes over sovereignty, borders, refugees, and other displaced persons and an endlessly debated "peace process" amid the ebb and flow of a war of attrition. Alternatively, the NP could have staggered on during the 1990s (and perhaps even beyond) as it had in the 1980s, repressing the opposition and thumbing its nose at outside pressure. Given the erosion of its support among Afrikaner intellectuals, this would have meant an increasingly authoritarian militarized society with scant hope for improvements in the economy. Yet it might have been survivable for a long time. True, the deteriorating political and economic climate supplied the NP with the impetus to start the negotiations and to stay the course, but it did not compel them to do so. Structural factors predispose things in one

---

[44] However, there is meaningful local and regional political competition. In the Eastern Cape, the United Democratic Movement (UDM) formed by Bantu Holomisa, who was expelled from the ANC in 1997, and Roelf Meyer, who had led the NP negotiating team in the transition, took away a substantial portion of the ANC vote to become the official opposition party in 1999. The Christian Democratic Party did the same thing in the Northern Transvaal. In both 1994 and 1999 Inkatha won elections in Natal, and the NP (in coalition with the Democratic Party after 1999) governs the Western Cape.

[45] After the first election much of the NP defected to other opposition parties, and in 2004 the party effectively ceased to exist when its leaders decided to join the ANC.

[46] See, for instance, Jung and Shapiro, "South Africa's Negotiated Transition," pp. 300–301.

direction or another, but agency is required as well. Had P. W. Botha remained at the NP helm, it is unlikely negotiations would have started in 1990 or, if somehow they had begun, ended successfully in 1993.

4.2. Missed Opportunity in the Middle East

Though in some ways more challenging, the commitment problems facing the principals in the Middle East in the early 1990s were not insuperable. Like Mandela and de Klerk in South Africa, Rabin and Arafat were both well placed to manage hostile flanks. Israelis saw Rabin as a war hero dedicated to Israeli security, better positioned than Shimon Peres to move the process forward. Arafat also had the clout of being a long-time Fatah leader-in-exile. Indeed, Rabin's decision to deal with Arafat directly through the "back channels" at Oslo was a clear recognition that the Palestinian delegation depended on and deferred to Arafat.[47] He risked a breakaway by his radical flank, but he quickly demonstrated his ability to gain the acquiescence of the majority and to marginalize the remaining opponents.

Yet the Middle East negotiations differed from those in South Africa from the perspectives of both sides. The Oslo formulation was widely seen as Arafat's attempt to shore up his personal power, and it was far from clear that when push came to shove many Palestinians would accept the agreement that could be extracted as superior to the status quo.[48] Nor was the Israeli side propelled by an imperative to consummate an agreement. Israel's decision to enter negotiations was based, in part, on the perception that a weakened Arafat would be easy to bargain with. The intifada and then significant U.S. pressure had moved the Israeli government into concessions in 1993, with an eye to getting an agreement rather than merely going through the interminable motions of the peace process. Like Arafat, Rabin seems to have been personally committed to reaching a settlement, but few can have doubted that Israel could cut and run if the going got rough.

This reality generated commitment problems that Arafat and Rabin both dealt with by burning bridges on their flanks. Convinced that Rabin was serious about a settlement that would involve a sovereign Palestinian state, and focused, perhaps, on his own political survival, Arafat accepted a partial agreement that postponed deciding the most important issues, such as control over Jerusalem, full establishment of a state, the

[47] Uri Savir, *The Process: 1,100 Days That Changed the Middle East* (New York: Random House, 1998), p. 5; Makovsky, *Making Peace with the PLO*, p. 39.
[48] Sayigh, *Armed Struggle and the Search for State*, pp. 658–60.

return of refugees, and water rights.[49] He also stepped decisively into the Rubicon by recognizing Israel's right to exist and committing himself to policing the West Bank to provide Israel security from Palestinian attacks. Opposition heightened, and the situation threatened to turn into a civil war in November 1994 when Palestinian police faced down several thousand Hamas supporters demonstrating outside the largest mosque in Gaza. In addition to the Islamist resistance, Arafat also faced increasing opposition from leftist and nationalist critics who decried the "Bantustan solution."[50]

Rabin also tried to face down hard-line opponents. Labour dominance in the Knesset allowed him to move forward in negotiations with little real attention to, or even acknowledgment of, opposition. But as he converged on the peace settlement, signing Oslo II in September 1995, an increasingly vitriolic opposition attacked his cooperation with Arafat, shouting "Death to Arafat" and portraying Rabin wearing Arafat's trademark kaffiyeh.[51] As Netanyahu remarked in that same month, "I don't want to say isolated, but we were in the minority. [Now] I think the government is in the minority."[52]

Rabin and Arafat demonstrated their commitment to the process, continuing cooperation even as they became targets of increasing attack. Rabin minimized Palestinian violations to help shore up the process. After a spate of bombings in 1995, for example, Arafat offered condolences while Rabin vowed to continue the peace process, telling Arafat, "We must work together to prevent terrorism, and you must remember that terrorists are not just our enemies, but yours as well."[53] Arafat showed similar patience when on February 25, 1994, Dr. Baruch Goldstein from Qiryat Arba walked into the Ibrahimi Mosque in Hebron's Tomb of the Patriarchs and fired on worshipping Muslims, killing twenty-nine and wounding nearly one hundred. Rather than call off the process, Arafat recalled that he told Rabin in a call following the massacre: "There are

[49] According to Edward Said, as early as 1992 Arafat seemed to be "staking his entire future on Rabin's electoral win." "Interview with Edward Said by Abdullah al-Sinnawi," al-'Arabi (Cairo), January 30, 1995, trans. Joseph Massad, in Edward Said, Peace and Its Discontents (London: Random House, 1995), p. 179.

[50] Ibid.; Usher, Palestine in Crisis, pp. 14–20, 25–34.

[51] On opposition in the settlements, see Robert Friedman, "Report from the West Bank: An Unholy Rage," New Yorker, March 7, 1994, pp. 54–56; Ehud Sprinzak, Brother against Brother: Violence and Extremism in Israeli Politics from Altalena to the Rabin Assassination (New York: Free Press, 1999); "Rabin Decides to Close Gazan Roads near Settlements, Arafat Condemns Attacks," New York Times, October 4, 1995; "Five Killed in Suicide Bombing of Bus 26 in Jerusalem," New York Times, August 21, 1995.

[52] Barton Gellman, "Likud Leader Hammers Rabin, PLO Premier; Hopeful Netanyahu Claims Ascendancy of Israeli Opposition," Washington Post, September 9, 1995, p. A22.

[53] "Rabin Decides to Close Gazan Roads"; see also Conni Bruck, "A Reporter at Large: The Wounds of Peace," New Yorker, October 8, 1995, pp. 64–91.

clearly fanatics in the settlements, and the government of Israel needs to take steps against them. They want to destroy the peace process."[54] That reaction, too, was met with harsh Palestinian criticism.

Had they been able to keep going, Arafat and Rabin might well have consummated an agreement whose benefits would have replenished their political capital on the South African model, but Rabin's murder in November 1995 put this possibility on ice.[55] However, in the end it was not Rabin's removal that thwarted the peace process. Rather, what froze negotiations was his successor Shimon Peres's inability to take advantage of the opportunities that negotiating in a flawed democracy can afford. His failure to call a snap election as soon as he replaced the fallen Rabin was surely one of the most consequential missed opportunities in the history of Middle East politics.[56] The evidence suggests that it might well have served the same function as de Klerk's March 1992 referendum, at a time when public opinion on both sides favored a two-state solution, and the outrage at Rabin's assassination had all but the most fanatical Israeli Right on the defensive.[57] Perhaps U.S. pressure could have moved Peres at this point, but the timing for this was not propitious in the run-up to the November 1996 U.S. presidential election.

True, many critical issues remained unresolved, but as the ambiguity around permanent power sharing during the South African referendum underscores, this does not mean that a workable settlement was unavailable. Indeed, in South Africa this ambiguity was essential to moving things forward. Had the South African negotiations fallen apart, many analysts would subsequently have said that the negotiations could not have succeeded because the whites would never have given up power

[54] Janet Wallach and John Wallach, *Arafat: In the Eyes of the Beholder* (New York: Birch Lane, 1997), p. 460.

[55] In our survey of business executives in 2003, twenty of twenty-five respondents believed that Rabin's assassination increased the likelihood that Oslo would fail. However, only twelve of them said that they recognized this in 1995.

[56] Fifteen of the top business executives we surveyed in 2003 thought this had been a strategic mistake by Peres. Nine of them thought his hard-line strategy in the run-up to the 1996 election harmed the prospects for peace.

[57] According to polls conducted by the Tami Steinmetz Center for Peace Research (TSC) at the University of Tel Aviv, the Oslo peace index of Israeli public opinion rose from 46.9 in October 1995 to 57.9 on November 8, immediately following Rabin's assassination. The index remained at 58 at the end of November, dropping to 55.8 in December. TSC, "Peace Index, 1995," http://spirit.tau.ac.il/socant/peace/ [06-18-2003]. In October 1995, 72.5 percent of Palestinians polled supported the peace process. JMCC, "JMCC Public Opinion Poll #10," http://www.jmcc.org/publicpoll/results/1995/no10.htm [06-18-2003]. For additional discussion of the missed opportunities for settlements under Rabin and Peres, see Ellen Lust-Okar and A.F.K. Organski, "Coalitions and Conflict: The Case of Palestinian-Israeli Negotiations over the West Bank," *Journal of Conflict Management and Peace Science* 19, no. 2 (2002): 23–58.

sharing. Plausible as such arguments might have sounded, they would have been wrong. Negotiations themselves shift conceptions of what is possible, which in turn changes what *is* possible.

In the event, Peres missed his opportunity—tacking instead to the right. He permitted the assassination of Yahya Ayyash in January 1996, which further contributed to the cycle of violence and closures on the West Bank and Gaza Strip. In addition, Peres responded to attacks from southern Lebanon by bombing Lebanese refugee camps in Operation Grapes of Wrath. At the same time, the wave of suicide bombings in the spring of 1996[58] led Israelis to seek a "firmer stance" in negotiations.[59] Likud was able to regroup while Peres alienated himself from Israeli supporters of the negotiations, as well as Israeli Arabs. Palestinian radicals thus helped secure the victory of the Israeli Right, and when elections were held in May 1996, Peres lost the race to become Israel's first directly elected prime minister by a mere twenty-nine thousand votes. In marked contrast to Peres, the incoming prime minister Benjamin Netanyahu had made no secret of his hostility to the Oslo Accords on which the negotiations had been predicated, leaving them on life support at best.

Facing defeated partners in peace, Arafat was massively weakened. Initially, he responded by attempting to push the peace process forward. He courted Netanyahu, waiting for the call and meeting that would eventually confer recognition on him as a legitimate negotiating partner. Netanyahu, facing U.S. pressure and an Israeli constituency pressing for a "secure peace," finally agreed not only to a meeting but also to signing the Hebron Accord and Wye Agreement. Arafat responded with increased concessions, but it was clear that Netanyahu was neither a willing nor a committed partner. Facing competing constituencies at home, he refused to implement the agreement and continued expanding settlements in the occupied territories. Israeli public support for an agreement was eroding.

Palestinians also became increasingly disillusioned with the peace process, and with the ability of the Palestinian Authority (PA) to deliver a positive solution. The Palestinian standard of living had fallen sharply since the signing of the 1993 accords. Palestinians faced economic and social difficulties, and an unresponsive, authoritarian PA. International support

[58] By March 1996, Israelis had experienced twelve suicide bombings during the Oslo process. Four of these came in February and March 1996 alone, killing fifty-nine Israelis. Aish HaTorah, "Myths and Facts," http://www.aish.com/Israel/articles/Suicide_Bombings .asp [06-18-2003].

[59] A June 1996 poll by the TSC found that 70.7 percent of Israeli Jews supported a firmer stance toward the Palestinians. TSC, "Peace Index June 1996," spirit.tau.ac.il/socant/peace/ peaceindex/ 1996/files/JUNE96e.pdf [06-25-2003].

from donors dropped as they lost confidence in the PA. Israel closed territories, continued expanding the settlements,[60] and dragged its feet in withdrawing from the occupied territories.[61] This compounded Palestinian alienation.[62] Support for the PA declined, with the majority of Palestinians coming to see it as corrupt.[63] The costs of selling any agreement with compromises thus rose dramatically for Arafat after the collapse of the Hebron Accord and Wye Agreement. Seventy percent of Palestinians polled in June 1999 continued to support the peace process, but their trust in Israel had declined.[64] Arafat faced opposition not only from Hamas and Islamic Jihad, but also from former Fatah supporters, academics, and the Palestinian middle classes who had been willing at least to "wait and see" through 1996.

Thus by the time Ehud Barak went to Camp David in 2000 intending to make major concessions, Arafat could no longer meet him halfway.[65] Elected in May 1999, Barak was riding a wave of anti-Netanyahu sentiment and knew his landslide victory had come largely in response to the

[60] The number of settlers rose from 99,065 in 1991 to 186,135 in 1999. Foundation for Middle East Peace, "Special Report," 11, no. 6 (November–December 2001), http://www.fmep.org/reports/2001/v11n6.html [06-18-2003].

[61] Had the aborted Wye Memorandum of October 1998 been implemented, Palestinians would have had control over 18.2 percent (Area A) of the West Bank and shared control over 21.8 percent (Area B). Israelis maintained full control over 60 percent of the territory (Area C). Of the scheduled transfers, only 1 percent was territory moved from Area C to Area A, and 3 percent of territory designated Area B remained in "nature reserves" in which Palestinians would be prohibited from building. This agreement was signed after the initially declared deadline for the establishment of a Palestinian state. Ministry of Foreign Affairs, "Wye Memorandum Agreement, October 23, 1998," http://www.mfa.gov.il/mfa/go.asp?MFAH07o10 [06-18-2003].

[62] Rex Brynen, *A Very Political Economy: Peacebuilding and Foreign Aid in the West Bank and Gaza* (Washington: USIP, 2000), pp. 140–44.

[63] A poll conducted by the Center for Palestine Research and Studies (CPRS), June 3–5, 1999, found that 71 percent of Palestinians believed the PA was corrupt, and 66 percent believed that the level of corruption would remain the same or increase in the future. CPRS, "Public Opinion Poll #41," www.pcpsr.org/survey/cprspolls/99/poll41a.html [06-18-2003].

[64] The CPRS poll conducted June 3–5, 1999, found that 70 percent of Palestinians surveyed supported the peace process, while 27 percent opposed it. At the same time, however, 66 percent of the respondents did not trust the peaceful intentions of the Barak government, in contrast to 23 percent expressing trust in the newly elected Israeli government. Similarly, 55 percent did not believe that final status negotiations would lead successfully to a permanent settlement, and 45 percent supported the continuation of armed attacks against Israel. Ibid.

[65] The extent to which concessions offered at Camp David were "major" and intended to meet Arafat halfway remains controversial. However, it appears clear that these concessions went beyond previous Israeli offers (much to many Israelis' dismay), and indeed exceeded offers that Arafat had previously found more acceptable.

Israeli demands to "end this process" and make an agreement.[66] As a directly elected prime minister, he enjoyed a degree of independent legitimacy, and the possibility existed of holding a referendum on an agreement even in the face of a hostile Knesset. That he was willing to make bold moves was readily apparent as, in an attempt to force a peace agreement with the Syrians, he announced the unilateral withdrawal from southern Lebanon. The attempt to conclude an agreement with Hafez al-Asad was bold and creative. It was apparently made in the belief that the Syrian treaty was easier to conclude than the Palestinian agreement, and that peace with the Syrians would ease the way for the latter treaty.[67] After the strategy failed, Barak turned fully to the Palestinian track in the spring of 2000, signaling his commitment to make more concessions than had any previous Israeli leader.[68] The resulting anger in the Knesset, marked by a failed no-confidence vote and threats to bolt the coalition, bolstered his credibility.[69]

The difficulty was that Arafat was now too weak to make concessions on such key issues as Jerusalem and the Palestinian "right of return." Palestinians' skepticism toward Barak's intentions had only heightened since the previous summer, as they saw themselves sidelined in favor of Syrian-Israeli negotiations. By the time Arafat came to Camp David in the summer of 2000, against his will and under strong pressure from Bill Clinton, his hands were tied. Survey data revealed most Palestinians to be opposed to the meetings, with little confidence in Arafat's negotiating team.[70] By then Arafat's only hope of maintaining Fatah dominance and his leadership position was by responding to Palestinian popular opin-

[66] Barak won the 1999 election for prime minister with 56.08 percent of the popular vote, vs. 43.92 percent for Netanyahu. See "Election Results 1999," *Jerusalem Post*, http://info.jpost.com/1999/Supplements/Elections99/final.html [06-18-2003].

[67] "Barak Survives No-Confidence Vote as Raids on Lebanon Resume," CNN.com World, February 14, 2000, http://www.cnn.com/2000/WORLD/meast/02/14/mideast.02/ [06-18-2003].

[68] Thus William Safire would attack Barak for making concessions in violation of his own election pledges by offering Arafat virtually all of the West Bank (including the Jordan Valley, which would have meant relocating forty thousand Israeli settlers), a virtual guarantee of a right of return to all Palestinians around the world, and shared sovereignty with a new Palestinian state over portions of Jerusalem, "unthinkable only a year ago." "Why Is Arafat Smiling?" *New York Times*, July 27, 2000, p. A25.

[69] "Barak Survives No-Confidence Vote in Parliament," CNN.com World, July 10, 2000, http://www.cnn.com/2000/WORLD/meast/07/10/mideast.summit.02/ [06-18-2003].

[70] A Jerusalem Media and Communication Centre (JMCC) poll conducted July 16–17, 2000, found that 52.8 percent of respondents did not expect the delegations to reach an acceptable final agreement, while only 37.3 percent expected an agreement. More important, when asked, "Are you confident or not confident in the Palestinian negotiating delegation in Camp David?" 34.7 percent lacked confidence and 7.8 percent "did not know." JMCC, "JMCC Public Opinion Poll No. 38 on Palestinian Attitudes towards the Camp David Summit, July 2000," www.jmcc.org/publicpoll/results/2000/no38.html [06-18-2003].

ion.[71] Unless Barak was willing to concede to Palestinian demands, which seemed vanishingly unlikely, Arafat would thus be unable to respond. This was clear to the lead writers for the *Economist* a week before the negotiations collapsed. Citing opinion polls giving only 32 percent support among Palestinians (with over 50 percent believing that he would be pressured into concessions at Camp David), they noted with great perspicacity that "the more he withstands the heat, the higher his stock will rise."[72] Former secretary of state James Baker reached the same conclusion in his postmortem following the collapse. Quoting Palestinian sources to the effect that "Arafat's ability to maneuver is nil,"[73] he concluded, "what was not enough for Mr. Arafat was too much for many Israelis, to whom any agreement will be submitted by referendum."[74] In short, the window of opportunity was no longer open because Arafat was not in a position to commit to anything that Barak could accept.

The Israeli-Palestinian negotiations demonstrate how easily potentially viable solutions to the commitment problem can be destroyed. Rabin had put himself and his leadership on the line, first in making and then in defending his decision to negotiate with the PLO. His solid, if slim, Labour majority in the Knesset enabled him to act with little regard for his opponents. The bridges he burned along the way suggested that he would do what was needed to deliver an agreement once one had been made. Arafat, who had his own reasons to negotiate, could thus anticipate that if he took the risk and signed the Oslo Agreement, Israel would fulfill its part of the bargain and move forward on the final status issues. Rabin took similar risks, even if somewhat less was at stake for him initially. He had reason to believe that Arafat would deliver on his commitments, given the political costs he had paid for entering negotiations. Certainly it was clear that if anyone could deliver the Palestinian side in 1995, it was he.[75] But the derailing of the process eroded his authority, and with

[71] According to a Palestinian Center for Policy and Survey Research (PCPSR) poll, 68 percent of Palestinians believed Arafat's overall position at Camp David was "just right," while 15 percent believed he had compromised too much. PCPSR, "Public Opinion Poll #1," July 27–29, 2000, www.pcpsr.org/survey/polls/2000/pla.html [06-18-2003].

[72] "The Ballad of Camp David," *Economist*, July 2, 2000, p. 43.

[73] For data supporting this conclusion, see PCPSR, "Public Opinion Poll #1."

[74] James A. Baker III, "Peace, One Step at a Time," *New York Times*, July 27, 2000, p. A25.

[75] Even those who question whether Arafat turned Hamas and the Islamic Jihad "loose" on the Israelis argue that he did so in order to increase his bargaining position and ultimately gain a better settlement. Few seriously question whether he really sought to end the conflict and see a Palestinian state develop before his imminent death. As he made clear in his March 2002 interview with Christiane Amanpour, he saw the establishment of the Palestinian state (including East Jerusalem) not only as his personal mission, but as the very definition of who he was. See http://www.cnn.com/2002/WORLD/meast/03/29/arafat .cnna/ [06-18-2003].

it his ability to deliver the Palestinian side in any agreement. Opponents of Oslo grew from small Islamist and leftist fringe groups into the mainstream of Palestinians, who came to believe that years of interim agreements had weakened them while providing no benefits. They continued to support "peace," but by 2000 the vast majority did not expect the then-current process to succeed.[76]

4.3. Northern Irish Vulnerability to Multiple Vetoes

Negotiations in Northern Ireland have faced two limitations. Moderate leaders have not had the success of Mandela and de Klerk in facing down their radical flanks, particularly on the Unionist side, and neither side has been sufficiently motivated by a deteriorating status quo to take the irreversible steps to consolidate agreement. The absence of an intifada or other serious threat to governability makes it remarkable that there has been an agreement at all, but unsurprising that the agreement lives in perpetual danger of falling apart.

Frustrated by the failure of the British government and the Unionists to negotiate seriously, the IRA suspended its cease-fire in February 1996 with a bomb explosion that injured one hundred people in London.[77] As in South Africa, violence was effective in galvanizing a recalcitrant negotiating partner, and three weeks later the Irish and British governments announced that inclusive all-party negotiations on Northern Ireland would follow elections to a negotiating Forum. Chaired by former U.S. senator George Mitchell, talks began in June 1996 under rules of "sufficient consensus," so that no proposal could pass if vetoed by Britain, Ireland, the Unionist UUP, or the Nationalist SDLP.[78]

These talks remained bogged down in party brinksmanship and infighting until a Labour landslide put Tony Blair into office in June 1997. Blair was free of the ties and debts to Unionist parliamentary partners that had hampered John Major's room to move the peace process. Blair immediately expressed his commitment to "solving" the Northern Ire-

---

[76] In July 2000, 75 percent of Palestinians polled supported the Palestinian-Israeli peace process, but 60 percent believed that lasting peace was impossible. Moreover, 66 percent of Palestinians polled also believed that Israelis do not believe lasting peace is possible with Palestinians. PCPSR, "Public Opinion Poll #1."

[77] Richard W. Stevenson, "Bomb Wounds 100 in London as IRA Truce Is Said to End," *New York Times*, February 10, 1996, http://www.nytimes.com/library/world/021096nireland-truce-ends.html [05-25-2000].

[78] The idea of sufficient consensus was drawn directly from the South African CODESA negotiations and predictably facilitated Unionist stonewalling. See Robert H. Mnookin, "Strategic Barriers to Dispute Resolution: A Comparison of Bilateral and Multilateral Negotiations," *Journal of the Institute of Theoretical Economics* 159, no. 1 (2003), http://www.mohr.de/jrnl/jite/jite1591.htm#Mnookin [06-18-2003].

land crisis. His first trip was to Northern Ireland, where he warned Sinn Fein that "the settlement train is leaving. I want you on that train. But it is leaving anyway and I will not allow it to wait for you. You cannot hold the process to ransom any longer. So end the violence now."[79] In June and July the British government worked hard behind the scenes to bring Sinn Fein into talks, to the growing ire of Unionists who feared Britain would sell them out to achieve peace. But the British and Irish governments recognized that no settlement would be enforceable without Sinn Fein's participation. Here the negotiators made a key decision that Israel and the United States had not made in 2003 when they sought to marginalize Hamas from the road map: to include all potential spoilers to the agreement.

But bringing Sinn Fein into talks jeopardized the political strength and negotiating position of Trimble's UUP. If Unionist support for negotiations crumbled, forcing Trimble to leave the table, the peace process would disintegrate. Moderators and guarantors were therefore careful to shore up the Unionist side, to protect it from its own right wing.[80] Moderators catered to the Unionist demand for IRA arms decommissioning, for example, by giving the issue prominence at the start of the talks.[81]

The IRA responded by announcing a second cease-fire on July 20, 1997, while continuing to refuse to decommission. Since the Unionists had made decommissioning a precondition of negotiations, Trimble took the risky decision to enter talks that could have gutted his support base. He had evidently reached a personal point of no return, as demonstrated by his private admission to Blair that "we are not in the mode of walking out."[82] On July 22, the debate over whether Sinn Fein should be admitted to talks without prior decommissioning came to a head in a vote. The UUP, the Democratic Unionist Party (DUP), and the UK Unionist Party (UKUP) all voted against it, with the result that when talks reconvened in September, Sinn Fein was at the table but the Unionist parties were gone.[83] The DUP and the UKUP had left for good, and tried to force the UUP to walk out through accusations that the party was betraying its people. Opinion polls showed that the UUP had popular support for remaining in the talks, but the party leadership was also under extreme pressure, even from within its own ranks.[84] This was the situation when the UUP

[79] George J. Mitchell, *Making Peace* (New York: Alfred Knopf, 1999), p. 101.

[80] Ibid., p. 104.

[81] No agreement was in fact reached over decommissioning, however, which of course continued to act as a stumbling block to implementation as late as 2003.

[82] Mitchell, *Making Peace*, p. 108.

[83] Ibid., p. 109.

[84] Ibid., pp. 111, 117.

finally entered negotiations under Trimble's leadership. Talks between the governments and the parties began seriously in October 1997.

Negotiations were organized in three strands. The first dealt with political arrangements within Northern Ireland, the second with North-South relations, and the third with relations between London and Dublin. Strand Two, concerning the relation between Ireland and Northern Ireland, was the most contested. In February, all parties agreed to an Easter deadline, and after a delay caused by cease-fire violations on both sides, the parties began serious negotiations in mid-March. As they came down to the wire, London and Dublin negotiated an agreement on Strand Two that was blatantly unacceptable to the Unionist side. At the insistence of the moderators, who argued that Trimble was not bluffing when he said he could not agree to this document, both sides returned to the table to renegotiate.[85] Strand Two was reworked in the final week before the deadline to include the controversial provisions demanded by each side: a North-South Ministerial Council and an elected Assembly expected to operate in mutual interdependence. The Good Friday Agreement, also known as the Belfast Agreement, was concluded in April 1998.

The accord included five main constitutional principles: Northern Ireland's future constitutional status, as part of Ireland or of the United Kingdom, would be in the hands of its citizens; the people of Ireland, north and south, could vote to unite; Northern Ireland would remain, for the time being, within the United Kingdom; Northern Irish citizens could choose to identify as Irish, British, or both; and the Irish state would drop its territorial claim on Northern Ireland.[86] A copy of the agreement was delivered to every household in Northern Ireland in anticipation of the referendum, and a clear majority in both Ireland (56 percent turnout; 94 percent approval) and Northern Ireland (81 percent turnout; 71 percent approval) approved it. This included majorities of both Unionists and Nationalists, although the Unionist majority was slim.[87]

As with the Oslo Accords, but unlike the ANC-NP agreement, the Belfast Agreement did not mark the end of negotiations and the beginning of implementation. For almost two years, London continued to govern Northern Ireland as implementation snagged on the controversial issues that had been left outstanding in the Good Friday Agreement. It seems clear that part of the obstacle to implementing the agreement was that a substantial portion of Unionists never believed that the status quo was unsustainable. Unlike the situation in South Africa, where polls revealed

---

[85] Ibid., p. 166.

[86] Darby, "Northern Ireland: The Background to the Peace Process," p. 7.

[87] Paul Bew, "Initiative to Trimble but His Edge over Opponents Is Thin," The Path to Peace Web site, April 1998, p. 1, http://www.ireland.om/special/peace/results/analysis/analysis10.htm [05-25-2000]. Fifty-five percent of Protestants approved the agreement.

that by the end of the 1980s most whites had concluded apartheid was no longer feasible, most Protestants in Northern Ireland continued to believe direct rule from London, or majority rule in which they would be the majority, were sustainable alternatives. They believed that a compromise with Nationalists could only weaken their position.[88] In this they were analogous to the Jewish settlers in the occupied territories who refuse to see flawed democracy as unsustainable. Achieving a settlement might require that their government force them to accept it.

But this is easier said than done in SAMENI settings. Given democratic constraints in the Unionist movement, Trimble and the moderates were unable effectively to face down the right-wingers who opposed agreement. From the outset, moderate Unionists had only a narrow margin of support for the accord. Exit polls from the May 1998 referendum on the agreement showed Protestants almost evenly divided between support and opposition. The Protestant middle class appeared ready to defect from the settlement over the early release of prisoners.[89] Whereas the March 1992 South African referendum returned a solid endorsement for continued negotiations, the results of the Northern Ireland referendum were sufficiently ambiguous that they could still be used to political advantage by those who opposed a settlement, highlighting again the fickle role of democracy in negotiations.[90] Although 96 percent of Catholics supported the agreement, only 55 percent of Protestants did.[91] Moreover, the Protestant vote was exceedingly fragile. According to the Northern Ireland Referendum and Election Study, one-quarter of all Protestants had considered changing their vote during the campaign, mostly from a yes to a no vote. Among Catholics, only 7 percent had considered changing theirs.[92]

Elections for the Northern Ireland Assembly were held in June 1998. The UUP won 28 seats, the SDLP 24, DUP 20, Sinn Fein 18, Alliance 6,

[88] In late 2000 the Northern Ireland Life and Times survey found that 14 percent of Protestants who voted yes in 1998 would now vote against the agreement because of declining support for devolution and lack of progress on decommissioning. Bernadette C. Hayes and Ian McAllister, "Who Voted for Peace? Public Support for the 1998 Northern Ireland Agreement," *Irish Political Studies* 16 (2001): 73–94, and Bernadette Hayes and Lizanne Dowds "Underpinning Opinions: Declining Levels of Support among Protestants for the Good Friday Agreement" (paper presented at roundtable discussion by Democratic Dialogue, Europa Hotel, Belfast, April 10, 2001).

[89] Hayes and Dowds, "Underpinning Opinions," p. 2; Frank Millar, "London Is Relieved but Difficulties Lie Ahead," p. 1, http://www.ireland.om/special/peace/results/road/ahead3 .htm [05-25-2000].

[90] Suzanne Breen, "United No Parties Set Their Sights on Assembly," http://www.ireland .om/special/peace/results/road/ahead3.htm [05-25-2000].

[91] Sydney Elliot and W. D. Flackes. *Conflict in Northern Ireland: An Encyclopedia* (Belfast: Blackstaff Press, 1999), p. 125.

[92] Hayes and McAllister, "Who Voted for Peace?" p. 81.

Women's Coalition 2, UKUP 5, Progressive Unionist Party 2, and anti-agreement Unionists 3. Although the UUP won a plurality of seats (but not of votes), its slim margin of victory actually represented a loss for the party, whose 1997 returns at Westminster presaged a win of as many as 39 seats, and only 16 for Ian Paisley's DUP. The 1998 election results suggested that the moderate center of Unionism was eroding. Moreover, the UUP was comparatively vulnerable as the antiagreement camp (DUP, UKUP, and AAU) also won, between them, 28 seats. Analysts had predicted before the election that the UUP would need to win at least 30 seats to avoid deadlock in the Assembly and to make the North-South Council work.[93] Therefore, although the UUP won the election and emerged as the largest party in the Assembly, antiagreement parties were also able to interpret the election result as a victory, in particular because the transfer system of voting favored the UUP.[94]

The election campaign also laid bare differences within the UUP over the agreement. Jeffrey Donaldson, a UUP member of Parliament at Westminster, emerged as the most important opposition figure within the party, but almost half of the leadership of the UUP openly opposed the accord. Some of these took seats in the Assembly, but they could not be counted on to vote the party line, further diluting the pro-agreement bloc.[95] Trimble barely squeaked by in elections for party leadership after 1998, as he faced powerful challenges over the issue of implementation of the accord. When Trimble agreed in 2000 that it might be possible to reenter government with Sinn Fein without prior decommissioning, Martin Smyth mounted an internal challenge for party leadership, which, though unsuccessful, exposed deep and continuing fault lines within the Ulster Unionist Party and the weakness of Trimble's support base.[96] Under pressure from Britain, Trimble nevertheless twice entered a power-sharing government without IRA decommissioning.

On August 15, 1998, a bomb exploded in Omagh, killing 28 people (mostly women and children) and injuring 220—the largest loss of life of any single act of violence during the Troubles. The Real IRA, a breakaway faction of the IRA opposed to the settlement, claimed responsibility and immediately apologized for the deaths, announcing the suspension

[93] Gerry Moriarty, "How the Parties Could Share Out Seats," p. 2, Path to Peace Web site, http://www.ireland.om/special/peace/results/road/ahead4.htm [05-25-2000].

[94] Gerry Moriarty, "Even Split for Anti, Pro-Agreement Parties," http://www.ireland.om/special/peace/results/news/news3.htm [05-25-2000].

[95] Bew, "Initiative to Trimble but His Edge over Opponents Is Thin," p. 1.

[96] Jonathan Tonge and Jocelyn A. J. Evans, "Faultlines in Unionism: Division and Dissent within the Ulster Unionist Council," *Irish Political Studies* 16 (2001): 113–14.

of all military operations. The act was so widely condemned, including by the IRA, that it backfired against hard-line Republicans—reminding everyone of the gruesome alternative to peace. Omagh played an important role in solidifying a commitment to peace across Northern Ireland and in marginalizing those from the Nationalist Right who would scuttle the process. After that, Sinn Fein and the IRA faced less of the hard-line censure that had limited Trimble's room to maneuver in the implementation phase of the process.

The UUP blocked Sinn Fein's entry to the Executive for sixteen months, insisting again on prior IRA decommissioning, while Britain, Ireland, and mediators continued to try to broker a compromise.[97] In November 1999, a slim majority of 58 percent of UUP delegates approved entry into a joint government, and the British and Irish governments transferred power from London to Belfast within days. Under a power-sharing formula, Trimble became first minister, and Seamus Mallon, leader of the Nationalist SDLP, the coequal deputy first minister. Ten other cabinet seats were divided proportionally among Ulster Unionists, the SDLP, Sinn Fein, and the DUP. The UUP was left deeply divided by the split vote, and the terms of entry included a clause committing the party council to reconvene in February to review the decision. If the IRA had not by then begun to disarm, the party would use its majority position to dismantle the government.[98]

As in South Africa, moderates in the opposition helped government reformers face down their recalcitrant flanks. When the IRA initially refused to move on decommissioning, London responded by suspending the Assembly in February 2000 to protect Trimble from another divisive UUP vote that threatened to sink his leadership. This made the IRA realize that it had to help Trimble survive, just as the ANC had helped de Klerk do so by agreeing to power sharing in the interim constitution, and Arafat had helped Rabin by dampening Palestinian response to the massacre in the Ibrahimi Mosque. Hours after the suspension, the IRA made its first commitment to dismantle its arsenal.[99] The result was that

---

[97] At the time, Trimble insisted that his hands were tied, and Ken Maginnis, a leading moderate within the party, agreed that the plan would split the party and was impossible to sell to rank-and-file supporters. Shawn Pogtchnik, "Ultimatum Irks Northern Ireland" *Detroit News*, July 4, 1999, http://www.detnews.com/1999/nation/9907/04/07049902.htm [05-25-2000].

[98] Warren Hoge, "Ulster Unionists Open Way for Ruling with Sinn Fein," *New York Times*, November 28, 1999, http://www.nytimes.com/library/world/europe/112899nireland-unionists.html [05-25-2000].

[99] Warren Hoge, "Britain Suspends System of Power Sharing in Ulster," *New York Times*, February 12, 2000, http://www.nytimes.com/library/world/europe/021200nireland-talks.html [05-25-2000].

in March Trimble won an internal challenge to his party leadership, if with only 57 percent support.[100]

But it was enough for him to move forward. In a bid to face down his opponents, Trimble announced his intention to sever ties with the Loyalist Orange Order. Although the move was part of a long-standing agenda to reduce the party's sectarian connections, the timing was clearly calculated to hive off naysayers within the party.[101] The IRA cooperated, agreeing to put their guns and bombs beyond use, and accepting weapons dump inspections by international assessors Cyril Ramaphosa and Martti Ahtisaari. The Unionists responded by supporting, by a two-thirds majority, Trimble's return to a power-sharing government with Sinn Fein.[102] The Ulster Unionist Council (UUC) finally voted at the end of May to resume implementation, and Britain transferred power back to the Northern Ireland Assembly and its twelve-person joint cabinet.[103]

Devolution was suspended three more times over the next three years, so that the power-sharing government in Northern Ireland was operational for only twenty of the possible fifty-four months that it might have functioned.[104] In September 2002 the UUC issued a statement affirming that the UUP would "not sit in government with unreconstructed terrorists," again demanding the total disbandment of all terrorist groups including the IRA.[105] In October 2002 devolution was suspended again because Trimble threatened to withdraw his ministers from the Executive in protest against the continued participation of Sinn Fein in government.[106] Blair had repeatedly backed the Unionist position, noting that the Irish Republic had refused to let Sinn Fein take seats in government without IRA dissolution, whereas Unionists in the North had been forced

[100] Warren Hoge, "Ulster Leader Holds On, but Power Lessens in Unionist Vote," *New York Times*, March 26, 2000, http://www.nytimes.com/library/world/europe/032600nireland-trimble.html> [05-25-2000].

[101] Frank Millar, "Trimble Stakes His Future on the Drive to Modernise," *Irish Times*, April 21, 2000, http://scripts.ireland.com/search/...wspaper/opinion/2000/0421/opt2.htm [05-25-2000].

[102] Suzanne Breen, "Most Ulster Unionists Want Trimble in Executive," *Irish Times*, May 12, 2000, http://www.ireland.com/newspaper/ireland/2000/0512/north4.htm [05-25-2000].

[103] Reuters, "Northern Ireland Rivals Try for Home Rule Again," *New York Times*, May 30, 2000, http://www.nytimes.com/reuters/international/international-irish-1.html [05-25-2000].

[104] Text of a Speech made by Gerry Adams, Monaghan, October 26, 2002, p. 6, CAIN Web Service, http://cain.ulst.ac.uk/events/peace/docs/ga261002.htm [11-11-2002].

[105] Text of "Document agreed at the Ulster Unionist Council meeting on Saturday 21 September 2002," CAIN Web Service, http://cain.ulst.ac.uk/issues/politics/docs/uup/uup210902.htm [11-11-2002].

[106] This occurred after a scandal in which Sinn Fein was accused of spying on other parties and the government at Stormont.

into a power-sharing arrangement with Sinn Fein.[107] Gerry Adams complained that London should not have the latitude to suspend the institutions of the Good Friday Agreement every time the UUP threatened to walk out, pointing out that Blair would be unlikely to do the same if Sinn Fein threatened to leave the government.[108] Trimble made the contrary case that Britain should not have suspended devolved government; that it ought instead to have suspended Sinn Fein.

Postagreement negotiations have nevertheless settled a number of other issues that were left outstanding in April 1998. In November 2001 the Royal Ulster Constabulary was renamed the Police Service of Northern Ireland, and the new Policing Board replaced the Police Authority. The UUP contested the arrangement, but the PSNI committed to recruiting on the basis of 50:50 representation.[109] This is potentially important. In South Africa the integration of the police force before the transition greatly eased enforcement problems. The IRA also made an important symbolic statement in July 2002, apologizing for killing and injuring non-combatants during the Troubles.[110] IRA decommissioning persisted as the main obstacle to implementation, however, leading analysts to assume that the relevant question was "What would have induced (or might in future induce) the IRA to disband as a paramilitary organization?"

But the South African experience suggests otherwise. South Africa's NP also insisted initially on ANC disarmament, but, when the ANC refused, talks proceeded almost without a pause. Considering that an international monitoring team repeatedly verified that IRA weapons were beyond use[111] and that Loyalists perpetrated most of the postaccord violence,[112] it was far from obvious that the IRA's refusal to change its rhetoric was a literal threat to security in Northern Ireland or Britain in the late 1990s and early 2000s.[113] Yet Tony Blair repeatedly suspended power-sharing governments out of sensitivity to Unionist demands. For instance, in May 2003 he again halted implementation by postponing

[107] Speech by Tony Blair, Harbor Commissioners' Office, Belfast, October 17, 2002, CAIN Web Service, http://cain.ulst.ac.uk/events/peace/docs/tb171002.htm [11-11-2002].

[108] Speech made by Gerry Adams, Monaghan, October 26, 2000.

[109] Chronology of the Conflict, CAIN Web Service, http://cain.ulst.ac.uk/othelem/chron/ch00.htm [06-05-2003].

[110] Full text of IRA statement of apology, July 16, 2002, CAIN Web Service, http://cain.ulst.ac.uk/events/peace/docs/ira160702.htm [06-05-2003].

[111] The IRA suspended contact with the Independent International Commission on Decommissioning (IICD) on October, 30, 2002. Full text of IRA statement, CAIN Web Service http://cain.ulst.ac.uk/events/peace/docs/ira301002.htm [11-11-2002].

[112] Hayes and McAllister, "Who Voted for Peace?" p. 88.

[113] DUP party member David Ervine argues, for example, that it was destructive of the UUP to insist on a condition that they should have known the IRA would be unable to comply with (interview, June 20, 2003).

legislative elections. He deemed insufficient Gerry Adams's statement that the IRA would "disarm fully as part of the Northern Ireland peace settlement if other parties to the accord fulfill their obligations,"[114] despite declarations by the Irish government and most pro-agreement parties that the insistence on disarmament caused more problems than it solved. American envoy Richard Haass also called for elections to take place "as soon as possible."[115] By July 2003, many politicians in Northern Ireland, including pro-agreement Unionists, agreed that postponing elections placed tremendous pressure on the settlement and seriously undermined the credibility of the agreement among voters.[116] Pro-agreement members of the Ulster Unionist Party were particularly concerned that party infighting would mean that postponed elections could favor those who opposed the agreement.[117]

SAMENI negotiations are prone to forms of myopia that lead participants to apply pressure in the wrong places. Blair's repeated suspension of power sharing was a failure of vision and nerve that ranks with Peres's missed opportunity in 1995, playing into the hands of those Unionist leaders for whom stonewalling against change has always been the name of the game. This is not to say that great and continuing pressure on the IRA would not have been needed to move the process forward. It is to say that Blair was uniquely placed, among recent British prime ministers, to bring no less essential pressure to bear on the Unionists. They, too, had to be told that the "settlement train is leaving the station." The relevant South African precedent here is not the failed CODESA idea of "sufficient consensus," which empowers and emboldens spoilers, and which, notably, fell apart twice without moving the process forward. Rather, it is that powerful players committed to a settlement must garner enough popular support to persuade spoilers that they will be marginalized if they do not join the process. Recall that the NP and ANC negotiated the core elements of the South African settlement in secret in 1992, and then announced them as nonnegotiable. Inkatha added its name to the ballot only days before the 1994 election, once Buthelezi finally realized that it could not be derailed.

This merits particular note in light of the fact that in other areas there have been moves toward the type of normal politics in Northern Ireland that are the ultimate goal of SAMENI negotiations. When government has been in session, much (though not all) of what goes on is politics as usual.

[114] Warren Hoge, "Sinn Fein Leader Pledges Full Disarmament of the I.R.A.," *New York Times*, April 28, 2003, p. A2.

[115] Brian Lavery, "US Envoy Wants Elections," *New York Times*, May 8, 2003, p. A2.

[116] Interviews with David McNarry and Dr. Esmond Birnie (UUP), Rachel Steert (Women's Coalition), David Ervine (DUP), and James Cooper (UUP).

[117] Interviews with Dr. Esmond Birnie and James Cooper (UUP).

Statements and proposed legislation about road safety, health care, unemployment, and pork barrel–type projects dominate the Web sites of all the major parties. The Women's Coalition and the Alliance Party explicitly eschew sectarian designation and are self-consciously attempting to generate a new political dialogue that will expand the possibilities of political identity in Northern Ireland. Polls indicate that a majority of Protestants and Catholics alike have also moved beyond the conflict in the new century, agreeing that issues like health service and unemployment are most pressing.[118]

To sum up, the obstacles to peace in Northern Ireland were as formidable in the 1990s as they were in the Middle East. Yet our analysis suggests in both cases that had different choices been made at critical junctures, things could have turned out differently, and there might have been settlements comparable to what was achieved in South Africa. Indeed, underscoring the fluidity of SAMENI negotiations and their critical dependence on contingencies of choice, we saw that the South African transition might well have derailed at various points, just as the others have done.

5. IMPLICATIONS

There is nothing intrinsic to the conflicts in the Middle East and Northern Ireland that renders them less tractable than South Africa's. People miss this because they focus on the alleged divided character of societies involved in these conflicts. They would do well to remember that similar claims about South Africa were conventional wisdom in the 1980s. The divided society lens directs attention either to the wrong features of the conflicts or to the wrong features of negotiations. Recognizing SAMENI conflicts as negotiated settlements in the context of flawed democracies redirects our attention to the importance of achieving agreements that can sustain popular support as a condition for making them stick. In what follows, we elaborate on the conditions that facilitate and undermine settlements, discuss the future prospects for the Middle East and Northern Ireland, and spell out some larger implications for conflict studies.

5.1. Lessons Learned

In contrast to conventional analyses of SAMENI conflicts, we find that successful negotiations do not depend on the nature of the solution. Rather, what is vital is that the solution—whatever its form—gains

---

[118] In the 1999–2000 Northern Ireland Life and Times survey, respondents were asked to identify the most important priorities for the new assembly: 40 percent chose improving health services and 37 percent cited employment. www.qub.ac.uk/ss/csr/nilt [06-05-2003].

enough legitimacy to convince potential spoilers that challenging it is too costly. This means building popular support for the new dispensation while it is being negotiated. It is far from clear that this could not have occurred had the negotiations between Rabin and Arafat been able to conclude in 1995, or had Peres adopted a different policy from the one he embraced immediately following Rabin's death. We saw in section 3.2 that at that time the two-state solution enjoyed considerable legitimacy. Blair was in an even stronger position to solve the enforcement problem by appealing to popular support in Northern Ireland after 1998, given his historic mandate in 1997 and the enthusiasm for the agreement in both communities. In the end, it is only the legitimacy of the agreement itself that can get potential spoilers to adhere to the conditions of a peace settlement.

Because a viable agreement must enjoy popular support, radicals and hard-liners cannot be marginalized until significant numbers of their supporters desert them and back the negotiations. This happened dramatically with de Klerk's referendum, and it could have happened, we noted, in the Middle East in 1995–96. Unfortunately, because analysts frequently underestimate the importance of democratic legitimacy to a negotiated settlement, they often focus on, and pin their hopes upon, moderate leaders who are willing to push a peace agreement forward— "sensible chaps" who are appealing to deal with—regardless of whether they have the requisite popular support. For instance, Gerry Adams's emergence on the scene in 1988 as a new kind of pragmatic IRA leader "with a human face" led to endless speculation about whether a settlement could now be anticipated. But Adams and his behavior were irrelevant until the Blair government came to power in the United Kingdom in 1997—given the dependence of the Tory governments on Unionist support under Thatcher and Major.

By the same token, both U.S. and Israeli negotiators often focus on Palestinian players who cannot reasonably be expected to deliver. The 2003 Middle East road map was a case in point. Arafat's corrupt government had lacked grassroots legitimacy since the mid-1990s, and the appointment of Mahmoud Abbas as prime minister was scarcely a solution to this problem. With its political legitimacy, not to mention its security apparatus, in tatters, the PA was in no position to rein in the violence that followed the Aqaba summit.[119] The more Abbas was praised as

---

[119] The Oslo process weakened Fatah and the PA vis-à-vis Hamas, which both provided critical social services to an increasingly impoverished Palestinian people. See Ian Fisher, "Defining Hamas: Roots in Charity and Branches of Violence," *New York Times*, June 16, 2003. Support for Hamas grew at Fatah's expense. In December 1996, support for Fatah was 35.2 percent and for Hamas 10.3 percent. Similarly, 41.2 percent of Palestinians most trusted Yasir Arafat, and 4.8 percent trusted Sheikh Yassin. Only 19.5 percent

"reasonable" in Jerusalem and Washington, the weaker he was bound to become in Ramallah. Caught as he was between a rock and a hard place, any popularity he could hope to sustain would depend on his delivering what Arafat could not: better living conditions, an end to curfews, and open borders—all of which are contingent on Israeli goodwill and U.S. pressure.

The presence of a strong radical flank need not itself bode poorly for peace, provided efforts are made to incorporate its members if they cannot be marginalized. That Hamas was not at the table in the early negotiations over the road map is the functional equivalent of the South African government's trying to strike a deal with Buthelezi in 1992, or of talks in Northern Ireland excluding Sinn Fein. Notwithstanding IRA failure to decommission as late as 2003, Sinn Fein support for the agreement was unwavering, as its electoral base grew in the years following the accord. Hamas and other violent Palestinian nationalist groups are doubtless aware that their strategy will never lead to outright victory over Israel, but their immediate target is not Israel. They are engaged in a struggle for control over the representation of the Palestinians, and failure of the peace process has solidified their support base.[120] Effective marginalization of Hamas is likely impossible in the foreseeable future. This means that any serious peace negotiations must involve dealing

---

of Palestinians did not trust anyone. By December 2001, support for Fatah had dropped to 26.1 percent, while that for Hamas had risen to 21.3 percent. Similarly, trust in Arafat declined to 24.5 percent, and that in Yassin rose to 12.8 percent. This trend has continued. JMCC, "Public Opinion Poll #43," http://www.jmcc.org/publicpoll/results/2001/no43.htm [06-25-2003]; JMCC, "Public Opinion Poll #18," http://www.jmcc.org/publicpoll/results/1996/no18.htm [06-05-2003]. A poll conducted by JMCC in April 2003 found that the majority of Palestinians believed that Abbas's appointment as prime minister would have little effect on the PA reform process: of respondents, 28.7 percent felt the appointment would further PA reforms, 17.4 percent felt it would hinder reforms, and 43.2 percent felt it would have no effect. It is telling that 67.8 percent of respondents believed that the creation of a prime ministry was due to external influences alone, 19.2 percent felt that it was due to external influences and a conviction that the reforms were in the interests of the Palestinian people, and only 6.2 percent believed the reform was undertaken purely in order to benefit the Palestinian people. Furthermore, only 1.8 percent of respondents named Abu Mazen as the Palestinian personality that they most trusted, vs. 21.1 percent for Yasir Arafat and 9.7 percent for Ahmed Yassin. JMCC, "JMCC Public Opinion Poll #48," April 2003, http://www.jmcc.org/publicpoll/results/2003/no48.htm#results [06-05-2003].

[120] By April 2003, Fatah remained the single most-trusted faction in Palestinian politics, with 22.6 percent, although overall support for Fatah trailed the combined support for Hamas (22.0 percent), Islamic Jihad (6.3 percent), Popular Front for the Liberation of Palestine (PFLP) (2.0 percent), and other factions (3.1 percent). However, more 34.3 percent responded they "don't trust anyone." JMCC, "JMCC Public Opinion Poll #48," April 2003, http://www.jmcc.org/publicpoll/results/2003/no48.htm#results [06-05-2003].

with them, perhaps in secret—at least initially.[121] Contrary to press reports at the time, Sharon's overture to the Palestinian Authority was not a case of Nixon going to China.[122] It was more like Nixon being dragged to Hong Kong.

Even when the right actors are on board, they may have to sell mutually incompatible solutions to their constituencies—at least until people realize that they can live with outcomes they had previously dismissed as unthinkable. Constructive ambiguity can help. There seems to be little question that in the Middle East obscurity about the final outcome, and even the interim steps, was essential for moving the process forward in 1995. Lack of clarity about such issues as the final status of Jerusalem, borders, settlements, and the right of return has been harshly criticized, but ambiguity about these issues was essential to creating a new reality in which Palestinians and Israelis accepted a two-state solution as legitimate. The South African success depended on the fact that the final agreement to abandon constitutionally mandated power sharing was not fully apparent earlier in negotiations. As this process illustrates, the very fact of participating in negotiations can loosen up fixed perceptions.[123]

If the SAMENI cases suggest that negotiations proceed best when the final details are left for later, they also suggest that there is urgency in getting to an agreement. That the South African negotiations moved quickly and concluded decisively contributed greatly to the result. Conversely, the slowing down of Middle East negotiations has repeatedly strengthened the hands of stonewallers and allowed windows of opportunity to close. The Bush administration seemed to appreciate this in the summer of 2003, when Secretary of State Colin Powell argued forcefully for the need to "move urgently," not giving time for the "terrorists to win."[124] Even the most committed moderates must outrun the radicals and reac-

---

[121] Hamas moderates have signaled their willingness to enter negotiations. See Amira Hass, "What the Doctor Orders," *Haaretz*, June 20, 2003, http://www.haaretz.com/hasen/pages/ShArt.jhtml?itemNo=307203& [06-22-2003].

[122] See John Diamond, "Sharon's Support for Road Map Historic," *USA Today*, May 26, 2003, p. 1, http://www.usatoday.com/news/world/2003-05-26-mideast_x.htm [06-24-2003].

[123] This is not to deny that constructive ambiguity can create implementation problems later. Northern Ireland and the Middle East have revealed all too clearly that it can. But without it they will not move forward, and the creative ingenuity of the players will never become focused on dealing with the implementation problems.

[124] "Powell Condemns Hamas Role," June 21, 2003, 00:53 GMT 01:53 UK, BBC News, http://news.bbc.co.uk/2/hi/middle_east/3008420.stm [06-24-2003]. Note that the 2003 Geneva Accord recognizes the importance of moving quickly toward a final settlement, which is specified with a degree of detail that would not have been possible but for the Oslo Accords.

tionaries who will be determined to prevent an agreement. The sooner a negotiated arrangement is seen as the new status quo, the less likely it is that recalcitrant forces will be able to destroy it.

5.2. Future Prospects

Taken together, these observations inform our expectations concerning the prospects for settlements in the Middle East and Northern Ireland. Despite continuing setbacks to the implementation of the Good Friday Agreement, the Northern Ireland conflict appears considerably closer to resolution than does that in the Middle East. Once decommissioning is seen in perspective, it becomes clear that the window of opportunity has been open for a good part of the time after 1998. Members of the Legislative Assembly speculate that support for the agreement has eroded in part precisely because it has been suspended so often that it seems unworkable.[125] The fact that it has been suspended by Westminster makes it seem additionally undemocratic in the sense of being more vulnerable to external than to electoral pressure. Blair was unwilling through 2004 to pay the political cost of putting real pressure on the Unionists, even though he had both the mandate and the leeway so to do. Moreover, it seems reasonable to think that he might have done so, and that there may well be future opportunities for him or others to implement some version of the Good Friday Agreement—though this will be notably harder to accomplish if there is not a Labour government in Westminster.

There seem to be three possibilities for Northern Ireland. Implementation could continue to move forward in fits and starts, but with everyday politics revolving less around the agreement and more around tangible improvements in areas like health care and employment. Polls show that popular support for the agreement has been diminishing ever since it was signed, but also that most people in Northern Ireland believe that social welfare and the economy are more pressing issues than the relative political status of Unionists and Republicans.[126] It remains to be seen whether the voting public will be able to move the parties toward a similar consensus. Alternatively, if the stalemate on decommissioning persists, there might be another big international push (possibly again led by the United States) to reach agreement on the outstanding issues. Publicity, attention, and deadlines would be used again, as they were in 1998, to generate a

---

[125] Author interview with Esmond Birnie. A poll conducted in January 2003 showed that only 36 percent of Protestants would still vote for the Good Friday Agreement. But 60 percent of Protestants would be willing to support the peace process if it could be made to work. Colin Irwin, "Devolution and the State of the Northern Ireland Peace Process," http://www.peacepolls.org [01-12-2004].

[126] http://www.qub.ac.uk/ss/csr/nilt [01-12-2004].

groundswell of support and excitement for implementation. A third possibility is a reversion to violence—even if the trend toward normal politics against the background of the Good Friday Agreement makes this outcome less likely. But completely ruling it out assumes more backbone from the British government than Blair exhibited in facing down Unionist recalcitrance in his first five years in office, and it takes too static a view of the IRA leadership, which could always revert to a military strategy.

Successfully maneuvering through the Middle East road map would require a great deal from Palestinian, Israeli, and international actors. The toll of the intifada, as well as the changing regional situation after the U.S.-Iraq war, led several key players to return to negotiations. At the same time, however, these very conditions limited the trust each side harbors for the other, and hence the likelihood that moderates can deliver an agreement. Prime Minister Sharon held his position largely owing to the weakness of the traditional Israeli peace camp. Given this reality, not to mention his history and ideology, he was unlikely to become a reformer.[127] Indeed, his 2002 decision to construct a massive fence in the West Bank was less likely meant to ensure an end of terrorism than to make conditions unbearable, thus stimulating Palestinian emigration from the occupied territories.[128] Yet, if he appeared less than eager to negotiate, he was capable of delivering. Deteriorating conditions had led many settlers to announce that they would accept evacuation from the settlements in return for economic compensation, thus weakening the right flank.[129] If Sharon had chosen to enter into the negotiations full steam ahead, he could likely have sidelined his right-wing supporters and offered Labour participation in his government.[130] As the historical champions of the

[127] We should not be surprised, therefore, by his equivocal statements on Israel's "occupation" of the West Bank in May and June 2003. John Kifner, "The Bush Plan: Put the Toughest Hurdles First," *New York Times*, June 8, 2003, sec. 4, pp. 1, 14; David K. Shipler, "Sharon Has a Map. Can He Redraw It?" *New York Times*, June 1, 2003, sec. 4, p. 1.

[128] Edward R. F. Shaheen, "The Map and the Fence," *New York Review of Books* 50, no. 11 (July 3, 2003), http://www.nybooks.com/articles/16411 [06-25-2003]. The fence is expected to affect the lives of 600,000 West Bank Palestinians. See "U.N. Estimates Israeli Barrier Will Disrupt Lives of 600,000," *New York Times*, November 12, 2003.

[129] According to a 2003 poll, 54 percent of settlers stated that they would resist forced dismantlement, but 74 percent would entertain moving inside the Green Line in return for compensation. Moreover, 71 percent of settlers thought a peace agreement should be reached (up from about 55 percent in 2002), and 44 percent accepted a Palestinian state (up from 19 percent the previous year). Israelis also increasingly see settlers as isolated in their struggle to secure settlement. The same survey found that about 64 percent of settlers expect themselves to be alone, and 75 percent of Israelis inside the Green Line see settlers as isolated in their struggle with the government. "Poll: 71% of Settlers Say There Will Be Deal with the Palestinians," *Ha'aretz*, July 23, 2003.

[130] Ellen Lust-Okar, "Israeli Elections 2003: What Likud's Victory Doesn't Tell You," *Yale Israel Journal*, Spring 2003, pp. 3–7.

peace process they would have little choice but to join. Sharon would have burned his bridges behind him, enhancing, from the standpoint of our analyses, the prospects for peace. That was not to be.

Success would require significant U.S. pressure on the Israeli administration to make concessions in the face of continuing right-wing domestic opposition and Palestinian violence. The Israeli government would eventually need to convince its own supporters that they would be better off with an agreement with the Palestinians and withdrawal from the occupied territories than they would be with either continued occupation of the West Bank and Gaza Strip (WBGS) or the ethnic cleansing of Eretz Israel. This had become a tall order by 2002, when Israeli support for the "transfer" of Palestinians living in the WBGS reached 46 percent, and the support for transfer of Palestinians living inside the Green Line stood at 31 percent.[131] It would perhaps be even more difficult, however, for Israelis to convince Palestinians that they would no longer solve immediate crises by rolling tanks into Palestinian towns or assassinating leaders with military aircraft. Without that conviction, it is difficult to see how support for any settlement would be forthcoming.

The tasks facing the Palestinians were equally difficult. Those intent on a settlement would need to restrain or incorporate the radical flank, demonstrating to Israelis not only that they could, but that they consistently would, ensure Israeli security. This was particularly difficult at a time when the security infrastructure of the Palestinian Authority had largely been demolished, and when support for the Fatah leadership and confidence in the Israelis were both at record lows. With a strong radical flank, the PA could not afford to sideline Hamas completely. Rather, it would need to gain at least tacit Hamas support, most likely by granting Hamas moderates what they have most fervently wanted: a place at the table. Because even this would be unlikely to satisfy the hard-liners who wanted only to see Israel pushed into the sea, the need for security remained. A successful solution would thus require a significant change in the attitudes of both Palestinian and Israeli hard-liners in the long run.[132]

[131] "Memorandum No. 61: Israeli Public Opinion on National Security," Jaffee Center for Strategic Studies, Tel Aviv University, July 2002. See also "Growing Popularity of a Transfer in Israel, Removing Palestinians from the West Bank and Gaza and Distributing Them throughout the Arab World," National Public Radio Morning Edition, October 21, 2002, http://www.npr.org/programs/morning/transcripts/2002/oct/021021.gradstein.html [06-25-2003].

[132] People-to-people programs and efforts to revise history textbooks are part of the efforts to change fundamental attitudes toward "the other" on both sides. See Fouad Moughrabi, "The Politics of Palestinian Textbooks," *Journal of Palestine Studies* 31, no. 1 (Autumn 2001): 5–19; Israel/Palestine Center for Research and Information program on Peace Education (see http://www.ipcri.org/index1.html); and "Teachers Greet the Enemy," *Jerusalem Post* (Internet edition), April 3, 2003, http://www.ipcri.org/index1.html [06-21-2005].

Western prognosticators rushed to hail Arafat's death in November 2004 as creating a window of opportunity for peace. Our account of the conditions needed for a settlement suggests that such optimism was misplaced. Mahmoud Abbas confronted many of the same legitimacy problems that had plagued Arafat by 2000. Yet the U.S. State Department and the Western press immediately zeroed in on him as someone with whom business could perhaps be done. Their inattention to figures like the imprisoned Marwan Barghouti (the most popular secular leader among Palestinians) underscores how little they grasped that it is the legitimacy of leaders, not their pliability to others' agendas, which is essential to a tractable settlement. For Arafat's death to have created an opportunity on the Palestinian side, not only Barghouti but also Hamas would have to have participated, becoming invested in solving the problem rather than in derailing potential solutions. Even in that eventuality, no settlement would have been feasible without significant changes in Israeli politics. In the years since the 2000 Camp David debacle, the Sharon government made it plain to all who were willing to look that it was more interested in a military victory than in a political settlement. Without a change in that attitude, there would be no more chance of a settlement in the Middle East than there had been in Northern Ireland before 1997.

The difficulty of achieving settlements in SAMENI settings should not surprise us. We have seen that the windows of opportunity that make such settlements possible open rarely, and they seldom stay open for long. Few politicians are willing to take the considerable risks involved in moving through them. Indeed, they often fail to see either the possibilities or how fleeting they might be. A better and more widespread understanding of the dynamics of SAMENI negotiations, and of their consistency with the logic of transplacements, might diminish that possibility.

5.3. Rethinking Conflict Studies

Conflict studies have long been informed in part by a debate, often implicit, over whether conflict is driven from above, by political elites manipulating followers to gross acts of violence, or from below, by ancient and primordial hatreds nurtured in families, communities, and places of worship. The study of conflict resolution is similarly riveted, and focuses either on elite dispositions to negotiate or on grassroots initiatives to foster tolerance. One of the functions of the imperfect democratic settings we study in these cases is to draw the link, both empirically and analytically, between the two levels of focus.

In the middle of a peace process, a society lacks both the security of hard-line retaliation (which represents the status quo ante) and that of a democratically legitimate settlement (which is the final goal). Suspended thus between a disappearing past and an unreachable future, elite politics often becomes polarized. In the politics of peace, as each side breaks into two or more factions, the most important contests are those that take place among the factions. And in these fights, a major weapon is popular support.

In both the Middle East and Northern Ireland the way forward seems primarily constrained not by elites or masses alone, but by the link between them. In both places those factions that reject a settlement, or that reject the particular settlement that is on the table, have gained ascendance since the heady days (1995 in the Middle East, 1998 in Northern Ireland) when a majority on all sides favored reconciliation. As negotiations have dragged on, a reforming center has lost ground partly because its members have failed to lock in their advantage by making peace work.

But paralysis may be no more sustainable than the status quo ante was once considered to be, and the specter of failure will continue to hang over these societies so long as some democratic peace is not reached. The factionalized character of the politics of peace draws the link between leaders and constituents even more starkly than does normal politics, and their mutual dependence offers the possibility of both vicious and virtuous cycles. A decisive swing in favor of a settlement will require some success—some sense that moving forward is better than moving backward. Achieving success lies in the hands of elites. But support for an agreement, or for implementation, which is what is needed before elites can move decisively toward peace without risk of losing power altogether, lies with their constituencies.

6. AFTERWORD: FIVE YEARS ON

Our conclusion, in 2005, that the window of opportunity remained open for a settlement in Northern Ireland proved correct. In July of that year, the IRA announced the end of its campaign and promised complete decommissioning of all its weapons. Under renewed pressure from Britain and the Irish Republic, the Northern Ireland peace process apparently concluded when the Democratic Unionist Party and Sinn Fein, the two largest parties in the Northern Ireland Assembly, formed a joint government in May 2007.

The stability of the 2007 settlement remains in question. The power-sharing arrangement reinforces the sectarian divide, rendering government a difficult balancing act. The moderate parties (UUP and SDLP) that initially negotiated the Belfast Agreement lost their majority in the Assembly in 2003 and were further weakened in 2007 elections that increased the majorities of the DUP and Sinn Fein. Each member of the

Legislative Assembly (MLA) is officially designated Nationalist, Unionist, or Other, and some resolutions can be passed only with cross-community support. This system gives veto power (and therefore the power to immobilize government) to any of the major players, creating the ever-present incentive for players to defect if they cannot realize their aspirations through the consensual structure. Any vote taken by the Assembly can be made dependent on cross-community support if a "Petition of Concern" is presented to the Speaker. Ministerial portfolios are divided among the parties in proportion to their strength in the Assembly, so that all parties with a significant number of seats are entitled to at least one minister.

The eruption of violence in the spring and summer of 2009 underscored the reality that sectarian animosity persists at high levels across Northern Ireland.[133] Many Protestant and Catholic communities are still separated by walls and other types of barriers.[134] Indeed, of the forty-one barriers that exist in Belfast, roughly half have been constructed or extended since the cease-fire in 1994. In residential areas, the construction and extension of barriers was ongoing even after the resumption of joint government in 2007.[135] According to surveys, even in 2008 residents strongly agreed "that the walls serve to help residents feel safer by keeping the communities separate," and the government had no plans to tear them down.[136] Think tank proposals for eliminating the walls envisioned a five-phase process, with no time line.[137]

Demographic changes should be expected to increase pressure on community relations and the power-sharing arrangement over time. As the Catholic minority grows, shifting the balance of legislative power from Unionist to Nationalist, the specter of unification with the Republic of Ireland will cause renewed tensions. The economic boom in the south,

[133] "Officer's Shooting near Belfast Raises New Fears," *New York Times*, March 9, 2009, http://www.nytimes.com/2009/03/10/world/europe/10ulster.html [09-01-2009]; "Real IRA Blamed for Belfast Riots," BBC News (July 14, 2009), http://news.bbc.co.uk/2/hi/uk_news/northern_ireland/8148955.stm [09-01-2009]; Henry McDonald, "Sectarian Riots Erupt in Belfast on Police Chief's Last Night in Charge" (September 1, 2009), http://www.guardian.co.uk/uk/2009/sep/01/northern-ireland-riots-hugh-orde [09-01-2009].

[134] For a breakdown of the type and location of interface barriers in Belfast, as well as an analysis of the background and changing context, see Neil Jarman, "Security and Segregation: Interface Barriers in Belfast," *Shared Space: A Research Journal on Peace, Conflict and Community Relations in Northern Ireland*, no. 6 (Belfast: Community Relations Council, 2008).

[135] Ibid., p. 22.

[136] A cohort of 1,037 people were polled in the Falls/Shankill, Short Strand/Templemore Avenue and Antrim Road/Tigers Bay areas. For details of the survey methodology and findings, see www.usirelandalliance.org [09-23-2008].

[137] Macaulay Associates, "A Process for Removing Interface Barriers," July 2008, http://www.macaulayassociates.co.uk/pdfs/peace_wall.pdf [09-18-2008].

which may have persuaded some Protestants of the merits of a closer relationship with the Republic, has been followed by one of the most dramatic slowdowns of the 2008–9 collapse. While nobody is predicting a return to the Troubles, governing Northern Ireland through power sharing will continue to be a tenuous balancing act that threatens perpetually to collapse.

Our predictions about the Middle East have held up depressingly well five years later. The two main criteria for moving things forward—strong American pressure on Israel to reverse the settlement policies on the West Bank and incorporation of Hamas into the negotiating process—are further from being realized than they were in 2004, despite President Obama's attempts to insist on a moratorium on new settlements in 2009. By that time enormous damage had been done by George W. Bush's declaration in April 2004 that all parties must henceforth accept changed "realities on the ground." This had amounted to a reversal of decades of American policy and a decisive show of support for Ariel Sharon's government.[138] As a consequence, any suggestion that Israel's unilateral departure from the Gaza Strip in September 2005 might prove to be a harbinger of comparable developments in the West Bank became vanishingly unlikely. Following Sharon's defection from Likud in the run-up to the 2006 Israeli elections, Kadima took over as Israel's governing party; so long as they retained control of Israeli policy and the U.S. government backed the idea that the 400,000-plus Jewish settlers would stay put in the West Bank, it remained highly improbable that sustainable support could be built among Palestinians for a two-state solution. Jimmy Carter might have attracted vitriolic attacks in the United States for including the term *apartheid* in the subtitle to his 2006 book on the peace process,[139] but it surely captured the reality Palestinians felt they were confronting.[140] Likud's return to power under Benjamin Netanyahu's leadership after the February 2009 Israeli election did nothing to change that.

In the second half of the 1990s Hamas had become an increasingly successful political force in Gaza and the West Bank. Yasir Arafat's corrupt and ineffective Palestinian Authority had lost popularity in the last years

[138] See President Bush's joint White House press conference with Ariel Sharon, April 14, 2004, http://www.whitehouse.gov/news/releases/2004/04/20040414-4.html [04-03-2006].

[139] Jimmy Carter, *Palestine: Peace not Apartheid* (New York: Simon and Schuster, 2006).

[140] The "Apartheid Wall" most dramatically symbolizes Palestinians' widespread sense of bantustanization In a 2006 survey conducted two years after the wall's construction began, only 19 percent of Palestinians believed Israel was building the wall to enhance security; 61 percent saw it as designed to enable Israel to take more land and water resources; and 26 percent thought it was intended to draw the final borders of Israel. "The Wall," Near East Consulting, July 5, 2006, http://www.neareastconsulting.com/surveys/wall/files/wall_eng_01.pdf [09-04-2009].

of his life. Hamas was operating as the de facto welfare state—especially in Gaza. Israel's killing many of its military leaders after 2003 and jailing charismatic figures like Raed Salah boosted their popularity. Nowhere was Hamas's increased political confidence and strength more clearly underscored than in the Cairo Accord with Arafat's successor Mahmoud Abbas in March 2005. Hamas agreed to a lull in terrorist operations *in exchange for* new elections to the PA, which would bring them to power the following year.[141] This was a dramatic shift from their boycott of the 1996 elections. Quite possibly it reflected their discovery of what groups like the Euskadi ta Askatasuna (ETA) Basque separatists had learned before them: that popular support tends to be eroded by extreme forms of terrorism.[142] Certainly Hamas's move was widely welcomed: 73 percent of Palestinians supported its decision to participate in elections, and over 61 percent thought that, if Hamas became part of the Palestinian Legislative Council, it would abide by council decisions.[143]

The most significant reality the Bush administration missed was that the Hamas leadership had for some time been signaling interest in an end to violence and a settlement with Israel. This began with a unilateral cease-fire agreed with the Palestinian Authority in June 2003. The cease-fire fell apart when a West Jerusalem bus bombing by a rogue Hamas cell from Hebron (disowned by the Hamas leadership) produced massive Israeli retaliation, including the assassination of Ismail Abu Shanab—the main Hamas architect of the cease-fire—among others. The bus bombing was a catalyst for concerted multilateral isolation of Hamas. The European Union put the whole organization (not just its military wing) on their terrorism blacklist; funds of sister organizations were sequestered in Israel and elsewhere; and economic support from Arab states declined sharply.[144]

The combination of military defeats and political strength led Hamas to declare a new truce in January 2005, indicating that it would be made permanent if Abbas—now PA president following Arafat's death—could get assurances of Israeli reciprocity and the release of Palestinian prisoners. Sharon rejected the offer, noting only that "quiet will be met with

---

[141] Ehud Yaari, "Fight Delay," *New Republic*, February 13, 2006, http://www.washingtoninstitute.org/templateC06.php?CID=899 [06-06-2006].

[142] See Ignacio Sánchez-Cuenca, "Nationalist Terrorism as a Constrained War of Attrition" (mimeo, Instituto Juan March and Universidad de Madrid, February 2005).

[143] JMCC, "JMCC Public Opinion Poll #55,", December 2005, http://www.jmcc.org/publicpoll/results/2005/no55.pdf [07-12-2006].

[144] Graham Usher, "The New Hamas: Between Resistance and Participation," *Middle East Report Online*, August 21, 2005, http://www.merip.org/mero/mero082105.html [06-06-2006].

quiet."[145] Hamas continued the truce nonetheless and, following its 2006 election victory, began floating trial balloons about being willing to recognize Israel as an "occupier state," the possibility of establishing a Palestinian state within "provisional borders" as outlined in the U.S. road map as an interim solution on the way to a two-state solution based on the 1967 boundaries, and a long-term (perhaps ten-year) *hudna* or truce.[146] The Hamas leadership was also quick publicly to reject Al Qaeda's offer of support and its advice never to make peace with Israel in the wake of its international isolation and ostracism after the party's 2006 election victory.[147] But the continued refusal to disarm or to accept Israel's legitimacy led Hamas's offers to fall on deaf ears in Jerusalem and Washington—where these remain preconditions for negotiations.

Notice a vital difference between the Middle Eastern and South African dynamics. When the apartheid government decided in 1990 to unban the ANC and all other political groups, release all political prisoners, and begin negotiations, the ANC had not recognized the government's legitimacy or suspended its armed struggle—let alone agreed to decommission weapons. Most white South Africans feared that the ANC was an agent of the USSR, not least because its leadership overlapped with that of one of the most Stalinist communist parties in the world. During the on-again-off-again negotiations over the next two years, the ANC refused requests to decommission weapons or to accept that the government's insistence on constitutionally mandated power sharing would ever be part of a settlement. At the time, power sharing was considered nonnegotiable by most whites—it was their Jerusalem. Nonetheless, the government continued negotiating with the ANC even after multiparty talks twice collapsed; negotiations led eventually to a settlement and democratic elections in 1994.

In the Middle East, the likely costs of not pressing forward, taking advantage of the gains that were on offer during the sixteen-month truce, were poignantly underscored in early June 2006. An apparently errant Israeli rocket killed eight civilians on a Gaza beach, leading Hamas leaders to suspend the truce—promising reprisal attacks on Israeli civilians.[148]

---

[145] Chris McGreal, "Islamists Halt Attacks on Israel," *Guardian*, January 24, 2005, http://www.guardian.co.uk/international/story/0,,1396958,00.html [06-20-2006]; "Officials: Israel Ends Targeted Killings," NewsMax.Com wires, January 26, 2005, http://www.newsmax.com/archives/articles/2005/1/26/11452.shtml [06-18-2006].

[146] Yaari, "Fight Delay."

[147] See "Hamas Rejects Al-Qaeda's Support," March 5, 2005, http://news.bbc.co.uk/1/hi/world/middle_east/4776578.stm [5-17-2006].

[148] Steven Erlanger, "Hamas Fires Rockets into Israel, Ending 16-Month Truce," *New York Times*, June 11, 2006, p. A1.

Cognizant of Al Qaeda's presence in Gaza, which had been growing as they moved toward being a government that might negotiate a settlement, Hamas leaders were protecting their flank.[149] Lacking any prospect of a tangible result, Hamas risked losing the symbols of Palestinian liberation to more radical groups like the Palestinian Islamic Jihad and Al Qaeda in Gaza just as the PLO had lost them to Hamas when Yitzhak Rabin's assassination scuttled the agreement he had been close to reaching with Arafat in 1995.

Indeed, denied the chance to be a partner in peace—at least without paying the high cost of entirely denouncing its position and disarming, Hamas increasingly turned toward its radical flank. Following the January 2006 elections, the United States reportedly encouraged Fatah not to conclude negotiations with Hamas on a national unity government, provided resources to strengthen Fatah against Hamas, and cut off funding to a Hamas-led government. In an "end of mission report," Alvaro de Soto, UN special coordinator for the Middle East peace process and personal representative of the secretary-general to the PLO and the PA, was particularly (and depressingly) telling:

A National Unity Government (NUG) . . . might have been achieved soon after the election, in February or March 2006, had the US not led the Quartet to set impossible demands, and opposed the NUG in principle. At the time, and indeed until the Mecca agreement a year later, the US clearly pushed for a confrontation between Fatah and Hamas.[150]

[149] Hazem al-Amin, "In the Palestinian Diaspora, They Joined Early . . . In the Territories, They Delayed in Receiving It" (pt. 1 of 2), *Al-Hayat*, April 7, 2006, http://english.daralhayat .com/Spec/04-2006/Article-20060407-74c40c9e-c0a8-10ed-0105-0034e1a86f7c/story. html [06-14-2006], and "In the Palestinian Diaspora . . . 'International Jihad' Accelerates Its Steps in the West Bank and Gaza, after 'National Jihad' Formed Its Government" (pt. 2 of 2), *Al-Hayat*, April 10, 2006, http://english.daralhayat.com/Spec/04-2006/Article-20060410-84272b88-c0a8-10ed-0105-0034bc562c62/story.html [06-14-2006]. See also Khaled Abu Toameh and Larry Derfner, "A Tough Neighborhood: Is al Qaeda Branching Out to the Palestinian Territories?" *U.S. News and World Report*, May 15, 2006, http:// www.usnews.com/usnews/news/articles/060515/15mideast.htm [06-14-2006].

[150] Alvaro de Soto, "End of Mission Report," May 2007, par. 55, http://image .guardian.co.uk/sys-files/Guardian/documents/2007/06/12/DeSotoReport.pdf [06-14-2007]. For further evidence of U.S. officials' unwillingness to engage Hamas, see Statement by United States Security Coordinator Lieutenant General Keith W. Dayton, Senate Foreign Relations Committee, March 15, 2006, http://www.senate.gov/~foreign/testimony/2006/ DaytonTestimony060315.pdf [08-02-2007]; "U.S. General Says Hamas Influence Waning in Gaza," USINFO.State.Gov, May 24, 2007, http://usinfo.state.gov/xarchives/display. html?p=washfile-english&y=2007&m=May&x=20070524114446NDyblehS0.419491 [08-02-2007]; NPR, *All Things Considered*, January 19, 2007; "Remarks by U.S. Security Coordinator LTG Keith Dayton, Update on the Israeli-Palestinian Situation and Palestinian Assistance Programs, House Foreign Affairs Middle East and South Asia Sub-Committee," May 23, 2007, http://foreignaffairs.house.gov/110/day052307.htm [08-02-2007].

As late as March 2007, the Palestinian public was overwhelmingly in support of the national unity government.[151] However, external pressure and domestic politics escalated the confrontation, leading to Hamas's violent takeover of the Gaza Strip in June 2007 and the effective creation of a divided Palestinian entity. Gaza's Hamas was pushed into a corner, cut off nearly entirely from economic and diplomatic relations, and with even humanitarian aid doled out in fits and starts. The West Bank Fatah, in contrast, was incorporated ever more closely into the peace process, awarded considerable EU and U.S. support, and applauded as it clamped down on Hamas militants, much as in the days of Arafat.

The result threatened to be the same as that during Arafat's latter years. Any hope that Mahmoud Abbas and Ehud Olmert would need each other enough to conclude an agreement was forlorn. The two parties stood side by side at Annapolis in November 2007, confirming their commitment to continuing negotiations and maintaining the outlines of the Quartet road map. Yet the map was poorly followed. Significant support from both the EU and the United States was funneled into the West Bank, helping to shore up Fatah-led administration there and training security forces—which frequently arrested Hamas sympathizers and activists. And the Israeli public benefited from the decrease in violent attacks from the West Bank, partly as a result of stepped-up security measures and the building of the security barrier. At the same time, however, settlement building continued in the West Bank through the end of the Bush administration, with 550 percent more new tenders issued in the first eight months of 2008 than in the entire year of 2007 (417 in 1–8/2008 vs. 65 in all of 2007). Moreover, the West Bank saw 1,000 new buildings in settlement areas, including approximately 2,600 housing units, with 55 percent east of the separation barrier.[152] The Israel Defense Forces (IDF) claimed to have removed 132 barriers since the Annapolis talks in 2007, but new checkpoints were also constructed. The result was an overall increase in barriers within the West Bank, from 563 in November 2007 to 630 in September 2008.[153] Freedom of movement, along with economic conditions, continued to deteriorate in the West Bank, as well as the Gaza Strip.

---

[151] PCPSR, "Public Opinion Poll #23," March 29, 2007, found that 88 percent of the public supported the makeup of the national unity government. http://www.pcpsr.org/survey/polls/2007/p23e1.html#nationalunity1 [12-24-2009].

[152] Peace Now, "Eliminating the Green Line—August 2008," http://www.peacenow.org.il/site/en/peace.asp?pi=61&docid=3380 [08-27-2009].

[153] BBC News, "In Figures: Since Annapolis," http://news.bbc.co.uk/2/hi/middle_east/7746905.stm [08-27-2009].

The chances of a settlement remain bleak. On the Palestinian side, Mahmoud Abbas may have the political will, but there is little reason to think that he enjoys the authority to conclude an agreement. In November of 2008 the PLO voted him the symbolic president of a Palestinian state, but he was unable to translate this into increased popular support for him or his party. By mid-2009 reports were surfacing that he would postpone elections scheduled for January of 2010, possibly by two years.[154] This was unsurprising. The Israeli invasion of Gaza in January of 2009 enabled Hamas to strengthen its position—using its control over smuggling tunnels into Egypt, its near monopoly on resources, and increased opposition to Israel to rally support. Although this support has dissipated somewhat since Israel's withdrawal, a peace treaty remains impossible as long as Washington and Tel Aviv refuse to include Hamas in negotiations.

It is also difficult to see whence an Israeli leadership would emerge that would be sufficiently strong and committed to settling the conflict. Benjamin Netanyahu and Likud came back into power following Israel's 2009 elections. Labour came in fourth with less than 10 percent of the vote, behind both Kadima and the ultra-right-wing nationalist Yisrael Beiteinu party led by Avigdor Lieberman—who joined Netanyahu's government as deputy prime minister and foreign minister. Under pressure from Obama, the Netanyahu government made some temporizing concessions on the acceptance in principle of a demilitarized Palestinian state. Although, as Lust and Shapiro argue in the next chapter, it makes strategic sense to call Netanyahu's bluff and begin negotiations on this basis, we remain skeptical that he has any serious intention of agreeing to anything Palestinians can accept. Past practice suggests he will go through the motions until the logic of Obama's reelection needs in the United States kicks in, causing him to reduce the pressure on Israel. And a second-term American administration can more easily be waited out.

In mid-2009 the Obama administration became involved in diplomatic cat and mouse with the Netanyahu government over freezing settlement expansion, on which the new American administration had volubly insisted. Obama also made a much-discussed speech in Cairo in June 2009, calling for a "new beginning" in Palestinian-Israeli and American relations.[155] These moves fed the perception in Israel that the new

---

[154] Yaakov Katz, "PA 2010 Elections Likely to Be Delayed," *Jerusalem Post*, July 13, 2009, http://www.jpost.com/servlet/Satellite?cid=1246443790046&pagename=JPArticle%2FShowFull [08-27-2009].

[155] Text: Obama's Speech in Cairo, *New York Times*, June 4, 2009, http://www.nytimes.com/2009/06/04/us/politics/04obama.text.html [09-29-2009].

American administration was hostile to Israeli interests.[156] They came as a shock to some because Obama had run a strongly pro-Israel campaign in 2008 and appointed Hillary Clinton, Rahm Emanuel, and Dennis Ross—all well known for their staunch support of Israel during the Clinton years—to key positions in his administration. But, despite the efforts of seasoned negotiator George Mitchell, the Obama administration soon learned that Netanyahu would up the ante by rejecting American demands for a settlement freeze. This forced Obama to decide whether he could afford a major confrontation with Israel's U.S. constituencies when American casualties in Afghanistan were on the rise and his major domestic legislative agenda for health-care reform was fracturing the Democratic Party on Capitol Hill and eroding his popular support.[157] Unsurprisingly, by the end of August 2009 Obama had abandoned his insistence on a freeze in the face of Israeli intransigence.[158] It was hard to conjure up the scenario in which Obama would find it worth squandering political capital and jeopardizing his reelection, given the low probability of success that had to be inferred from the alignment of political forces in Israel.

South Africa's fourth national election, held in April 2009, was both a striking affirmation of the nascent democratic regime and a remarkable consolidation, by the African National Congress (ANC), of its power. True, the ANC's 65.9 percent share of the vote was 4 percentage points less than the share it had won five years earlier. The decline cost the party 33 seats in Parliament, leaving it with 264 seats—three short of the two-thirds majority required unilaterally to change the constitution. The opposition Democratic Alliance (DA), led by Cape Town Mayor Helen Zille, won 16.7 percent of the vote and gained 17 seats for a total of 67—its strongest showing ever. The DA also took control of the Western Cape provincial government, importantly curtailing the ANC's regional power.

Significant as these developments were, the larger story of the 2009 election was that South Africa's nascent political institutions had weathered their most serious constitutional crisis to date, and that the ANC

[156] "Poll: 4 Percent of Jewish Israelis See Obama as Pro-Israel," *JTA* (August 28, 2009), http://jta.org/news/article/2009/08/28/1007507/percent-of-jewish-israelis-that-see-obama-as-pro-israel-continues-to-decline [09-29-2009].

[157] See "Obama Weekly Approval Average Now 52%, a New Low," Gallup (August 24, 2009), http://www.gallup.com/poll/122468/Obama-Weekly-Approval-Average-New-Low.aspx?CSTS=tagrss [08-30-2009].

[158] Barak Ravid, "U.S. Drops Demand for Israel Building Freeze in East Jerusalem," *Haaretz*, August 27, 2009, http://www.haaretz.com/hasen/spages/1110507.html [08-29-2009].

had survived the most internally threatening leadership crisis in its history. The dynamics by which these developments took place were less than prepossessing, but this scarcely differentiated South African politics from what we have witnessed in struggling democracies like Mexico or Iraq—not to mention such established democracies as Britain or the United States—in recent decades.

Although less commented-upon than the leadership struggle within the ANC, South Africa's successful navigation of a potentially destabilizing constitutional crisis between 2007 and 2009 is perhaps the more consequential development. Focusing on what did not happen—on the dog that did not bark—does not typically command our attention. Yet it is worth reflecting on what was avoided in the run-up to the 2009 election. In mid-2005, supporters of President Thabo Mbeki began floating trial balloons on the possibility of changing the constitution to enable him to run for a third term as president. Initially he refused to rule out the possibility, but by early 2006 enough ANC bigwigs had weighed in against the idea that he was forced to back down.[159] During the same period, Mbeki's long-simmering conflict with his deputy president, Jacob Zuma, came to a head. Zuma was a populist who built an independent base of support in the trade union movement and the left-leaning ANC Youth League. Zuma had long been a thorn in Mbeki's side, and, when the opportunity presented itself owing to a series of rape and corruption allegations, Mbeki fired Zuma in June 2005.[160]

But Mbeki broke a primal rule: if you are going to shoot an elephant, you had better be sure to kill it. Zuma was acquitted of some of the charges, in some cases based only on technicalities, and succeeded by various legal maneuverings in getting the others postponed and ultimately dropped.[161] He mounted a challenge to Mbeki's leadership, provoking Mbeki to seek an additional term as leader of the ANC—even though he could not be president of the country for a third term. Zuma prevailed at a raucous ANC National Convention in Polokwane in December 2007, creating the anomaly that the country's president was no longer the leader of his political party. The potential for this to precipitate a major political crisis was manifest in South Africa's quasi-parliamentary system, in which the president is elected by, and relies on the continued confidence of, Parliament. Mbeki became increasingly isolated as his supporters were replaced in key ANC structures by Zuma's people. Mbeki

[159] See "S.A.'s Mbeki Rules Out Third Term" (February 6, 2006), BBC News On Line, http://news.bbc.co.uk/2/hi/africa/4684752.stm [05-25-2009].

[160] See "South African Leader Sacks Deputy" (June 14, 2005), BBC News On Line, http://news.bbc.co.uk/2/hi/africa/4092064.stm [12-24-2009].

[161] See "Timeline: Zuma's Legal Problems" (April 6, 2009), BBC News On Line, http://news.bbc.co.uk/2/hi/africa/7153378.stm [12-24-2009].

resigned the presidency in September 2008 after being "recalled" by the ANC's National Executive Committee, following a court finding (that would later be reversed) of improper interference in Zuma's corruption prosecution. The remaining charges against Zuma were dropped as a result of the alleged procedural improprieties, but he could not easily become president immediately because he was not a member of Parliament. Mbeki was replaced by the moderate deputy president, Kgalema Motlanthe, until Zuma could be installed in the presidency following the April 2009 elections.

At first blush, that a man with Zuma's checkered past has become president of South Africa might not seem to be a cause for celebration. But it is worth remembering that this occurred at the very time that the last vestiges of democratic process were being dismantled by Robert Mugabe not very far to the north. President Mbeki scarcely distinguished himself by conspicuously refusing to deploy South Africa's soft power to try to tip the scales against Mugabe's power grab and the attendant destruction of civil liberties in Zimbabwe, but it is notable how scrupulously procedural propriety was observed at home. No major player even hinted at overstepping the boundaries of his constitutional authority in the delicate power transitions from Mbeki to Motlanthe, and from Motlanthe to Zuma. Political opponents were not arrested. Press freedom was not curtailed. The April elections, marked by a high 77 percent turnout, were quickly declared to be free and fair by South Africa's Independent Electoral Commission and by international observers—still a comparative rarity in contemporary Africa.[162] No doubt this orderly transfer of power owed a good deal to the precedent set by Nelson Mandela in choosing to relinquish the presidency in 1999, but it is notable, nonetheless, that the potential for a major political crisis was averted.

From our perspective here the notable fact is that the system weathered the transition with comparative ease. Mbeki relinquished power without a fuss, and Zuma did not attempt an end run around the constitution. To be sure, the country remained a considerable distance from passing Huntington's two-turnover test for a consolidated democracy, but the possibility was beginning to come into view. Certainly it was clear that the transition that had begun so improbably almost two decades earlier had been consummated successfully. This divergence from the outcomes in Northern Ireland and the Middle East underscores the radical contingency that attends SAMENI negotiations. There are many more ways for

---

[162] See "IEC Declares Election Free and Fair" (Tuesday April 28, 2009), http://www .sagoodnews.co.za/politics/iec_declares_election_free_and_fair.html [05-28-2009], and "South African Election Free and Fair—African Union," *Harare Tribune*, April 25, 2009, http://www.hararetribune.com/world/southern-africa/629-south-africa-election-free-and-fair-african-union.html [05-28-2009].

them to go wrong than for them to go right. Rare combinations of luck and leadership are needed for windows of opportunity to open when key players are able and willing to move through them. South Africa stands for the proposition that this is nonetheless possible even in unlikely circumstances, suggesting that democrats should never discard hope—even when they have few reasons for optimism.

CHAPTER FOUR

Players, Preconditions, and Peace: Why Talks Fail and How They Might Succeed

Ellen Lust and Ian Shapiro

AVIGDOR LIEBERMAN, leader of Yisrael Beitenu, Netanyahu's deputy prime minister and foreign minister, swore on the eve of February 2009 elections, "We will not have direct or indirect negotiations with Hamas nor a ceasefire."[1] This assertion was scarcely novel, but it illustrates how parties to Middle East peace negotiations consistently undermine the possibility of success. They do so by excluding the actors they regard as likely to press demands they will not want to meet, and by insisting on preconditions that adversaries must accept before negotiations will start. Lieberman's insistence on excising from the process the very group that withstood the 2008–9 Israeli assault to maintain control over Gaza, and decisively won Palestinian elections only three years before, is counter-productive.

But it is not unique. Both the Bush and Obama administrations have insisted on a variety of conditions that Hamas must meet if it is to partici-pate in negotiations, and both the Palestinian Authority and Hamas have made their participation contingent on Israel's acceptance of various con-ditions with respect to West Bank settlements. Drawing on the argument developed in chapter 3, we show here that excluding players and insisting on preconditions are both misguided strategies. We explain why this is so and suggest a better path forward for all the players involved in the Palestinian-Israeli conflict. Unless they take it, the chances of success are negligible. Moreover, Israel's already compromised democratic creden-tials will be further weakened. Demographic changes will turn its Jewish population into a shrinking minority within the territories it controls. And the fragile sprouts of democracy within the West Bank and Gaza will likely be obliterated by continuing war and civil strife.

---

[1] Benjamin Pogrund, "More Roadblock than Roadmap in the Middle East: As the Coali-tion-Building Begins, the Only Certain Thing That Can Be Said of Israel's Election Result Is That Peace Was Not the Winner," *Guardian*, February 11, 2009, guardian.co.uk [03-24-2009].

POWERFUL PLAYERS

Excluding powerful players from the negotiating table in the Middle East, often labeling them terrorists or pariahs, has left a trail of failed attempts at solving the Palestinian-Israeli conflict. Israeli and U.S. refusal to talk to PLO "terrorists" during the 1970s and 1980s perpetuated the stalemate just as the attempts to sideline Hamas do today. Palestinians make the same mistake. The PLO aims to exclude Hamas and use successful negotiations to defeat their opponent. In the words of Sa'eb Erekat, chief negotiator for the Fatah-dominated PA: "If I have an end game agreement showing the two-state solution, Hamas will disappear. If I don't, I will disappear."[2] The difference between the PLO and its Israeli and U.S. counterparts is not its intent—all seek to isolate their enemies before negotiations even begin—but rather its power; the PLO can exclude Hamas only with support from Israel and the United States. Yet these strategies, which the Obama administration supports, are misguided.

Powerful players sitting on the sidelines have every incentive to turn their full energies to undermining agreements. They do so partly because they know that compromise agreements will fall short of their goals, and—as we explore shortly—because excluded from the process, they have little reason to moderate their demands. They also do everything they can to destroy settlements because they stand to lose politically if the settlement succeeds. The concluding of even the most agreeable settlement, if done without them, chips away at their political authority. Yasir Arafat was painfully aware of this in the early 1990s, when the United States and Israel formally excluded the PLO from joining the joint Palestinian-Jordanian delegation attending the Madrid Conference of November 1991. Sitting in Tunisia, Arafat knew that he was better off concluding even an inferior agreement at Oslo than allowing the subsequent negotiations in Washington to succeed without him.

Those who advocate ignoring extremists usually hope that this will strengthen the hands of moderates, but more often it has the opposite effect. All groups—even the most radical—are internally divided. They confront a common adversary, but they are almost always also engaged in power struggles among themselves. Radical hard-liners have tactical reasons to want the moderates within their ranks to be seen as compromising the goals of the movement for no gain. Moderates, on the other hand, are often willing to make serial concessions in order to achieve small "confidence-building" victories, hoping that this process may lead eventually to agreement on thornier matters. If the radical hard-liners pull the rug out from under them, moderates are open to charges of in-

---

[2] Q&A with Sa'eb Erekat, Ha'aretz.com, September 4, 2009, www.haaretz.com/hasen/pages/QA.jhtml?qaNo=147&m=147 [12-24-2009].

eptitude, if not collaboration with the enemy—strengthening the hand of the radicals.

Refusing to engage powerful antagonists in negotiations also makes it difficult to determine when settlements are possible. In the presence of opportunity, previously hidden splits within movements often break out into the open. Contending factions use political statements, negotiations, and violence to outmaneuver one another. Their statements often appear contradictory, and third parties latch on to one or another statement as evidence of the group's "true" intentions. Doing so typically misses the reality that the group is internally divided. The challenge is not to determine "the group's" position, but to understand the veracity of moderates' claims and assess their ability to face down adversaries opposed to a settlement.

Sadly, both the Obama and Netanyahu administrations seemed oblivious to these realities in 2009. In July of that year they turned a cold shoulder to Hamas leader Khaled Meshaal's offer to "cooperate with any American, international or regional effort" to negotiate a settlement along the lines of a two-state solution. Instead the White House continued to stand by the Quartet's position that Hamas is not an appropriate partner for negotiations.[3] Benjamin Netanyahu dismissed the offer on the grounds that Meshaal "remains rooted in an extremist theology which fundamentally opposes peace and reconciliation."[4] Absent engagement, these expectations can neither be tested nor be proven wrong.

The few successes there have been in Middle East diplomacy have involved including strong pariah players. President Carter brought Anwar Sadat and Menachem Begin together, an historic achievement that took regional war off the table. A decade and a half later, George H. W. Bush's administration forged a new multilateral peace process that eventually led to the Oslo Agreement. Vital to their success was the involvement of players previously considered beyond the pale. Talking to Sadat had been anathema before the events leading up to Camp David. Bush Senior brought a reluctant Syria to the negotiating table for the first time in 1991. Including these players meant facing down stiff opposition. Israel's government did not like it. Nor did Israel's U.S. constituencies.

A South African comparison is illuminating here. In 1990 President F. W. de Klerk recognized the importance of including potential veto

---

[3] The Quartet, consisting of the United States, Russia, the EU, and the UN, was established in Madrid in 2002 by then Spanish prime minister Aznar. Former British prime minister Tony Blair has been the Quartet's special envoy since mid-2007.

[4] "Hamas Chief Outlines Terms for Talks on Arab-Israeli Peace," *Wall Street Journal*, July 31, 2009, http://online.wsj.com/article/SB124899975954495435.html?mod=djemITP#printMode [10-02-2009]. See also Taghreed El-Khodary and Ethan Bronner, "Addressing U.S., Hamas Says It Grounded Rockets," *New York Times*, May 4, 2009, http://www.nytimes.com/2009/05/05/world/middleeast/05meshal.html [10-02-2009].

players in peace negotiations, and he took on considerable opposition in order to do so. Many whites, particularly in the National Party, regarded Inkatha, the ethnic Zulu party based primarily in the eastern part of the country, as the more benign force. They believed that its leader, Mangosuthu Gatsha Buthelezi, had been comparatively pliable in his dealings with the government. He seemed open to considering power-sharing arrangements, and less likely than the African National Congress, with its historical ties to the USSR and continuing connections with the South African Communist Party, to challenge white economic privilege and the fundamentals of a market economy. Many whites saw Buthelezi as the kind of black leader they could talk to. But de Klerk was well aware from the polling and other sources that the ANC commanded widespread support among blacks throughout the country. He knew that even in the Zulu heartland of Natal, the ANC might give Inkatha a run for its money. Recognizing that no settlement was going to stick unless the ANC ultimately helped implement it, de Klerk resisted the opposition and negotiated with the ANC.[5]

Yitzhak Rabin also understood the importance of standing up to naysayers and negotiating with all critical players when he negotiated with the PLO during and after the Oslo Accords of 1993. As we explained in chapter 3, those negotiations came exceedingly close to producing a settlement, but Rabin's assassination by a Jewish extremist in December 1995 derailed them. Ironically, but accurately, it was Rabin himself who had once observed that "peace is not made with friends. Peace is made with enemies, some of whom—and I won't name names—I loathe very much."[6]

President Obama appears to grasp the importance of this approach. During his campaign he argued that not engaging enemies is a mistake.[7] Even when his willingness to negotiate with Iran drew strong attacks from John McCain, he held firm. Once in office the Obama administration agreed to talks with Iran. Obama held fast to this position in

---

[5] For discussion of how de Klerk developed the resources to face down the naysayers in the National Party, see our discussion in chapter 3, pp. 102–7.

[6] Clyde Haberman, "Mideast Accord: The Secret Peace / A Special Report; How Oslo Helped Mold the Mideast Pact," *New York Times*, September 5, 1993, http://query.nytimes.com/gst/fullpage.html?res=9F0CE6DA113AF936A3575AC0A965958260&sec=&spon=&pagewanted=2 [01-22-2009].

[7] Interview with Martin Indyk, "Obama Must Take a Regional Approach on Gaza Violence," Council on Foreign Relations, January 12, 2009, http://www.cfr.org/publication/18204/obama_must_take_regional_approach_on_gaza_violence.html [1-24-2009]. See also Richard N. Haass and Martin Indyk, "Beyond Iraq: A New U.S. Strategy for the Middle East," *Foreign Affairs*, January/February 2009, http://www.foreignaffairs.org/20090101faessay88104/richard-n-haass-martin-indyk/obama-s-middle-east-agenda.html [1-23-2009].

the face of mounting conservative pressure, even after Iran's leadership crisis, following the disputed June 2009 elections, heightened tensions between the United States and Iranian president Mahmoud Ahmadinejad, along with his hard-line backers in the Republican Guard.[8] Yet by October 2009 Iran had agreed to open its newly revealed uranium enrichment plant near Qum to international inspection, and to send most of its openly declared enriched uranium to Russia for conversion to reactor fuel.[9] Iran continued playing cat and mouse with international inspectors and the West, testing missiles and perhaps nuclear components while at the same time keeping diplomatic channels open for discussions on exchanging the bulk of their enriched uranium for nuclear fuel rods.[10] The Obama administration kept up the pressure by mobilizing international support for sanctions while at the same time remaining open to talks with the regime.[11]

Nor was this approach limited to Iran. In some ways more surprisingly, in 2009 the Obama administration was seriously considering negotiating with Taliban members in Afghanistan.[12] Its willingness to consider talks with nongovernmental actors, who are manifestly committed to ideologies seen as anathema to U.S. interests and ideals, exhibits an understanding that political solutions require including all sides at the table.

Yet when it came to Israel-Palestine, Obama hewed to the failed approach of the Clinton and G. W. Bush administrations. Writing in *Foreign Affairs* in 2007, then-senator Obama acknowledged that achieving a two-state solution to the Palestinian-Israeli conflict was more vitally important than ever. But his proposed strategy was to prevent "the reinvigoration of Hamas," and to "help the Israelis identify and strengthen those partners who are truly committed to peace, while isolating those who

[8] See "Iran: Obama Not Giving Up," News24.com (July 6, 2009), http://www.news24.com/Content/World/News/1073/0c451f9ee43842009e3746759f48993f/Iran_Obama_not_giving_up [07-07-2009].

[9] Steven Erlanger and Mark Landler, "Iran Agrees to Send Enriched Uranium to Russia," *New York Times*, October 2, 2009, http://www.nytimes.com/2009/10/02/world/middleeast/02nuke.html [10-02-2009].

[10] See Steven Edwards, "Iran Missile Tests Puts Pressure on Israel, the West," *National Post*, December 16, 2009, http://www.nationalpost.com/news/story.html?id=2349195 [12-23-2009]; "Secret Document Exposes Iran's Nuclear Trigger," *Times* (London), December 14, 2009, http://www.timesonline.co.uk/tol/news/world/middle_east/article6955351.ece [12-23-2009]; and "Iran Agrees to Nuclear Fuel Swap," *New York Times*, December 12, 2009, http://www.nytimes.com/aponline/2009/12/12/world/AP-Iran-Nuclear.html [12-23-2009].

[11] See Spencer Ackerman, "Obama Administration Prepares Iran Sanction Options," *Washington Independent*, December 21, 2009, http://washingtonindependent.com/71561/obama-administration-prepares-iran-sanction-options [12-23-2009].

[12] Helene Cooper and Sheryl Gay Stolberg, "Obama Ponders Outreach to Elements of the Taliban," *New York Times*, March 8, 2009.

seek conflict and instability."[13] His first phone call as president, reportedly made to Mahmoud Abbas,[14] signaled that Obama was determined to deal with the conflict. But his subsequent decision to focus his energies on Abbas, and the administration's unwillingness to react positively to Hamas's overtures for inclusion, demonstrated that his approach to the Palestinian-Israeli conflict would continue to diverge from his strategies in Iran and elsewhere.

In part, this is not surprising. For Obama to begin negotiating with Hamas would mean confronting powerful lobbies within the United States and Israel determined to marginalize Hamas. The political upheaval surrounding the withdrawal of Charles Freeman as Obama's nominee to chair the National Intelligence Council (even though it had no particular Middle East portfolio) on the grounds that he was perceived to be insufficiently pro-Israel was simply one visible sign of the enormous political pressure Obama faces to treat the Palestinian-Israeli conflict as he has done.[15] Any American politician thinking about reelection has strong incentives not to resist it.

Yet this does not alter the reality that a successful settlement that excludes Hamas is no longer possible. In the early 1990s the PLO was in a position to deliver a settlement, but this possibility was tragically derailed by Rabin's assassination. Since that time its loss of support among Palestinians has been huge. President Clinton discovered this at Camp David in 2000. At the time, Arafat was widely criticized for rejecting terms that he had been willing to accept from Rabin five years earlier, prompting many to repeat Abba Eban's old line that the PLO "never misses an opportunity to miss an opportunity."[16]

Far from reflecting Arafat's irrationality though, his intransigence signaled his knowledge that he could no longer deliver Palestinians' support for a compromise. His visibly corrupt Palestinian Authority had lost legitimacy. Years of humiliation at the hands of successive Israeli governments plus the failure to deliver material improvements had eroded his personal popularity among Palestinians. The growth and popularity of other groups, particularly Hamas, had accelerated. Arafat would not have lasted a week

---

[13] Barack Obama, "Renewing American Leadership," *Foreign Affairs,* July/August 2007, http://www.foreignaffairs.org/20070701faessay86401-p10/barack-obama/renewing -american-leadership.html [1-24-2009].

[14] "President Obama's First Phone Call Was to President Abbas," *Times* (London), January 22, 2009, http://www.timesonline.co.uk/tol/news/world/us_and_americas/us_elections/ article5563280.ece [02-02-2009].

[15] Charles Lane, "A Parting Shot That Maligns Obama, Too," *Washington Post,* March 15, 2009.

[16] See Charles M. Sennott and Charles A. Radin, "Arafat Illness Spurs Struggle for Influence: Key Palestinians Jockey over Possible Successors," *Boston Globe,* November 5, 1004, http://www.boston.com/news/world/articles/2004/11/05/arafat_illness_spurs_struggle_for_ influence?pg=full [05-05-2006].

in Palestinian politics had he signed at Camp David in 2000.[17] Unlike the situation during and after Oslo, there was no coalition of powerful Palestinian constituencies committed to the success of Camp David. Groups whose support was necessary to sell any agreement had become disbelievers, convinced that Israel would neither sign a fair agreement nor implement what it signed. Palestinian negotiators, with one eye on the summit and another back home, went to Camp David almost apologetically, determined to demonstrate that this time they would not be duped.[18]

By the time of the 2006 elections Hamas had become a well-organized, pragmatic political movement. A number of its leaders were clearly looking for a deal and even sought to prove themselves better negotiating partners with Israel than the PLO. Abu Tayyar, number two on the Hamas electoral list, was unequivocal: "We'll negotiate [with Israel] better than the others, who negotiated for 10 years and achieved nothing."[19] It would have made better sense to let them succeed, thereby marginalizing the more militant elements who had no interest in a settlement.

Of course few Palestinians—including Hamas supporters—expected that Hamas would sweep the January 2006 elections so completely. In elections that saw nearly 75 percent turnout, voting for 414 candidates and 11 electoral lists, Hamas gained a resounding victory: 74 of the 132 seats, compared to the 45 won by Fatah. Hamas won only 44 percent of the popular vote, gaining a disproportionate number of seats because of Fatah's fragmentation.[20] As 2009 wore on, Hamas lost some of the very high levels of popular support it had achieved following its success against the Israeli invasion in January of that year, and Fatah gained some prestige from its successful conference in August. But none of this changed the obvious reality that Hamas could not be defeated and it could not be ignored. While neither Israel nor the United States would admit this publicly, it was clearly understood in Israeli intelligence and military circles that "there is no obvious alternative to continued Hamas rule in Gaza."[21]

[17] See our discussion in chapter 3, pp. 110–14.

[18] Hussein Agha and Robert Malley, "Camp David: The Tragedy of Errors," *New York Review of Books*, July 12, 2001, http://www.nybooks.com/articles/archives/2001/aug/09/camp-david-the-tragedy-of-errors/?pagination=false [06-25-2010].

[19] He continued: "In the past, it was said that we don't understand politics, only force, but we are a broad, well-grounded movement that is active in all areas of life. Now we are proving that we also understand politics better than the others. . . . We are not saying 'never.' The question of negotiations will be presented to the new parliament and, as with every issue, when we reach the parliament it will be discussed and decided in a rational manner." Abu Tayyar, quoted in "Enter Hamas: The Challenges of Political Integration," ICG Middle East Report No. 49 (January 18, 2006): 21–22.

[20] Khalil Shikaki, "Results of PSR's PLC Exit Poll," February 15, 2006, p. 1, Palestine Center for Policy and Survey Research, www.pcpsr.org [12-24-2009].

[21] See Howard Schneider, "What to Do with Hamas?" *Washington Post*, October 7, 2009, http://www.washingtonpost.com/wp-dyn/content/article/2009/10/06/AR2009100602146.html [10-07-2009].

Attempts by the United States, Israel, and the Fatah-led PA to isolate or eliminate Hamas have not only been unsuccessful, but they have also led to missed opportunities. In the early months after Hamas's 2006 election victory, Alvaro de Soto (former under-secretary-general, United Nations special coordinator for the Middle East peace process, and personal representative of the secretary-general to the PLO) argued that a national unity government was possible. The problem, he noted, was that the United States led the Quartet "to set impossible demands, and opposed the national unity government in principle."[22] Rather than support the establishment of a national unity government, which would have reflected the relative parity of Hamas and Fatah and provided a platform for compromise, Israel and the United States attempted to reverse Hamas's victory. They cut off aid to Hamas-controlled areas while supporting Fatah, in a vain attempt to build their popularity.

Ramping up sanctions and targeting the Palestinian population within Hamas-controlled territory made life for Gazans ever more desolate. As the director of the UN's Relief and Works Agency operations in the Gaza Strip noted, "While the imprisonment and impoverishment of the civilian population in Gaza [was] not the publicly stated policy objective, it [was] nonetheless its principal effect." By summer 2008, 90 percent of Gaza's industrial companies had closed their doors, leaving more than eighty thousand Gazans without jobs and 80 percent of the population below the poverty line. Shortages of fuel and other supplies stalled transportation, diminished water supplies, made garbage collection impossible, left schoolchildren without books, and fostered inflation.[23] Many Gazans did indeed start blaming Hamas for their difficulties.[24] Yet, while their public support was souring, Hamas's political and military position remained strong. Control over tunnels, employment, and ever-scarce resources continued to strengthen them. By taking the political options off the table for Hamas and threatening their viability as a fledgling government that could serve its citizens, Israel and the United States were cornering Hamas. If political success was not going to be an option, like any national liberation movement Hamas would revert to military options. It cannot be surprising that Hamas responded to this situation with force.

[22] Alvaro de Soto, "End of Mission Report," May 2007, par. 55, http://image.guardian.co.uk/sys-files/Guardian/documents/2007/06/12/DeSotoReport.pdf [06-14-2007].

[23] John Ging, director UNRWA Operations Gaza, "The Humanitarian Emergency in Gaza: 'A Shocking and Shameful Situation,'" Testimony to the International Development Committee House of Commons, April 30, 2008, http://www.un.org/unrwa/news/statements/DUO/HumanEmer_30Apr08.html [01-23-2009].

[24] Palestine Center for Policy and Social Research, "Palestinian Public Opinion Poll No. 28," June 12, 2008, http://www.pcpsr.org/survey/polls/2008/p28e.html#head4 [01-23-2009]; JMCC, "JMCC Public Opinion Poll No. 66, November 2008," http://www.jmcc.org/publicpoll/results/2008/no66-eng.pdf [01-23-2009].

Stopping Hamas from governing would in any case have been a tall order, and Operation Lead only increased Hamas's legitimacy and heightened the challenge.[25] Within days of Israel's withdrawal, Khaled Meshaal was claiming that "the Gaza Strip has scored a victory. The enemy has failed and the resistance, together with our people and nation, has scored a victory."[26] Such crowing may seem at first a stark contrast with his subsequent appeals to join negotiations—and indeed, support for Hamas has diminished somewhat, as we have noted. Yet the fundamental lesson remains clear. Hamas's resistance in Gaza demonstrated that they have the ability to undermine or support a settlement. Just as Sadat had done in the 1973 War, Hamas showed it can inflict costs on Israel. By the same token, it can play a key role in any lasting settlement. Hamas might not be as popular as the ANC became in the 1970s and 1980s in South Africa, but it is too powerful to ignore.[27]

SETTING PRECONDITIONS

Insisting that adversaries must accept specific conditions before negotiations can take place—to bring them back from beyond the pale—is no less destructive than attempting to exclude potential veto players before negotiations. Preconditions can include publicly accepting the other side's legitimacy; ending and renouncing violence; decommissioning arms; agreeing in advance to certain features of a final agreement (or at least

[25] In the short run, the war increased Hamas's legitimacy and popular support. Israeli analyst Aluf Benn was correct when he noted at the start of the war that a draw would enhance Hamas's legitimacy. Griff Witte and Jonathan Finer, "Battered Gaza Still in the Grip of Hamas: Islamist Group Retains Strength Despite War," *Washington Post*, January 24, 2009, p. A07, http://www.washingtonpost.com/wp-dyn/content/story/2009/01/23/ST2009012303518. html [01-24-2009]. See also Palestinian Center for Policy and Survey Research, "Palestinian Public Opinion Poll No. 31," March 9, 2009, http://www.pcpsr.org/survey/polls/2009/p31epressrelease.html [03-24-2009]. Aluf Benn, "No Quick Fix in Sight," *Haaretz*, January 3, 2009, http://www.haaretz.com/hasen/spages/1052027.html [01-05-09].

[26] "Hamas Leader Urges West to Talk," BBC News, January 21, 2009, http://news.bbc.co.uk/2/hi/middle_east/7843465.stm [01-22-2009]. See also "Israel's Offensive a Holocaust: Mishal," *Gulf Times*, January 11, 2009, http://www.gulf-times.com/site/topics/article.asp?cu_no=2&item_no=265904&version=1&template_id=57# [03-22-2009].

[27] Other commentators who have reached this conclusion include Nathan Brown and Michael Thomas, "What to Make of Hamas, Part III," *Council for National Interest*, July 31, 2009, http://www.cnionline.org/what-to-make-of-hamas-part-iii/ [10-02-2009], and Nathan Brown, "The Green Elephant in the Room: Dealing with the Hamas Party-State in Gaza," *Carnegie Endowment Web Commentary*, June 2009, https://www.carnegieendowment.org/publications/index.cfm?fa=view&id=23225 [10-02-2009], and "Palestine: The Schism Deepens," *Carnegie Endowment Web Commentary*, August 20, 2009, http://www.carnegieendowment.org/publications/index.cfm?fa=view&id=23668 [10-02-2009].

agreeing to take specified demands off the table); and agreeing to a date by which negotiations must be concluded. It is no surprise that both sides seek such preconditions to provide themselves safety nets, assure nervous constituencies, and shape eventual outcomes. Tempting as insisting on preconditions often is, doing so ignores the reality that preconditions are welcome targets for players on both sides who oppose negotiations to scuttle them.

Since assuming office President Obama has repeatedly insisted on preconditions for involving Hamas in peace negotiations. At the same time as he acknowledged Hamas's support on the ground in a speech in Cairo in June 2009, Obama argued that "to play a role" Hamas must "put an end to violence, recognize past agreements, recognize Israel's right to exist."[28] Secretary of State Hillary Clinton has also embraced this approach, declaring that "until Hamas renounce[es] terrorism and recognizes Israel, negotiating with Hamas is unacceptable for the United States."[29]

This logic might seem sound, but it does not work. When negotiations are accompanied by preconditions, spoilers on both sides violate the conditions, preventing settlements. Former South African president F. W. de Klerk spelled out why when interviewed about the success of his negotiated settlement with the African National Congress between 1990 and 1992.[30] De Klerk pointed out that in early 1990, when the South African government unbanned the African National Congress, released all political prisoners, and undertook to negotiate a settlement, this was done without preconditions of any kind. Specifically, the ANC was not required to recognize the legitimacy of the apartheid state or the National Party government, or to renounce violence.

Three months later, the ANC leadership also acted unconditionally to suspend its armed struggle and begin negotiating a transition to democracy with the government. The two sides had incompatible ideas about what this would mean, with the government committed to constitutionally mandated power sharing and the ANC standing firm for an "ordinary democracy." Both sides insisted to the media and their own constituencies that these were nonnegotiable, but they negotiated nonetheless. And although the government periodically demanded that the ANC decommission its military wing, Umkhonto we Sizwe, Nelson Mandela's refusal to do this never ended negotiations. Even when the roundtable talks involving all "stakeholders" were torpedoed by white extremists who op-

---

[28] "Obama Calls for End to 'Cycle of Suspicion and Discord' and 'a New Beginning,'" *New York Times*, June 5, 2009.

[29] Hillary Clinton, "Clinton's Remarks to the AIPAC Conference," Real Clear Politics, June 4, 2008, http://www.realclearpolitics.com/articles/2008/06/clintons_remarks_to_the_aipac.html [01-23-2009].

[30] F. W. de Klerk, interview with Ian Shapiro, Cape Town. December 9, 2003.

posed a democratic transition, and by the ethnic Zulu Inkatha Freedom Party, whose leaders hoped for a partition in which they would control the eastern part of the country, the government and the ANC continued secret negotiations until they reached their now famous settlement.

Insisting on preconditions for negotiations, which both Israel and the United States have done since the mid-1990s, has led to a series of missed opportunities and strengthened the hands of those elements within Hamas who oppose a settlement. By the same token, it has been no less shortsighted for both the PLO and Hamas leaderships to refuse to negotiate with Israel's Netanyahu government on the grounds that the two-state solution he finally proposed in June 2009 includes what for them are unacceptable features—notably that the Palestinian state would be demilitarized, and that its leaders must abandon any claims by Palestinians to right of return to the Israeli state. To insist that Israel discard these positions before talks can begin is, in effect, to create preconditions from the other side.

Again the South African example is instructive. In late 1991 and early 1992 F. W. de Klerk lost a series of by-elections to the Hard Right, whose attacks on him intensified as his not-so-secret bilateral talks with the ANC became common knowledge. De Klerk responded by calling a snap referendum on the question whether to negotiate a settlement, which he won resoundingly. At the time the ANC heaped scorn on the referendum as one more meaningless "whites only" vote. They also declared it to be an irrelevant sideshow because de Klerk insisted throughout the referendum campaign that he would never give away constitutionally mandated power sharing—which the ANC regarded as unacceptable. Nonetheless, the ANC continued negotiating, and, though they accepted constitutionally mandated power sharing in the interim constitution, they got the National Party to abandon it in the negotiations on the final constitution. Mandela was astute enough to grasp that constitutionally mandated power sharing was the Afrikaners' Jerusalem in 1992. It was unthinkable for them to give it up, and de Klerk needed it to bring his constituencies to the negotiating table.

A large part of the art of negotiation involves finding ways of rendering the unthinkable thinkable, as this example underscores. What many saw as a major deal-breaker in 1992 turned out to be a comparatively minor bump in the road. The disappearance of communism from the agenda, the ANC's agreement to an amnesty process (that later became famous), the experienced benefits of no longer being an international pariah, and the mere passage of time without catastrophic breakdown helped white South Africans realize that strict majority rule was much more likely to give them Brazil than Cuba. Unthinkable as giving away mandated power sharing was in 1992, that concession pales by comparison with the National Party's choice twelve years later to put itself out of business by joining the ANC.[31] You could have gotten pretty good odds against that in 1996.

A moral of this story for the contemporary Middle East is that political adversaries should never ossify stumbling blocks, either by refusing to negotiate on account of them or by issuing ultimatums and other preconditions that invariably become targets for spoilers. Netanyahu's June 2009 move to offer a demilitarized Palestinian state was quickly, and predictably, dismissed as a cynical ploy both by Palestinians and by right-wing Israeli politicians like Tzipi Livni.[32] They might well have been right, but that is not a reason to avoid calling his bluff by moving forward.

Likewise with the Netanyahu government's continued defiance of Palestinian, U.S., and world opinion on settlement building. The Obama administration made a substantial error in visibly demanding a settlement freeze and then no less visibly backing down when Netanyahu, in the fall of 2009, first insisted on "natural" growth and then authorized hundreds of new settlements.[33] The administration was right not to allow the settlements to impede talks, and it should continue to resist Mahmoud Abbas's attempt to turn the freeze into a precondition for talks.[34] But the United States should have been applying massive and consistent pressure on the Netanyahu government—withholding aid and opening the door to sanctions—to get Israel to abandon the settlement policy that clearly renders an eventual agreement ever more difficult to achieve.

We cannot know whether de Klerk's insistence that he would never move on power sharing was a cynical ploy to snooker his right flank or something he sincerely believed at the time; in the end it does not matter much. The more consequential point is that it moved the negotiations forward in ways that changed the reality on the ground irreversibly. As we saw in chapter 3, many other things had to happen as well for the

---

[31] Basildon Peta, "Party of Apartheid Merges with ANC," *Independent*, August 9, 2004, http://www.independent.co.uk/news/world/africa/party-of-apartheid-merges-with-anc-555878.html [07-09-2009].

[32] See "Netanyahu's Announcement Seen by Many as Major Reversal, but Swiftly Rejected by Palestinians," CBS World, July 14, 2009, http://www.cbsnews.com/stories/2009/06/14/world/main5087808.shtml [07-10-2009], and "Netanyahu Not after Two States: Livni," PressTV, July 6, 2009, http://presstv.com/detail.aspx?id=99975&sectionid=351020202 [07-10-2009].

[33] Matthew Lee, "US Seen Easing Israeli Settlement Demands," Associated Press, August 27, 2009, http://www.google.com/hostednews/ap/article/ALeqM5hd9kAxAmPQiepMZBmilJL5AMwbnwD9ABG7Q80 [09-07-2009].

[34] "No Talks without Full Settlement Freeze: Abbas Aide," Reuters, August 31, 2009, http://www.reuters.com/article/worldNews/idUSTRE57U1W420090831 [09-07-2009]; "Abbas Says Israel Freeze of Settlements a Must," *New York Times*, September 25, 2009, http://www.nytimes.com/reuters/2009/09/25/world/international-uk-un-assembly-abbas.html [09-25-09].

South African agreement to be consummated—any number of which might have gone awry. There are many more ways for negotiations to break down than for them to succeed. But without steps of this kind—by their nature into the dark—failure is assured. Whatever their histories and motives might be, players who take such steps begin opening windows of opportunity. Whether they prove willing or able to step through them is another matter, but even if in the end they do not, perhaps someone else will replace them—someone who turns out to have the motive and the means to do so.

REASON FOR HOPE?

By 2009 Hamas had for some time been calling for negotiations and suggesting its willingness to accept a settlement along the lines of a two-state solution. The question was whether a settlement was possible. Many remained skeptical, arguing that—despite Hamas's rhetoric—nothing had changed. Yet there were good reasons to think this skepticism was debatable, if not misplaced.

Continuing efforts to compromise Hamas's ability to govern will surely be counterproductive. In the aftermath of the 2008–9 war, Hamas again signed up to a one-year truce, this time brokered by Egypt.[35] They have since sought to restrain more militant forces, halting rocket attacks on Israel.[36] Most notably, Hamas leaders are now calling openly to be included in negotiations, signaling their willingness to accept a two-state solution. The United States and Israel should take advantage of this opportunity.

Israel's failure to destroy the Hamas leadership might be a plus for implementing an eventual agreement. If and when the possibility of a settlement emerges, leaderships on both sides will have to be strong enough to face down rejectionists and implement the settlement. Hamas demonstrated its ability to do this during the 2008 cease-fire. In the four months between July and October of that year, Hamas reined in rogue groups and all but stopped missile attacks. According to Israeli government statistics, only twenty missiles were launched from Gaza in that period.[37]

[35] "Hamas Agrees to Year Long Gaza Truce from Thursday," *Haaretz*, February 2, 2009, http://www.haaretz.com/hasen/spages/1060589.html [02-02-2009].

[36] Ali Waked, "Sources in Gaza Say Group Wants to Show Control in Region, Not Escalate Situation While Negotiations Ongoing," *Ynetnews*, March 5, 2009, at http://www.ynetnews.com/articles/0,7340,L-3681908,00.html [03-22-2009].

[37] "The Hamas Terrorist War against Israel," Israeli Ministry of Foreign Affairs, January 1, 2009, http://www.mfa.gov.il/MFA/Terrorism-+Obstacle+to+Peace/Palestinian+terror+since+2000/Missile+fire+from+Gaza+on+Israeli+civilian+targets+Aug+2007.htm [01-25-2009].

Israel was to have eased the blockade in response, but the government refused.[38] This led to mutual escalation, marked by increased violence on both sides, and the failure to renew the cease-fire in December.[39]

The Obama administration must recognize that a settlement between Israel and the Palestinians will come only if the United States takes the lead in pressing for negotiations among the critical players. We have to work with adversaries who have signaled an interest in a settlement, and who have a realistic chance of delivering one. This is far more important than spelling out what the terms of the settlement will be, which the United States should actively refrain from doing. Selecting partners because they seem benign to us, or malleable to our purposes, invariably fails. In Gaza and the West Bank, Fatah unquestionably lost the 2006 elections to Hamas. Since that time, Washington and Tel Aviv have behaved as if this were a "problem" that could be "fixed," first by undermining the possibility of a national unity government and then by strangling Hamas and bolstering Fatah. The Gaza invasion was the logical conclusion to this self-defeating strategy. Three days after the Israeli withdrawal from Gaza, the Associated Press was reporting that Palestinians had reopened tunnels for weapons smuggling, and Hamas had begun distributing new aid to its beleaguered population.[40] It is clear that Israel cannot achieve peace, or even victory, by eliminating Hamas. They must negotiate with the very party that they insist is "the enemy of peace in the region."[41]

[38] "Trapped: Collective Punishment in Gaza," Amnesty International. August 27, 2008, http://www.amnesty.org/en/news-and-updatesfeature-stories/trapped-collective-punishment-gaza-20080827 [01-25-2009]. "Israel and the Occupied Palestinian Territory," Amnesty International Submission to the UN Universal Periodic Review, December 1–12, 2008, http://www.amnesty.org/en/library/asset/MDE15/029/2008/en/55336154-59a1-11dd-bc96-55b5ceea4018/mde150292008eng.html [01-25-2009].

[39] Steve Weizman, "Hamas Formally Suspends Truce: Gazans Accuse Israel of Breaches; 2 Sides Trade Fire," *Washington Post*, December 20, 2008, p. A1, http://www.washingtonpost.com/wp-dyn/content/article/2008/12/19/AR2008121903265.html [01-25-2009].

[40] Isabel Kershner, "Hamas to Start Paying Gaza Residents Compensation and Reconstruction Aid," *New York Times*, January 23, 2009, http://www.nytimes.com/2009/01/23/world/middleeast/23mideast.html?emc=eta1 [01-23-2009]; Alfred deMontesquiou, "Gaza Tunnels Back in Business," Associated Press, January 22, 2009, http://www.google.com/hostednews/ap/article/ALeqM5gI3mvb6-rK7nAuNIXPLr-sl0nDngD95S8RMG0 [01-23-2009].

[41] Foreign Minister Tzipi Livni, cited by Barak Ravid, "Olmert to Clinton: Israel Will Do All It Can to Prevent Gaza Smuggling," *Haaretz,* January 22, 2009, http://www.haaretz.com/hasen/spages/1057898.html [01-23-2009].

CHAPTER FIVE

Containment and Democratic Cosmopolitanism

THE ARGUMENT OF THE previous chapter was well summed up by John F. Kennedy in his inaugural address: "Let us never negotiate out of fear, but let us never fear to negotiate."[1] As President Kennedy's dictum emphasizes, willingness to negotiate should not be confused with weakness in the face of threatening opponents. Readiness to do what is needed to prevail against potentially catastrophic threats has to be part of any country's approach to international politics, but, as Kennedy showed in his handling of the Cuban missile crisis, it is vital to do this without escalating conflicts unnecessarily. Kennedy acted decisively to contain the threat, ramping up a quarantine against Cuba while reserving the option of an armed response as his strategy of last resort. We now know how lucky the world is that Kennedy, chastened by the disastrous advice he had received from his generals the previous year advocating the Bay of Pigs invasion, rejected the advice of his Joint Chiefs for a preemptive strike against Cuba in 1962. The Soviet forces already there had tactical nuclear weapons with orders to use them to repel any invasion. This would likely have sparked a superpower nuclear exchange, given the prevailing rules of engagement.[2]

The idea of containment as the basis of national security was initially developed by George Kennan, a career foreign service diplomat and then director of the Policy Planning Staff for President Truman, in response to the emerging Soviet threat after World War II. Kennan's argument was spelled out in "The Sources of Soviet Conduct," published in *Foreign Affairs* in 1947, signed by "X," but widely known as his work.[3] It provided the core ideas that structured U.S. national security policy in dealing with the Soviets during the Cold War. Kennan held that containing the Soviet Union until its dysfunctional economy and unsustainable global ambitions led it to implode would be sufficient to protect the United States and its allies, a view that was widely seen as vindicated by the end of the Cold

---

[1] John F. Kennedy, "Inaugural Address," January 21, 1961, http://www.bartleby.com/124/pres56.html [07-22-2009].

[2] See Arthur Schlesinger, Jr., "Bush's Thousand Days," *Washington Post*, April 24, 2006, p. A17.

[3] X, "The Sources of Soviet Conduct," *Foreign Affairs*, July 1947, www.foreignaffairs.org/19470701faessay25403-p0/x/the-sources-of-soviet-conduct.html [12-23-2009].

War. But after the 9/11 attacks the Bush administration declared containment obsolete in the face of global terrorist threats, likening its defenders to appeasers, just as John Foster Dulles and Dwight Eisenhower had done in attacking the original containment doctrine in the early 1950s. The Bush administration instead proposed a doctrine of aggressive unilateralism and preemptive war, which they used to justify the U.S. invasion of Iraq in the spring of 2003.

In 2007 I published *Containment: Rebuilding a Strategy against Global Terror*, in which I argued that they were wrong, and showed how and why containment should be adapted to the threats faced by the United States in the post–Cold War world.[4] My goal in this chapter is to build on the argument of that book and put forward a more general defense of containment as the national security policy of choice for cosmopolitan democrats. I take *cosmopolitan democrats* to be people who are committed to the view that democracy is the best system of government, and who favor its preservation and diffusion around the world. I develop this argument from an American perspective, but it could equally be developed from that of any other democracy.

Whereas Kennan was interested in containment as a response to the threat posed to the United States by the Soviet Union, mine is a more general account of the presumptive policy for dealing with the violent threats democracies face in the post–Cold War world. This changed context entails some differences with Kennan on how best to go about containment, though there are also surprising continuities with his views. In what follows I develop the theoretical underpinnings of my account more fully than I did in the book. I also meet the objection that containment takes an unjust nation-state system, from which the United States has derived ill-gotten gains, for granted—and might even help perpetuate it.

Some equate the commitment to cosmopolitan democracy with the project of creating a world government. In part 1, I take up, and dispatch, the three main arguments that have been put forward in support of world government: those based on claims about the nature of public coercion, those that appeal to observations about the moral arbitrariness of the existing division of the world into nation-states, and those rooted in the principle of affected interest—the idea that one's right to a say in a decision should be based on the importance of the interest that one has at stake. I turn to containment's normative basis in part 2, where I expound upon containment's elective affinity with the democratic principle of nondomination. This leads to a discussion, in part 3, of the pros and

---

[4] Ian Shapiro, *Containment: Rebuilding a Strategy against Global Terror* (Princeton: Princeton University Press, 2007).

cons of democratization through forcible regime change, where I make the case that this can be justified only in a highly restricted set of circumstances of the sort presented by Japan and Germany after World War II. In most circumstances, including those embroiling the United States in the Middle East during much of the first decade of the twenty-first century, the nature of democratic legitimacy makes external imposition inescapably problematic.

In part 4, on global containment, I show why, in the age of rogue regimes, weak states, and mobile terrorist threats, containment requires cooperation with other states and legitimation through international institutions. This falls notably short of the idea of world government discussed earlier, though it involves steps in the direction of strengthening the international rule of law. In parts 5 and 6, I take up the argument that containment is objectionable on the grounds that it legitimates a status quo that incorporates the ill-gotten gains of the containing power. Compelling as such arguments about ill-gotten gains concededly are, I argue that they do not dethrone containment as the national security policy of choice for cosmopolitan democrats. Better than the going alternatives, containment fits with the imperatives of governments to protect their populations, preserve existing democratic institutions, and support the diffusion of democratic values and practices around the world.

1. Cosmopolitanism and World Government

Some will question why a committed cosmopolitan democrat should defend any *national* security policy. Should our cosmopolitanism not commit us instead to the creation of a global democracy that would render any account of the appropriate relations among states beside the point, if not already obsolete? Not necessarily, or so I argue here. A cosmopolitan commitment to democracy does involve endorsing the view that democracy is the best system of government, and supporting democracy's spread across the globe, but it is a huge leap from embracing this commitment to arguing for a world government. Making the latter move is neither desirable nor feasible, as one can see by examining the main arguments that have been put forward in support of world government.

One argument is connected only indirectly to democratic government. It turns on a claim about the nature of coercive force. Its logic was most clearly spelled out by Robert Nozick in his discussion of the emergence of unified national governments. Nozick's key claim was that coercive force is a natural monopoly. Accordingly, he argued that, within a given territorial area, competing enforcement authorities cannot coexist in equilibrium. Eventually, one will either wipe out or co-opt the others.[5] The survivor will then be a Weberian state—one that monopolizes the legitimate use of force within a given territory.

Why is this relevant to democratic world government? The reason is suggested by the historical democratization of nation-states. Perry Anderson established long ago that what we now think of as the developed countries of Europe did not move from feudalism to democracy, but rather from feudalism to absolutism to democracy.[6] Other scholars, prominent among them David Held, have detailed the process whereby the centralization of power within nation-states came before their democratization.[7] It is the concentration of authority that motivates the democratic project. Held has suggested elsewhere that, at a minimum, advancing the cause of global democracy would require creation of a global rule of law via an international *rechtsstaat* for analogous reasons.[8] Pressing the analogy to the formation of national democracies seems to suggest the necessity for a world state to make the international *rechtsstaat* a practical reality.

Nozick was not thinking about world government, but, if his argument is valid, an obvious question to ask is, why is there not a world government now? Nation-states are the global analogues of his competing mutual protection associations within a given territory. The Nozickian global expectation should therefore be that one nation would eventually co-opt or edge out the others, yet it fails to happen.

Nozick's answer would presumably involve reference to available technologies of force. As their geographical reach expands, the relevant territorial area over which a monopoly can be exercised grows with it. World government has not arrived yet, but, on this telling, we will move steadily toward it as weapons too powerful to be ignored can more easily be delivered anywhere in the world. Presumably it was reasoning of this sort that Bertrand Russell had in mind in 1947 when he pushed for

---

[5] Robert Nozick, *Anarchy, State and Utopia* (New York: Basic Books, 1974), pp. 54–119.

[6] Perry Anderson, *Lineages of the Absolutist State* (London: Schocken Books, 1979).

[7] David Held, *Democracy and the Global Order: From the Modern State to Cosmopolitan Governance* (Cambridge: Polity Press, 1995). This does not mean, of course, that centralized authoritarian states necessarily democratize as the modernization theorists believed. See Seymour Martin Lipset, "Some Social Requisites of Democracy: Economic Development and Political Legitimacy," *American Political Science Review* 53, no. 1 (1959): 69–105, and David Apter, *The Politics of Modernization* (Chicago: University of Chicago Press, 1967). Just as authoritarian regimes can survive in national states, the same problem might arise with a world state.

[8] David Held, "The Transformation of Political Community: Rethinking Democracy in the Context of Globalization," in*Democracy's Edges*, ed. Ian Shapiro and Casiano Hacker-Cordón (Cambridge: Cambridge University Press, 1999), pp. 84–111.

the United States to declare a world government following its first use of nuclear weapons against Japan.[9]

But the Russell-Nozick story lacks plausibility, at least without large qualifications that would leave us scant reason to anticipate world government's arising from the feasible worldwide deployment of lethal force any time soon. For one thing, the existence of a lethal weapon that can technically be deployed anywhere does not mean that it is practically deployable. Proliferation of such weapons might make the costs of deploying them too high, given the retaliatory possibilities. Hence the logic of Mutually Assured Destruction that gave rise to deterrence during the Cold War.

Of course Russell's argument anticipated that. His premise was that the United States should take advantage of the window of opportunity created by America's nuclear monopoly after the bombing of Hiroshima and Nagasaki precisely because that monopoly would otherwise be temporary. "It is obvious," Russell insisted, "that the only way in which war can be permanently prevented is the creation of a single government for the whole world, possessed of all the more powerful weapons of war." In order to do its job, the world government would have to be "irresistible; even the greatest of separate powers should be incapable of fighting against it with any hope of success." Limiting the development of nuclear weapons should therefore not be part of the agenda. "The more deadly are the weapons monopolized by the international authority, the more obvious will be its capacity to enforce its will, and the less will be the likelihood of resistance to its decrees."[10]

But Russell offered no mechanism through which a nuclear monopoly might be translated into a world government. He conflated overwhelming military superiority with the capacity to achieve day-to-day control of populations. The Vietnam War made it plain that there is a vast difference between the two, even if the Soviet experience in Afghanistan and the post-2002 U.S. experience there and in Iraq reveal governments to be slow learners of this lesson. If the most powerful country on earth declared itself a world government, conflicts currently labeled as wars might be relabeled as insurgencies or civil wars—but there is no reason to suppose that there would be fewer conflicts or that they would be any less deadly.

The Russell-Nozick view also ignores many economies of smallness in enforcement. Perhaps some combination of increases in surveillance and enforcement will make a worldwide *Nineteen Eighty-Four* scenario feasi-

---

[9] Bertrand Russell, *Towards World Government* (London: Thorney House, 1947).
[10] Ibid., p. 5.

ble some day, but we are a long way away from that. As the literature on community policing reveals, effective law enforcement depends vitally on local knowledge and relationships.[11] This is essential for generating relevant information, but also for the perceived legitimacy of enforcement. As Fernand Braudel, James Scott, and others have pointed out, often the state's monopoly is incomplete and its legitimacy is at least questioned by significant sectors of the population.[12] Without that legitimacy, subject populations can be expected to defect—either through crime or by reaching for such weapons of the weak as terrorism. In short, it is doubtful that coercive force *is* a natural monopoly, and correspondingly dubious that its evolution will or should drive the world in the direction of a single government.[13]

A different argument for world government appeals to norms about legitimacy. The starting point here is the arbitrary division of the world into nation-states. Countries have been forged by wars and other historical accidents, with a huge proportion of the world's power and wealth residing in the hands of the small number of people who inhabit the strongest and richest nations. The vast majority of the world's population is effectively excluded from these resources. It is a system of global apartheid. None of the going conceptions of legitimacy plausibly lend themselves to its defense. Various fictions about social contracts are just that, since no nation has actually been ushered into existence by a consensual agreement.[14] Nor have democratic procedures been followed in

---

[11] See David Thacher, "Conflicting Values in Community Policing," *Law and Society Review* 33, no. 4 (2001),: 765–98, and Archon Fung, *Empowered Participation: Reinventing Urban Democracy* (Princeton: Princeton University Press, 2004).

[12] See Fernand Braudel, *The Mediterranean and the Mediterranean World in the Age of Philip II*, vol. 1 (Berkeley and Los Angeles: University of California Press, 1996), pp. 53–59, and *The Perspective of the World: Civilization and Capitalism, 15th to 18th Century*, vol. 3 (New York: Harper and Row, 1984); and James Scott, *Weapons of the Weak* (New Haven: Yale University Press, 1985), and *Domination and the Arts of Resistance* (New Haven: Yale University Press, 1990).

[13] Even in the United States, groups like the Amish have often managed to defy the will of the state with respect to their educational practices. For decades before the famous *Wisconsin v. Yoder* 406 US 205 (1972) litigation local authorities had all but given up trying to enforce mandatory high school education on them. The *Yoder* litigation came about only as a by-product of a school rationalization plan in Wisconsin that had nothing to do with the Amish. See Richard Arneson and Ian Shapiro, "Democratic Autonomy and Religious Freedom: A Critique of *Wisconsin v. Yoder*," in Ian Shapiro, *Democracy's Place* (Ithaca: Cornell University Press, 1996), pp. 137–74.

[14] See Thomas Pogge, *Realizing Rawls* (Ithaca: Cornell University Press, 1989); Charles Beitz, *Political Theory and International Relations* (Princeton: Princeton University Press, 1999).

the manufacture of any nation.[15] Utilitarianism is notoriously at odds with the nation-state-based distribution of power and resources in the world.[16] In sum, no good arguments have been put forward to justify this massively unequal system.

If we concede this last claim, *arguendo*, it scarcely amounts to a case for world government. Distributive injustice among people inhabiting different nations should be redressed, to be sure, because justice is predicated of individuals—not of states. But abolishing nation-states in favor of world government is not a plausible path to advance toward this destination. Massive, and sometimes even increasing, inequalities persist within nation-states—including those with democratic political systems based on a universal franchise. Why this happens is a continuing puzzle for political economists.[17] Whatever the explanation for the maldistribution, it seems implausible that creating a worldwide polity would do anything to alleviate it. On the contrary, the enforcement difficulties and collective action obstacles to change within so large an entity would likely multiply.

Sometimes the arbitrariness objection is not about access to economic resources so much as to the distribution of citizenship itself. Why should the accidents of birth privilege some to be citizens in benign countries while others are condemned to live where life is nasty, brutish, and short? Why should the former get the windfalls associated with belonging to one country while the latter suffer the costs of another? If the claim here is really about the maldistribution of life chances associated with different citizenships, then considerations like those just adduced about economic resources apply: there is no better reason to suppose that a move to world government would reduce the maldistribution of noneconomic factors that influence life chances than that it would reduce the maldistribution of economic resources.

There is, in any case, something of a non sequitur involved in moving from the premise of different advantages stemming from different citizenships to the conclusion that national citizenship should be abolished. It is a bit like saying that because some people have better eyesight than others, the world would be a better place if everyone were rendered

---

[15] See Ian Shapiro and Casiano Hacker-Cordón, "Outer Edges and Inner Edges," in *Democracy's Edges*, ed. Ian Shapiro and Casiano Hacker-Cordón (Cambridge: Cambridge University Press, 1999), pp. 1–15.

[16] See Shelly Kagan, *The Limits of Morality* (Oxford: Oxford University Press, 1991), and Peter Singer, *One World: The Ethics of Globalization* (New Haven: Yale University Press, 2004).

[17] For a review of the literature see Ian Shapiro, *The State of Democratic Theory* (Princeton: Princeton University Press, 2005), pp. 104–45.

blind. The existence of different national citizenships with differing values might support an argument for the most liberal sustainable immigration policies, or for compensation of those with less desirable national citizenships by those with more desirable ones, but not for the abolition of national citizenship as such. To establish the desirability of *that*, one would have to carry the additional burden of showing that people would actually be better served by being global citizens only.

If, however, the argument really is about the objectionability of the very idea of national citizenship (as distinct from benefits or costs instrumentally associated with it), it is unclear just what the basis for the objection is. Citizenship in anything short of a world state involves exclusion of some, to be sure, but exclusion is not by itself objectionable. Unrequited love leads to exclusion, but it is a form of exclusion that we routinely expect people to accept. One might say that exclusion from a civic status is different, but it is unclear why. More than two decades ago Michael Walzer made a compelling case that it is not the unequal distribution of a good as such that is objectionable, but rather the translation of that inequality into the wherewithal to dominate others.[18] If this translatability were absent from national citizenship, it would be hard to make the case that nations are illegitimate, or that they should not be free to create and enforce exclusive forms of citizenship. It is the translatability of national citizenship into instruments of domination that is objectionable, not national citizenship as such.

These considerations suggest a third rationale for world government, one that appeals to the principle of affected interest. Democratic legitimacy is rooted in the notion that the people affected by a decision should have a say in making it. One reason why national decision making can be troubling is that so often it operates at variance with this principle. In an increasingly global economy, decisions about trade, employment, fiscal, and monetary policy in one country have huge ramifications for people who live elsewhere. This is not to mention the spillover effects of environmental degradation, natural resource depletion, and military adventures. As power is increasingly exercised on a global basis, the need to harness its exercise through global institutions becomes stronger. If the principle of affected interest is the wellspring of democratic legitimacy, how can we justify making national governments the repositories of decision making in an increasingly interdependent world?

This is a powerful argument, but it does not support replacing national governments with a world government. For one thing, while everyone on earth might in some sense be affected by a decision, some people will

---

[18] Michael Walzer, *Spheres of Justice: A Defense of Pluralism and Equality* (New York: Basic Books, 1984), pp. 3–30.

have basic interests at stake in many decisions while others will not.[19] It is the former who have the strongest claim to participation in decision making. As I have argued elsewhere, what matters here is not the size of the interest at stake, as, say, in the amount of money, but rather its importance for people's survival and their capacity to live normal lives under democratic conditions.[20]

Those with basic interests at stake in a given decision might not map well onto national populations, but a remedy that gave people with negligible interests the same say as those with basic interests at stake in the matter at hand would scarcely solve this problem. We would not want people who do not rely on publicly funded health insurance for their medical treatment to have the same say in determining which procedures should be covered by the insurance as those who have no choice but to rely on it.[21]

Moreover, if the goal is—as I agree that it should be—for decision making better to reflect the preferences of people with basic interests at stake, sometimes this will involve devolution to subnational units rather than supernational ones. Recent arguments for devolution from Westminster to Scottish and Welsh assemblies appeal to this idea. And sometimes, when it does make sense to shift a decision to a larger unit, it will be to a regional body like the European Union rather than a world legislature. The principle of subsidiarity embraced in the EU recognizes this implicitly. It creates a presumption of deference to more local decision making, and then decisions move up the ladder of subsidiarity if and when protecting relevant affected interests requires this. No doubt there will be disagreements about where particular decisions should be located on the ladder, requiring, in turn, procedures for resolving those disagreements. But the pertinent point here is that, rather than world government, the principle of affected interest suggests disaggregating the demos decision by decision. Indeed, some decisions—such as whether to terminate life support for the terminally ill—should be devolved to even smaller decision-making units like families and perhaps (by living wills and durable powers of attorney) to single individuals.[22]

The proposition that cosmopolitan democrats should abjure the nation-state in favor of world government is therefore not sustainable—at

---

[19] I define basic interests by reference to the wherewithal to survive and thrive in the economy as it can reasonably be expected to operate over the course of one's lifetime and in the polity governed as a democracy. See *Democratic Justice* (New Haven: Yale University Press, 1999), pp. 85–90, and chapter 8 of this volume.

[20] See Shapiro *Democratic Justice*, pp. 85–90, 161–63, 186–90.

[21] For additional discussion as illustrated by the flawed deliberative sessions of the reform of Oregon's health-care system in the early 1990s, see *The State of Democratic Theory*, pp. 23–28.

[22] For additional discussion, see *Democratic Justice*, pp. 219–29.

least not by means of the arguments that have typically been adduced in its support. This means that cosmopolitan democrats cannot reasonably avoid embracing some account of the appropriate relations among governments. In what follows I deal with that part of this subject that concerns the role of national security policy in preserving democracy where it exists and helping foster it—when possible—where it does not. This focus should not be taken to imply that I see national security policy as exhausting the international obligations of governments from a cosmopolitan democrat's point of view. Most obviously, there are obligations to give foreign aid and undertake humanitarian intervention that would be part of a fuller account of the appropriate relations among states. Each of these has its own rationale and is appropriately governed by distinctive considerations. National security policy is one piece of the puzzle—a piece that has generally been neglected by cosmopolitan democrats for reasons that I discuss in part 5.

2. Containment's Normative Basis

In *Containment* I argued that the ideal of nondomination that appropriately structures relations among individuals also provides the right basis for thinking about the relations among states.[23] This is not true without qualification. As I note in part 3, there are circumstances in which it makes sense actively to assist indigenous democrats who are seeking to overthrow authoritarian regimes. In those circumstances containment is sometimes better abandoned in favor of a more activist approach to undermine nondemocratic states. But for the most part, a stance of refusing to be dominated by other states is the best point of departure to think about the national security dimensions of relations among states.

How does containment serve the goal of nondomination in international politics? For George Kennan, this question was thrown up by events. Writing at the end of World War II when troops were being demobilized and budgets cut, he was acutely aware that national security would have to be pursued with an eye to husbanding scarce resources. This would not be a world in which the United States could afford to dominate the global security environment. In such a context, Kennan argued, the United States would be best able to ensure its security by building a world that no one could dominate.

In part this was a judgment about the USSR. Convinced that the Soviet system was dysfunctional, and that its own overextension would lead it eventually to implode, Kennan argued that all we had to do was hem the

---

[23] Shapiro, *Containment*, chap. 6.

Soviets in and wait them out. In holding that the Soviet goal of worldwide hegemony was doomed while any comparable American goal would be unsustainably expensive, Kennan was building—however unwittingly—on traditional republican arguments to the effect that empires invariably become overextended and collapse.

Kennan's particular twist was to invert the logic of divide-and-rule into the service of resisting domination. We might call it the principle of divide-and-refuse-to-be-ruled. Kennan thought it a mistake to conceive of our Cold War adversary as the World Communist Movement. The country that threatened the United States and its allies was the Soviet Union. There were conflicts and potential conflicts within the communist camp that could work to the Americans' advantage as they faced down that threat. Kennan thus welcomed the rise of Titoism in Yugoslavia; this was the kind of internal challenge to Soviet hegemony that would promote competition within the Soviet camp, weaken the Soviet grip on Eastern Europe, and complicate the USSR's battle for hearts and minds in the developing world. In defending this view Kennan opposed John Foster Dulles and other proponents of "rollback," who proposed the aggressive worldwide confrontation of communism. In *Containment* I make an analogous case to Kennan's about the imprudence of the Bush administration's invocation of an "Axis of Evil"—lumping together vastly different adversaries, giving them reasons to bury their differences, and to form united fronts against the capitalist democracies in general and the United States in particular.

For Kennan, the goal of creating a world that no one could dominate was strategic all the way down. The multilateral clusters of national powers to which it would lead offered Americans the best available guarantee of security from foreign attack. But normative considerations, rooted in democratic theory, dovetail neatly with Kennan's case. Early in the *Discourses* Machiavelli argues that it is better to give power to the common people because, unlike the aristocracy whose desire is to dominate, their desire is not to be dominated.[24] Institutionalizing a course of actions to prevent domination has been a principal aim of democratic theory since Machiavelli's time, at the root of debates over entrenching measures that are essential to the operation of democratic politics, regulating the reach of private interests in politics, and ensuring representation of disempowered minorities.

Containment extends the neo-Machiavellian case for nondomination to the realm of national security. The essential idea is to stop the bully without yourself becoming a bully. In this it appeals to the impulse to

[24] Niccolò Machiavelli, *The Discourses* (ca. 1517) (Harmondsworth: Penguin, 1970), § I.5.

refuse to be dominated rather than the impulse to dominate. It is this rootedness of containment in the idea of nondomination that gives it an elective affinity with democratic politics, conferring legitimacy on it at home and abroad. At home, containment can provide people with security without saddling them with unsustainable military obligations, and it can lead people to support democracy beyond their borders without arrogating to themselves the task of toppling regimes in other countries. Abroad, containment can be seen as a policy that requires acceptance by others of the legitimacy of existing democracies. It also signals that, so long as this is compatible with ensuring their own survival into the future, democratic governments will join forces arrayed against domination beyond their borders by helping to protect other democracies, resisting the expansion of tyranny, and supporting viable democratic resistance to authoritarian regimes.

Containment is more behavioral than ideological in the sense that its focus is on what potential adversaries actually do internationally rather than on their internal political arrangements or the beliefs of their leaders. Political theorists might discern in it an element of a stripped-down "political, not metaphysical" disposition, inasmuch as it seeks a basis for interacting with others that does not depend on persuading them of the validity of your beliefs or the folly of theirs.[25] In Kennan's case this was born of the conviction that arguing with Soviet leaders about the merits of international issues was a waste of time because they could never be persuaded of the values and commitments of America's political leaders.[26] He thought the Soviets would, nonetheless, respond to the logic implicit in containment even if they were unwilling or unable to acknowledge that they were doing this. He thought this supplied the best basis for dealing with them.

However true this might have been of Soviet leaders during the Cold War, in the post–Cold War era it seems even more obviously so of adversaries whose beliefs are sharply at odds with those of most Americans, and who lack any history of democratic politics. Seeking to convert them to our worldview seems, at best, naive. The fusion of communism and anti-American nationalism proved to be a potent mixture in Indochina and much of Africa and Latin America during the Cold War. There is every reason to expect the fusion of Islam and anti-American nationalism to be no less potent. Just as the Vietnam conflict solidified anti-Americanism in Southeast Asia, so the 2003 Iraq invasion has done it across the Middle East.

[25] See John Rawls, *Political Liberalism* (New York: Columbia University Press, 1993), pp. 131–254.

[26] This was the subject of his famous eight-thousand-word "long telegram" when he was a diplomat in Moscow in 1946 that first got the attention of the Truman administration.

The George W. Bush administration played into this dynamic, contributing to the "clash-of-civilizations" construction of what is at stake.[27] In the aftermath of 9/11 and in the 2002 *National Security Strategy of the United States*[28] the administration insisted that the war on terror is a war on people who hate "freedom" and hate us for who we are.[29] In a series of speeches in late 2005, President Bush began explicitly connecting the war on terror to variants of radical and militant Islam.[30] In this he was genuflecting in the direction of neoconservatives like David Frum and Richard Perle, who have long insisted that militant Islam is the principal cause of terrorism, that it is widely endorsed across the Muslim world and among Muslim minorities in the West, and that its goal is to "overthrow our civilization and remake the nations of the West into Islamic societies, imposing on the whole world its religion and its law."[31]

This analysis defies most expert opinion, which recognizes that since 1980 more terrorism, including suicide bombing, has been perpetrated by secular groups than by religious fundamentalists,[32] and that even Islamic terrorist leaders like Osama bin Laden see themselves as engaged in a "defensive jihad" in response to American policies in the Middle East rather than an "offensive jihad" geared to the global spread of

---

[27] See Samuel P. Huntington, *The Clash of Civilizations and the Remaking of World Order* (New York: Simon and Schuster, 1998).

[28] *The National Security Strategy of the United States of America* (The White House, 2002), http://www.whitehouse.gov/nsc/nss.pdf [09-03-2007].

[29] "Americans are asking, why do they hate us? They hate what we see right here in this chamber—a democratically elected government. Their leaders are self-appointed. They hate our freedoms—our freedom of religion, our freedom of speech, our freedom to vote and assemble and disagree with each other." George W. Bush, Address to a Joint Session of Congress and the American People, September 20, 2001, http://www.whitehouse.gov/news/releases/2001/09/20010920-8.html [12-24-2009]. President Bush also commented after the 2004 Madrid bombings that "These people kill because they hate freedom and they hate what Spain stands for." George W. Bush, Interview by Television of Spain, March 12, 2004, http://63.161.169.137/news/releases/ 2004/03/20040312-19.html [04-07-2006].

[30] See President Bush's Address at the National Endowment for Democracy, October 6, 2005, http://www.whitehouse.gov/news/releases/2005/10/20051006-3.html [06-18-2006]. Bush continued to deny it was intrinsic to the Islamic religion, but—as with mentioning Iraq in the same paragraph as 9/11 while denying that he was asserting they were connected, the likely result, and perhaps event the intent, was manifest.

[31] David Frum and Richard Perle, *An End to Evil: How to Win the War on Terror* (New York: Random House, 2003), p. 42.

[32] See Stephen Hopgood, "Tamil Tigers," in *Making Sense of Suicide Missions*, ed. Diego Gambetta (Oxford: Oxford University Press, 2005), pp. 43–76; Robert Pape, *Dying to Win: The Strategic Logic of Suicide Terrorism* (New York: Random House, 2005); and Mia Bloom, *Dying to Kill: The Allure of Suicide Terror* (New York: Columbia University Press, 2005).

Islam.[33] Feeding the idea of a clash of civilizations is as self-defeating with respect to Islam as Kennan believed it to be with respect to international communism.

Containment also presupposes a normative reason to prefer the stripped-down "political, not metaphysical" attitude to others' beliefs. In one respect this attitude calls to mind the logic of the secret ballot, which shields people from any expectation that they should justify their political views to others. There are, to be sure, deliberative strands of democratic theory that call for more or less ambitious attempts at justifying one's beliefs in terms that others will accept.[34] Yet even deliberation's enthusiastic proponents do not contend that in politics deliberation should be *required* of people, or that the results of "deliberative polls" and other deliberative mechanisms should actually be binding on the decisions of a democratic polity. This marks their acknowledgment, however tacit, that it is the act of deciding rather than the mental processes behind it that is essential to democratic legitimacy.[35]

Whatever one's view of deliberativist philosophical ventures, it is notable that democracies do not institutionalize them. Indeed, as John Ferejohn and Pasquale Pasquino have noted, we tend to require more in the way of reason giving the further away we get from the ballot box. For instance, on their telling we expect judges to give reasons for their decisions just because they are not backed by the legitimation of the ballot box.[36] Whether or not Ferejohn and Pasquino are right that this is the reason, it is clear that democracy requires us to accept the political choices of others regardless of their reasons for those choices, so long as they do not impose them on us in violation of democratic processes. By an analogous token, containment is indifferent to the beliefs of others, so long as the actions that flow from those beliefs do not threaten our ability to operate democratically on the basis of our own beliefs.

[33] The definitive treatment of this subject is former intelligence officer Michael Scheuer's *Imperial Hubris: Why the West Is Losing the War on Terror* (Dulles, VA: Potomac Books, 2004).

[34] See Jürgen Habermas, *The Theory of Communicative Action*, vol. 1, *Reason and the Rationalization of Society* (Boston: Beacon Press, 1984), and "Three Normative Models of Democracy," *Constellations*, no. 1 (1994): 1–20; Amy Gutmann and Dennis Thompson, *Democracy and Disagreement* (Cambridge, MA: Harvard University Press, 1996); and James Fishkin, *The Voice of the People: Public Opinion and Democracy* (New Haven: Yale University Press, 1995).

[35] *The State of Democratic Theory*, pp. 21–49.

[36] See John Ferejohn and Pasquale Pasquino, "Constitutional Courts as Deliberative Institutions: Towards an Institutional Theory of Constitutional Justice," in *Constitutional Justice East and West: Democratic Legitimacy and Constitutional Courts in Post-Communist Europe in a Comparative Perspective*, ed. Wojciech Sadurski (The Hague: Kluwer Law International, 2002), pp. 21–36.

3. Containment and "Regime Change"

Containment occupies a midpoint on a continuum between isolationism and proselytizing regime change. Containment's primary imperative for democratic governments is to protect their people and resist threats to their survival as democracies. This particularist impulse does not signal indifference to democracy's fate around the world. A commitment to containment is compatible with a cosmopolitan democratic commitment to resisting the expansion of tyranny in the world. It involves willingness to help protect other democracies, to resist expansionist ambitions of tyrannical regimes, and to assist democratic oppositions in authoritarian countries.

But why protect one's own democracy *first*? This priority does not rest on the supposition that American lives are more valuable than other lives, or that American democracy is more important than democracy elsewhere (even if my argument will be attractive to people who believe those things). Rather, it reflects the reality that no government will long be in a position to protect others or to foster democracy elsewhere unless it can protect its own people and preserve its country as a democracy. In this the imperative for the United States to secure American democracy first is analogous to John Locke's injunction that each individual strive to preserve mankind to the extent that this is compatible with his or her self-preservation. This did not mean, for Locke, that a given person's survival was more important than that of any other. On the contrary, Locke's signature and revolutionary view was that we are all equal in God's eyes. It was simply a matter of who had primary responsibility for what.[37] Containment's particularism is thus compatible with a cosmopolitan commitment to democracy that would suggest securing French democracy first as a French national security priority, securing South African democracy first as a South African national security priority, and so on.

But I want to advance a stronger claim: containment is not only *compatible* with a cosmopolitan commitment to democracy; containment is the best available national security policy for cosmopolitan democrats to embrace. Taking the time to establish that containment is superior to isolationism from this point of view scarcely seems necessary; for present purposes I will simply assume that cosmopolitan democrats would prefer containment over isolation. The more contentious question is whether

---

[37] "Every one, as he is bound to preserve himself, and not to quit his station willfully, so by the like reason, when his own preservation comes not in competition, ought he, as much as he can, to preserve the rest of mankind." John Locke, *Second Treatises of Government*, in *Two Treatises of Government and a Letter Concerning Toleration*, ed. Ian Shapiro (New Haven: Yale University Press, 2003), chap. II, § 6, p. 102.

I am right that containment beats a policy of toppling authoritarian regimes in order to replace them with democracies.

The advantages of my view should become evident once we reflect on the difficulties associated with imposing regime change in the name of democracy. Japan and what came to be West Germany after World War II are often mentioned in this connection, in support of the contention that viable democracy can and sometimes should be imposed from the outside. But Germany and Japan were highly unusual cases in that both had waged aggressive war on the United States and its allies with the result that the legitimacy of the allied destruction of their regimes was widely accepted internationally, and even by many among their domestic populations. Having destroyed the regimes, we did indeed assume the obligation of building democracies in those countries if this was feasible. It is worth noting that this took a massive commitment of American resources and a military presence over many decades, even though both Germany and Japan had prewar experience with democracy.

Going to war in order to implement regime change, when you have neither been attacked nor been threatened with imminent attack, is an altogether different proposition. If the justification for doing this is that democracy is better than authoritarianism, you face the conundrum that democracy gets its legitimacy from support for the regime by those over whom power is exercised. There are two related problems here: the new regime lacks legitimacy because it is not the creation of those who are subject to it, and your motives as an invading power are inescapably suspect. The second problem compounds the first, leading the new government all too easily to be seen as the puppet of an imperial power.

It is true that all democratic transitions require decisive action from above at critical junctures. The U.S. Constitution was rammed through in violation of the Articles of Confederation. The terms of the South African transition were negotiated in secret by the leaderships of the ANC and the National Party government, with dissenting voices in the Inkatha Freedom Party and the white Right told to like it or lump it once the deal was done. But what differentiates such cases from external impositions was the existence of large domestic constituencies whose members supported the democratic transition. Moreover, the transitions were not undertaken exclusively from above. As was detailed in chapter 3, they involved an interactive dynamic in which political elites were careful to build support for their actions in key constituencies as they went along.

When the installing agent is an outside power, the legitimacy hurdles are inevitably much higher. By what authority does it act? What are its real motives and agenda? How can it claim to be acting in the name of democracy when it is forcing the domestic population to accept the institutions it is imposing?

One way in which an outside power may mitigate these difficulties is by acting in concert with, and at the behest of, an indigenous democratic opposition. But as John Stuart Mill warned a long time ago, if the opposition forces are too weak to overthrow the regime, then the chances that they will be able to establish a viable democracy are low.[38] Whether the relevant support exists in fact will often be a difficult judgment call, since opposition movements might well overestimate their chances of success. This renders external intervention inherently fraught with risk.

One rule of thumb is that internal oppositions seeking outside assistance should receive more serious consideration than expatriate oppositions. Internal oppositions are more likely to have accurate information, and, more important, unlike expatriate oppositions they have to live with the consequences if a planned insurrection fails. This gives them the incentive to get accurate information about their chances of success. Expatriates, particularly those who have been away for many years, are more likely to have suspect information and to be prone to the wishful thinking that comes of talking disproportionately to people with views similar to one's own.[39] The expatriate Cubans who assured the Kennedy administration before the Bay of Pigs that the population would rise up against Castro warranted considerable skepticism by this test. Likewise with the assurances offered by Ahmad Chalabi and his associates about how Americans would be received in Iraq in 2003.

The importance of acting at the behest of indigenous oppositions is not simply a matter of their power; it extends also to questions of legitimacy. Trying to force regime change from the outside when this is not called for by local opposition forces is likely to do little more than hand propaganda victories to the regime. The Clinton administration's sanctions against Iraq had this effect, allowing Saddam Hussein to make political hay by displaying starving babies on television. Contrast that with sanctions against South Africa imposed by Congress over Ronald Reagan's veto in 1986. The administration's argument that they would do more harm than good to South Africa's dispossessed blacks while leaving the regime untouched was undercut because the ANC had been calling for sanctions since 1959.[40] Comparable considerations suggest that external pressure might be plausible in the service of democracy promotion in Burma but not in North Korea.

[38] See John Stuart Mill, "A Few Words on Non-intervention," in John Stuart Mill, *Essays on Politics and Culture* (New York: Anchor Books, 1963), pp. 381–82.

[39] See Cass Sunstein, "The Law of Group Polarization," *Journal of Political Philosophy* 10, no. 1 (2002): 175–95.

[40] "South Africa," *Foreign Policy in Focus* 2, no. 22 (January 1997), http://www.fpif.org/pdf/vol2/22ifsafr.pdf [07-14-2009].

In Iran, following the disputed election of June 2009, the Obama administration was attacked from various quarters for failing to come out in strong support of the reformists who insisted that the election had been stolen. What Obama's critics missed was that at no time did Mir-Hossein Mousavi or any of his supporters seek American intervention, sanctions, or even declarations of support. Presumably they understood, as did Barack Obama, that this would weaken their hand in the Iranian struggle, not strengthen it. This does indeed mean, as some critics of my book have noted, that my argument disallows intervention to promote regime change in the worst regimes, those in which no opposition of any kind is permitted to survive. This is true, but ought entails can. Toppling a dictatorship that will likely be replaced by another dictatorship following an interregnum of war or civil war imposes enormous human cost with no discernible benefit in the way of reducing domination.

Democrats should be disposed toward helping in the creation of new democracies as part of their agenda to reduce domination, but they should do this mindful of the reality that democratic legitimacy comes primarily from within and from below. Outsiders must remain in the subordinate position of assisting indigenous democratic forces, lest the outsiders morph into new agents of domination. Their actions will have been self-defeating if they are backed into installing puppet regimes that lack legitimacy on the ground.

4. GLOBAL CONTAINMENT

In the post–Cold War world of rogue regimes, weak states, and mobile terrorist organizations, facing down the expansion of tyranny might require a military response to belligerence—even when this does not involve strict self-defense against an imminent threat. Democrats should be willing to support international containment for this purpose. Saddam Hussein's 1991 invasion of Kuwait is a case in point. It was unprovoked aggression that clearly called for a response by those committed to resisting the spread of domination in the world. But just because it was not a matter of self-defense for the United States and its allies, the question inevitably arose: by what authority could they act?

For such action to garner legitimacy it must involve widespread international participation, with strong involvement from the local region, and this action must be authorized through international institutions. This view involves major departures from the classic conception of containment. George Kennan had no time for international institutions such as the UN, which he believed would be sidelined in any serious conflict between the United States and the Soviets. He was also distrustful of alliances, believing they would hamper the United States unnecessarily, and, in the case of NATO, that it would needlessly militarize the standoff with the Soviets in Europe. But that was then and this is now. Containing aggressive tyranny that can emerge, unpredictably, in different parts of the world requires a response that is transnationally coordinated and internationally authorized.

Coordinated transnational action with strong regional participation is needed partly for pragmatic reasons. Countries in the neighborhood of a failed or rogue regime are likely to have vital interests at stake and to be potential spoilers if their cooperation is not secured. If it is secured, this will help scotch the perception that the far-off power is acting from imperial motives. Participation from Arab countries in the region in the U.S. effort to oust Iraq from Kuwait in 1991 was beneficial for all of these reasons. The lack of comparable cooperation with the U.S. invasion of Iraq in 2003 has compounded American difficulties there significantly. The Iraq Study Group understood this when it recommended, in December of 2006, that the administration begin working with Syria and Iran to secure Iraq's southwestern and southeastern borders.[41] Iraqi prime minister Nuri al-Maliki was equally clear about this in late 2007.[42] Otherwise, no effective postoccupation containment strategy is conceivable for the terrorism that will emanate from the failed state that Iraq has become.

This is not to deny that Iran will also need to be contained, any more than the Nixon administration's opening to China as part of its containment of the Soviet Union eliminated the need to continue containing China. Taking advantage of common interests does not imply that there is, or a need to pretend that there is, an identity of interest. Rather, it suggests that the United States should take advantage of common interests where this is possible, while reserving the right to work with others to contain external aggression and the financing and export of terror.

It will typically be true that pursuing containment on a global basis will require cooperation from others. It is sometimes said that the containment regime against Saddam Hussein's Iraq was failing by 2002—as revealed by the fact that he agreed to the return of UN weapons inspectors only once American troops were massing on his border. If we grant this, *arguendo*, it also reveals the limits of unilateral action. As a containment regime, the U.S. action was unsustainable. Everyone knew that we could not keep the troops there at battle readiness throughout the summer of 2003. This presented the Bush administration with only two

---

[41] James Baker III et al., "The Iraq Study Group Report" (December 2006), pp. 25–40, http://bakerinstitute.org/Pubs/iraqstudygroup_findings.pdf [09-11-2007].

[42] Waleed Ibrahim, "Iraq PM Defends Government, Urges Regional Cooperation," *Washington Post*, September 9, 2007, http://www.washingtonpost.com/wp-dyn/content/article/2007/09/09/AR2007090900356.html?referrer=emailarticle [09-11-2007].

options: invade or withdraw. Had he pursued the latter course, Saddam could have continued the cat and mouse by expelling the weapons inspectors again. The fear of being seen as a paper tiger on the world stage boxed the administration into invading.

If, instead, President Bush had put together the kind of coalition his father had assembled in 1991, then troops from different nations could have been rotated in and out, keeping up the pressure. To this it might be objected that too few powers would have agreed to participate to make this viable. Perhaps so, but that suggests, in turn, that the Americans were exaggerating the threat. If other major powers would not participate and Iraq's neighbors did not feel sufficiently threatened to get involved either, that should have been a warning that the WMD threat in Iraq might indeed be illusory. This widespread reluctance on the part of those who would be most immediately and seriously threatened by a newly rearmed Iraq should have prompted hard scrutiny of what turned out later to have been the hyped intelligence claims of those bent on finding a justification for war.

Regional participation is important also for normative reasons. Nations bordering on an expansionist power will have major, possibly vital, interests at stake. The principle of affected interest thus gives them a strong claim to a say and to a role in the defensive response. To this it might be objected that, if they are not themselves democracies, why should democrats respect the appeal of the governments of regional powers to the principle of affected interest? Why should democrats care about Kuwait's interests, let alone those of Syria or Iran?

But the failure of others to respect the principle of affected interest is not a good reason for democrats to flout it. Moreover, democrats have an interest in encouraging nondemocracies to adopt democratic norms and to play by democratic rules when they operate internationally—whether in institutions like the UN or in informal consultations and coalitions. The more governments accept the norm's legitimacy in one context, the more they legitimate it, willy-nilly, in others—making it harder for them to resist domestic demands for democratic reform.

Authorization through international institutions also matters for reasons both practical and normative. On the practical front, it will often be the officials from the UN and other international agencies on the ground who have access to pertinent information. This is especially likely to be true as far as weak and failed states are concerned, where it is often the local representatives of international institutions who will know the details of different warlords' capacities and agendas, where the weak points in borders are, and other relevant street-level information. Moreover, international authorization of containment coalitions enhances their stability. It is harder for a country to withdraw from participation when it has become committed through an international legal process than when it is merely a coalition "of the willing"—of which some future administration might take a different view. The socialist victory in the 2004 Spanish election is a case in point.

But the most important reasons for international authorization are normative. If major powers act either unilaterally or via coalitions of the willing when they are not themselves under threat of imminent attack, they lack principled authority for their actions. As a result, they are likely to be seen as imperialistic, opportunistic, or both. The 1991 Gulf War and the 2001 action against Afghanistan garnered worldwide support in significant part because they were authorized by the UN Security Council. This stands in stark contrast to the 2003 Iraq war, which continues widely to be seen as a rogue American action against a country that posed no regional or global threat. Rather than undermining the UN at every turn, as the Bush administration did, the major democratic powers should strengthen the UN and then work through it to face domination down. Cosmopolitan democrats should press their governments to get behind that enterprise. This is a far cry from the aspiration to create a world government discussed earlier. But it is a modest move in the direction of enhancing the international rule of law.

5. Containment and Legitimating the Status Quo

A different worry about containment derives from its apparent indifference to past injustices perpetrated by the nation doing the containing. Those who recognize that the United States has been a source of great harm and oppression in the world over the past several decades might be reluctant to engage with the question: what should America's national security policy should be *now*? The worry is that whoever engages with the question inevitably becomes tarred with the brush of legitimating the unjust actions that have helped bring about this status quo. A strategy for securing America today is all too easily seen as a strategy for securing ill-gotten gains.

This concern merits serious attention, not least because ignorance of the harm for which the United States bears responsibility limits awareness of how malevolently we are seen in much of Africa, Asia, and Latin America. But one can grant much of this critique of American global behavior over the past half century yet still recognize that we are bound to pose the question: and what now? Whatever combination of decisions, forces, and events brought the United States to its present geopolitical position; we still have to choose what our policies will be going forward. That the United States has often failed as a global force for democracy in the past makes all the more urgent the task of coming up with principles and strategies for it to be such a force in the future. This is why it is important to adopt a national security policy that is rooted in democratic principles, and which commits the United States henceforth to opposing oppression and aiding the legitimate diffusion of democracy around the world.

To be sure, much of the strategy for supporting democracy and diffusing it around the world involves the medium term: building international institutions, supporting the economic development necessary to turn weak states into viable ones, and being seen to be working to ameliorate injustice around the world. But endorsing these medium-term commitments cannot mean that we can simply ignore national security in the more immediate sense that requires governments to provide for essential safety from violent attack. A lesson to be drawn from the events since 9/11 is that if those who favor progressive democratic change in the world fail to develop a viable national security agenda, others will. In order to be in a position to develop and implement policies that promote progressive democratic change, democratic governments must come up with policies that can plausibly provide basic security to populations under their control and preserve their political institutions into the future.

6. Cosmopolitanism Revisited

Containment might make cosmopolitan democrats uncomfortable because it seems to legitimate the nation-state system we have inherited. But I have sought to show here that such discomfort is misplaced. Democracy finds its legitimacy and appeal in the principle of affected interest, to be sure, and this principle is often sharply at odds with a default assumption in favor of national decision making. Despite the fact that democratic nondomination is predicated of individuals rather than states, we saw in part 1 that none of this adds up to a case in support of world government. My argument in parts 2 and 3 was that containment, which occupies a midpoint on a continuum between isolationism and proselytizing regime change, is the national security policy of choice for cosmopolitan democrats. Containment is desirable because of its elective affinities with the democratic principle of nondomination. Containment also makes pragmatic and normative sense as the best bet for securing the populations and institutions of democratic countries, and for promoting the diffusion of democracy around the world.

In part 4, I noted that the containment doctrine inherited from George Kennan stands in need of modification for the post–Cold War world in ways that buttress the development of a global rule of law. This falls well short of the idea of world government favored by some cosmopolitan democrats, but it is a nod in their direction inasmuch as effective rule of law in a given domain is in any case a precondition for viable democratic politics there. This aspect of my argument would have been captured better had my book's subtitle alluded to a *global response to terror* rather than a *response to global terror*.[43] The alternative links containment more explicitly to the project of sustaining democracy on a global basis by requiring international authorization for containment that moves beyond strict self-defense by a nation in response to actual or imminent attack. And my proposed alternative also opens the way to the forward-looking view of national security policy sketched in part 5. Culpable as the United States has been in the injustices of the past, we are nonetheless bound to ask what the best national security policy is from now on. For cosmopolitan democrats, the view of containment sketched here is the best answer to that question.

[43] This subtitle would also have been preferable on the minimizing-hysteria front. As one audience member pointed out at a discussion of my book at the London School of Economics, the "global terror" formulation tends to amplify the threat. It deflects attention from the reality that in any of the advanced capitalist democracies one is much more likely to be killed in an auto accident than in a terrorist attack.

CHAPTER SIX

The Political Uses of Public Opinion: Lessons from the Estate Tax Repeal

Mayling Birney, Ian Shapiro, and Michael J. Graetz

IN THE PREVIOUS chapter it was noted that citizens in democracies are not generally expected to justify their views to others. But this does not mean that politicians are uninterested in understanding those views. On the contrary, each year politicians pour millions of dollars into polling, focus groups, and other instruments to inform themselves about every nook and cranny of public opinion. They have an obvious, and much studied, motivation for doing this: the need to win elections. Less often attended to than the role of public opinion in electoral strategies is the subject that concerns us here: how does public opinion influence what politicians do when they are in office? More specifically, what impact does it have on the laws they enact? The answer to this question is ultimately connected to electoral politics, but, as we explain in this chapter, in ways that are paradoxical and not well understood.

We explore our subject in the course of examining the surprising case of the repeal of the federal estate tax in 2001. This repeal benefited only a tiny minority of wealthy Americans: those bequeathing, or inheriting from, estates larger than $1 million. Logically, one might have anticipated, as congressional Democrats did for a long time, that such a regressive measure would provoke a popular backlash. If enacted at all, it would be done in the dead of night, like a congressional pay raise, or after being buried quietly within a larger bill. Yet, as of the late 1990s, estate tax repeal somehow acquired a populist flavor and became a high priority for mainstream as well as conservative politicians. Beginning in 2000, the House and Senate repeatedly voted in stand-alone measures to repeal the estate tax, as shown in figures 6.1a and 6.1b. While, owing to budgetary constraints, the actual repeal that was signed into law in June 2001 was phased in gradually and was only temporary,[1] as shown in table 6.1, the repeated achievement of broad bipartisan sup-

---

[1] The omnibus tax reform bills passed by both houses included a phaseout of the estate tax followed by full repeal. However, the specifics of the phaseout, other tax cut provisions, and the overall price tags of the omnibus bills differed substantially, so that aspects had to be compromised. During conference committee, behind closed doors, the decision was

port was an astonishing success for repeal advocates. As the battle for a permanent repeal has persisted, Republicans and some Democrats have continued to view this highly regressive measure as a winning issue with the public.

Our goal here is to unravel this conundrum and explore its implications for our understanding of how public opinion affects political outcomes. Our investigation is unorthodox in that, in addition to the usual public sources, archival research, and scholarly literature, we engaged in some one hundred interviews, the great majority not for attribution, with congressmen, senators, political aides, civil servants, journalists, interest group representatives, analysts, and others with different stakes in the outcome. We found that, although political scientists often view public opinion and interest group activity as separate influences on the policy-making process, public opinion is in fact a weapon that can be deployed, more or less effectively, by interest groups that are struggling to shape what Congress does. Our study revealed that interest groups expended great effort to identify the wide-ranging contours of public opinion and used this knowledge to shape politicians' perceptions of public opinion on the issue.

In part 1 we demonstrate the extent to which the direction of public opinion on the estate tax is open to interpretation—something that was apparently not well understood until recent years—and we show how polls were strategically deployed to "interpret" it for politicians. Indeed, as we elaborate in part 2, the evidence suggests that interest groups even structured their very policy position around their efforts to manage elite perceptions of public opinion on the estate tax. Members of the Family Business Estate Tax Coalition, which in 1995 began exerting pressure to diminish estate taxes, have since become strangely wedded to the repeal stance—even as significant obstacles remain to achieving permanent repeal, and readily available reform options might better serve their interests. They seem to fear that, were they to abandon the goal of repeal, they would lose the momentum they have gained from framing public opinion around principles that are associated with repeal so effectively, but that are not associated with reform options geared to reducing the estate tax burden. In part 2 we also present a fuller portrait of how interest groups and political leaders actively shaped politicians' understandings of latent public opinion to serve their own policy goals.

We see the recent successes of interest groups in shaping politicians' perceptions of public opinion as vital to developing broad political support for repeal. In fact, this effort to repeal the tax is the first serious one since

---

unexpectedly made to sunset the entire tax cut, including the estate tax provisions, after ten years. This effectively resulted in a one-year repeal in 2010.

Fig. 6.1a. House votes on estate tax repeal

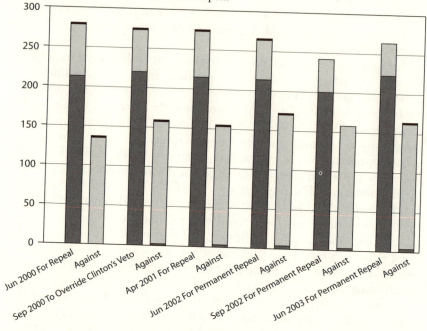

Fig. 6.1b. Senate votes on estate tax repeal

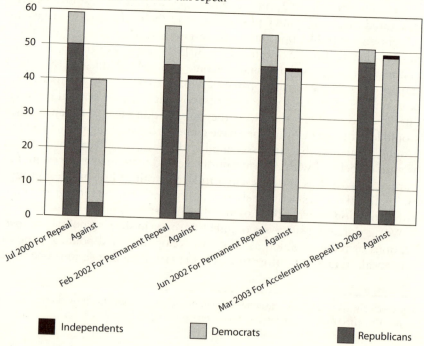

TABLE 6.1
Key Changes to the Federal Estate and Gift Taxes (Signed into Law in June 2001)

	Estate Tax Exemption Level	Top Estate Tax Rate	Gift Tax Exemption Level	Top Gift Rate	Basis for Assets Assets	State ET Automatic Credit
2002	$1,000,000	56%	$1,000,000	56%	stepped-up	12%
2003	$1,000,000	49%	$1,000,000	49%	stepped-up	8%
2004	$1,500,000	48%	$1,000,000	48%	stepped-up	4%
2005	$1,500,000	47%	$1,000,000	47%	stepped-up	deduction
2006	$2,000,000	46%	$1,000,000	46%	stepped-up	deduction
2007	$2,000,000	45%	$1,000,000	45%	stepped-up	deduction
2008	$2,000,000	45%	$1,000,000	45%	stepped-up	deduction
2009	$3,500,000	45%	$1,000,000	45%	stepped-up	deduction
2010	REPEALED	n/a	$1,000,000	35%	carry-over	n/a
2011 (law reverts to 2001 law)	$1,000,000	55% (60%. some estates > $10,000,000).	$1,000,000	55%	stepped-up	16%
			$1,000,000	55%	stepped-up	16%

the budget surpluses of the 1920s. The timing and persistence of this effort cannot be explained by the reach and rates of the tax alone, as these have been more or less constant for decades, and the estate tax was notably more onerous in the 1970s.[2] Other factors, beyond the actual burden of the tax, contributed to the attraction of repeal in recent years. Undoubtedly, the strength of the economy in 2000 and 2001, the fact that the government was running budget surpluses, demographic changes in the profiles of the wealthiest Americans, and Republican ascendance in Washington made it a propitious time for abolishing the estate tax. Yet these factors still do not explain why estate tax repeal, rather than other longer-standing conservative tax priorities that garner more support from corporate America and supply-side economists, succeeded. When the role of interest groups in shaping elite perceptions of public opinion is also considered, the timing and persistence of the repeal effort begin to make more sense.

[2] The estate tax burden was greatest in the 1970s, when the exemption rate fell below half a million dollars (in 2001 dollars) and the maximum tax rate rose as high as 77 percent. In the years after the federal estate tax was enacted in 1916, fewer than 1 percent were subject to it and sometimes fewer than 0.5 percent; and in recent decades, about 2 percent of the population has paid the estate tax. Since the 1930s, the percentage of national wealth held by those who are subject to the estate tax has not changed much. As estimated from estate tax returns themselves, the top 1 percent of Americans are estimated to have held between 20 and 25 percent of the country's wealth since the 1940s, save for several years beginning in the late 1970s when the figure dropped to around 18 percent. The wealth share of the top 0.5 percent has remained roughly 6 percent of the country's wealth since 1946. Wojciech Kopczuk and Emmanuel Saez, "Top Wealth Shares in the United States, 1916–2000: Evidence from Estate Tax Returns," NBER Working Paper, 10399 (2004).

1. INTERPRETING PUBLIC OPINION: PRINCIPLE OR PRIORITY?

Starting in the late 1990s, interest groups and political parties employed opinion polling strategically to understand the contours of public opinion on the estate tax. They wanted to know how it varied according to the frameworks, symbols, and principles invoked; with reference to the particular reform or repeal options presented; and in juxtaposition with other priorities. In improving their understanding of these contours, activists could promote to politicians the interpretation that best served their goals. Advocates of repeal were especially active and effective in this regard. With an eye to what such polling revealed to those actively engaged in the debate, in this section we examine the partisan and nonpartisan poll data that were inserted into the public debate on the estate tax. We located, through extensive archival research and interviews with political actors, the publicly released national polling data on the estate tax that date from 1997 to 2003. This period encompasses the time when estate tax repeal had its greatest momentum on the national stage. In 1997, following the passage of an estate tax reform provision to raise the unified exemption from $600,000 to $1 million, the new goal of many estate tax opponents became estate tax repeal; and both houses of Congress have held floor votes on the issue of estate tax repeal.

Many analysts, and even strong advocates of repeal, reported being surprised by how wide-ranging were the contours of opinion that became apparent. After all, considering that only the wealthiest 2 percent of Americans pay the estate tax, and that the estate tax is the most progressive part of the tax code, the vast majority of the public could only lose from estate tax repeal. Yet many polls show that most people support repeal when it is presented as a stand-alone issue—even those least likely to pay the tax and most likely to be beneficiaries of the roughly $30 to $40 billion it raises each year. This amount of revenue boosts the federal budget by 1 to 2 percent, nearly enough to fund, say, the Department of Homeland Security or the Department of Education. Is the explanation that people do not understand their self-interest? There is indeed clear evidence that, in light of misunderstanding and misinformation, many do not. Yet, while this is an important component of the explanation for public support for estate tax repeal, polls show that, even when people are disabused of their illusions on this score, support for repeal remains surprisingly strong. Principled judgments about fairness, which were often primed by question wording, are at least as important as appeals to self-interest. That said, when asked to consider its priorities or the possibility of a higher exemption, the public's verdict typically shifts dramatically, to the extent that the large majority was then found to *support* retaining the estate tax in a reformed version.

1.1. Perceived and Misperceived Self-Interest

If we were to impute preferences based on accurately perceived expectations of economic self-interest, those who never expect to pay the estate tax should favor keeping it, given the likelihood that repeal would entail either a relative shift of the tax burden to them, or a reduction in services that might benefit them. It would be reasonable to anticipate no more than a modest showing in support of repeal: the small percentage of persons who might realistically risk paying the tax upon death, plus their likely heirs. Yet many polls since the late 1990s have shown widespread public support for estate tax repeal, in the realm of 60 or 70 or 80 percent. Moreover, supporters appear to be spread more or less equally across income groups, contrary to what self-interest would predict.[3]

More sophisticated economic models may impute preferences based on potentially inaccurate perceptions of economic self-interest; and misperceptions certainly do help to explain a good portion of the public support for estate tax repeal. People know very little about estate tax levels and rates and rules, as evidenced by a January 2000 Gallup poll, in which most people (53 percent) admitted they simply didn't "know enough to say" whether the "federal inheritance tax" was too high, too low, or about right. Obtaining accurate information can be difficult, especially when others have an incentive to mislead you. With little background knowledge, many people seem to guess that nearly everyone is taxed at death—a misperception sometimes encouraged by question wording. For example, in a 2003 National Public Radio / Kaiser Foundation / Harvard Kennedy School (henceforth NKK) survey, two-thirds of respondents either thought "most people have to pay" the estate tax (49 percent), or said they didn't know (18 percent); and 62 percent of those opposing the estate tax said one reason was because "it affects too many people." Controlling for socioeconomic and demographic factors, and general attitudes toward the tax code, Joel Slemrod uses results from this survey to estimate that the misconception that most families pay the estate tax "increases the likelihood of favoring abolition by 10.6 percent."[4]

[3] Lower-income persons support repeal of the estate tax at nearly the same rate as others. A 2001 McLaughlin poll showed support for repeal from 76 percent of those with incomes under $40,000 versus 81 percent of those with higher incomes. Joel Slemrod finds a similar result in his analysis of the 2003 NKK survey. Joel Slemrod, "The Roles of Misconceptions in Support for Regressive Tax Reform," in *Brookings Institution Briefing: Do Misperceptions Guide the Tax Policy Debate?* (Washington, DC, 2003).

[4] The analysis is a linear probability regression that controls for the belief that the current tax system is complex and/or unfair, age, gender, race, education, and income. The only variables that are found to be significant for support of estate tax repeal are misconceptions about who pays and being over age sixty-five. Slemrod, Joel. "The Role of Policy

In keeping with this, surveys consistently show that the number of people in favor of repeal drops when respondents are given information on exemption levels or how many people pay. For instance, in the NKK poll, 60 percent of respondents say they want to eliminate the estate tax when the exemption level is not specified. Yet the percentage who favor repeal drops to 48 percent when respondents are asked to consider an estate tax with an exemption of at least $1 million—which is what the actual exemption was slated to be even before the repeal law passed. When asked to consider an estate tax with an exemption of at least $5 million—which was one of the proposed reforms rejected in the Senate—even fewer, 35 percent, still favor repeal.

Precisely how misperceptions about the estate tax change people's views is difficult to say, but it may be through affecting a person's perception of self-interest in repeal or through affecting her unselfish evaluation of the social fairness of the tax. In practice, these reasons are entangled because, even provided with correct information, people may misunderstand their own self-interest, and their perceptions of social justice may correspond to their misperceived self-interest. For instance, once people were given more information about who pays the estate tax, and had heard arguments both for and against repealing it, the percentage of those believing that they or someone in their household would have to pay the tax fell from 37 to 30 percent in a 2002 Greenberg Research Poll, while support for repeal correspondingly dropped from 60 percent to 47 percent. Some of the change in views might thus be attributed to a change in respondents' perceptions of self-interest.

Yet more remarkable than the difference made by the presence of correct information is the difference that is *not* made. After all, a full 30 percent of informed people still believed someone in their household would have to pay the estate tax. This result is even more extreme than another often-cited July 2000 Gallup poll showing that 17 percent of informed respondents believe they will personally benefit from estate tax repeal, even after being told that only estates valued at over $1 million would be subject to estate tax. In the 2003 NKK poll, 69 percent of those supporting repeal said a reason that "it might affect [me] someday." Like stereotypical lottery ticket holders, Americans seem wildly optimistic in their judgments about their likely future wealth.[5]

Misconceptions in Support for Regressive Tax Reform," *National Tax Journal* 59, no. 1 (March 2006): 57–75.

[5] Larry Bartels provides further evidence that opinion on the estate tax is largely based on "simple-minded and sometimes misguided considerations of self-interest" that correspond closely to a person's "subjective sense of their own tax burden." Larry Bartels, "Democracy with Attitudes," in *Electoral Democracy*, ed. M. B. MacKuen and G. Rabinowitz (Ann Arbor: University of Michigan Press, 2003). In a detailed analysis of the 2002

1.2. Principles of Fairness

Despite the important role of evaluations based on self-interest—and confused self-interest—they do not seem to account for the majority of public support for estate tax repeal. A surprisingly high percentage of people—26 percent in the NKK poll—still want repeal even with an exemption of $25 million or more.[6] People's particular judgments about tax fairness are central to accounting for the high support for repeal, and repeal proponents learned to "message" their goal in terms of principles of fairness. We do not discount the possibility that public opinion on the estate tax could also have migrated in recent decades, especially as inflation, demographic changes, social changes, and economic changes have meant that people of more diverse backgrounds would likely come within the reach of the estate tax. However, we cannot determine the extent of any such shifts since, with few exceptions, similarly worded poll questions have not been asked over time.[7]

Whatever underlying shifts there may have been in public opinion, our analysis here shows that the dramatic disparities in publicly reported polling results over the past few years depended principally on framing and phrasing rather than timing. For instance, a December 1999 poll by the Democratic Emily's List found that only 37 percent of voters defined their stance as "favorable" when asked, "When you hear that George W. Bush wants to eliminate the inheritance tax, is your reaction to that fa-

---

National Election Study survey, Bartels finds that the perception that one's own tax burden is "too high" accounts for about a third of the net support for repeal; and, ironically, "this apparent misplaced self-interest is most powerful among people whose own economic circumstances make them least likely to have any positive personal stake in repealing the estate tax." Larry Bartels, "Homer Gets a Tax Cut: Inequality and Public Policy in the American Mind," (paper presented at the Annual Meeting of the American Political Science Association, Philadelphia, 2003). Note also that the economic and stock market boom in and around 2000 may have contributed somewhat to people's optimism. Moreover, the shift away from traditional defined-benefit pension plans toward 401(k), defined-contribution, and other individual retirement savings plans mean that some people might feel wealthier since they hold their own retirement assets.

[6] Although this 26 percent is less than half of the 60 percent of NKK respondents who supported repeal when no exemption level was specified, we cannot conclude that all those whose stance on repeal depended on the particular exemption level are self-interested. Some of them may instead view a higher exemption as more just.

[7] No real difference exists in responses to a question about "eliminating the inheritance tax" that was asked, in identical form, by the Pew Research Center in September 1998 and August–September 2000. A 10 percentage point difference does exist between responses to a question asked, in identical form with a margin of error of +/– 3.1 percent, by McLaughlin and Associates in September 2000 and January 2001. But responses to similar questions asked by Gallup in June 2000 and November 2002 yielded a 10 percentage point difference in the *other* direction.

vorable, neutral, or unfavorable?" One month later, a poll by the Republican consultants McLaughlin and Associates found that 79 percent of likely voters approved when asked, "Do you approve or disapprove of abolishing the estate tax, also known as the 'death tax'?" In yet another contrast, a neutral Gallup poll that was conducted within three days of that poll found that only 41 percent of adults felt the estate tax was too high when they were asked, "Thinking about the federal inheritance tax, do you consider this tax too high, about right, too low, or don't you know enough to say?" Though each of the questions is simply worded, they differ via invoking "George W. Bush," delivering negative connotations with the words "abolish" and "death," and encouraging respondents to be comfortable saying they don't know.

The strategic and disciplined use of the term "death tax," rather than "estate tax," has received particular attention as an innovation of repeal proponents. The terminology certainly seems to shift the issue to new ground: the tax is presented as one "on death—and not as one on wealth."[8] At one point in 1999 or 2000, the Republican leadership in fact issued a directive to its membership to use only the term "death tax" to refer to the estate tax. One of the major advantages of the term is that, in contrast to the term "estate tax," it makes the tax sound as though it applies to everyone; after all, everyone dies, but few people think of themselves as having "estates." In addition, the term also conjures up an image of government invasiveness during families' most terribly wrenching times. Not surprisingly, people react less favorably to the term. In a 2002 Greenberg Research poll, people rated the "estate tax" at 37.9 on a favorable-feelings scale of 1 to 100, but the "death tax" scored an even lower 31.3. However, as these numbers suggest, the impact of the term on public opinion seems to have actually been relatively modest. To control for the impact of the "death tax" terminology in question wording, the 2002 National Election Survey asked the question in two parallel forms and reported a difference of barely more than 2 percentage points; 67.8 percent favored "doing away with the estate tax," and 70.0 percent favored "doing away with the death tax."[9] The 2003 NKK poll found a larger difference, of 6 percentage points, when it added the phrase "that some people call the death tax" to a question about the estate tax. Yet a March 2001 CBS News / New York Times Poll that explained who pays the tax, thus negating any impact the term might have on its perceived scope, showed essentially no difference when it compared the use of the term "estate tax" to "estate/death tax."

[8] Joshua Green, "Meet Mr. Death," *American Prospect*, May 21, 2001.
[9] Bartels, "Homer Gets a Tax Cut."

More support for repeal was gained when it was related to principles of fairness, which might be firmly and easily evaluated by anyone, regardless of their familiarity with this particular tax. In a representative democracy, people may tend to defer to experts on questions they see as economic, but they are unlikely to do so on moral questions. Speaking about double or triple taxation has been particularly effective.[10] The rhetoric portrays the estate tax in moral rather than financial terms: as an unfair double tax, not as a fair means of preventing extraordinary wealth from altogether escaping taxation. In a January 2001 McLaughlin poll, even once informed of the exemption level and rate of the estate tax, 86.9 percent of voters agreed that it was "unfair for the government to tax a person's earnings while it is being earned and then tax it again after a person dies." Note that this is not a question about the estate tax itself, but the coupling of the estate tax with double taxation implies that the one is the other.

This coupling technique was often used in poll questions and in the public presentation of poll responses to produce the perception of towering opposition to the tax—upwards of 70 or 80 percent. It was even used to claim gay and lesbian support for repeal on the grounds that they were denied the benefits of the estate tax's 100 percent spousal deduction.[11] In truth, it is not the estate tax that discriminates against gays and lesbians, but rather the prohibition of their marrying. Of poll questions that coupled the issue of the estate tax with the unfairness of double taxation, the only result we saw with support of less than 70 percent was a May 2001 McLaughlin one in which 60 percent of likely voters thought it unfair to apply an estate tax of 40 percent or greater to *billionaires*. McLaughlin conducted this poll specifically to argue that "voters view the estate tax as wrong on principle"; indeed, the stance was more widespread among those earning less than $40,000. Figure

---

[10] While it is not precise to characterize the estate tax as equivalent to double taxation, since it captures revenue from many assets that would otherwise entirely elude tax, it is true that the estate tax may also double-tax some assets. The claim of double taxation is premised on the belief that the assets in an estate have already been taxed once under the income tax. Repeal opponents claim that the estate tax acts as a backstop to the income tax, covering assets that have escaped taxation, including capital gains, which are passed on at the time of death and are exempt from taxation because of the step-up in basis.

[11] In an April 2001 memorandum to "Interested Parties," Frank Luntz makes this claim on the basis of a poll of six hundred likely gay and lesbian Americans, in which 97 percent "believe that just like traditional married couples, they too should have the right to pass along their assets to their partner without paying up to 55% in death taxes," 72 percent believe the estate tax is "discriminatory," and 82 percent want to see it eliminated. Frank Luntz, "The Environment: A Cleaner, Safer, Healthier America," in *Straight Talk* (Washington, DC: The Luntz Research Companies, 2002).

6.2 shows results from those questions that ask about the "fairness" of the estate tax or about whether it is "fair" or not—producing results even more dramatic than did another effective framing technique, which was to ask about repeal as a stand-alone issue. Also worth noting is that, regardless of prompting, it appears that people opposed to the tax may have often evaluated it with reference to principles of tax fairness. Of those who supported repeal in the 2003 NKK poll, 92 percent say a reason is that "the money was already taxed once and it shouldn't be taxed again"—which is 18 percent more than the cohort who credit the next most popular reason (that "it might force the sale of small businesses and family farms").

Indeed, messages that emphasized the burden of the estate tax on family farms and small businesses were also especially resonant, possibly because the American Dream preserves a romantic perception of their bootstrapping spirit, because of a dispassionate recognition that enterprises are commonly heavy in business assets but low in cash flow, or because so many people own a small business or farm, or have a close family member who does.[12] In reality, most of the estate tax burden does not fall on family-owned businesses or farms; in 1998, only 1.6 percent of taxed estates held half or more of their value in family-owned business assets, and only 1.4 percent held half or more of their value in farm real estate or assets.[13] Notwithstanding this, the public was more likely to want to repeal the tax for these particular groups than for all people. The message of these findings was clear: it was in the interests of the Republican Party leadership and repeal proponents to try to associate relief for small businesses and farmers with complete repeal, and it was in the interests of the Democratic Party leadership and others who opposed all-out repeal to try to disassociate the two options.

Not all arguments polled by the pro-repeal side proved to be effective at winning public approval. Sociotropic arguments—which tried to trade on public support for what benefits the economy—are one example. A March 2001 poll by three business school professors, for example, found only one-third believing the tax reduces economic growth, almost 40 percent believing it does not, and over a quarter with no opinion.[14] An earlier

---

[12] In the 2002 Greenberg Quinlan poll, 36 percent of respondents said they or a family member had a small business, and 23 percent said they or someone in their family owned a family farm.

[13] Joel Friedman and Andrew Lee, "Permanent Repeal of the Estate Tax Would Be Costly, Yet Would Benefit Only a Few, Very Large Estates" (Washington, DC: Center on Budget and Policy Priorities, 2003).

[14] Keith Lantz, A. Lee Gurley, and Kenneth Linna, "Popular Support for the Elimination of the Estate Tax in the United States," *Tax Notes Today* 99 (2003): 1263.

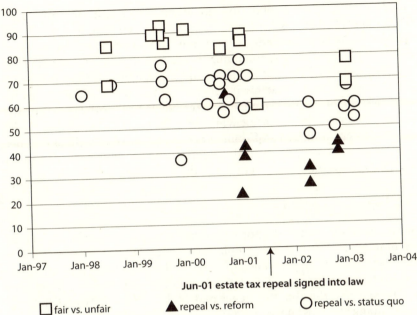

Fig. 6.2. Poll results on estate tax repeal: framing the issue as a question of fairness or a choice between options. This chart includes publicly released national polling data, from 1997 through the end of 2003, in which respondents were asked to evaluate the repeal or the fairness of the estate tax. The pollsters and poll sponsors are identified in the appendix to chapter 6. Data sources include the publications and press releases of the polling organizations and the Roper Center for Public Opinion Research at the University of Connecticut.

1998 poll by the pro-repeal Americans Against Unfair Family Taxation found that 53 percent of respondents believed that the estate tax would hurt the economy; but they and other organizations did not bother to poll the question thereafter. During the late 1990s, proponents of repeal de-emphasized arguments about economic effects in favor of appeals to perceptions of self-interest and moral claims about fairness.

Polls were also actively used to explore which messages or frames would most appeal to certain segments of the population. Extremely valuable—and surprising even to many advocates of repeal—was the finding that males and females, people of all age groups, people of all different income levels, and blacks and whites often gave more or less the same responses to many questions. This suggested the potential to enlist unexpected groups in support of the repeal effort. However, responses of people with different profiles did sometimes differ in informative ways. Blacks and Hispanic Americans, for instance, were less convinced than whites and Asian Americans by the argument that "death taxes are unfair to heirs, small businesses, and family farms and should be eliminated"; in one poll, only 48.5 percent of blacks and 55.3 percent of Hispanic Americans agreed with that statement, compared to 66.8 percent of whites and 87.8 percent of Asian Americans.[15] Yet blacks' support for repeal was entirely comparable to that of whites in response to a question framing estate tax repeal in terms of double taxation.[16] Certainly these numbers made it clear that there was little likelihood of intense hostility from minorities against the move to get rid of the estate tax.

1.3. A Matter of Priority

As we discuss in part 2, supporters of the estate tax seem initially to have maintained a sense of false complacency in the face of the repeal effort, expecting that, if only people correctly understood who was subject to the estate tax, nearly everyone would oppose repeal. This belief was way off the mark, as the above evidence makes clear. Eventually realizing that maintaining the existing estate tax was an untenable political position, by 2000 estate tax supporters took the stance of backing a more immediate and permanent reform of the tax—through raising the exemption, lowering rates, and/or excluding farmers and small businessmen—as an alternative to repeal. They struggled even to defend this moderated position, which they argued for principally on the grounds of the great progressivity of the estate tax. That only the very wealthiest Americans are subject to the tax may appeal to the less wealthy either out of self-interest or on principle, that is, as a desirable outcome. Either way, progressivity clearly convinces some people; and yet this remains only a limited group. Still nearly half of the *supporters* of the estate tax explicitly declined to justify their views in these terms in the NKK poll.

Despite the limited appeal of petitions for progressivity, supporters of the estate tax did not promote other principle-based arguments widely. Notably, they found the public unresponsive when the estate tax was de-

[15] These numbers are from an October 2000 Zogby International poll of 2,526 registered voters. Respondents were asked to agree with one of the following statements: "On estate or death taxes: Statement A: Death taxes are unfair to heirs, small businesses, and family farms and should be eliminated. Statement B: Since death taxes affect only a small percentage of small businesses and family farms, the tax process can be easily changed without exempting large estates and businesses."

[16] In a September 2000 McLaughlin and Associates poll of 1,000 likely voters in which respondents were asked, "Do you think it is fair or unfair for the government to tax a person's earnings while it is being earned, and then tax it again after a person dies?" 87.9 percent of whites and 91.6 percent of blacks considered it unfair.

fended on the grounds that "America is founded on the notion of equal opportunity for all," and "eliminating the estate tax creates a two-tiered society where some individuals do better than others based on inherited wealth rather than hard work." Although the equality-of-opportunity principle formed the basis of the successful defense of the estate tax in the 1920s, during the only other serious attempt in history to repeal it, the justification scored a disappointing 4.6 on a scale of 0 ("completely unconvincing") to 10 ("extremely convincing") in a 2002 Greenberg poll. In fact, only one of several principled justifications for the estate tax was viewed as "convincing" in that poll, scoring a 6.4. This rather surprising argument was that repeal should be opposed because, as the tax "has been eliminated and put back in place four times in the past, making estate planning impossible," it would be better to have a "permanent reform that simplifies this tax once and for all and keeps 99 percent of taxpayers exempt." With this discovery, the opponents of repeal now had their own somewhat misleading message for tapping into public frustration with government incompetence.[17]

Ultimately, advocates of retaining the estate tax found that their position received the most support when questions encouraged respondents to consider their priorities rather than their principles, as illustrated in figure 6.2. One way to do this was to pit estate tax repeal against more broadly beneficial tax cuts. For instance, in the 2002 Greenberg poll, supporters of the estate tax rated as most convincing (scoring 7.3) the argument that "We should cut taxes for the middle class by abolishing the marriage penalty and making college tuition and job training costs tax deductible, rather than giving more tax breaks to multi-millionaires." This is consistent with the fact that, in annual Gallup polls from 1997 through 2001, no more than 6 or 7 percent of Americans ever ranked estate tax repeal as their highest tax cut priority, whereas typically more than 30 percent prioritized "a tax cut for moderate and low-income Americans."

A second way to encourage respondents to voice their priorities was to allow them to choose an option between the two extremes of repealing or maintaining the existing estate tax. For instance, in a February 2002 Gallup poll, after being told that "federal inheritance taxes currently apply only to estates valued at more than $1 million," 55 percent of people wanted either to maintain the existing estate tax or to reform the tax to exempt family farms and small businesses—substantially more than the 39 percent who wanted repeal. The following week, a Bloomberg poll found that 47 percent of people preferred a raised exemption level

---

[17] They neglected to mention that every one of these occasions occurred more than a century ago, during times of war or national crisis, when the estate tax was resorted to as an intentionally temporary measure; and in fact, frequent reforms to the estate tax are what have made planning most difficult.

of $3 million to all-out repeal, slightly more than the 42 percent with opposite preferences. In addition, when people learned more about the estate tax, they seemed more likely to accept it; in 2002, a Greenberg poll found that, after being informed about the existing estate tax, and hearing strong arguments for both sides, two-thirds of people, 67 percent, preferred reform to repeal.

1.4. Theoretical Perspectives on Interpreting Public Opinion

Public support for estate tax repeal, as expressed in polls, has clearly been responsive to question wording and "framing effects"—to the degree that what the public truly wants is open to interpretation. This is generally consistent with how political scientists have long understood public opinion, particularly on policy issues, which is as something less than fully fixed and rational. At one extreme, theorists such as Philip Converse have viewed responses to opinion polling as tantamount to a confusion of "non-attitudes."[18] Others, such as Benjamin Page and Robert Shapiro, have argued that public opinion might be stable and clear on some high-salience policy issues,[19] if not necessarily on issues of lower salience like the estate tax repeal. In the case of the estate tax, public opinion may not obviously favor a particular policy position, but the polling of it reveals identifiable contours. That is, within a given framework—whether one that presents the issue as a principle of fairness or one that presents it as a matter of priority—public opinion does seem to follow roughly consistent patterns. Even the term "death tax" had limited impact on poll results. The relatively robust contours suggest the hypothesis that public judgments, even when hasty and misinformed, may be more responsive to reasons or recognized political symbols[20] than to vague associations. They are consistent with those theories that view people as holding a stable core of attitudes, even while their preferences on policy positions are not fixed.[21]

[18] Philip Converse, "The Nature of Belief Systems in Mass Publics," in *Ideology and Discontent*, ed. D. E. Apter (New York: Free Press, 1964).

[19] Benjamin I. Page and Robert Y. Shapiro, *The Rational Public: Fifty Years of Trends in Americans' Policy Preferences* (Chicago: University of Chicago Press, 1992).

[20] David O. Sears, "The Role of Affect in Symbolic Politics," in *Citizens and Politics: Perspectives from Political Psychology*, ed. J. H. Kuklinski (New York: Cambridge University Press, 2001).

[21] Bartels, "Democracy with Attitudes"; James A. Kuklinski and Norman L. Hurley, "It's a Matter of Interpretation," in *Political Persuasion and Attitude Change*, ed. D. C. Mutz, P. M. Sniderman, and R. C. Brody (Ann Arbor: University of Michigan Press, 1996); John Zaller and Stanley Feldman, "A Simple Theory of Survey Response: Answering Questions versus Revealing Preferences," *American Journal of Political Science* 36, no. 3 (1992): 579–616.

Yet some of the contours of public opinion on the estate tax are surprising from the standpoints of prevailing political science views. Notably, even though the subject is taxation—the quintessential pocketbook issue—people's preferences are largely based on beliefs that have nothing to do with self-interest. This is in sharp contrast to the well-known economic median voter theorem, which imputes preferences based on self-interest, implying erroneously that we would see just a small percentage of support for estate tax repeal. What we find is consistent with the view of D. O. Sears and C. L. Funk, who argue that self-interest has little effect on policy judgments unless the personal stakes are substantial and clear.[22] Many rational choice models nevertheless treat economic policy positions as reflective of self-interest, though this is not a necessary approach even within a rational choice framework. For instance, a variation on the economic median voter theorem, Downs's theory of rational ignorance, provides an important partial explanation for the extensive support seen. This theory justifies why, given the costs of obtaining correct information, it can be rational to remain ignorant and to base judgments on rough-and-ready shortcuts; thus sensible individuals might make guesses about the scope of the estate tax that misjudge their self-interest regarding the issue. Indeed, when optimistic misperceptions about future self-interest are taken into account, public opinion on the estate tax becomes somewhat more understandable. These misperceptions favored opponents of the estate tax, as both sides of the debate clearly understood. Still, they remain far from adequate for explaining the high levels of support for estate tax repeal.

Many people were inclined to see the estate tax in terms other than self-interest, and repeal proponents found that an effective strategy was to associate their position with principles of fairness that resonated with those whose support they sought. In doing this, they turned a seeming liability—the low salience of their cause—into a major opportunity. Low salience may have meant, consistent with a dynamic John Zaller has addressed,[23] that people were less likely to have thought about the estate tax, and less likely to have readily accessible facts and considerations in their minds that might resist arguments, associations, and information presented to them in poll questions. Estate tax defenders also tried to find principled messages that resonated with large majorities of the public, but were not nearly as successful. Why not? One reason, as discussed further in the upcoming section, is that they were generally less organized,

---

[22] D. O. Sears and C. L. Funk, "The Role of Self-Interest in Social and Political Attitudes," in *Advances in Experimental Social Psychology*, ed. M. P. Zanna (New York: Academic Press, 1991).

[23] John Zaller, *The Nature and Origins of Mass Opinion* (Cambridge: Cambridge University Press, 1992).

less innovative, and more on the defensive. They did not invest nearly as much in testing messages and remaking their image. Had they done so, they might have engineered a different outcome consistent with the stable existence of the estate tax since 1916. For instance, to encourage senators to support strategic "message" amendments that pitted the estate tax repeal against spending priorities like prescription drug benefits, they might have polled this trade-off; yet they never did so. The eventual realization that progressivity-based arguments were of limited appeal, and the discovery that their position could be defended as a once-and-for-all simplification of the tax code, provide evidence that strategic investment in public opinion research can yield high payoffs.

Yet, at the same time, was there also something inherently more difficult about winning over public opinion for the policy position they were advocating? In some ways, the supporters of the estate tax did have a particularly awkward position to argue, misconceptions about who pays the tax aside. To begin with, people have high animosity toward taxes as a general category. When asked, in a February 1998 Zogby poll, which one of three taxes they disliked the most, only 7 percent named the estate tax, but 31 percent of people volunteered—without any prompting—that they "hate all taxes." This suggests that it may be much easier to get people to state a position against a tax than it is to get them to state a position for it. In addition, many people seem uncomfortable with "class warfare," as the opposition dubbed it, notwithstanding that the public seems receptive to this argument applied to corporate taxation. Moreover, Americans have very little resentment against the wealthy and, as a whole, believe strongly in the achievability of the American Dream.[24] In the popular imagination, they are the success stories, like Bill Gates or Oprah Winfrey, the sorts of people you want to root for, not resent.

The decision to defend the estate tax on the basis of its progressivity seems to have saddled the supporters of the estate tax with a fundamental liability. This is that they were arguing for an inherently divisible position: that the wealthy should pay higher taxes, to a *degree*. In order for people to agree with them, they needed not only to accept the existence of the estate tax, but also to accept that the proposed rates or exemptions represented the right balance between the competing considerations of fairly giving to the poor and fairly taking from the rich. Yet the "right balance" is always a difficult call, inherently open to compromise and dependent on particular details. Moreover, a progressive outcome can be achieved in any number of ways, begging the question of why it should

---

[24] Jennifer Hochschild, *Facing Up to the American Dream: Race, Class, and the Soul of the Nation* (Princeton: Princeton University Press, 1996).

be sought through an estate tax. Meanwhile, in emphasizing principles of fairness, the other side was advocating an indivisible position, in which a judgment about the right or wrong approach was a straightforward call that could be made on the basis of simple convictions. This innovation of indivisibility was not one taken by supporters of the tax.

Consequently, they eventually resorted to framing the estate tax as a matter of *priority*. This allowed them to draw upon the flip side of the issue's relatively low salience, which was its relatively low priority in people's minds, turning this to their advantage. Most people were not compelled by the idea of estate tax repeal, and they preferred estate tax reform or other tax reforms. In essence, the reform advocates introduced choices—tapping into a combination of crosscutting and self-interested preferences—as a defensive maneuver. Inconveniently, but unsurprisingly, this strategy was most effective after respondents were educated about who pays the tax. Better informing the general public, of course, would be an overwhelming task owing to the low salience of the issue, but at least in certain districts this might be a conceivable, if daunting, option. That aside, the main objective of introducing choices and priorities into polling questions was not necessarily to find a practical way to change public opinion at large. In simply yielding favorable polling results, such questions could help take back the mantle of public opinion, and pressure legislators and the media with the shift.

The data on public opinion suggests, but ultimately leaves unexplored, some other interesting hypotheses about what might characterize the contours of public opinion on the estate tax or taxes more generally. First, at least in the case of the estate tax, more people responded favorably when presented with arguments about justice in *processes*, such as the principle that double taxation is wrong or that people should be allowed to pass on wealth to their children.[25] Sociotropic arguments about justice in *outcomes*, which tried to link the estate tax to progressivity or to economic growth, did not resonate with as many people. Whether or not this represents a general pattern—or one particular to tax issues, to low-salience issues, to trust in government,[26] to timing, to demographics, or to other

[25] In a different context, that of trying to distinguish "easy issue" voters from "hard issue" voters, Carmines and Stimson noted that some people may find it easier to think about processes than about outcomes. They differentiate "easy" issues from "hard" issues on the basis of three factors: being "symbolic rather than technical," more likely to "deal with policy means than ends," and "long on the political agenda." Edward G. Carmines and James A. Stimson, "The Two Faces of Issue Voting," *American Political Science Review* 74, no. 1 (1980): 78–91.

[26] Stanley Feldman, for instance, hypothesizes that when people have low trust in government, they are more likely to place weight on principles of process justice than on those of outcome justice. The reasoning behind this is that the latter depends more heavily on government intervention. However, in the case of the estate tax, this reasoning does not

conditions—is a good research question. Second, people responded more favorably to justifications that invoked more personal, concrete examples or symbols, such as images of how the estate tax affects family businesses and farmers, than to justifications that were expressed in abstract, numerical terms, such as explanations about how few people would pay the estate tax under an exemption level of $3 million. Indeed, taking this approach to the extreme, Republican strategist Frank Luntz advises in a memorandum, "A compelling story, even if factually inaccurate, can be more emotionally compelling than a dry recitation of the truth."[27] Finally, while it is clear that people dislike taxes in general, the existence of a large minority of the public that consistently desires estate tax repeal raises the question of whether certain types of taxes may be especially likely to make Americans bristle. Is it more offensive to be taxed at death than during life? Is there agreement about what constitutes "confiscatory" tax rates? Is there something inherently more objectionable about taxing assets or legacies—wealth that people may have long owned—as opposed to new income flows or transactions?

2. Leveraging Public Opinion for Policy Goals

By actively testing different messages, repeal proponents learned how better to frame their position to appeal to various segments of the population, as we have seen. The objective of these polls was not to be responsive to the public, but to learn how to make the public appear responsive to their goals. Yet how did these results enter into the policymaking process, if at all? Our analysis in this section shows that poll results were leveraged to help change the ideological profile of repeal and bring together a broad coalition around repeal. In conjunction with organized activity, repeated polling was used to generate momentum around repeal, through heightening awareness of the parameters of latent public opinion. This momentum both assured politicians that they needn't worry about a potential public backlash, and helped to hold the repeal coalition together. On top of this, favorable polling results impressed the potential opposition as an intimidating storehouse of political ammunition, compelling additional support in key districts and deterring some of the opposition and competing lobbyists from entering the fight.

always apply. The idea that repealing the estate tax would lead to more economic growth, for instance, assumed less government intervention. Stanley Feldman, "A Conflicted Public? Equality, Fairness and Redistribution" (paper presented at the Conference on Inequality and American Democracy, Princeton University, 2003).

[27] Luntz, "The Environment."

Opponents of repeal also eventually tried to do the same for their position, but they were a dollar short and a day late—conducting and releasing their first moderately detailed public poll in 2001, more than a year after repeal had already passed both the House and Senate, when most legislators had already committed to a position. From 1997 through 2003, pro-repeal advocates conducted eleven separate publicly released polls on the repeal or the fairness of the estate tax, compared to only three by its defenders. They also lacked the broad-based membership to claim to represent or influence particular districts. This is not to say that Democratic pollsters did not privately poll the issue and test it with focus groups in earlier years. They did, and because their studies affirmed the low priority of the issue, they reported feeling secure that the repeal issue would not derail their candidates in the short term. Presumably because that was their main concern, whatever other valuable information these polls revealed was neither made public nor, it seems, applied to the development of a strategy for the policy debate over the longer term. In contrast, as elaborated upon here, repeal advocates' leveraging of apparent public opinion was relentless, effective, and audacious in the degree to which it aimed to remake the image of estate tax repeal.

2.1. From Extreme to Mainstream

In the early 1990s, repeal of the estate tax was a fringe issue of the extreme Right, with only a handful of notably conservative cosponsors in the House and Senate. The orthodox wisdom was that any attempt to repeal the estate tax would be a debacle, an apparent move by shady politicians to do favors for their rich friends, at the expense of ordinary Americans. Yet, by June 2000, some of the most liberal members of the House were cosponsors of repeal; and 65 Democrats had voted for its passage. The situation was similar in the Senate, where the bill passed the Senate 59–39, with the support of 9 Democrats. Even some of the most committed advocates of repeal were surprised by the degree of bipartisanship, although they had worked for years to change the image of repeal and to broaden support.

The initial realization that repeal might be politically feasible emerged, for some, only after a 1992 Gephart-Waxman proposal to expand the estate tax produced a completely unforeseen public relations fiasco and was hurriedly withdrawn by Democrats.[28] Before then, even some key

[28] See HR 4848, the Long Term Care Family Security Act of 1992, introduced on April 9, 1992, and sponsored by Representatives Waxman and Gephardt, which included a provision that would reduce the unified credit against estate and gift taxes from $600,000 to $200,000.

repeal advocates had assumed that the public and politicians would strongly favor the estate tax. Repeal was initially left out of the 1994 Republican Contract with America, and it moved to the top of the Republican agenda only after successful experiences pursuing estate tax reform united and emboldened, rather than assuaged, repeal advocates. The estate tax reforms in 1997 and 1998 raised the exemption levels and created relief for family farms and small businesses. The latter was accomplished through the Qualified Family Owned Business Interests (QFOBI) provision,[29] but this turned out to be so confusing and difficult to apply that many on both sides of the issue had contempt for its workability. Some early champions of repeal sensed that what had been politically unthinkable in the past might become unstoppable as they learned better how to leverage public opinion, diversify their coalition, and remake the image of repeal.

Even as wealthy families and ideologically conservative groups contributed to the repeal effort, it was the wholesome, hardworking image of farmers and small businessmen that became its face. The key repeal coalitions recruited, as illustrated in figure 6.3, substantial breadth and weight. They were led by the National Federation of Independent Businesses (NFIB), the American Farm Bureau (AFB), the National Association of Manufacturers (NAM), the National Cattleman's Beef Association (NCBA), the Food Marketing Institute (FMI), the Newspaper Association of America (NAA), and the Policy and Taxation Group. Excepting the last group, which was funded by several wealthy families, all these were groups with nationwide chapters or members; and nine coalition members were listed in *Fortune Magazine*'s "Power 25" Washington interest groups. Their prioritization of estate tax repeal, especially when reform would have exempted nearly all their memberships, is striking considering that relatively few farmers and small businesspersons are affected by the tax. This is particularly so because the reform proposals might have been permanent, without the 2010 sunset clause that rendered the actual achievement of repeal questionable for most of its supporters.

Just as with most segments of the public, many lay members of these groups misunderstood their self-interest in repeal, or viewed the estate tax as unfair; and repeal advocates encouraged these beliefs. A survey in 1996 found more than 60 percent of family-owned businesses reporting that paying estate taxes would limit business growth and threaten their survival, with a third believing the tax liability would require them to sell all or part of their business.[30] Yet the Congressional Research Ser-

[29] The Qualified Family Owned Business Exemption (QFOBE) was created in 1997 and modified into the Qualified Family Owned Business Interests (QFOBI) deduction in 1998.

[30] Joseph Astrachan and Roger Tutterow, "The Effect of Estate Taxes on Family Business, Survey Results," *Family Business Review* 9 (1996): 303–14.

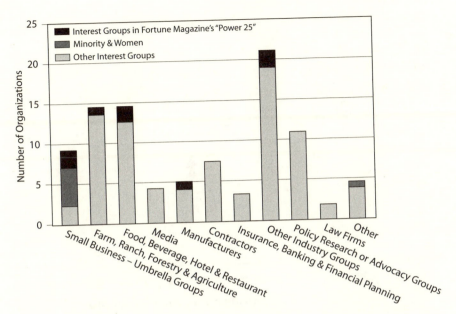

Fig. 6.3. The coalition for estate tax repeal as of January 2002. This nonexhaustive chart includes the seventy-seven members of the American Family Business Estate Tax Coalition, plus other groups that vocally supported repeal of the estate tax.

vice estimates the 1998 estate tax affected 7.5 percent of farm-owner decedents and 4.4 percent of business-owner decedents, and that "only a tiny fraction, almost certainly no more than a percent or so, of heirs of business owners and farmers would be at risk of being forced to liquidate the family business to pay estate and gift taxes."[31] Indeed, in an investigative piece for the *New York Times*, David Cay Johnston found that the American Farm Bureau could not direct him to any instance of a farm that had been sold to pay the estate tax, nor could he uncover one on his own reporting.[32]

Efforts by repeal advocates to diversify their profile were stimulated and backed by the results of public opinion polls that claimed overwhelming support for repeal across major demographic and political groups. Their polls and focus groups revealed valuable information about which principles appealed most to whom, and which frames were most effective. In addition to promoting specific angles—such as using "death tax" rhetoric

[31] Jane G. Gravelle and Steven Maguire, "Estate and Gift Taxes: Economic Issues," Congressional Research Service Report RL30600 (2001).
[32] David Cay Johnston, "Focus on Farms Masks Estate Tax Confusion." *New York Times*, April 8, 2001.

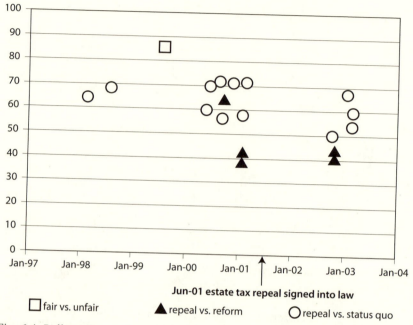

Fig. 6.4. Poll results on the repeal of the estate tax: frames used by neutral poll sponsors. This chart includes publicly released national polling data, published by neutral poll sponsors from 1997 through the end of 2003, in which respondents were asked to evaluate the repeal or the fairness of the estate tax. The pollsters and poll sponsors are identified in the appendix to chapter 6. Data sources include the publications and press releases of the polling organizations and the Roper Center for Public Opinion Research at the University of Connecticut.

or invoking the wholesome image of farmers—repeal proponents advocated framing repeal as a stand-alone issue in polls and congressional roll call votes. This approach effectively pitted repeal against the status quo. Perhaps unwittingly, neutral polling organizations like Zogby and Gallup repeated this framing and promoted it by disproportionately using it in their polling. This occurred even though, by 2000, the estate tax debates in Congress and in the Election 2000 presidential campaign were explicitly between repeal and reform, not between repeal and the status quo. Figure 6.4 shows that in the eighteen months prior to the June 2001 repeal of the estate tax, neutral polling organizations used the stand-alone framing that repeal advocates promoted, rather than presenting the choice as between repeal and reform, in seven of the ten poll results they released on estate tax repeal.

Polls were also more directly used as hooks to approach minority or-ganizations or sympathetic politicians. Thus gay and lesbian support was claimed after the findings of an April 2001 poll showing that 72 percent of likely gays and lesbians believe the tax is discriminatory, and that 82 percent would support a law to get rid of it even though they knew that they might not benefit.[33] Claiming widespread public support was a key part of the larger project to diversify the image of repeal, and the coali-tion became skillful at working with Democrats and interest groups that would not usually be thought of as natural allies for the cause. Frank Blethen, publisher of the liberal-leaning *Seattle Times* and an early key organizer for estate tax repeal, helped to persuade minority newspaper publishers to join the coalition for repeal and furnished local newspapers around the country with free copy-ready political ads against the death tax. The NFIB arranged for emotional testimony against the estate tax from unexpected faces like Chester Thigpen, an elegant, eighty-three-year-old African American from Mississippi, the grandson of slaves, who had built an environmentally friendly tree farm business on the same land he was born on. Although he advocated reform, not repeal, his story was repeatedly circulated in the case for repeal. Patricia Soldano of the Policy and Taxation Group, and the savvy political strategists she hired, saw that it was possible and important to garner support from minority business owners, environmentalists, women's business groups, and gays and lesbians.

In addition, knowing that politicians are most sensitive to public opin-ion associated with their district, repeal advocates used targeted polls to claim the support of spatial, not only demographic or political, constitu-encies. For instance, in April 2001, McLaughlin published the results of state-level polls on estate tax repeal, and the approval ratings of senators, taken in Iowa, Louisiana, New Mexico, Montana, and South Dakota. These polls were no doubt meant to deliver reinforcement and pressure to Senate Finance Committee chair Charles Grassley (R-IA), Finance Committee ranking member Max Baucus (D-MT), and John Breaux (D-LA), all of whom supported the estate tax repeal and would shortly have the choice of bargaining for it, against other tax cuts, as members of the June 2001 omnibus tax bill conference committee. These polls also targeted Democratic minority leader and repeal opponent Tom Daschle (D-ND), wary repeal supporter Mary Landrieu (D-LA), and the states' other senators.

On top of this, members of the coalition operated an "inside-outside" strategy of grassroots mobilization at the district level. The coalition was

[33] See n. 11 above.

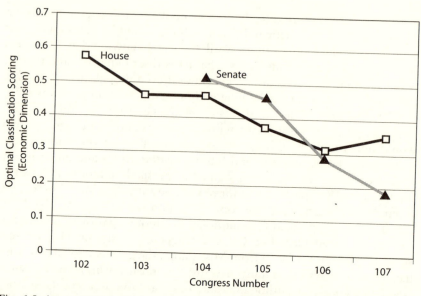

Fig. 6.5. Average ideological position of repeal bill sponsors. This chart uses the first dimension of Keith Poole's Optimal Classification data, which represents the rankings of legislators on a liberal-conservative dimension, based on their past voting records in the chamber. The scoring scale ranges from 1 (most conservative) to −1 (most liberal).

not only diverse in profile, but also spatially diverse enough to deliver a personalized message to elected officials across different types of constituencies. In this case, the NFIB and AFB were an ideal duo, with the former having its strongest influence in the House, and the latter having its strongest influence in the Senate, where farmers are overrepresented by virtue of the number of low-population states with farming interests. Coalition groups looked to contacts on the Hill for guidance as to which members of Congress or the Senate should be targeted. Then, understanding that "members of our organizations are the best lobbyists," they arranged not only large eruptions of letters and phone calls, but also in-person contacts from local civic groups and well-respected and successful local persons. These would ideally be "the owner of the local hardware store," the kind of person an elected official "likes to be seen with," or someone he or she has "known for thirty years." Not all of them would pay the estate tax, but these well-regarded individuals—the "grasstops" of the grassroots—caught the attention of members of Congress and contributed to the sense of a citizen uprising by hardworking, dignified, intelligent Americans who were being unfairly victimized.

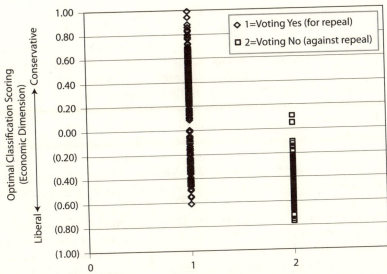

Fig. 6.6. Ideological distribution of legislators voting on HR 8 in the 106th Congress: June 9, 2000, roll call vote. This chart uses the first dimension of Keith Poole's Optimal Classification data, which represents the rankings of legislators on a liberal-conservative dimension, based on their past voting records in the chamber. Sixty-eight legislators with a negative (liberal) OC score voted yes, whereas only two legislators with a positive (conservative) OC score voted no. Thus the mean OC score of those voting yes is 0.27, whereas the mean score of those voting no is –0.44.

The public image of repeal was so completely remade that politicians stood to gain, not lose, from associating themselves with the moral high ground it had claimed and its array of all-American supporters. This made it even easier for politicians with ideological sympathy for repeal—particularly those who wanted to roll back the progressivity of the tax code—to prioritize the legislation. Other politicians signed on to the bill to please certain constituents, interest groups, fellow representatives, or party leaders, at the same time feeling comfortable that, not only would there be no eventual public backlash, there might well be public approval. "No one is going to lose his seat over supporting repeal," one congressman said to us. Conservative strategist Grover Norquist, borrowing a tactic used by environmental protection groups, decided to give politicians an added impetus to prematurely fingerprint themselves on the issue and included it in the political "scorecards" published by his group, Americans for Tax Reform. Even those who didn't want the estate tax to be repealed, but did believe it needed to be significantly reformed, understood the power of the image now being associated with repeal. Some of them told us that, even though they both hoped and expected the repeal bill would later be compromised in favor of a reform option, they supported it because they saw it as the only way to put the estate tax back on the agenda. As the bill gained momentum, moderates and Democrats were reassured by the presence of familiar company on the bill's list of sponsors, including moderate John Tanner (D-TN), who served as the bill's lead Democratic cosponsor, and liberal Neil Abercrombie (D-HA), both of whom were frustrated with their party's failure to court small businesses. Surprisingly to many, repeal was even backed by the Congressional Black Caucus, though not unanimously, apparently to protect the capital accumulation of the first large wave of black entrepreneurs and businessmen.

Led on the Hill by Congresswoman Jennifer Dunn (R-WA) and Senator Jon Kyl (R-AZ), repeal advocates steadily built support across the spectrum. Figure 6.5 charts how dramatically the issue shifted on the ideological spectrum by comparing, across Congresses, the ideological rankings of the average repeal bill sponsor, using Keith Poole's Optimal Classification (OC) system.[34] The OC data represent a calculation of the liberal-conservative ideological rankings of individual legislators based on their past voting record in the chamber. In the 102nd Congress, only 3 extremely conservative legislators supported repeal, but by the 106th Congress, the *average* sponsor—of 244 in the House and 47 in the Senate—was a mainstream Republican. Figure 6.6, which uses OC scores to show the distribution of House legislators' votes in June 2000, demonstrates the extraordinary degree to which repeal was rebranded to penetrate deep into the Democratic Party. It gained the support of not only conservative Democrats, but also liberal ones who, on most budgetary bills, would not be seen on the side of conservative Republicans.

2.2. The Running Room of Public Opinion

The positive public image of estate tax repeal gave its supporters running room that the other side didn't have, largely because they were hamstrung by a failure effectively to manage their own public image in the eyes of politicians. Initially, supporters of retaining the estate tax paid little attention to changing views about public opinion, instead focusing on countering misinformation and pro-repeal arguments on the Hill. Not until early 2001, years after the repeal effort had begun in earnest, after estate tax repeal had already passed both houses by large majorities, and

---

[34] Keith Poole, "Non-Parametric Unfolding of Binary Choice Data," *Political Analysis* 8 (2000): 211–37.

only after the Democrats had lost the White House, did supporters of the estate tax put large resources into recrafting its public image. Only then did they pay for strategic polling and launch a coordinated image-oriented campaign. Yet they had trouble developing a public image that could compete with the repeal advocates' rainbow coalition. Many life insurance providers were strongly opposed to estate tax repeal, but because this was fundamentally out of a self-interest in their estate-planning and insurance business, it undeniably would "look bad" to take too high a profile a stance. So they hesitated about whether and how to take action. Labor organizations were preoccupied with other priorities and uninterested in opposing tax cuts that are, in fact, supported by many of their lay members, actual self-interest aside. Many charitable organizations also were wary of estate tax repeal because they expected repeal to lead to a steep decline in charitable bequests, but not all of them felt free to speak against the repeal for fear of seeming greedy and alienating wealthy donors or board members. Debating their options internally, they, too, hesitated.

Supporters of the estate tax at last received a public relations boost in February 2001, when, assisted by a Boston-based group called Responsible Wealth, Bill Gates, Sr., George Soros, Steven Rockefeller, and over a hundred other wealthy businessmen, public figures, and philanthropists published a statement opposing repeal. Warren Buffett insisted even more vehemently on the tax's importance in making success dependent on merit rather than inheritance. The unexpected statements caught the public eye, but the supporters of the estate tax still lacked a very compelling image; they appeared to be a collection of the ultrawealthy plus highbrow liberal think tanks. Moreover, despite this public stance, they did not supply significant funding to groups like OMB Watch and Responsible Wealth to run extensive and repeated polls that might dislodge the framing of the issue that was, by then, deeply entrenched in media treatments and politicians' perceptions. The Gates ad was shrewdly countered by Black Entertainment Television founder Bob Johnson, who organized some fifty prominent African American businessmen to sign their own syndicated advertisement defending repeal as conducive to capital formation in the black community. In addition, a new group called Disabled Americans for Death Tax Relief emerged to declare the millionaire opponents of repeal "callous and heartless" for denying disabled persons the "full financial help" of their parents. Clearly, supporters of the estate tax were not going to find it easy to create the more appealing public image, but now they were battling for it.

Led by Responsible Wealth and OMB Watch, some charitable sector organizations, insurance sector representatives, and others joined up in 2001 to coordinate an active, savvier opposition campaign. Their financial investment and organizational resources paled in comparison to those of the other side, but they were able to make headway, as late in the debate as it was. Among other things, they invested in polling different messages on the estate tax issue and were able to report that, when given choices, the American public preferred reform to repeal by a ratio of two to one. This finding, in combination with a worsening federal budgetary situation, the new priority of a war on terrorism, and the strategic introduction of Democratic proposals to reform the estate tax at last gave some of the cover of public opinion to legislators who wished to vote against permanent repeal. In June 2002, six senators who had previously voted for repeal nevertheless voted against making the repeal permanent.

In contrast, the Republican leadership had been leveraging public opinion to their advantage for years. In both the House and the Senate, Republicans did not miss opportunities to force stand-alone votes, against tradition on tax bills. This was an issue that they clearly saw as politically difficult for many Democrats. They had learned the previous year that a large omnibus tax bill has a sticker-shock problem. Members can oppose it as simply being too expensive. Moreover, individual members could claim that they supported aspects of the bill, but not others, and so—contrary to logrolling logic—were obliged to oppose the whole. Yet the message behind one's vote on a stand-alone bill is clear, and many members did not want to be on the record against repeal. Others simply found it difficult to vote no on tax cut after tax cut. This fingerprinting strategy was especially important once the White House changed hands and some Democrats discovered that what they thought of as "free votes"—votes that would ingratiate some, even as the legislation would assuredly be vetoed by President Clinton—were no longer so. As well as the pressures that had earlier impelled them to support repeal, they now had to confront the public relations risk of being seen as flip-floppers if they backtracked.

Supporters of repeal had leverage because they could make a credible threat to take the issue public in campaigns against politicians who did not support their bills. They had amply demonstrated their ability to tap into public attitudes in opinion polls, as well as to direct effective district or state-level agitation by interest groups. In fact, they later made good on some of these threats. For instance, public relations stunts and death tax–related ads on the radio, in print, and/or on television were launched against repeal opponents such as Senator Paul Wellstone (D-MN), Senator Patty Murray (D-WA), Senator Jean Carnahan (D-MO), presidential candidate Governor Howard Dean (D-VT), and Senate Minority Leader Tom Daschle (D-SD). In the ad targeting Daschle, who lost his 2004 reelection bid by a single percentage point, an announcer leverages his vote against repeal to tap into widespread resentment of overtaxation: "You're born. You go to school. You work hard. You raise a family. You pay your taxes. And when you die, the IRS can tax you again, taking as much as 55 percent of everything you've saved for your children. It's called the death tax. And it's wrong. . . . Isn't a lifetime of taxes enough?"[35]

Beyond deterring the opposition to repeal, positive public perceptions of estate tax repeal also played a role in keeping competing tax cut lobbyists at bay. The apparent popularity the issue had gained by 2000 encouraged presidential candidate George W. Bush to include it in his proposed tax cut plan and to mention it frequently in his campaign speeches, to resounding applause. Once in office, his first tax cut proposal included the same four elements he had pitched in his campaign: income tax rate cuts, marriage penalty relief, a child tax credit, and estate tax repeal. Enthused by Bush's successful entrance into the White House, Republicans in Congress were ready to be deferential to their new president and his tax relief package. Long-standing and more broadly beneficial proposals such as a capital gains tax cut or alternative minimum tax reform were sidelined in part because they were less arousing. Also, aware that it would cut a bad public image to provide corporate tax breaks ahead of individual tax relief, the White House ordered corporate lobbyists not to try to put their priorities into this bill, promising them a later corporate tax relief bill. Thus, although, by itself, public opinion was not sufficient to move estate tax repeal to the top of the agenda, it cleared space for advocates, giving them the running room that others did not have. The estate tax made this "cut," and others, not only because politicians could agree with it or had something to gain from supporting it, but also because they had come to believe it couldn't hurt them in the eyes of the public.

2.3. All or Nothing

By insisting on repeal, rather than aiming for any of a number of estate tax reform options, estate tax opponents had strengthened their tactical hand. First, as we discussed earlier, the public responded most favorably to principled arguments for repeal when considered as a stand-alone issue, so this indivisible stance helped to construct an image of widespread public support. Second, anticipating that they might need to compromise in order to get past the multiple veto points—the House, Senate, president, and complex budgetary rules—it may have been prudent to stay with as extreme a position as could be managed, particularly in the

[35] The ad was paid for by the Club for Growth Advocacy, a 527 organization founded in 2001 to "educate the public and lobby for policies that promote economic growth." The sum of $25,000 was dedicated for this particular run, April 14–25, on statewide cable networks.

years before unified party control was achieved in 2000. Third, the repeal stance was vital for holding together the coalition of interest groups and ideologues driving the legislation. Anything less would have splintered the coalition, because they would have disagreed about what form any reform should take, and their sets of interests would have ceased to overlap. Repeal was their least common denominator. Farmers, for instance, would generally have preferred a higher exemption level to address their concerns about the valuation of inherited land, while large family businesses would have preferred lower estate tax rates since they are less likely to be fully exempted by a higher exemption level. As will be explained, farmers were also extremely averse to proposals to tie repeal to the implementation of carryover basis, a rule that would subject many a bequeathed asset to larger capital gains taxes by setting the original purchase value, rather than the market value at the time of inheritance, as the tax basis. Meanwhile, conservative ideologues seemed interested in repeal above all, motivated by the prospect of eradicating an entire tax, and the most progressive one at that.

Yet, especially in 2001 and afterward, the coalition experienced serious centrifugal pressures because some groups, particularly those with large memberships who were doing the legwork, were not necessarily well served by continuing to be wed to repeal. Although legislators had repeatedly voted for an enduring repeal, the June 2001 omnibus bill that did pass included only a one-year repeal in 2010, and then a reinstatement of the estate tax—at 2001 levels—in 2011. Because of a combination of stubborn minority opposition in the Senate and budgetary constraints, it became highly uncertain whether a full and permanent repeal of the estate tax would ever be passed. Any of a number of foreseen and unforeseen obstacles might overwhelm it: the economy has since worsened; the war on terrorism and in Iraq has taken front stage and eaten into the budget; other tax cut priorities threaten to close out the estate tax repeal; the Democrats won the House and Senate in 2006; and Senate scoring rules make an extension of repeal dramatically more costly, on the books, as 2011 draws closer.

In addition, the risks of staying in the repeal coalition are even higher for those who object to carryover basis, which would be the cheapest rule to implement in conjunction with any repeal. The current law allows the capital appreciation of inherited assets to be based on market value at inheritance, a practice called stepped-up basis, rather than being based on the original purchase value, a practice called carryover basis. Yet the quid pro quo for the one-year repeal had been the replacement of stepped-up basis with carryover basis, lending momentum to the possibility that the quid pro quo for any permanent repeal might also be carryover basis. Although in practice it can be difficult to capture tax on carryover amounts, this issue was of particular concern to farmers and proprietors of independent newspapers, whose businesses often have few liquid assets but considerable accumulated net worth. Many were strongly opposed to giving up stepped-up basis, even if it meant accepting an estate tax reform rather than repeal, and some thought the issue might split the coalition. The issue in fact led to a split among farmers; as the AFB continued to lead the repeal coalition, another major farm group, the National Farmers Union, whose members are on average less wealthy, began vocally to support a reform option that would immediately raise the exemption to $4 million per person ($8 million per couple) and modestly lower rates.

Once coalition members understood the trade-offs, why didn't they show more interest in the compromise proposals? These included legislation dramatically and permanently to raise the exemption to $5 million or more, or to entirely exempt family farms and small businesses from the estate tax while maintaining stepped-up basis. Arguably, their memberships would have much preferred these immediate changes to the risks inherent in pursuing permanent repeal. When questioned about the reasons for their continued allegiance to total repeal in light of these options, some coalition members emphasized the importance of staying unified, pointing out that they had already been much more influential as a whole than they could have been in parts. Some referred to a lack of trust in the Democrats or their reform options, noting that inflation would erode any proposed threshold, and that it can be difficult to craft workable devices, as shown by their previous experience with QFOBI. Others alluded to potential costs of turning on Republican allies on the Hill who would be needed for other legislative priorities.

In addition, some interest group members emphatically justified their stance with the conviction that the estate tax is morally wrong, suggesting how completely they had embraced the framing in which the pro-repeal forces had invested so much. While we have no doubt that the actions of organized interests were centrally motivated by other considerations, is it possible that the principle kept their troops fired up and purposeful? Some literature in political psychology suggests that participation in groups tends to move like-minded people to more extreme points in the direction indicated by their predeliberative commitments.[36] If so, glue is perhaps the right metaphor in this regard. Principles and ideologies may help hold together organized groups, and perhaps even move members to subordinate individual interests to a common purpose, but they are not sufficient on their own to move political agendas.

[36] Cass R. Sunstein, "Deliberative Trouble? Why Groups Go to Extremes," *Yale Law Journal* 110, no. 71 (2000): 71–119.

Perhaps they magnify intensity of cause after commitments have been made for other reasons.

Regardless, standing by the principle of repeal was viewed by coalition members as important for keeping *policymakers* receptive. By premising their message on the idea that the tax is just "wrong," they had generated the appearance of overwhelming public support, built a broad coalition, and shifted politicians' thinking about the estate tax. The matter was viewed less and less as a distributive issue about which horse trading and compromise can be acceptable,[37] and more and more as an issue of moral principle, about which compromise seems inherently hypocritical. That they could do this with such a highly progressive tax is impressive as well as ironic, given that money is inherently divisible. To compromise now risked weakening their carefully crafted public image and accepting the legitimacy of "splitting the difference." Thus the need to assure politicians that their stance could resonate with the public, in conjunction with the strategic desire to maintain a unified alliance among diverse interest groups and ideological politicians, may have increased the likelihood of achieving an all-or-nothing outcome, versus a marginal reform.

2.4. Perspectives on the Role of Public Opinion in Policy Debates

Public opinion seems to have played a key role, but not a direct role, in the repeal of the estate tax. Aware of the relatively low priority of the estate tax issue in the public eye, most politicians are unlikely to have felt immediate pressure due to public opinion. After all, the public as a whole was not particularly engaged, and the contours of its opinion could be interpreted in support of either reform or repeal. Thus the dynamic of this debate does not correspond to the dynamic in a thermostatic model of policymaking, in which politicians respond to public opinion with policy changes, at least on higher-salience or priority issues; and public opinion in turn responds to policy change.[38] Still, perceptions of the underlying contours of public opinion did appear to matter for the estate tax outcome.

In particular, politicians were alert to latent public opinion—to use V. O. Key's phrase:[39] how the public might view the issue should salience be

---

[37] Nicholas Miller, "Majority Rule and Minority Interests," In *NOMOS XXXVIII: Political Order*, ed. I. Shapiro and R. Hardin (New York: New York University Press, 1996).

[38] Christopher Wlezien, "The Public as Thermostat: Dynamics of Preferences for Spending," *American Political Science Review* 39 (1995): 981–1000; Page and Shapiro, *The Rational Public*.

[39] John Zaller, "Coming to Grips with V. O. Key's Concept of Latent Opinion," in *Electoral Democracy*, ed. M. MacKuen and G. Rabinowitz (Ann Arbor: University of Michigan

raised, or should active efforts be made to influence their views. Many legislators, wary especially because repeal could be portrayed as a favor to their wealthy friends, were reluctant to act unless there were solid indicators that latent public opinion would not rise up to haunt them. For advocates of repeal, it was critical to manage public opinion to combat the long-standing conventional wisdom on Capitol Hill that supporting estate tax repeal would be costly with voters. They drew adeptly upon common misperceptions of self-interest and coupled repeal with principles of fairness to generate the appearance of extremely high support for repeal. Their very position of a hard-line stance on repeal was chosen, and adhered to, after they took into account several factors that included the degree to which that position might resonate with the public. Understanding that politicians feel pressure to create policies that benefit groups with positive social constructions,[40] repeal advocates also crafted an image as independent farmers, hardworking small businessmen, and entrepreneurial minorities.

Reform advocates struggled to take back the mantle of public opinion. To do so, they relied on the flip side of low salience, which was the issue's low priority in people's minds. Note that while both the low salience and low priority of an issue might contribute to a low overall intensity of public opinion on that issue, the two are distinct concepts and played different roles in this policy debate. The low salience worked to repeal advocates' advantage because it meant that many people had not given the matter much thought, allowing more scope for careful framing to have effect. The low priority of repeal meant that nearly everyone preferred other tax cuts to repeal, as well as that healthy majorities supported estate tax reform options over repeal.

Each side's opposing claim to represent public opinion was plausible because the contours of public opinion on this issue were so wide. Yet it may not be unusual that public opinion appears to be quite different depending on which lens is invoked.[41] Charged issues are often contentious precisely because there are two highly compelling ways to look at them. For instance, studies have shown that while only 20–25 percent of poll respondents say that too little is being spent on "welfare,"

Press, 2003); V. O. Key Jr., *Public Opinion and American Democracy* (New York: Alfred Knopf, 1961).

[40] Anne Schneider and Helen Ingram, "Social Construction of Target Populations: Implications for Politics and Policy," *American Political Science Review* 87, no. 2 (1993): 334–37.

[41] Lawrence R. Jacobs and Robert Y. Shapiro, "Presidential Manipulation of Polls and Public Opinion: The Nixon Administration and the Pollsters," *Political Science Quarterly* 110 (1995–96): 519–38; Benjamin Ginsberg, "Polling and the Transformation of Public Opinion," In *The Captive Public*, ed. B. Ginsberg (New York: Basic Books, 1984); Walter Lippman, *The Phantom Public* (New York: Harcourt, Brace and Co., 1925).

63–65 percent say that too little is being spent on "assistance to the poor."[42] How, if at all, people square the tensions in holding these two views simultaneously is a complex matter that activists on neither side of the issue try to resolve. Instead, they advertise the aspect of majority opinion that is favorable to their cause. In the hurly-burly of political conflict, publicized opinion polls are less authentic measures of public opinion than they are rocks that activists throw at one another to signal their reach.

On the estate tax issue, the battle to produce favorable polling results was part of the larger war to manage politicians' perceptions of the lens through which the public would view the issue. Advocates of repeal were especially effective at all aspects of this war. They communicated the framings of public opinion that best served their objectives; diversified the coalition to change their image from privileged to all-American; implied, through coordinating an active inside-outside strategy, that the issue had a reasonably high level of public salience and priority, at least among the "grasstops"; and presented a credible threat that they could, and would, move district-level public opinion on the issue as a last resort. Boosting these efforts was the fact that neutral polling organizations, perhaps unwittingly, disproportionately took up the stand-alone framing promoted by repeal advocates—even though the political debate pitted repeal against reform, not repeal against the status quo. In changing how legislators saw the issue on an ideological spectrum, and how legislators thought the public would react to it, advocates changed legislators' calculations of the likely electoral costs and benefits of their positions.

Advocates of repeal may have been especially effective at signaling the latent threat of a public backlash because they invested, over several years, in polling, framing, and "grasstops" organizing. This required financial and membership resources, and as reported by people on both sides of the issue, the repeal advocates were advantaged in at least three stages. Wealthy individuals and interest groups were willing to provide seed money to initiate message framing and organize the coalition; they had the money for frequent polls and the organization to coordinate "grasstops" activism; and, in some districts, they had the funds to heighten salience on repeal and turn it into a potent campaign issue. This raises the question of whether those with greater resources have the better ability to claim the mantle of public opinion. If so, it may not be that unusual to see, as we did in this case, great asymmetry in the skillfulness with which intense interests on each side manage their public image. Repeal advocates could credibly threaten to fire up latent public opinion to discipline legislators. This disciplining might take place through either preelectoral

[42] Bartels, "Democracy with Attitudes."

rational anticipation, in which legislators change their stance to increase the probability of their reelection, or postelectoral turnover, in which those who stick to unpopular stances are voted out of office.[43]

Regardless of which side was more effective, on neither side of the debate did concentrated interests or political leaders try to circumvent public opinion to achieve their objectives. This idea that public opinion matters for policy outcomes stands in contrast to theories that, at the other extreme from the thermostatic model, see public opinions on policy issues as nonconsequential. Among these are the views that public opinion is irredeemably difficult to interpret[44] or itself the product of manipulation by a "power elite."[45] Other theorists contend that, even if public opinion is viewed as stable and well formed, it still may not matter for lower-salience or lower-priority policy issues; politicians may not expect voters to sanction them, because of crosscutting preferences over other issues that matter to them,[46] strong habitual stability in party or candidate allegiances,[47] or other factors. With these ideas in mind, some theorists contend that policy outcomes are determined by the activities of interest groups or politicians who, especially on relatively low-salience issues, can either disregard or manipulate public opinion.[48]

What we observed suggests an alternative theory of political outcomes in which interpretations of latent public opinion can enable or obstruct change, but these interpretations are largely driven by interest group activity and political leadership. If so, the contours of public opinion, in interaction with organized activity selectively to reveal and perhaps even shape latent opinion, determine how much "running room" policy leaders have to maneuver. If issue advocates can convince politicians that latent public opinion is favorable to their proposal, or at least not against it, they may widen the range of politically acceptable outcomes to en-

[43] James A. Stimson, Michael B. Mackuen, and Robert S. Erikson, "Dynamic Representation," *American Political Science Review* 89, no. 3 (1995): 543–65.

[44] Converse, "The Nature of Belief Systems"; E. E. Schattschneider, *The Semi-Sovereign People* (New York: Holt, Reinhart & Winston, 1960).

[45] See G. William Domhoff, "The Power Elite, Public Policy, and Public Opinion," in *Navigating Public Opinion: Polls, Policy, and the Future of American Democracy*, ed. J. Manza, F. L. Cook, and B. I. Page (Oxford: Oxford University Press, 2002); J. W. Kingdon, "Politicians, Self-Interest, and Ideas," in *Reconsidering the Democratic Public*, ed. G. E. Marcus and R. L. Hanson (University Park: Pennsylvania State University Press, 1993).

[46] John Roemer, "Does Democracy Engender Justice?" In *Democracy's Value*, ed. Ian Shapiro and Casiano Hacker-Cordón (Cambridge: Cambridge University Press, 1999).

[47] Angus Campbell, Philip E. Converse, Warren E. Miller, and Donald E. Stokes, *The American Voter* (New York: John Wiley, 1960).

[48] John Geer, *From Tea Leaves to Opinion Polls: A Theory of Democratic Leadership* (New York: Columbia University Press, 1996); Mancur Olson, *The Logic of Collective Action: Public Goods and the Theory of Groups* (Cambridge, MA: Harvard University Press, 1971).

compass their proposal, creating an opening for policy leaders to run with the issue. Gaining adequate running room does not imply that a policy proposal will pass—district pressure from interest groups and the ideological preferences of politicians certainly matter more for giving impetus to legislation—but it would imply that politicians are no longer wary that public opinion could be turned against them regarding it. Systematic studies across issues could help identify which factors, such as low salience or the existence of multiple public opinion contours, most contribute to large potential running room.

This "running room" view bears some resemblance to a latitude theory of public opinion, but it is distinct, with different implications. In latitude theory, public opinion may constrain policymakers from pursuing policies outside of some zone of acceptability, lest they "suddenly encounter a catastrophic avalanche of protest"; but so long as politicians stay clear of the "electrified fence," public opinion is not a constraint.[49] In our view, public opinion does exhibit contours that limit how the public might respond to various framings of the issue, but whether or not politicians have an accurate picture of the contours, as well as whether they assess them as unthreatening or as electrified barriers, depends largely on interest group and partisan activity. Moreover, there is considerable room for political advantage and maneuver within the contours, and sometimes the chance to alter them. In contrast to the predictions of latitude theory, even when public opinion contours are constant, the potential for public opinion to enter the debate as a constraint, and in which direction, may change dramatically. Given this wide potential for change, when interest groups are committed to gaining support for legislation (as distinct from when their focus is on influencing an election), they may often find it more direct and cost-effective to invest in altering politicians' perceptions of public opinion, rather than in altering public opinion itself.

In the case of estate tax repeal, before repeal advocates refashioned the issue's public image, the conventional wisdom had indeed been that a hurricane of public outrage would blast politicians who supported repeal. Yet the coalition for repeal eventually did such an effective job at convincing legislators that public opinion was on their side, and could reliably be maintained that way, that the conventional wisdom was all but reversed. Many legislators then wondered if it would be acceptable to uphold the estate tax—or if that would contribute to their being branded as tax-and-spend types—as Daschle was by some. At that point, supporters of the estate tax became desperate to ensure that their side still had

[49] Gregory Andrade Diamond, "Implications of a Latitude-Theory Model of Citizen Attitudes for Political Campaigning, Debate, and Representation," in *Citizens and Politics: Perspectives from Political Psychology*, ed. J. H. Kuklinski (New York: Cambridge University Press, 2001).

running room too; this is why it was so important to demonstrate the low priority of the issue in the public eye. Although they have probably not succeeded in spinning the issue to the point that a repeal vote looks very costly—as had so long been assumed would be the case—their efforts at least helped reassure politicians that a vote for reform, rather than repeal, could be rendered as a respectable, safe position.

Thus the case of estate tax repeal suggests a dynamic in which the impact of latent public opinion may largely depend on interest group activity, at least on lower-salience issues. This view is distinct from both classic and modern models of policymaking that stress the direct influence of either organized interests or public opinion on politicians. It is compatible with, but still distinct from, views that highlight the influence of political leaders on public opinion, such as Lawrence Jacobs and Robert Shapiro's study of two high-salience issues, Clinton's health-care reform initiative and the Republican Contract with America. They emphasize, similar to what we find, that "crafted talk" is used to make existing policy agendas seem more agreeable to the public.[50] However, while in their cases political leaders have a read on public opinion and try to use the media as a conduit for communicating their messages to the public, in this case we find that interest groups joined political strategists to serve as critical intermediaries for interpreting public opinion to politicians.

In this view of politics, organized interests, as well as politicians, possess substantial potential for political entrepreneurship. In particular, interest groups can help clear and sow the locations of perceived minefields of public opinion. Their potential to be successful in doing so might be higher on lower-salience issues, for which the balance of political organizing may be more likely to be asymmetrical, and public opinion less fixed and less well understood. However, since low-salience issues may also be low-priority issues, opponents of a proposal may have a good deal of potential to be entrepreneurial in countering with alternative frameworks.

The importance that interest groups placed on interpreting public opinion to politicians seems, in the case of the estate tax, to have been one factor contributing to the coalition's strange adherence to total repeal, even when such a stance was contrary to the interests of most of its members. At that point, suddenly changing one's tune was seen as a public image risk that outweighed the perceived risk of continuing to pursue an all-or-nothing outcome. The repeal coalition chose to go for broke in 2001, betting and hoping that they would be able to win again down the stretch.

[50] Lawrence R. Jacobs and Robert Y. Shapiro, *Politicians Don't Pander: Political Manipulation and the Loss of Democratic Responsiveness* (Chicago: University of Chicago Press, 2000).

As time wore on after the repeal, much received wisdom held that Congress would find a way to craft a compromise that would preserve an exemption of between $5 million and $7 million and a 45 percent rate before the tax came to be repealed in January 2010 and then automatically restored at its considerably more punitive 2001 level a year later: a $1 million exemption and a 55 percent top rate (rising to 60 percent on some estates). As the first of these deadlines approached at the end of 2009, the Senate Democratic leadership turned out not to be up to the task, perhaps because it had its hands full enacting health-care reform—the Obama administration's top domestic priority. The result was that the tax was indeed repealed in its entirety as the first decade of the new century drew to a close. The stakes remained high, however, because just as the proponents of repeal managed to block the passage of a compromise to keep the tax alive, it was far from clear that their opponents would be unable to block its reinstatement at 2001 levels a year later.[51] Plenty of running room remained, and it was impossible to tell who the eventual winners and losers would be.

[51] Carl Hulse, "Estate Tax Is Expiring but Death Won't Last," *New York Times*, December 19, 2009, http://www.nytimes.com/2009/12/18/us/politics/18cong.html?_r=1&emc=eta1 [12-23-2009].

CHAPTER SEVEN

The Constitutional Politics of Abortion in the United States

ONE OF DEMOCRACY'S greatest challenges is to devise ways to manage conflicts among people who harbor intense disagreements over public policy. This challenge is thrown into sharp relief by the American battle over abortion rights. As with the estate tax discussed in the previous chapter, beliefs about the rightness or wrongness of abortion are more intensely held by activists than by the mass public.[1] Until the early 1970s, when the federal courts became involved, this battle was fought out in legislative politics. But it was in state legislatures rather than in Congress because abortion regulation was exclusively a matter of state law. Bringing the federal courts in has added a dimension to the battle among organized interests different from what we saw in the estate tax controversy, one that provides a window on the subject of this chapter: the advantages and limitations of involving constitutional courts in divisive social conflicts.

Elite driven as it might be, the American debate over abortion is both passionate and relentless. Rooted in powerfully held beliefs, it seems to pit irreconcilable worldviews against one another. Religious convictions that a fetus is a person, and abortion therefore murder, run headlong into the categorical insistence that life begins at birth. Those who believe that global poverty, climate change, and demographic explosion are humankind's most intractable problems find themselves incredulous at spiritual leaders who travel the world railing against abortion and even contraception. Government policies to limit birthrates through abortion and family planning are seen by some as enlightened and necessary; for others they amount to wanton interference with inviolable human rights. Strongly held convictions that women are entitled to sovereign control of their bodies collide with equally resolute beliefs that pregnancy brings with it the responsibility—however unwelcome—to carry a fetus to term. Even murder has seemed justified in the eyes of some in order to prevent the performance of an abortion. "No judicial decision in our time," writes Ronald Dworkin of the Supreme Court's 1973 decision in *Roe v. Wade*,

---

[1] See Morris Fiorina, Samuel Adams, and Jeremy Pope, *Culture Wars? The Myth of a Polarized America* (New York: Pearson Longman, 2005), pp. 34–54.

which established that women have a constitutionally protected right to abortion, "has aroused as much sustained public outrage, emotion, and physical violence, or as much intemperate professional criticism."[2]

Alasdair MacIntyre goes further, remarking that the most striking feature of the modern abortion debate is its interminable character. The views that are pitted against one another are "conceptually incommensurable" in that although they are internally consistent, they rest on rival premises which "are such that we possess no rational way of weighing the claims of one as against the other."[3] The ambivalence and conflicting emotions that people feel about abortion were well reflected in a 1989 *Los Angeles Times* national opinion poll. It reported that although 61 percent of Americans think abortion is morally wrong and 57 percent think it is murder, 74 percent nonetheless believe that "abortion is a decision that has to be made by every woman for herself."[4] This inconsistency might reflect the reality that abortion is less important to most voters than it is to the activists who join battle over the issue. Perhaps people worry less about resolving conflicting impulses on matters that are less important to them than on matters that are more important. In any case, American ambivalence about the morality and legality of abortion has persisted. A 2000 *Los Angeles Times* poll again found that 57 percent of those questioned considered abortion to be murder, yet fully half of that 57 percent nonetheless believed in allowing women access to abortion.[5]

For all their contradictory impulses—indeed, perhaps partly because of them—it seems that people also expect to resolve the abortion debate. They argue in books, legislatures, and the media. They take issue with one another's reasoning and adduce statistics that they believe to be decisive for one or another aspect of the issue. Even as they sense, perhaps, that the abortion debate is beyond resolution, at some level many people cannot accept this. There *must* be a reasonable resolution of the debate, they seem to think; the question is how to arrive at it.

The U.S. Supreme Court has been engaged in a struggle over the abortion question for the better part of four decades. The 1973 decision in *Roe v. Wade*, supported by a majority of seven to two on the Court, seemed at the time to create a decisive resolution to the controversy. However, those who expected this decision to settle the matter by removing the abortion question from the realm of charged political debate

[2] Ronald Dworkin, "The Great Abortion Case," *New York Review of Books*, June 29, 1989, p. 49.

[3] Alasdair MacIntyre, *After Virtue: A Study in Moral Theory*, 2nd ed. (Notre Dame, IN: University of Notre Dame Press, 1984), pp. 6–8.

[4] Reported in Dworkin, "The Great Abortion Case," p. 49.

[5] Allisa J. Rubin, "Americans' Narrowing Support for Abortion," *Los Angeles Times*, June 18, 2000, http://articles.latimes.com/2000/jun/18/news/mn-42249 [04-21-2009].

were quickly disappointed; if anything *Roe* seemed to intensify and further polarize the public abortion debate. Nor has there been stability in the Supreme Court's view of the abortion question in the years since *Roe* was handed down. The right recognized in that decision was reaffirmed by a bare majority on the Court in *Planned Parenthood v. Casey* in June 1992, but both the content of the right in question and the jurisprudential basis on which it rests have evolved substantially.[6] Indeed, the reasoning on which the original *Roe* decision rested has largely been abandoned by the Court.

Part of the evolution in the Court's understanding of the right to abortion reflects changes in its personnel. In 1973 Justices William Rehnquist and Byron White were the only dissenters from the majority opinion authored by Justice Harry Blackmun. Within two decades Rehnquist was chief justice, and most of the original *Roe* majority had departed. Warren Burger, William Douglas, William Brennan, Potter Stewart, Thurgood Marshall, Lewis Powell, and Blackmun had all retired (as had the other dissenter from the majority holding in *Roe*, Justice White), and been replaced by Justices John Stevens, Antonin Scalia, Sandra Day O'Connor, Anthony Kennedy, David Souter, Clarence Thomas, Ruth Bader Ginsburg, and Stephen Breyer. All the replacements other than Ginsburg and Breyer (appointed by President Clinton in 1993 and 1994) were Republican appointees who were in varying degrees uncomfortable with the reasoning in *Roe*, the outcome, or both. Indeed, even Ginsburg was known to be uncomfortable with aspects of the reasoning (see below). This group of justices continued to serve together for over a decade until the summer of 2005 when Justice O'Connor announced her retirement and Chief Justice Rehnquist passed away—opening the way for President George W. Bush to replace them with Justice Samuel Alito and Chief Justice John Roberts.

The evolution of the right to abortion since *Roe* has been affected by factors in addition to the changing faces on the bench. It is possible to discern in that evolution attempts by various members of the Court to reconcile the apparently irreconcilable, to find a middle ground that could satisfy at least some of the contending parties who have sought to influence the Court's handling of the abortion issue. Several justices have struggled mightily in this regard. How successful they have been will be taken up in parts 2 and 3 below, when I explore the evolution of the Court's abortion jurisprudence and its implications for a democratic theory of the Court's role in a constitutional democracy such as ours. This is followed, in parts 4 and 5, by a discussion of the future of the constitutionally protected right to abortion in light of the intervening

[6] 112 S. Ct. 1791 (1972).

analysis. As a prelude to that, I begin with a sketch of the right's historical evolution.

1. History of the Constitutional Right to Abortion

There is a significant respect in which debate about constitutional protection for the right to abortion on the Supreme Court is detached from the public abortion debate. Kristin Luker is surely correct when she says of the public abortion debate that it is fundamentally "a debate about personhood."[7] The slogans and posters at demonstrations outside abortion clinics, at pro-life and pro-choice rallies, and in much of the discussion in the media might reasonably lead one to assume that the central question at issue is, indeed, about whether or not a fetus is a person. In fact no justice on the Supreme Court has ever been committed to the view that the Constitution should regard a fetus as a person, and if the Court were ever to embrace that view, the implications would be more radical than even the most ardent opponents of *Roe* appear to realize.[8] Indeed, litigants on both sides of the abortion controversy have shied away from entertaining even the argument that abortion methods should minimize any pain experienced by the fetus. Pro-choice litigants worry, perhaps, that this is a slippery slope toward granting the fetus the status of a person. This is not necessarily true, as is indicated by the fact that we accept laws mandating the humane killing of animals without thereby giving animals legal rights. On the other side, it is not clear that the abortion methods that pro-life litigants find most objectionable—such as partial birth abortion—cause more pain than alternative abortion methods.

[7] Kristin Luker, *Abortion and the Politics of Motherhood* (Berkeley and Los Angeles: University of California Press, 1984), p. 5.

[8] Judith Jarvis Thompson has famously argued that the common perception that whether or not one is in favor of abortion depends on whether or not one thinks "a fetus is a person" is false. She argues that if a woman awoke one day to discover that a brilliant but sick violinist had been attached by tubes to her kidneys and that the attachment had to be maintained for nine months if the violinist was not to die, the woman would have no moral obligation to maintain the attachment against her will. "A Defense of Abortion," *Philosophy and Public Affairs* 1, no. 1 (Fall 1971): 47–66. Ronald Dworkin points out that Thompson's argument, although influential among philosophers, is not legally dispositive because "abortion normally requires a physical attack on a fetus, not just a failure to aid it, and, in any case, parents are invariably made an exception to the general doctrine [that one ordinarily has no affirmative legal duty to save a stranger] because they have a legal duty to care for their children." *Life's Dominion: An Argument about Abortion, Euthanasia, and Individual Freedom* (New York: Knopf, 1993), p. 111. For a more elaborate discussion of the legal implications of Thompson's argument, see Donald Regan, "Rewriting *Roe v. Wade*," *Michigan Law Review* 77, no. 7 (1979): 1569–1646.

If the Court were to decide that a fetus is a legal person within the meaning of the U.S. Constitution and its amendments, this might well bring with it an obligation to *proscribe* abortion as a matter of federal constitutional law—at least in a large class of circumstances. Jurists and legal commentators who argue that the decision in *Roe* is unconstitutional and that it should be repealed are not partisans of that view.[9] Rather, they are advocates of restoring the status quo ante that existed before *Roe*'s passage, when the law of abortion was regulated differently in different states—sometimes by state legislatures and sometimes as a matter of state constitutional law. This status quo ante had been quite varied, ranging from liberal states like New York that had permitted abortion, to states like Texas that had blanket prohibitions, to various intermediate regulatory regimes.[10] Opposition to *Roe* from such justices as Rehnquist, White, Scalia, and Thomas has not, therefore, been tantamount to opposition to abortion rights as such. Rather, it has been opposition to federalizing the abortion rights question as a matter of constitutional law.[11]

That government should regulate or limit women's access to abortion in order to protect the fetus is a relatively recent idea in American law and politics. Historically, its emergence seems to have been linked to the increase in abortions sought by white, Protestant, married, middle- and upper-class women (as opposed to poor women of other races) in the mid- to late nineteenth century, and to the threat to the existing social order that these developments implied.[12] Prior to this, abortion had been regulated—but the argument for regulation was that it protected the health of the mother. Abortion was a dangerous procedure that often led to infection and death. However, as Justice Blackmun noted in his majority opinion in *Roe*, by 1973 medical developments were such that

[9] See, for example, Justice Rehnquist's dissent in *Roe*, in which he concedes that he has "little doubt" that statutes proscribing abortion in all circumstances would not survive constitutional scrutiny. 410 U.S. 113, at 173 (1973).

[10] Prior to *Roe* no American state had ever regarded the fetus as a legal person. As Dworkin points out, even states with the most stringent antiabortion laws did not punish abortion as severely as they did murder—which they ought to have done had they conceived of a fetus as a constitutional person. Nor did they try to prevent women from procuring abortions in jurisdictions where it was legal. Dworkin, "The Great Abortion Case," p. 50. This issue is discussed further below in connection with partial birth abortion.

[11] This leaves open the question what other branches of the federal government might do. The state-centered approach to abortion legislation was eroded somewhat by the Partial-Birth Abortion Ban Act, which was signed into law by President George W. Bush in November 2003, discussed below. But nothing in that legislation, or in the Court's 2007 upholding of it in *Gonzalez v. Carhart*, 550 U.S. 124 (2007), raises supremacy clause issues beyond the federal proscription of this rare abortion procedure.

[12] See James Mohr, *Abortion in America: The Origins and Evolution of National Policy* (Oxford: Oxford University Press, 1978), especially chaps. 3 and 4.

statistically a woman was at greater medical risk if she carried the child to term than if she had an early abortion.[13]

This altered reality set the context for the Court's analysis of the right to abortion in *Roe*, in which the justices held unconstitutional a Texas statute that had made it a crime to "procure an abortion" unless the life of the mother is threatened by the continuation of the pregnancy. For reasons that will be taken up later, such statutes were held to violate the due process clause of the Fourteenth Amendment.[14] First let us get clear on the holding. Blackman's majority opinion deals with abortion differently during each of the three trimesters of a normal pregnancy:

(a) For the stage prior to approximately the end of the first trimester, the abortion decision and its effectuation must be left to the medical judgment of the pregnant woman's attending physician.

(b) For the stage subsequent to approximately the end of the first trimester, the State, in promoting its interest in the health of the mother, may, if it chooses, regulate the abortion procedure in ways that are reasonably related to maternal health.

(c) For the stage subsequent to viability the State, in promoting its interest in the potentiality of human life, may, if it chooses, regulate, and even proscribe, abortion except where it is necessary, in appropriate medical judgment, for the preservation of the life or health of the mother.[15]

This trimester-based test greatly limited the power of states to regulate abortion. Before the end of the first trimester abortion could no longer be regulated at all; prior to the point of viability it could be regulated only in the interests of the health of the mother; and even after viability if a state chose to regulate or proscribe abortion, acting on its interest "in the potentiality of human life," this could be trumped if the attending physician made an "appropriate" judgment that this was necessary for the "life or health" of the mother.

In *Roe* the Court acknowledged that the state has an interest in potential human life, but circumscribed that right and effectively subordinated it to the woman's right to an abortion, even (if with qualification) after the point of viability. In the years following *Roe*, various modifications to the constitutional right that it created were added by the evolving majority on the Court. Critics argued that the Court's recognition of a state interest in potential human life was empty, given how heavily circumscribed it was by the constitutionally protected right to abortion recognized in

[13] 410 U.S. 113 (1973), at 149.
[14] The due process clause states, "No state shall . . . deprive any person of life, liberty or property, without due process of law."
[15] 410 U.S. 113 (1973), at 164–65.

Roe. But the fact that this interest was nonetheless acknowledged would turn out to be important in the subsequent history of the Court's abortion jurisprudence.

In a number of respects the right recognized in *Roe* was secured and expanded. In *Doe v. Boulton,*[16] also decided in 1973, the Court struck down restrictions on places that could be used to perform abortions, giving rise to the modern abortion clinic. Three years later, in *Planned Parenthood v. Danforth,*[17] the Court denied states the authority to give husbands veto power over their wives' decisions to abort pregnancies, and also held that parents of unwed minor girls could not be given an absolute veto over abortions. In 1979, in *Colautti v. Franklin,*[18] the Court affirmed its intention to give physicians broad discretion to determine when a fetus can live outside the womb. The justices said that although a state may seek to protect a viable fetus, the determination of viability must be left to doctors. In 1983 the Court placed additional limits on the types of regulations that states may place on abortion. In a trio of decisions, *City of Akron v. Akron Center for Reproductive Health,*[19] *Planned Parenthood of Kansas City v. Ashcroft,*[20] and *Simopolous v. Virginia,*[21] by a six-to-three vote a majority on the Court denied states and local communities the power to require that women more than three months pregnant have their abortions in a hospital, and struck down regulations that, among other things, imposed a twenty-four-hour waiting period between the signing of an abortion consent form and the medical procedure. Three years later (this time by a five-to-four vote that reflected the conservative drift on the court that was by then well under way), a bare majority struck down Pennsylvania regulations that had required doctors to inform women seeking abortions about potential risks and about available benefits for prenatal care and childbirth.[22] In 1987, the justices split four to four in *Hartigan v. Zbaraz,*[23] thereby letting stand a lower-court decision invalidating an Illinois law that might have restricted access to abortions for some teenagers.

Despite the elaboration and deepening of the woman's constitutional right to abortion brought about by these decisions, the Court had also begun to limit that right in various ways long before the *Roe* majority

[16] 410 U.S. 179 (1973).

[17] 428 U.S. 476 (1976).

[18] 439 U.S. 379 (1979).

[19] 462 U.S. 416 (1983).

[20] 462 U.S. 476 (1983).

[21] 462 U.S. 506 (1983).

[22] *Thornburgh v. American College of Obstetricians and Gynecologists,* 476 U.S. 747 (1986).

[23] 484 U.S. 171 (1987).

began eroding. One important area of constraint concerned abortion funding. In 1977, the Court ruled, in *Maher v. Roe*,[24] that states have no constitutional obligation to pay for "non-therapeutic" abortions, and three years later a five-to-four majority held, in *Harris v. McRae*,[25] that, even for medically necessary abortions sought by women on welfare, neither states nor the federal government is under any constitutional obligation to provide public funding. In 1979, in the first of what was to turn out to be a string of decisions regulating the rights of dependent minors to abortion, an eight-to-one majority on the Court held in *Bellotti v. Baird*[26] that states may be able to require a pregnant, unmarried minor to obtain parental consent to an abortion so long as the state provides a "bypass" procedure, such as allowing the minor to seek a judge's permission instead. In 1981 a six-to-three majority held, in *H.L. v. Matheson*,[27] that states may require physicians approached by some girls who are still dependent on their parents, and too "immature" to decide such matters for themselves, to try to inform parents before performing abortions. Two 1990 decisions, *Hodgson v. Minnesota*[28] and *Ohio v. Akron Center for Reproductive Health*,[29] further elaborated the law of parental notification. In the Ohio case, a six-to-three majority upheld the state law requiring notification of at least one parent so long as it provided a judicial bypass, but in the Minnesota case a five-to-four majority made it clear that statutes requiring both parents to be informed before a minor can have an abortion would not survive in the future.

By the time of the 1990 decisions, much of the reasoning underlying *Roe* had been compromised by the watershed decision in *Webster v. Reproductive Health Services*[30] handed down by a multiply divided Court eleven months earlier. With that decision, majority support for *Roe* on the Court seemed finally to have evaporated—as Justice Blackmun pointed out in a furious dissent. In its controlling opinion, the *Webster* Court upheld a Missouri statute requiring that before a physician performs an abortion on a woman who he has reason to believe is twenty or more weeks pregnant, he shall first determine whether the unborn child is viable. More important than this comparatively minor new restriction of a woman's right to an abortion was that the plurality launched a frontal assault on *Roe*'s trimester-based framework of analysis that had been law for the preceding decade and a half.

[24] 432 U.S. 464 (1977).
[25] 448 U.S. 297 (1980).
[26] 428 U.S. 132 (1979).
[27] 430 U.S. 398 (1981).
[28] 497 U.S. 417 (1990).
[29] 497 U.S. 502 (1990).
[30] 492 U.S. 490 (1989).

Justice Blackmun's throwaway remark in *Roe* that the state has an interest in "the potentiality of human life" had come back to haunt him. In Chief Justice Rehnquist's hands it became a stake that he seemed poised to drive into *Roe*'s heart. In an opinion signed also by Justices Kennedy and White, Rehnquist flatly rejected Roe's "rigid" framework as "hardly consistent with the notion of a Constitution cast in general terms, as ours is, and usually speaking in general principles." Rehnquist went on to say that the plurality "did not see why the State's interest in protecting potential life should come into existence only at the point of viability, and that there should therefore be a rigid line allowing state regulation after viability but prohibiting it before viability."[31]

Justice O'Connor had announced her opposition to *Roe*'s trimester framework as early as 1985,[32] and Justice Scalia's only objection to the plurality opinion in *Webster* was that it should have gone further and done explicitly what he insisted it did implicitly, namely, overrule *Roe*. This appeared to mean that there were now five votes in favor of overruling *Roe*, even if the five justices in question were not yet all prepared to reach that matter on the grounds that the Missouri statute in question did not in fact try to regulate abortions prior to viability. The principle had been conceded, even if what Scalia dismissed as the Court's "newly contracted abstemiousness" meant that "the mansion of constitutionalized abortion-law, constructed overnight in *Roe v. Wade*, must be disassembled doorjamb by doorjamb."[33] No more impressed than Scalia by what he saw as the plurality's "feigned restraint," Justice Blackmun (dissenting also for Brennan and Marshall) declared that the majority decision in *Webster* "implicitly invites every state legislature to enact more and more restrictive abortion regulations in order to provoke more and more test cases, in the hope that sometime down the line the Court will return the law of procreative freedom to the severe limitations that generally prevailed in this country before January 22, 1973." Thus, "not with a bang, but a whimper," Blackmun concluded, "the plurality discards a landmark case of the last generation, and casts into darkness the hopes and visions of every woman in this country who had come to believe that the Constitution guaranteed her the right to exercise some control over her unique ability to bear children."[34]

That some of Blackmun's own formulations in *Roe* could be used to undermine its result in *Webster* is characteristic of the haphazard (some might say dialectical) way in which constitutional interpretation often

---

[31] 492 U.S. 490 (1989), at 518–19.

[32] See her dissenting opinion in *Thornburgh v. American College of Obstetricians and Gynecologists*, 476 U.S. 747 (1985), at 828.

[33] 492 U.S. 490, at 537.

[34] Ibid., at 538, 557.

evolves over time. Perhaps this very fact should have alerted Blackmun to the possibility that all was not lost from his point of view. Although *Roe*'s trimester framework had been jettisoned, and a majority on the Court had embraced the idea that states may assert an interest in protecting "potential" human life even before the point at which a fetus is viable, this did not necessarily mean that the constitutional protection of a woman's right to an abortion would soon follow the trimester framework into the annals of constitutional history. Everything would now depend on what the nature of states' interest in potential life would turn out to consist in. Until that was determined, just what the impact of *Webster* would be on a woman's constitutionally protected right to an abortion could not be known. This would remain unclear for almost three years.

In retrospect we can say that there were clues dating back to the 1970s. In *Maher v. Roe* the Court had declared that the right recognized in *Roe* "protects the woman from unduly burdensome interference with her freedom to decide whether to terminate her pregnancy."[35] This notion that state interference with a woman's right to an abortion must not be "unduly burdensome" had first appeared in 1976 in *Bellotti v. Baird*, in which the Court had held that states may not "impose undue burdens upon a minor capable of giving informed consent."[36] Since that time, various members of the Court, including several majorities, had held that no state may "unduly burden the right to seek an abortion,"[37] that the constitutional right affirmed in *Roe* "protects the woman from unduly burdensome interference with her freedom to decide whether to terminate her pregnancy,"[38] that informed-consent requirements for first-trimester abortions will be upheld if they do not "unduly burden the right to seek an abortion,"[39] and that the state interest in protecting human life "does not, at least until the third trimester, become sufficiently compelling to justify unduly burdensome state interference."[40] In 1982 Justice O'Connor made it clear in her dissent in *City of Akron v. Akron Center for Reproductive Health* that, for her at least, the issue of abortion revolved around finding restrictions that do not "infringe substantially" or impose "unduly burdensome" interference on the woman's right to an abortion,[41] a view that she reasserted in *Hodgson v. Minnesota* in the course of arguing that only when a state regulation imposes an "undue

---

[35] *Maher v. Roe*, 432 U.S. 464 (1977), at 473–74.
[36] 482 U.S. 132, 147 (1976).
[37] *Bellotti v. Baird*, 433 U.S. 622, 640 (1979).
[38] *Maher v. Roe*, 432 U.S. 464 (1977), at 473–74.
[39] *Bellotti v. Baird*, 428 U.S. 132, 147 (1976)
[40] *Beal v. Doe*, 432 U.S. 438–46 (1977).
[41] 462 U.S. 416, 461–62 (1982).

burden" on a woman's ability to make the abortion decision does the power of the State reach into the heart of the liberty protected by the due process clause.[42]

In view of these formulations, it should perhaps not come as a surprise that Justices O'Connor and Kennedy—who had declined Justice Scalia's invitation to overrule *Roe* in *Webster*—would be part of a centrist bloc on the Court (the other member being Souter) committed to reformulating the constitutional right to abortion by reference to an "undue burden" standard rooted in the due process clause of the Fourteenth Amendment. This was the step taken in *Planned Parenthood v. Casey*, handed down in June 1992, in which a once more multiply divided Court reaffirmed *Roe*'s basic holding while detaching it from Blackmun's now defunct trimester-based framework of analysis, and tethering it instead to the notion of undue burden.[43] The *Casey* decision left many matters unresolved. Indeed, it created new areas of uncertainty in the constitutional law of abortion, as we will see. But two fundamental matters about which *Webster* had generated considerable confusion were now clarified. The first was that "the essential holding of *Roe v. Wade* should be retained and once again reaffirmed."[44] This meant not only that the Constitution guarantees women a right to abortion that no legislature has the power to destroy, but also that the Court had decided not completely to reject Blackmun's original reasoning that had located the constitutional protection in question in a right to privacy thought to be entailed by the due process clause. This was a notable development, because Blackmun's reasoning had been much criticized in the academic literature, and several of the newer appointees to the Court—not to mention Chief Justice Rehnquist—were on record as being unimpressed by it. This was perhaps the main reason that *Webster* was thought by so many to be the beginning of the end of *Roe*, prompting the introduction of legislation intended to reverse *Webster* in Congress and turning abortion into a lightning-rod political issue in the run-up to the 1992 presidential election.

In the event, declaring that "liberty finds no refuge in a jurisprudence of doubt,"[45] the plurality invoked the doctrine of *stare decisis*. This doctrine rests on the notion that "no judicial system could do society's work if it eyed each issue afresh in every case that raised it," and that consequently once a decision has become part of the law on which people have come to rely, it should not lightly be overturned. *Stare decisis* is not an "inexorable command" to uphold every precedent, and it might reasonably be ignored if a rule has "proved to be intolerable simply in

---

[42] 497 U.S. 417, 458–59 (1990).
[43] 112 S. Ct. 2791 (1992).
[44] Ibid., p. 2796.
[45] Ibid., p. 2803.

defying practical workability," if it is "subject to a kind of reliance that would lend a special hardship to the consequences of overruling and add inequity to the cost of repudiation," or if "facts have so changed or come to be seen so differently, as to have robbed the old rule of significant application or justification."[46] But the plurality held that none of these considerations applied in the case of *Roe*, so that it should be upheld, even though "[w]e do not need to say whether each of us, had we been Members of the Court when the valuation of the State interest [in protecting potential life] came before it would have concluded, as the *Roe* Court did, that its weight is insufficient to justify a ban on abortions prior to viability even when it is subject to certain exceptions."[47] By appeal to this reasoning, the plurality in *Casey* held that a woman does have a constitutionally protected right to an abortion until the point of viability, and that after that point states have the power to "restrict abortions," provided the law contains "exceptions for pregnancies which endanger a woman's life or health."[48]

The second matter resolved by *Casey* was that the state's interest in protecting potential life would be seen as subordinate to the woman's constitutionally protected right to an abortion. The plurality's discussion of this issue did not amount to a definitive account of the status of the state's interest or of the woman's, but it set some limits on what states may do in regulating abortions. Following the point of viability, threats to the woman's life or health could trump legitimate abortion restrictions rooted in the state's interest in protecting potential life. Depending on how broadly "health" is defined (in particular whether it includes psychological well-being), and bearing in mind that it will generally be a physician of the patient's choosing who decides whether the woman's health is threatened, this had the potential to turn out to be a substantial constraint on the state's power even after the point of viability.[49]

The *Casey* decision amounted to a rejection of *Roe's* underlying logic not only because the trimester-based analysis was explicitly abandoned, but also because the state's interest in potential life was held unequivocally to begin before the point at which the fetus is viable. The state's interest is conceived as strengthening as the fetus develops, justifying gradual increases in interference by the state with the constitutionally protected rights of pregnant women over the course of their pregnan-

---

[46] Ibid., pp. 2808–9.

[47] Ibid., p. 2817.

[48] Ibid., p. 2791.

[49] This is distinct from the issue of who has the authority to determine what the safest abortion procedure is in circumstances when an abortion is legitimate. This would be litigated in the partial birth abortion cases in 2000 and 2007, and is taken up at pp. 245–48 below.

cies. Before the point of viability, the Court's "undue burden" test rules out "[u]necessary health regulations that have the purpose or effect of presenting a substantial obstacle to a woman seeking an abortion."[50] But this does not mean that the state is powerless to try to influence a woman's decision to abort in the early stages of pregnancy. "What is at stake," the *Casey* plurality insisted, "is the woman's right to make the ultimate decision, not a right to be insulated from all others in doing so."[51] From the onset of a pregnancy states "may enact rules and regulations designed to encourage [a woman] to know that there are philosophic and social arguments of great weight that can be brought to bear in favor of continuing the pregnancy."[52] So long as neither the purpose nor the effect of the regulations in question is to place an "undue burden" on women by imposing "substantial obstacles" on their choice in favor of abortion, states may try to get women to reflect on that choice and encourage them to consider alternatives.[53]

Just what would count as an undue burden in particular cases was by no means clear, and was bound to invite further litigation—as the dissenters in *Casey* were quick to point out. In *Casey* itself the Court held that a Pennsylvania statute placed an undue burden on women if it required a married woman seeking an abortion to sign a statement that she had notified her husband, but a variety of the Pennsylvania statute's other provisions survived the test. These included provisions designed to ensure that the woman was giving informed consent to the procedure by requiring that she receive certain information at least twenty-four hours before undergoing the abortion procedure; that for a minor to undergo an abortion there must be informed consent from at least one parent at least twenty-four hours before the procedure (with provisions for a judicial bypass procedure); and that abortion clinics could be obliged to comply with various reporting requirements. The spousal notification requirement was thought to differ from the others in that although most women would tell their husbands voluntarily what their intentions were, women who are victims of physical and psychological spousal abuse "may have very good reasons for not wishing to inform their husbands of their decision to obtain an abortion."[54] If the Court was clear that this tipped the scale of undue burden while the twenty-four hour waiting period did not, the reasoning behind the distinction was less than entirely lucid. In particular, the justices seemed to have run together the quite different considerations of trying to ensure that the woman makes

[50] 112 S. Ct. 2791 (1992), at 2821.
[51] Ibid.
[52] Ibid., p. 2818
[53] Ibid.
[54] Ibid., p. 2828.

a well-thought-out decision (that is, one that *she* would not subsequently come to regret), and the state's right to further *its* interest in potential life by regulating the woman's abortion choice. For this and other reasons *Casey* raised as many questions as it settled, as subsequent litigation soon began to reveal.[55]

For the next eight years the Supreme Court was silent on the abortion question, apparently content to wait for litigation under the new regime to play out in the lower courts. Then the justices revisited the subject in *Stenberg v. Carhart*,[56] taking up the highly charged procedure that had come to be labeled by its critics as "partial birth abortion." This comparatively rare procedure was defined in the Nebraska statute that banned it as "intentionally delivering into the vagina a living unborn child, or a substantial portion thereof, for the purpose of performing a procedure that the [abortionist] knows will kill the . . . child and does kill the . . . child." Comparable statutes had been enacted in thirty state legislatures. The challenged Nebraska statute made it a felony to conduct a partial birth abortion unless it was necessary to save the life of the mother. Conviction would lead to automatic revocation of a physician's license to practice medicine. The Eighth Circuit Court of Appeals had upheld the district court's finding that the statute was unconstitutional, and the Supreme Court affirmed this result in a contentious five-to-four decision.

Justice Kennedy, who had been part of the majority in *Casey*, now voted with the dissenters.[57] Justice O'Connor, the main architect of *Casey's* undue burden test, made it plain that although she was voting to strike down the challenged Nebraska statute, this was because it was overbroad and lacked an exception for the health (in addition to the life) of the mother. Otherwise she would have held it constitutional, which, given Kennedy's stance, suggested that a five-to-four majority on the Court might be willing to uphold a more restrictive partial abortion statute with an exception for the mother's health. Much turned, therefore, on why the majority thought the Nebraska statute overinclusive, and on just what would be needed to assure protection of the mother's health.

The two issues are distinct. *Casey* had held that, prior to viability, abortion regulations must not unduly burden or obstruct a women's right to abortion. The challenged statute could be read to include "dilation and evacuation" (D&E) procedures commonly used in previability second-

---

[55] See *Fargo Women's Health Organization v. Schafer*, 113 S. Ct. 1668 (1993), and *Planned Parenthood v. Casey II*, 114 S. Ct. 909 (1994).

[56] 192 F.3d 1142, emphasis supplied.

[57] This did not affect the outcome because Byron White, who had dissented in *Casey*, had been replaced by Ruth Bader Ginsburg, who endorsed *Casey's* application in *Stenberg*, in the interim.

trimester abortions as well as the rare "dilation and extraction" (D&X) method, often used after sixteen weeks, that Nebraska sought to ban.[58] Accordingly, the Court applied *Casey*'s undue burden test and found the statute wanting because the D&E method is seen as safer than the available alternatives for previability abortions performed between twelve and twenty weeks of gestation. This is the least controversial part of the decision because Nebraska never sought to outlaw the D&E procedure. The issue dividing the majority from the dissenters was whether the Court should construe the statute more narrowly to render it constitutional, or should strike it down and in effect require Nebraska to enact a more narrowly drawn statute.

The comparative dangers of different abortion procedures also lie at the core of the more contentious part of the decision, that involving the D&X procedure. This concerns certain late-term abortions where D&E is no longer effective owing to the more advanced pregnancy, and where the fetus presents feet first. The doctor pulls the fetal body through the cervix (hence the term "partial birth"), collapses the skull, and extracts the fetus through the cervix. The procedure was defended at trial as safer than the alternatives for the woman in circumstances involving nonviable fetuses, for women with prior uterine scars, and for women for whom induced labor would be particularly dangerous. As a result, the majority found that the lack of a health exception rendered the Nebraska statute unconstitutional.

At issue between the majority and the dissenters was the status of the evidence that the D&X procedure is the safest available method in some circumstances and must therefore be protected by a health exception. *Roe* had insisted on the inclusion of such an exception when states regulate abortion procedures, and *Casey* had affirmed that there must be exceptions when abortion is "necessary, in appropriate medical judgment, for the preservation of the life or health of the mother."[59] But what constitutes appropriate medical judgment? It had long been a criticism of *Roe* that this escape clause created abortion on demand. "Appropriate medical judgment" had been interpreted as the judgment of the attending physician, and there would always be a physician willing to say that carrying a pregnancy to term would in some way be harmful to a woman's physical or psychological health. Part of the opposition to *Casey* had derived from the fact that the decision limited this escape clause by holding that states may regulate abortion so long as this does not burden women unduly. The dissenters in *Stenberg* differed among themselves as to whether the *Casey* rule should have been

---

[58] The D&X procedure is sometimes referred to as the "intact D&E" procedure, though I will use D&X here.

[59] 505 U.S., at 879.

adopted. They were united, however, in insisting that *Stenberg* rendered the *Casey* rule meaningless because the interpretation of "appropriate medical judgment" seemed sufficiently capacious to re-create abortion on demand by establishing an attending physician's veto over all abortion regulation.

The objection here was not to the proposition that part of the idea of an undue burden includes the notion that a woman should not be required to endure a less safe procedure when a safer one is available. Whatever else it might mean, undue burden seems to include that idea. Rather, the objection goes to the question: who should decide safety? Dissenting justice Kennedy objected that the majority had deferred to the judgment of the attending physician, re-creating abortion on demand and to that extent rendering *Casey*'s modification of *Roe* meaningless. Justice Thomas added that the majority did not establish its assertion that a "substantial body" of medical opinion supports the proposition that the D&X procedure is safer than the alternative in any circumstances. By what logic or authority, he asked, should the Supreme Court second-guess the judgment of the Nebraska state legislature on this factual question? And in an "I told you so" mood, Justice Scalia insisted that "those who believe that a 5-to-4 vote on a policy matter by unelected lawyers should not overcome the judgment of 30 state legislatures have a problem, not with the application of *Casey*, but with its existence. *Casey* must be overruled."

In 1994 the Republicans had taken control of both houses of Congress for the first time in a generation. This led to the opening of a new front in the battle over abortion rights in national politics. There had been skirmishes even before *Stenberg* was handed down, but the decision galvanized pro-life forces to craft a national ban on partial birth abortion that could pass muster on the Court. The House and Senate passed partial birth abortion bans in 1996 and 1997, but these had been vetoed by President Clinton. When George W. Bush took office in January 2001, the stars were aligned for enactment of a nationwide ban. This occurred on November 5, 2003, when President Bush signed the Partial-Birth Abortion Ban Act, which had been passed by both houses of Congress, into law.

The new federal statute addressed some infirmities that the Court had identified in the Nebraska law struck down in *Stenberg*. Congress responded to the overbreadth problem by explicitly excluding D&E abortions as well as inadvertent D&X extractions—where the physician ends up performing a partial birth abortion that was not intended. The politicians responded to the women's health issue by holding hearings on the relative safety of the D&X procedure and then declaring in the statute that a "moral, medical, and ethical consensus exists" to the effect that partial birth abortion "is a gruesome and inhumane procedure that is never medically necessary and should be prohibited."[60]

In the litigation that inevitably followed, the lower federal courts revealed that they were unimpressed. The Partial-Birth Abortion Ban was struck down by district courts in California and Nebraska. Their decisions were upheld by the Eighth and Ninth Circuit appellate courts in 2005 and 2006. But the Supreme Court granted certiorari, and in April 2007 it handed down a new decision overturning the lower court decisions, sustaining the constitutionality of the federal Partial-Birth Abortion Ban Act, and all but reversing the Court's own precedent that had been set seven years earlier in *Stenberg*.

The new decision, *Gonzales v. Carhart*,[61] partly reflected changes in the Court's personnel—O'Connor and Rehnquist having been replaced by Roberts and Alito. Both had been artfully imprecise about their views on the constitutionality of abortion during their Senate confirmation hearings, but both were well known as Catholic conservatives, and few Court-watchers were surprised when the five-to-four majority that had upheld the constitutionality of the D&X procedure in *Stenberg* was replaced, in *Gonzales*, by a five-to-four majority that took the opposite view.

Chief Justice Rehnquist's replacement by John Roberts had left the abortion arithmetic on the Court unaffected, but Sandra Day O'Connor had been both the architect of *Casey*'s undue burden test and the swing vote in its application in *Stenberg*. Justice Alito now joined a majority opinion penned by Justice Kennedy in which the Court held that Congress had indeed solved the overbreadth problem by exempting the D&E procedure and indemnifying physicians who performed D&X abortions inadvertently. Moreover, the lack of a health exception was held to have been cured by the congressional finding that the D&X procedure is never medically necessary.

The Court's basis for deferring to the congressional finding was not entirely clear. As Justice Ginsburg noted in stinging dissent, the *Congressional Record* was replete with testimony contradicting the finding in the act that the D&X procedure is never safer than the alternative—not to mention evidence from other professional sources such as the American College of Obstetricians and Gynecologists. The act incorrectly asserts that no medical schools taught the D&X procedure when in fact many of the leading ones did. Moreover, as if to underscore the cursory and result-driven nature of the hearings, none of the physicians who testified that

[60] 18 U.S.C. § 1531 (2000 ed., Supp. IV), p. 767.
[61] *Gonzales v. Carhart*, 550 U.S. 124 (2007).

the D&X procedure is never medically indicated had in fact performed it.[62] The federal courts have a long history of refusing to defer to manifestly implausible legislative findings, and the lower courts followed that precedent in this case. But the new majority on the Supreme Court did not, holding instead that in the face of professional disagreement over the medical merits of the procedure, Congress was free to take the position that it did.

2. Abortion Jurisprudence

Much of the heat generated by the abortion controversy stems from its symbolic role in American politics. Arguments over "life" versus "choice" serve as proxies for conflicts over the role of women in American society, the controversial status of "traditional" and "family" values, and the place of religion in American politics.[63] However, part of the heat has been internally generated, by the manner in which *Roe* was decided and the privacy argument on which it rested. This stemmed partly from the sweeping nature of the holding in *Roe*, and partly from the fact that the right of privacy on which Justice Blackmun based his argument is nowhere mentioned in the Constitution.

Arguments about privacy and reproductive freedom are rooted in the Supreme Court's 1965 decision in *Griswold v. Connecticut*.[64] *Griswold* had been the culmination of a fifty-year battle to organize formal opposition to birth control statutes.[65] A seven-to-two majority on the Court struck down an 1879 statute that had made it illegal "to use any drug or article to prevent conception," holding that a zone of privacy encompassing the marital relationship outweighs any legitimate state interest in preventing sexual immorality.[66] This decision provided part of the logical foundation for Justice Blackmun's reasoning in *Roe*, in which he maintained that the zone of privacy encompasses decisions about abortion as well as contraception. But *Griswold* applied to married couples only; by itself this could not generate the right to *individual* privacy on which *Roe* rests. The bridging argument was supplied in *Eisenstadt v. Baird* in 1972 when Justice Brennan, writing for the majority, observed of the contra-

---

[62] 550 U.S. 124, at 131.

[63] An excellent treatment of this subject is Luker, *Abortion and the Politics of Motherhood*, especially chaps. 3–7.

[64] 381 U.S. 479 (1965).

[65] For an account of this history, see David J. Garrow, *The Right to Privacy and the Making of "Roe v. Wade"* (New York: Lisa Drew Books, 1993).

[66] 381 U.S. 479–84 (1965).

ception cases that if "the right of privacy means anything, it is the right of the *individual*, married or single, to be free from unwanted governmental intrusions in matters so fundamentally affecting a person as the decision whether to bear or beget a child."[67]

The *Griswold* result has often been criticized as poor constitutional jurisprudence, and Blackmun's extension of it to *Roe* has never been secure. The principal charge with which its defenders have had to deal is that *Griswold* is alleged to be an example of "judicial legislation"—that in deciding it the Court set itself up as a kind of superlegislature. There are two possible responses to this line of criticism for those who support the outcome in *Roe*. One is to insist that what the Court did in *Griswold* is not unusual. Every clause of the Bill of Rights has to be interpreted in light of background philosophical assumptions.[68] Moreover, this line of response goes, few critics of *Griswold* would want to live with the full implications of abandoning the notion that there is a constitutionally protected right to privacy. Indeed critics of *Roe*, such as President Reagan's solicitor general Charles Fried, usually deny that *Griswold* should be overruled.[69] As Ronald Dworkin—perhaps the most articulate defender of *Griswold* and its extension to *Roe*—has noted, it is difficult to discern a principled basis for this view. Once *Griswold* is accepted, it seems inevitably to lead to *Roe*, partly because the technologies of contraception and abortion overlap (and may do so increasingly over time),[70] and partly because it is difficult to articulate compelling grounds for distinguishing the two cases from one another.

The Court's reasoning in *Griswold* was that decisions affecting marriage and childbirth are of such an intimate and personal character that people must be free to make the decisions for themselves. As Dworkin notes, decisions regarding abortion are at least as private as those concerning contraception; indeed in one respect they are more so because the abortion decision "involves a woman's control not just of her sexual relations but of changes within her own body, and the Supreme Court has recognized in various ways the importance of physical integrity."[71] Accordingly, Dworkin defends both *Griswold* and *Roe*, as well as the Supreme Court's refashioning of the *Roe* doctrine in *Casey*, by reference to an "undue burden" standard that places gradually more stringent

---

[67] *Eisenstadt v. Baird*, 405 U.S. 453 (1972), emphasis in original.

[68] See Ronald Dworkin, *Taking Rights Seriously* (Cambridge, MA: Harvard University Press, 1977), pp. 14–80.

[69] As he maintained in oral argument before the Court in *Webster* in 1990.

[70] Some intrauterine devices and many popular birth control pills destroy fertilized ova if they fail to prevent fertilization.

[71] Dworkin, *Life's Dominion*, p. 107.

burdens on the woman seeking an abortion as pregnancy advances, designed to get her to reflect on the seriousness of her proposed abortion and to further the state's interest in protecting potential human life.[72]

To defend *Roe* on the grounds that it cannot be distinguished from *Griswold* in a principled way is to appeal to what is at bottom an ad hoc argument, as conservatives like Robert Bork have been quick to point out.[73] The *Griswold* doctrine has also been rejected by radical feminists as male ideology that contributes to the subjugation of women.[74] Indeed, in other contexts—such as in arguing for the passage of marital rape statutes—feminists have been concerned to weaken the common-law presumption that the marital relationship shields "intimate" behavior from the criminal law.[75] Partly for these reasons, an alternative line of response to the perceived weakness of *Griswold* and *Roe* has been put forward by defenders of the right to abortion, one that jettisons the privacy argument altogether and relies instead on the constitutional commitment to equal protection of the laws, explicit in the Fourteenth Amendment, and implied in the due process clause of the Fifth Amendment.

The equality argument turns on the claim that restrictions on abortion discriminate against women by placing constraints on their freedom that men do not have to bear. This was the view defended by then appellate court federal judge Ruth Bader Ginsburg in her 1993 Madison Lecture at New York University, which prompted some sharp questioning in her confirmation hearings for the Supreme Court because it revealed her discomfort with *Roe*'s privacy doctrine.[76] On Ginsburg's

---

[72] Though Dworkin would apply the standard more permissively than does the Court. For instance, his view is that the Court should have struck down the mandatory waiting periods that were upheld in *Casey*. Dworkin, *Life's Dominion*, p. 172–74.

[73] Bork argued in his confirmation hearings for the Supreme Court that both *Roe* and *Griswold* should be overruled. This view has the merit of internal consistency, but it was so far out of the mainstream of even conservative jurisprudential opinion that it led many conservative Democrats and Republicans in the Senate to oppose what turned out to be his failed nomination.

[74] See Catharine MacKinnon, *Feminism Unmodified: Discourses on Life and Law* (Cambridge, MA: Harvard University Press, 1987), pp. 93–102, and Robin West, "Jurisprudence and Gender," *University of Chicago Law Review* 55, no. 1 (1988): 67–70.

[75] On the changing law of marital rape in the United States, see Michael Freeman, "If You Can't Rape Your Wife, Who[m] Can You Rape? The Marital Rape Exception Reexamined," *Family Law Quarterly* 15, no. 1 (Spring 1981): 1–29; Deborah Rhode, *Justice and Gender* (Cambridge, MA: Harvard University Press, 1989), pp. 249–51; Rene I. Augustine, "Marriage: The Safe Haven for Rapists," *Journal of Family Law* 29, no. 3 (1990–91): 559–90; and Sandra Ryder and Sheryl Kuzmenka, "Legal Rape: The Marital Exception," *John Marshall Law Review* 24 (1991): 393–421. On the English evolution of the exception, see P. M. Bromley and N. V. Lowe, *Family Law*, 7th ed. (London: Butterworths, 1987), pp. 109–12.

[76] Ruth Bader Ginsburg, "Speaking in a Judicial Voice" (mimeo, Madison Lecture, New York University Law School, March 9, 1993). For the hearings, see Senate Committee

account, abortion regulations affect "a woman's autonomous charge of her full life's course—her ability to stand in relation to man, society, and the state as an independent, self-sustaining citizen."[77] Ginsburg argued that the *Roe* Court should have "homed in more precisely on the woman's equality dimension of the issue," enabling it to argue that "disadvantageous treatment of a woman because of her pregnancy and reproductive choice is a paradigm case of discrimination on the basis of sex."[78] It is true that equal protection arguments had been of declining effectiveness in the Burger (and, subsequently, Rehnquist) Courts, but Ginsburg pointed out that in the very term *Roe* was decided, the Supreme Court had a case on its calendar that could have served as a bridge, "linking reproductive choice to disadvantageous treatment of women on the basis of their sex."[79] Accordingly, she saw the decision to opt for the *Griswold* line of reasoning in *Roe* as a missed opportunity to place the right to abortion on a firmer conceptual and constitutional footing.[80]

Whatever the jurisprudential basis for the right to abortion, it is arguable that it was the manner in which *Roe* was decided—as much as the content of the decision—that was to render its legitimacy suspect. After all, in *Roe* the Court did a good deal more than strike down a Texas abortion statute. The majority opinion laid out a detailed test to determine the conditions under which any abortion statute could be expected to pass muster; in effect Justice Blackmun authored a federal abortion statute of his own. Ginsburg makes a powerful case that decisions of this kind tend to undermine the Court's legitimacy. She thinks that it is sometimes necessary for the court to step "ahead" of the political process to achieve reforms that the Constitution requires, but if it gets too far ahead, it can produce a backlash and provoke charges that it is overreaching its appropriate place in a democratic constitutional order.[81]

on the Juiciary, *Nomination of Ruth Bader Ginsburg to Be an Associate Justice of the United States Supreme Court: Report together with Additional Views*, 103rd Cong., 1st sess., 1993, Exec. Rept. 103-6, pp. 17–19.

[77] *Nomination of Ruth Bader Ginsburg*, p. 17.

[78] Ginsburg, "Speaking in a Judicial Voice," pp. 24, 28. For a more elaborate defense of the equality-based view, see Sylvia A. Law, "Rethinking Sex and the Constitution," *University of Pennsylvania Law Review* 132, no. 2 (1983–84): 1002–13.

[79] Ginsburg, "Speaking in a Judicial Voice," p. 24. The case, *Struck v. Secretary of Defense*, 409 U.S. 947 (1973), was remanded for consideration of mootness.

[80] It is of course possible that Blackmun canvassed this possibility and could not find support for it among his brethren on the Court, though—given his failure even to mention it—it seems more likely that, like Ronald Dworkin, Blackmun simply thought Griswold compelling.

[81] Ginsburg, "Speaking in a Judicial Voice," pp. 30–38.

This line of reasoning about the Court's role has been more fully developed by Robert Burt.[82] He contrasts the Court's handling of the abortion question with its approach in the school desegregation cases of the 1950s. In *Brown v. Board of Education* the justices declared the doctrine of "separate but equal" to be an unconstitutional violation of the equal protection clause,[83] but they did not describe schooling conditions that would be acceptable. Rather, they turned the problem back to Southern state legislatures, requiring them to fashion acceptable remedies themselves.[84] These remedies came before the Court as a result of subsequent litigation, were evaluated when they did, and were often found to be wanting.[85] But the Court avoided designing the remedy itself, and with it the charge that it was usurping the legislative function. Indeed, as Gerald Rosenberg has detailed, desegregation of Southern schools was substantially achieved by legislatures.[86] In *Roe*, by contrast, as Ginsburg puts it, the court "invited no dialogue with legislators. Instead, it seemed entirely to remove the ball from the legislators' court" by wiping out virtually every form of abortion regulation then in existence.[87]

On the Ginsburg-Burt view, *Roe*'s sweeping holding diminished the Court's democratic legitimacy at the same time as it put paid to various schemes to liberalize abortion laws that had been under way in different states. Between 1967 and 1973 statutes were passed in nineteen states liberalizing the permissible grounds for abortion. Many feminists had been dissatisfied with the pace and extent of this reform, and they mounted the campaign that helped bring about the result in *Roe*. Burt concedes that in 1973 it was "not clear whether the recently enacted state laws signified the beginning of a national trend toward abolishing all abortion restrictions or even whether in the so-called liberalized states, the new enactments would significantly increase access to abortion for anyone." Nonetheless, he insists that "the abortion issue was openly, avidly, controverted in a substantial number of public forums, and unlike the regimen extant as recently as 1967, it was no longer clear who was winning the battle."[88] Following the *Brown* model, the Court might have struck down the Texas abortion statute in *Roe* (whether by appeal to Blackmun's privacy argument or to the equality argument favored by

---

[82] Robert A. Burt, *The Constitution in Conflict* (Cambridge, MA: Harvard University Press, 1992), pp. 344–52.

[83] *Brown v. Board of Education I*, 347 U.S. 483 (1954).

[84] *Brown v. Board of Education II*, 349 U.S. 294 (1955).

[85] Burt, *Constitution in Conflict*, pp. 271–310.

[86] Gerald N. Rosenberg, *The Hollow Hope: Can Courts Bring About Social Change?* (Chicago: University of Chicago Press, 1993).

[87] Ginsburg, "Speaking in a Judicial Voice," p. 32.

[88] Burt, *Constitution in Conflict*, p. 348.

Ginsburg and others) without going on to develop and apply Blackmun's trimester framework. This would have set some limits on what legislatures might do in the matter of regulating abortion without involving the Court directly in designing that regulation. On the Ginsburg-Burt view, this would have left space for democratic resolution of the conflict that would have ensured the survival of the right to abortion while at the same time preserving the legitimacy of the Court's role in a democratic constitutional order.[89]

3. Implications of "Undue Burden"

It is ironic, perhaps, that although *Casey* was decided before Ruth Bader Ginsburg's elevation to the Supreme Court, that decision brought the Court's stance into line with the Ginsburg-Burt view of the manner in which the Court should approach the abortion question. By affirming the existence of a woman's fundamental constitutional right to an abortion, recognizing the legitimacy of the state's interest in potential life, and insisting that states may not pursue the vindication of that interest in a manner that is unduly burdensome to women, the Court set some basic parameters within which legislatures must now fashion regulations governing abortion. The *Casey* dissenters were right to point out that there would be a degree of unpredictability and confusion as different regulatory regimes are enacted in different states and tested through the courts.[90] Particularly given the developmental dimension to the test—which permits increasingly burdensome regulation as pregnancy advances—this is inevitable. On views of adjudication that encourage efficiency and clarity above all else, this might seem to be a reprehensible invitation to further litigation.[91] On the Ginsburg-Burt view, however, that *Casey* invites litigation may be

---

[89] Ibid., pp. 349–52.

[90] In his partly dissenting opinion, Rehnquist—joined by White and Scalia—said of the controlling opinion in *Casey*: "The end result of the joint opinion's paeans for praise of legitimacy is the enunciation of a brand new standard for evaluating state regulation of a woman's right to abortion—the undue burden standard. . . . *Roe v. Wade* adopted a 'fundamental right' standard under which state regulations could survive only if they met the requirement of 'strict scrutiny.' While we disagree with that standard, it at least had a recognized basis in constitutional law at the time *Roe* was decided. The same cannot be said for the 'undue burden' standard, which is created largely out of whole cloth by the authors of the joint opinion. It is a standard which even today does not command the support of a majority of this Court. And it will not, we believe, result in the sort of 'simple implementation,' easily applied, which the joint opinion anticipates." 112 S. Ct. 2791, at 2866 (1992).

[91] See Rehnquist's remarks immediately following those quoted in the preceding footnote. For a more general defense of efficiency in appellate federal adjudication, see Richard Posner, *The Federal Courts: Crisis and Reform* (Cambridge, MA: Harvard University Press,

a cost worth paying. It places the onus on democratically elected legislatures to come up with modes of regulating abortion that do not unduly burden women, and it forces them to do this in the knowledge that the statutes they enact will be tested through the courts and thrown out if they are found wanting. This gives legislators incentives to devise regimes of regulation that minimize the burdens placed on women when they seek to vindicate the state's legitimate interests in protecting potential life. It also assigns the federal courts a legitimate role in a constitutional democracy. "Without taking giant strides and thereby risking a backlash too forceful to contain, the Court, through constitutional adjudication, can reinforce or signal a green light for social change."[92]

By adopting the Ginsburg-Burt approach to the manner in which abortion regulations are reviewed, the Court has arguably begun to belie Alasdair MacIntyre's claim mentioned at the outset of this chapter that the different sides in the abortion controversy operate from incommensurable worldviews between which rational adjudication is impossible. On the contrary, as the debate has moved away from metaphysical imponderables—about when life begins and whether a fetus is a person—and toward consideration of what constitutes an undue burden on a woman's constitutionally protected rights, it has become plain that there is a good deal of room for rational argument about the legal right to abortion. That abortion can be a politically polarizing issue does not mean that it has to be polarized, and it is certainly an advantage of the *Casey* approach that it pushes the debate away from issues that cannot be resolved in a pluralist culture, and toward areas where compromise and accommodation might be available.

Questions of approach aside, the substance of the "undue burden" standard offers possibilities for limiting abortion regulations that may be more robust than critics of *Casey* have realized. Certainly it seems to be a plausible interpretive strategy to claim in the wake of *Casey*, as Dworkin does, that any regulation of abortion decisions should be deemed unnecessarily coercive and therefore "undue" if the same "improvement in responsibility of decisions about abortion could have been achieved in some different way with less coercive consequences."[93] This line of reasoning suggests that if plaintiffs can show that less restrictive regulations can achieve states' expressed goals in regulating abortion, existing regulations will have to be struck down. Knowing this, legislatures contemplating the passage of abortion statutes will have incentives

---

1985), pp. 169–315. For criticism of Posner's view, see my "Richard Posner's Praxis," *Ohio State Law Review* 48, no. 4 (1987): 1009–26.

[92] Ginsburg, "Speaking in a Judicial Voice," p. 36.

[93] Dworkin, *Life's Dominion*, p. 173.

not to adopt more stringent regulations than those that can be justified as necessary.

Yet perhaps the most important and least noticed feature of the "undue burden" standard around which the constitutional law of abortion has come to revolve since *Casey* is its potential to reinvigorate the egalitarian considerations that Blackmun sidestepped when he looked to *Griswold*'s privacy doctrine as the foundation for his opinion in *Roe*. The reason for this is that it will likely prove exceedingly difficult to hammer out a jurisprudence of due and undue burdens without reference to equitable considerations. A hint of this can be found in the *Casey* opinions. The dissenters in that case point out that it is hard to discern a principled basis for the Court's holding, on the one hand, that spousal notification requirements impose undue burdens on women because some women may face abusive husbands, while holding, on the other, that parental consent requirements do not—even though, presumably, some pregnant teenagers will face abusive parents.[94] Dworkin extends this critique, pointing out that it is no less difficult to find a principled basis for the Court's rejection of the claim that a twenty-four-hour waiting period fails the undue burden test, even though it is conceded by the Court to place a comparatively heavy burden on poor women. If a restraint that does not make abortion practically impossible for anyone, nonetheless "makes it sufficiently more expensive or difficult that it will deter some women from having an abortion that they, on reflection, want," it should fail the undue burden test on his view.[95] Dworkin's logic is hard to resist, once the Court has embraced the idea that a regulation that may impose severe costs on *some* women fails to pass constitutional muster for that reason. This argument is not explicitly egalitarian, but it is implicitly so because it suggests that abortion regulations may not impose burdens on poor women merely in virtue of their poverty.

Dworkin's reasoning is rooted in the reality that it is difficult—perhaps impossible—to make sense of the idea of "dueness" without reference to the idea of equality. This is perhaps nowhere better illustrated than in the evolution of the concept of due process in American criminal procedure, and it might be illuminating, here, to mention some possible parallels between that history and the future of the undue burden standard in the constitutional law of abortion.

The famous 1963 case of *Gideon v. Wainwright* centered on the question whether states must supply indigent criminal defendants in capital cases with legal counsel paid for by the government.[96] The Court held

[94] 120 L. Ed. 2d 674 (1992), at 774–97.

[95] Dworkin, *Life's Dominion*, p. 173.

[96] For an excellent account, see Anthony Lewis, *Gideon's Trumpet* (New York: Vintage, 1966).

that they must, partly on the grounds that wealthy defendants typically are in a position to hire counsel.[97] In the decades following *Gideon* the notion that the poor, in pursuit of their constitutionally protected rights, should not have to shoulder burdens that the rich do not have to bear became embedded in the notion of criminal due process. As a result, robust protections were built into the law of criminal procedure in the 1960s and 1970s relating to the right to counsel for appeals as well as trials, for noncapital offenses if a defendant is to be imprisoned if found guilty, and related areas.[98] It is true that egalitarian readings of the due process clause in criminal procedure were subsequently cut back by the Burger and Rehnquist courts.[99] This underscores the reality that the law does not always evolve in a single direction. It is by no means necessary that robustly egalitarian interpretations of the idea of "dueness" will always prevail in this area or any other. Nonetheless, egalitarian considerations have not been entirely abandoned by the Court in this area, and at times even conservative courts have expanded upon them—as in the 1985 holding that an indigent defendant who offers an insanity plea should be allowed his own court-appointed psychiatrist at the government's expense.[100] Once again the idea of "dueness" in the due process clause was unpacked by reference to equality.

It does not take great leaps of imagination to discern the creative possibilities for analogous reasoning as the federal courts unpack the meaning of "undue burden" in the constitutional law of abortion. The notion that a burden is less than due if it imposes substantial costs on *some* women has a foothold in the language of the controlling opinion in *Casey*, as we have seen, though, as was the case with due process in criminal procedure, the implications of this are contradictory in the Court's opinions and have yet to be fully worked out. One obvious area that might be explored concerns abortion funding. Just as Clarence Earl Gideon's constitutional right to counsel was held to require the government to appoint counsel at its own expense for indigent defendants in certain circumstances, so one can imagine analogous arguments' being explored in the abortion context. What the parallel class of circumstances would turn out to be is difficult to discern in advance, but the case of rape—where the pregnant woman has no presumptive responsibility at all for her pregnancy—is an obvious place to start. From the standpoint of radical feminists this might seem like a small potential gain given what has been lost since *Webster*

[97] 372 U.S. 335 (1963).

[98] For examples, see *Douglas v. California*, 372 U.S. 353 (1963), and *Argesinger v. Hamlin*, 407 U.S. 25 (1972).

[99] See *Scott v. Illinois*, 440 U.S. 367 (1979); *Ross v. Moffitt*, 417 U.S. 600 (1974); *United States v. Cronic*, 466 U.S. 648 (1984); and *Strickland v. Washington* 466 U.S. 668 (1984) .

[100] *Ake v. Oklahoma*, 470 U.S. 68 (1985).

and *Casey*, but since the Court has never looked favorably on plaintiffs seeking abortion funding in the past, a potential gain in this area should not be judged insignificant from their point of view.

We do not exhaust the egalitarian possibilities by playing out the implications of the notion that regulations imposing substantial burdens on *some* women should fail the "undue burden" test. *Casey* identifies two sources of the state's interest in regulating abortion: to ensure that the woman has given her informed consent to the abortion procedure, and vindicating the state's interest in protecting potential life. The first of these interests is individual-regarding in the sense that the state may encourage the woman contemplating an abortion to reflect on the seriousness of her proposed course of action and consider alternatives to it, so long as this does not unnecessarily burden her decision. The state's interest here is in the quality of the woman's decision: that it should be authentic and informed. As already indicated, egalitarian considerations implicitly affect the evaluation of regulations designed to achieve this goal because the same regulations that will not be burdensome to wealthy women may impose substantial costs on poor women.

A different—and potentially more powerful—type of egalitarian consideration arises, however, once we reflect on the state's regulating abortion in order to vindicate its interest in potential human life. This opens up the possibility of reviving the equal protection considerations that Ginsburg, MacKinnon, West, and others think were lost when Blackmun decided to base *Roe* on Griswold's privacy doctrine. Why, it can and will be asked, should states be permitted to vindicate *this* interest in any way that imposes the costs of so doing disproportionately on some women, or, indeed, on women rather than men? The possibilities offered by this line of thinking are difficult to discern in the abstract. Clearly, the Court in the 1990s and 2000s remained unreceptive to the feminist view that virtually all regulation of abortion discriminates against women and should be rejected for that reason.[101] But the opportunity for an equal protection argument lurks in the logic of *Casey*, if not in its language, and it seems at least possible that this logic might generate substantial constraints on abortion regulations in the future.

4. The "Partial Birth" Controversy

Within eight years of the *Casey* decision there were signs that egalitarian considerations were shaping the Court's abortion jurisprudence. The opening paragraph of Justice Stephen Breyer's majority opinion in its

[101] See n. 74 above.

controversial partial birth abortion decision, *Stenberg v. Carhart*, noted that millions "fear that a law that forbids abortion would condemn many American women to lives that lack dignity, depriving them of *equal liberty* and leading those with least resources to undergo illegal abortions with the attendant risks of death and suffering."[102] The decision in *Gonzales v. Carhart*, which reversed the *Stenberg* outcome, did not repudiate this egalitarian logic. True, aspects of Justice Kennedy's majority opinion could be read as paternalistic, if not patronizing, toward women—notably his assertion that women who do not fully appreciate what the D&X procedure involves might subsequently be traumatized if they learn this after the fact. As Justice Ginsburg noted in dissent, this is scarcely a basis to distinguish the D&X from the D&E procedure, and it assumes that women are somehow incapable of making decisions in their own best interests.[103] But the majority left unchallenged the notion that undue burden requires all women to have access to the safest available abortion procedure, thereby affirming, at least implicitly, a commitment to women's equality.

The argument concerned whether the D&X procedure is truly safer in some circumstances. In *Stenberg* the lower courts had found that there is, indeed, a substantial body of medical authority in support of the attending physician's judgment that the D&X procedure was the safest available in certain circumstances. This was contested by the dissenting justices Kennedy, Rehnquist, Thomas, and Scalia. Rather than debate the conflicting views about the science with the dissenters, the majority would have done better to take the position that, as a disputed question of fact, this is best settled by the trial court. If the Nebraska legislature had considered the evidence of the relative safety of different procedures, the time to establish this was at trial, and if Dr. Carhart disputed the science on which its judgment was based, he, too, would have had to persuade the trial court. Perhaps the Nebraska legislature never considered the matter at all, in which case the notion that it is better placed than an appellate court to make this determination, as the dissenters contended, would be beside the point.

Reviewing courts do not listen to witnesses or hear expert testimony. As a result, they are generally not expected to second-guess lower courts' findings of fact. Unless the record contains overwhelming evidence that they cannot be believed, the factual findings below are generally to be taken as given. And even when there is reason to doubt them, the appropriate remedy is to remand the case to the trial court for rehearing, not to make a different determination of the facts during the process of

---

[102] 192 F. 3d 1142, emphasis supplied.
[103] 129 S. Ct. 1610 (2007) at 1648–49.

appellate review. From this perspective it is the dissenters in *Stenberg*, not the majority, who inappropriately relied on their own (lack of) expertise in the adjudication of contested factual questions.

The *Stenberg* dissenters did not openly challenge the notion that, in circumstances where an abortion is legitimate, undue burden requires the safest available procedure to be allowed. But it is difficult not to conclude that they did not accept it. Some of the rhetoric surrounding the various arguments suggests that the dissenters objected to the D&X procedure on the (unacknowledged) ground that they believe it verges on infanticide: delivery of all but the head of the fetus before the skull is crushed comes uncomfortably close to creating a human being in order to avail the woman of a safer procedure for terminating her pregnancy. Though they did not say so, this might have been the nub of their conclusion that D&X is objectionable in a way that D&E is not.

The difficulty with this view is that "uncomfortably close" glosses over whether or not the contention is that a partially delivered fetus is, as a legal matter, a person. Were the Court to take the view that it is, then the D&X procedure would indeed be infanticide. Murdering someone to enhance a woman's medical safety is illegal, and the Court would be bound to proscribe it. But the Nebraska statute did not assert that a fetus is a person under these (or any) conditions, and the Court has systematically refrained from deciding for itself when life begins. If it did, this would take the Court into wholly different territory from the debate over whether or not the decision in *Roe* should be reversed. Doctors who perform abortions once the threshold to life had been crossed would be guilty of murder, and the women who have those abortions would be guilty as accessories to their crimes. Litigants, lawyers, politicians, and judges not have seen fit to press in this direction. In this they reflect public opinion. As we saw at the outset, although most Americans oppose abortion, even more do not want to see people prosecuted for it.

Congress upped the ante in response to *Stenberg* by entering the field with an explicit finding that the D&X procedure is never medically necessary, and embedding this finding in its Partial-Birth Abortion Ban legislation of 2003. This action is surely due some weight. The question is: how much? The federal courts have never been willing to defer completely to legislative findings of fact. As Justice Thomas himself put it while serving on the District of Columbia Court of Appeals before his elevation to the Supreme Court, "If a legislature could make a statute constitutional simply by 'finding' that black is white or freedom is slavery, judicial review would be an elaborate farce. At least since *Marbury v. Madison* . . . that has not been the law."[104] In view of the demonstrable factual errors,

---

[104] *Lamprecht v. FCC*, 958 F. 2d, 382, 392 (DC Circuit 1992).

conclusory assertions, and marginally qualified witnesses that accompanied this congressional finding already mentioned, it is scarcely surprising that the lower courts had not been persuaded. Indeed, it is notable that Justice Kennedy's majority opinion does not defend the congressional fact-finding exercise. Rather, it takes the view that there is "medical uncertainty" over the question whether D&X is safer for women in some circumstances, and that this uncertainty "does not foreclose the exercise of legislative power."[105] Perhaps not, but nor does it entail that the courts should defer to that power when it is based on manifestly implausible findings.

Whether the outcome in *Gonzales* had in fact moved the Court any closer to abandoning *Casey*'s reaffirmation of a woman's constitutionally protected right to an abortion was left unclear. Justice Ginsburg's dissent suggested that it had, and commentary from such pro-choice scholars as Ronald Dworkin sounded an ominous note in this regard.[106] True to form, given his prior opinions, Justice Thomas wrote a terse concurrence reiterating his view "that the Court's abortion jurisprudence, including *Casey* and *Roe v. Wade*, has no basis in the constitution."[107] Justice Scalia joined the Thomas concurrence. This, too, was no surprise. But whereas in the past Rehnquist's name would have been there as well, neither of the new justices chose to associate himself with the Thomas-Scalia view. This might have signaled agreement with Kennedy that *Casey*'s guarantee of abortion rights remains intact even though the undue burden test was not met, in their judgment, in the matter at hand. But it might have signified that either or both of the new justices were undecided on the larger issue or, if decided, disinclined to tip their hands for the moment. Only time would tell.

5. ABORTION JURISPRUDENCE AND DEMOCRACY

How should democrats evaluate the Court's reversal of itself in *Gonzales*? Let us concede, *arguendo*, Justice Ginsburg's claim that Congress was implausibly perfunctory in its "finding" that the D&X procedure is never medically indicated. Does that mean the Court should have struck down the congressional statute?[108] How, if at all, should democratic considerations influence our answer to this question?

---

[105] 127 S. Ct. 1610 (2007) at 1618.

[106] Ronald Dworkin, "The Court and Abortion: Worse Than You Think," *New York Review of Books* 54, no. 9 (May 31, 2007).

[107] 127 S. Ct. 1610 (2007), at 1639–40.

[108] Note that I am skirting the supremacy clause questions, as did the litigants and the Court. These issues will eventually have to be addressed. The traditional conservative view

One answer, consistent with *Stenberg*, might be that the trial court that heard the evidence was unimpressed by Congress's empirical "findings." This view might seem to be recommended by the long-established maxim that trial courts' findings of fact should not be second-guessed by appellate courts. There are exceptions to this maxim, when such findings in the trial court are so implausible that they could not reasonably support the holding in question, but that was not claimed here. The entire focus was on what Congress was alleged, after hearings, to have found.

Things are complicated, however, by the fact that the legislature had clearly spoken in response to the Court's action in *Stenberg*. Should this not cast the trial court's findings of fact in a different light? On the Ginsburg-Burt view of the Court's role endorsed here, returning the matter to the legislature is what is supposed to happen, and, because it happened in this case, arguably the Court should have accepted the result.

Notice, however, that Congress did not dispute the Court's account of what undue burden requires. Indeed, Congress's felt need to establish that the D&X procedure is never medically indicated as safer evinces its implicit acceptance of the notion that if a safer procedure is available in circumstances where abortion is permissible, then forcing a woman to endure a less safe procedure imposes an undue burden on her. Everything therefore turns on what deference, if any, is due to the congressional finding of fact.

As Justice Thomas's remark quoted earlier indicates, it would be absurd for such deference to be entirely unqualified. Had the Southern state legislatures responded to *Brown* during the 1950s by staging bogus hearings to conclude that their separate school districts were not in fact unequal, the federal courts would not have capitulated. Nor should they have done so on the Ginsburg-Burt view. Rather, they should have been expected to evaluate these claims along with other factual allegations presented by the parties at trial. The point of sending the matter back to the legislatures was to ask them to fashion a policy that comes within the constitutional constraint, not to subvert that constraint.

The congressional findings at issue in *Gonzales* were readily impeachable at trial because they ignored the views of relevant professional as-

was that *Roe* should be repealed, re-creating the pre-1973 world in which abortion was a matter for state law. That status quo ante is no longer straightforwardly available, however, Congress having entered the fray. Among the complexities that will have to be addressed is that at least seven states have enacted laws protecting a woman's right to end her pregnancy regardless of *Roe*, and nine have language in their state constitutions that has been interpreted by courts as guaranteeing that same protection. See Christine Vestal, "States Probe Limits of Abortion Policy," *State Politics and Policy*, stateline.org (June 22, 2006), http://www.stateline.org/live/ViewPage.action?siteNodeId=136&contentId=121780 [02-17-2010].

sociations; because Congress did not hear from a single physician who had any experience with the procedure; and because the record contained demonstrably false assertions—notably the claim that no major medical school teaches the procedure when many leading schools in fact did. That the trial court was persuaded by different testimony that contradicted the congressional findings is a signal to the legislature that such perfunctory factual hearings will likely be accorded the deference that they merit.

The trial court might, of course, have found differently had the government presented a more convincing case. In that event the Partial-Birth Abortion Ban Act of 2003 would have been upheld at trial. As things turned out, it was not, and the U.S. Supreme Court had no more business reversing that finding than it would have done in reversing the trial court's rejection of the Nebraska partial birth abortion ban statute seven years earlier. The dissenters in *Stenberg* were part of the majority in *Gonzales*, but this was because the composition of the Court, not the merits of the issue, had changed. It remained as true in 2007 as it had been in 2000 that those who see and hear witnesses and testimony are best placed to judge their credibility, and that reviewing courts should therefore second-guess trial courts on questions of fact only when it is manifest that they have abused their fact-finding authority. That was never alleged by any litigant below or in any opinion in *Gonzales*.

Democratic defenses of judicial review are motivated by the recognition that all decision-making procedures are flawed. Majority rule is the decision procedure of choice in many circumstances, but it can nonetheless produce results that are at odds with democracy's principled commitment to nondomination. When they function well, courts blunt the resulting tension—prompting legislatures to devise creative solutions to it. Courts do this by setting out criteria for the avoidance of domination in particular contexts, to which those who utilize majoritarian procedures must then accommodate themselves. The notion of undue burden is one such criterion in the abortion context. It has been elaborated to include the idea that when an abortion is permissible, it imposes an undue burden on women to require them to endure a less safe procedure when a more safe procedure is available. It is a mark of the legitimacy that this standard has achieved that Congress did not seek to challenge it.

CHAPTER EIGHT

Democratic Justice: A Reply to Critics

DEMOCRACY AND JUSTICE are often mutually antagonistic ideas. Whatever our conception of justice might be, there is no guarantee that democratic procedures will converge on it. As a result, achieving just outcomes might often seem to require a readiness to subvert democracy. By the same token, if democratic procedures are embraced as desirable this might well involve accepting that they will generate injustices. Yet most democrats are also committed to some idea of justice, and few defenders of justice believe that it can be pursued regardless of democratic institutions and decision making. This tension between the requirements of democracy and those of justice has been recognized at least since Plato wrote the *Republic,* and no definitive resolution of it has ever been put forward. Yet my central contention in *Democratic Justice* is that democracy and justice are best pursued together.[1]

This is partly for political reasons. Justice must be sought democratically if it is to garner legitimacy in the modern world, and democracy must be justice promoting if it is to sustain allegiance over time. But, in addition to these political considerations, I argued that there is a philosophical link between justice and democracy, rooted in the fact that the most plausible accounts of both ideals involve commitments to the idea of nondomination. Power and hierarchy are endemic to human interaction, making the possibility of domination ever present. The challenge is to find ways to limit domination while minimizing interference with legitimate hierarchies and power relations.

This goal of limiting domination while interfering with legitimate hierarchies as little as possible led me to the notion of democracy as a subordinate or conditioning good: one that shapes the terms of human interaction without thereby determining its course. Pursuing democratic justice involves deferring to *insider's wisdom* as much as possible, getting people to democratize the collective pursuit of other goods for themselves. Imposed solutions are unlikely to be as effective as those designed by insiders, and their legitimacy will always be in question. Imposed solutions are solutions of last resort. When adopted, they are best pursued

---

[1] Ian Shapiro, *Democratic Justice* (New Haven: Yale University Press, 1999).

indirectly and designed to minimize interference with people's pursuit of other goods.

In the applied chapters of *Democratic Justice*, I explored how this could be done in different phases of the human life cycle, from childhood through the adult worlds of work and domestic life, retirement, old age, and approaching death. In the course of developing this account, I spelled out the implications of the theory for pressing debates about authority over children, the law of marriage and divorce, abortion and population control, the workplace, basic income guarantees, health insurance, retirement policies, and decisions made by and for the infirm elderly.

Democratic Justice, with its applied focus on civil institutions, is the first of three volumes on justice. The second, *Democracy and Distribution*, will deal with income and wealth. I sketched the elements of the main argument in chapter 5 of *The State of Democratic Theory*, published in 2003. The third volume on justice will deal with public institutions. The focus will be on representative arrangements, the relations among governmental institutions, and a full statement and defense of my democratic theory of judicial review, a preliminary sketch of which is supplied in the previous chapter.

These books are part of my ongoing effort to defend a conception of justice that can be realized by democratic means, in tandem with developing an account of democratic institutions and practices that can have a fighting chance of doing the job. Part of my motivation for this dual approach is pragmatic. Perhaps there is a "right" answer to the question "what is just?" that has been, or will be, discerned by someone with an unusually acute philosophical mind. But if ever there was an era for philosopher kings, ours is not it. Benevolent dictators are considerably more likely to shed their benevolence than their love of power—making them poor bets for advancing the cause of justice. Moving toward justice—or away from injustice—will have to happen through democratic institutions if it is to happen at all. They are the font of political legitimacy in today's world.

But my motivation is also principled. It reflects my argument for the existence of an internal relationship between the ideas of democracy and justice: both are rooted in commitments to the ideal of nondomination. Theorists from Joseph Schumpeter to John Roemer to Giuseppe Di Palma who have urged that popular expectations about advancing justice be decoupled from democracy are not merely unrealistic, people being what they are. These theorists also fail to appreciate that those expectations are well founded. Part of democracy's legitimacy derives from the expectation that it will help create a less unjust world by reducing domination, and democrats demand justice because they sense that this is a convincing way to resist domination—or so I argue.

My account of democratic justice has attracted its share of critical fire, some of which I take up in this chapter. In responding to criticisms, my main focus is on those that enable me to move the enterprise forward—by scotching misperceptions, incorporating and building on suggestions, or otherwise refining my arguments. I should start, therefore, by thanking my critics. For the most part my arguments have been carefully and appreciatively read, and my critics have supplied me with both the occasion and the wherewithal to improve them.[2] In what follows I consider objections related to four main themes: rights and basic interests; economic inequality; deliberative democracy; and public institutions.

RIGHTS AND BASIC INTERESTS

In "Liberal Theory and the 'Loyal Opposition' in *Democratic Justice*" Steven Shiffrin objects that I am "a rights theorist in a democrat's clothing."[3] This objection seems to me to be largely semantic. What divides liberals from democrats is not whether or not they are committed to rights, but rather which rights they endorse and why. Liberals characteristically take the view that rights are anterior to politics, insisting that a large part of the challenge of institutional design is to insulate them from politics. Democrats usually adopt the contrasting view that rights are artifacts of collective arrangements. They see the task as trying to structure politics so as to reflect the interests of the governed. Of course this involves the creation of rights: most obviously rights of democratic

[2] In a couple of instances where my views have been misconstrued, as by James Fishkin on apartheid and inequality of opportunity, and by Steven Shiffrin on loyal opposition, this does not require much of a response since the critics in question acknowledge my actual views later in their respective commentaries. Accordingly, I will not dwell on these issues except to reiterate that apartheid ran afoul of several of my presumptions against hierarchy (it was avoidable and ossified; it created massive externalities and exit costs for those on whom it was imposed); that systematic inequality of opportunity of the kind invoked by Bernard Williams's warrior society violates my injunction against non-self-liquidating hierarchies at least; and that with respect to loyal opposition my argument is that unless there are opportunities for loyal opposition, disloyal opposition will be both forthcoming and legitimate. As I put it on p. 48 of *Democratic Justice*, "the more democratically those who win in battles over collective decisions conduct themselves in victory, the stronger is the obligation on the defeated to ensure that their opposition be loyal rather than disloyal— and vice versa."

[3] Steven Shiffrin, "Liberal Theory and the 'Loyal Opposition' in *Democratic Justice*," *The Good Society* 11, no. 2 (2002): 79.

participation and opposition. But the justification for the existence of these rights is that they are instrumental to the democratization of power relationships, not that they are extrapolitical entities (of what metaphysical origin?) attaching to individuals.

If you ask democrats why it is desirable or legitimate to democratize power relationships, they will give different answers. Some will say that this is more important than protecting the rights liberals characteristically value. Some will say that democracy offers the best way to vindicate those rights. Some will give other reasons. In my case, the argument of *Democratic Justice* is that if the power relations constituting a collective order are not democratized, it is difficult to see why that order will, or should, command the allegiance of those on whom it is imposed. The reason is that democratization of power relations provides the best available insurance for vindicating people's basic interests. And unless institutional arrangements hold out the plausible promise of achieving that goal, there is little reason to expect them to garner legitimacy or support over time.

This raises the question: what are basic interests, and how do we identify them? Several commentators raise questions about my deployment of the idea. From some perspectives it might, indeed, fairly be said that my account of basic interests in *Democratic Justice* is both incomplete and undertheorized. In response I will say that I proceeded as I did because I have become persuaded of the merits of a pragmatic approach to argument in political theory, which I would sum up with the dictum: pursue justification only in the context of exploring concrete problems, and only as needed to respond to particular skeptical challenges. It is perhaps worth a brief excursus to explain the thinking behind this stance.

I cut my philosophical teeth in the Anglo-American tradition of political philosophy. We were taught to act on the injunction, whose merits were—ironically—treated as self-evident, that everything should be justified from the ground up. First let me persuade you of my metaphysics and epistemology, then my theory of science, then my ethics and social theory, and then, having done all that, I will convince you of the wisdom of my political theory. Over the past two decades I have become convinced that this is a mug's game, partly because of the endemic plurality of philosophical outlooks, and partly because I see no evidence in the history of the tradition to suggest that this is the way in which arguments in political theory gain traction and influence. The reason Plato, Hobbes, Marx, Mill, and Rawls (many others could be named) garner widespread attention as political theorists has much more to do with their destinations than with their starting points. Accordingly, my approach in *Democratic Justice* was to focus centrally on the creative challenge of trying to make the destination compatible with—and indeed attractive from—multiple points of view. This tactic reflects my affinity with Rawls in his "political, not metaphysical" mode and with Cass Sunstein's advocacy on behalf of incompletely theorized agreement.[4]

With respect to basic interests, my approach was to describe them in a comparatively thin fashion partly so as to minimize their controversial character. I argued that children have a basic interest in the security, nutrition, health, and education needed to develop into, and live as, normal adults. More particularly, I argued that people have a basic interest "in developing the capacities required to function adequately and responsibly in the prevailing economic, technological, and institutional system, governed as a democracy, over the course of their lives."[5] Many would want to insist on more robust conceptions of basic interests, but the more one adds, the more controversial the list inevitably becomes.

This is not to say that my account of basic interests is inconsequential or uncontroversial. As I note in my response to James Fishkin's egalitarian critique below, the economic requirements of basic interests are either unmet, or in serious jeopardy, for over two-fifths of the U.S. population and for billions of the world's population. It would not be difficult to make a convincing case that the educational and human capital aspects of basic interests scarcely fare much better. Basic interests might constitute a minimal list, but minimal does not mean negligible.

As for controversiality, I do not doubt that every conceivable account of basic interests is controversial among some (including the refusal to embrace any such conception—as with the neoclassical economist's unwillingness to countenance interpersonal comparisons of well-being). Indeed, this is partly why deferring the development of one's political theory until a particular conception has won the philosophical high ground amounts to waiting for Godot. And, as Clarissa Hayward is right to point out in her comment on *Democratic Justice*, recognizing endemic disagreement is foundational to its argument for normative as well as for empirical reasons.[6] Yet in Hayward's account there are only two possible ways out of this conundrum: either to ground democratic procedural standards in practices that are taken to be universal, therefore appealing to a consensus centered on procedures, or to theorize intuitions and values shared by most—although not all—social actors, which implies adopting a definition of justice endorsed by the majority.[7] Yet I mean to avoid this stark Hobson's choice she poses between appealing to some-

---

[4] See *Democratic Justice*, pp. 231–32, and Cass R. Sunstein, "On Legal Theory and Legal Practice," in *NOMOS XXXVII: Theory and Practice*, ed. Ian Shapiro and Judith Wagner DeCew (New York: New York University Press, 1995), pp. 267–87.

[5] *Democratic Justice*, pp. 85–86.

[6] Clarissa Hayward, "Comment on Ian Shapiro's *Democratic Justice*," *The Good Society* 11, no. 2 (2002): 82–85.

[7] Ibid., p. 85.

thing like Habermas's performative contradiction and having all basic interests be decided by majority rule.[8] The former is too rationalist and the latter caves in too quickly to pure proceduralism. Instead of either of these, the distinctive tack in *Democratic Justice* is to take a power-centered approach to basic interests.

Other resourcist views, such as John Rawls's, Amartya Sen's, and Ronald Dworkin's, affirm the importance of a list of basic or instrumental goods from the perspective of achieving multiple conceptions of the good life. My distinctive focus is on the ways in which the resources needed to vindicate basic interests are implicated in the project of democratizing power relations. Consider the interest in being sufficiently well-educated to understand, critically evaluate, and so vote intelligently on the policy choices likely to confront someone's society over the course of a lifetime. The views of parents who want to deprive their children of such an education out of a fundamental hostility to democracy should ultimately be overridden, because their stance involves denying their children the wherewithal to participate effectively in the democratic order. On my account, we all have a basic interest in the existence of such an order and in developing the capacities to participate effectively within it. No doubt education has many other important consequences for the promotion of human flourishing, but from the perspective of democratic justice these belong in the realm of superordinate goods. The state's responsibility is to vindicate children's basic interests in ways that interfere as little as possible with parents' responsibility for their children's best interests. But if attempts to craft an accommodation fail, the state's responsibility to ensure that children's basic interests are vindicated must prevail.

Nancy Rosenblum is thus right to describe me as a muscular democrat in "*Democratic Justice* 'all the way down'" if by this she means to identify me with the view that, at the end of the day, rights of democratic control should be defended against antidemocrats by force if necessary.[9] This I take to be part of our justification for responding to the Osama bin Ladens and Timothy McVeighs of this world as we do. Their terrorist tactics no doubt provide us with an independent justification, but even without them it would be right forcibly to resist an individual or entity that threatened to destroy democratic political arrangements. Similar considerations led me to argue in *Democratic Justice* that democratic institu-

---

[8] A "performative contradiction" arises when a person's assertion undermines itself—as when someone says "I am mute" or "all my statements are untrue." In Hayward's usage here, she intends it to capture the notion that people who appeal to reasons in order to reject the claim that reasoned agreement is a feature of legitimate arguments could be said to be caught in a performative contradiction. Ibid., p. 84.

[9] Nancy Rosenblum, "*Democratic Justice* 'all the way down,'" *The Good Society* 11, no. 2 (2002): 65.

tions should be entrenched to the extent possible, particularly in settings where they have been in recent serious jeopardy, such as Germany after World War II and South Africa following the collapse of apartheid.[10] And if, as in the Algerian example, an elected government outlaws opposition and is otherwise subversive of democratic institutions and practices, it, too, should be resisted. As I have said, opposition should be "loyal" to existing institutions only to the extent that government is.

My use of "ultimately" and "at the end of the day" in the preceding paragraphs is meant to signal two kinds of caveat that open up a third path between Hayward's alternatives. The first concerns my injunction to limit the coercive dimensions of muscular democracy as much as possible through burden shifting and other institutional devices designed to ensure that the state vindicates basic interests in ways that interfere as little as possible with the other activities people engage in. Hence my argument that, in the United States, parents should enjoy both standing and forums to challenge the ways in which public officials enforce basic interests—with the burden of persuasion shifting to the officials. They must establish that there is no other way to meet their legitimate goals that is less subversive of what the parents believe to be the children's best interests. How weighty that burden should be varies with the importance of the basic interest at stake. Building on the thinking behind the U.S. Supreme Court's tiers-of-scrutiny reasoning, my suggestion was that the more important a basic interest, the more deeply entrenched it should be.[11] Those essential to the operation of a democratic order should be at or close to the top of the list.

Does this mean that people should be prohibited from advocating antidemocratic outcomes in democratic politics? No. As I intimated in *Democratic Justice* (and will discuss more fully in volume 3 on public institutions), the alternatives to a strongly libertarian policy on permissive freedoms of speech and association are all worse.[12] In effect this means that those who advocate the end of democracy must be tolerated, however hypocritically they make use of democratic freedoms to do this. They can be remonstrated against and voted against, but suppressed only if they plausibly threaten actually to impede democracy's operation.[13] To be sure, this can be a difficult line to walk, and it can present exceedingly tough choices in practice, but the alternative is to vest incumbent bureaucrats and politicians with the dangerously tempting power to decide that political dissent they find objectionable or inconvenient should

---

[10] *Democratic Justice*, pp. 19–21.

[11] Ibid., pp. 56, 83, 185.

[12] Ibid., pp. 40–41.

[13] On this subject, see Alexander Kirshner, "Militant Democracy" (PhD diss., Yale University, 2011).

be repressed as hostile to democracy. We need only mention the case of J. Edgar Hoover and McCarthyism in the 1950s, or the repression of legitimate opposition via spurious appeals to protecting democracy in regimes ranging from the old Soviet Union to Zimbabwe in 2008, to make this point.

Although those who reject democracy *tout court* should be resisted, forcibly if necessary, those who accept it but challenge government's prevailing interpretation of what is essential to its operation should be free to contest this through the democratic process. Unwilling as we should be to countenance rejection of democracy's foundational institutional legitimacy, we should anticipate, even welcome, the (inevitable) contestation over just what democracy requires. Amish parents have no special claim qua parents to insist that their children should forgo education after age fourteen because by then they have learned what they need to survive in the Amish subculture, or, indeed, even on the grounds (never alleged in *Wisconsin v. Yoder*) that education of their children to age fourteen is sufficient to vindicate their basic interests outside the Amish community.[14] However, as citizens Amish parents should indeed be free to try to convince a majority of Wisconsinites that education beyond age fourteen is unnecessary for basic interests protection. *Pace* Hayward, were they to succeed—though it seems vanishingly unlikely that they would—then the law there should indeed be changed on that point.[15]

Rosenblum takes *Democratic Justice*'s commitment to fight domination in all spheres of human activity to be an endorsement of what she describes as the logic of congruence. Congruence, as she defines it, requires that groups and associations "from families to churches to social groups conform to liberal democratic values 'all the way down.'"[16] Certainly I never invoked any such logic in *Democratic Justice*, arguing instead that the goal is to democratize the power dimensions of human association while keeping to a minimum interference with the other (superordinate) goods that people pursue. Rosenblum quotes me correctly to the effect that democracy is a foundational good in that "no prior or more basic institutional commitment rightly commands our allegiance." However, she neglects the rest of my view, which is that this does not mean that no prior *moral* commitments rightly command our allegiance, and my concomitant insistence that "we should resist every suggestion that just

---

[14] See Richard Arneson and Ian Shapiro, "Democratic Autonomy and Religious Freedom: A Critique of *Wisconsin v. Yoder*," in Ian Shapiro, *Democracy's Place* (Ithaca: Cornell University Press, 1996), pp. 137–74.

[15] For present purposes I assume that decisions about the amount of education required for democratic participation are appropriately made in state legislatures. An argument might be made that such questions belong in the federal legislature.

[16] Rosenblum, "*Democratic Justice* 'all the way down,'" p. 66.

because democracy is a foundational good, it is the only good for human beings, it is the highest human good, or it should dominate the activities we engage in."[17] Democracy operates best, I argue, when it facilitates our other activities, not when it displaces them, so that the ongoing creative challenge for democrats is to find ways to democratize the multiple domains that structure social life while retaining democracy in a subordinate or conditioning role.[18]

Comparable considerations apply to Georgia Warnke's discussion of school vouchers and Christian Scientists' beliefs about medical care in "Children and Ian Shapiro's *Democratic Justice*." Warnke takes exception to my insistence that Christian Scientists should not be allowed to deny medical care to their children on the grounds that "presumably Christian Scientists and other religious groups would consider spiritual needs just as important as physiological ones." As far as vouchers are concerned, she observes that "poor and minority parents who support vouchers are not looking out only for the best interests of their children. They are also looking out for their basic interests in receiving an adequate education, a basic interest for which they think the state has failed to provide."[19]

Starting with the Christian Scientists, we should distinguish the case when parents act in their appropriate second-guessing roles with respect to children's basic interests from when they act as primary fiduciaries of children's best interests. As I argue in *Democratic Justice*, although parents and the state are appropriately viewed as primary fiduciaries of children's best and basic interests respectively, each also has a role as secondary fiduciary with respect to the interests over which they do not have primary fiduciary responsibility.[20] The secondary fiduciary's second-guessing role is warranted by the fact that children are incapable of effective opposition, while the primary fiduciary role is warranted by reason of children's limited ability to participate in making decisions that affect them. Second-guessing parents should indeed have standing to go into court and argue that the state is not fulfilling its responsibility to children in underwriting their health care—perhaps when they are turned away

[17] *Democratic Justice*, p. 21.

[18] I am even more puzzled by Rosenblum's discussion of what she describes as an "obtuse" moral psychology motivating her logic of congruence, which I would never think of endorsing and from which even she says I am "largely absolved." Grateful as I am for this—albeit partial—absolution, I should note that a number of the terms she uses in quotation marks in a manner that might be taken to indicate that they are mine are not. "Zero-tolerance," "seedbed of virtue," "bootcamps of citizenship," "spilling-over," and "soulcraft" do not appear in my book and have nothing to do with any of my arguments.

[19] Georgia Warnke, "Children and Ian Shapiro's *Democratic Justice*," *The Good Society* 11, no. 2 (2002): 88, 89.

[20] *Democratic Justice*, pp. 78–84.

from an emergency room owing to their parents' lack of health insurance coverage. But Warnke goes further, saying that in rejecting medical care for their children Christian Scientists may "take themselves to be looking out, not just for their children's best interests in spiritual salvation, but also for their basic interests in spiritual survival, a form of survival they take to be more important than merely physical survival." But parents qua parents have no right unilaterally to redefine basic interests to include spiritual salvation.

Perhaps there is not really much disagreement here, since Warnke appears to concede that "courts cannot allow Christian Scientists to substitute prayer for their children's medical care." She does say that they should "encourage the use or development of different sorts of medical therapies that are more compatible with Christian Scientist belief."[21] It is hard to know what these might be when it is known that a child is going to die if he or she does not get a blood transfusion. In any event, I have already agreed that public officials should be required to vindicate basic interests in the least intrusive manner possible with respect to parents' fiduciary responsibilities, a requirement that should be enforceable through courts and administrative agencies, and in other appellate forums. But, at the end of the appeals process, government should be entitled, indeed obliged, to vindicate basic interests as its legitimate agent interprets them.

The issue Warnke raises concerning vouchers and inner city schools is considerably tougher. As I acknowledged in *Democratic Justice*, the difficulty is that many public schools in the United States do indeed fail to vindicate basic interests of children in their charge.[22] However, when the concerned parents, acting in their second-guessing roles, opt for exit rather than voice, things are likely to become worse for the children who remain. If local governments adopt voucher plans to facilitate this kind of opting out, their actions should therefore be challengeable in courts or administrative forums by parents and others representing these remaining children. The burden should shift to the defenders of the voucher schemes to establish that implementing them will not have a deleterious impact on the education of those who remain. Public schools are not sacrosanct from the perspective of democratic justice; vindicating basic educational interests is. If different institutional arrangements can do a better job of providing basic education than presently failing public schools, arguably they should be tried.[23]

We should remember that parents' concerns tend, quite properly, to be limited to the prospects for their own children, while public officials

[21] Warnke, "Children and Ian Shapiro's Democratic Justice," p. 90.
[22] *Democratic Justice*, pp. 108–9.
[23] This is discussed further in chapter 2 of *The State of Democratic Theory* (Princeton: Princeton University Press, 2003).

are expected to attend to the basic interests of all the children for whom they are responsible. Both perspectives are needed, but they are not substitutes for one another. Governments are properly charged with ultimate responsibility for ensuring that people develop the capacities needed to function as normal adults in a democracy. There is invariably room for argument, debate, and experimentation over just what that requires, and there should always be institutional forums in which people can seek to influence it. But that is quite another thing from unilateral action to defect from the process, which is justified, if ever, only in extreme cases of institutional failure.

I agree with Warnke that there will be circumstances in which every institutional remedy fails, and parents feel compelled to step in and act unilaterally as the second-guessing fiduciaries of their children's basic interests. As I put it in *Democratic Justice*, "Parents who opt for voice instead of exit may expend much energy to little effect, and their children might be adversely affected for life as a result." I acknowledged there that it is difficult to blame them in such circumstances for choosing fail-safe solutions of last resort, but noted that recognizing this is merely an acknowledgment of "the devastating consequences of institutional failure. The presence of serious externalities and collective action problems are a significant part of why the state is needed to protect children's basic interests to begin with. As a result, we can scarcely be surprised that these difficulties run rampant when government fails to do its job."[24]

A different reason that democratic debate over how to meet basic interests should be expected and welcomed derives from the fact that basic interests are partly tied to prevailing economic and technological arrangements. They include what Marx once described as a "historical and moral element." In the information age, effective participation and opposition in a democracy might well require different kinds of education from what was needed in previous eras. In some respects people might need to know more, in others less, and different types of knowledge might become salient as technological conditions evolve. Indeed, just what kinds of knowledge are necessary is likely to be contestable partly because it is unclear. This reality supplies us with additional reasons for thinking it important for the political system to remain open to ongoing debates about just what democracy requires, pursuing a middle way between Hayward's alternatives.

Comparable considerations apply to basic interests in other realms. For instance, democracy cannot operate meaningfully within the firm if power disparities render workers so vulnerable to managers that they do not feel free to dispute their decisions. There may be other justice

[24] *Democratic Justice*, p. 109.

reasons for supporting a comparatively robust social wage as one element of basic interests, but from the perspective of democratic justice in the workplace the central reason is that a robust social wage reduces employee vulnerability. As a result, when the social wage is high, then less intrusive measures are needed to condition the power dimensions of work democratically. And since the goal is always to do this in ways that are least subversive of superordinate goods, those working to advance the cause of democratic justice in the workplace should support expansion of the social wage.

To affirm this is not to deny that there should be democratic decision making over what the elements of the social wage should be, or, when arbitrators or courts do intervene more rather than less aggressively on the side of labor in industrial disputes owing to the thinness of the social wage, that their activities should not be democratically constrained. I argued in chapter 3 of *Democratic Justice* that, in order to build and maintain legitimacy in democracies, courts and other second-guessing agencies must always act in democracy-sustaining ways. This means reining in imperial tendencies in the interpretative doctrines they deploy as much as possible, returning decisions to elected branches for revision rather than revising them themselves, and generally operating as reactive players whose goal is to induce others to find ways to avoid practices that foster illegitimate exclusion and permit domination. Vanguardism undermines democratic legitimacy. It should always be the reluctant strategy of last resort.

For Iris Marion Young, the problem is not *Democratic Justice*'s definition of basic interests or its focus on ending domination in all spheres of human endeavor, but rather its particular approach to the locus of domination: she criticizes me for focusing on power relations within particular institutions and practices instead of "structures."[25] Like Shiffrin's discussion of rights, this objection seems to me to be largely semantic. By *structural* Young means the ways in which the "organization, rules and practices within one institutional sphere condition the relationships, actions, and options in others."[26] But this is the idea of a power externality as I deploy it in chapter 6 of *Democratic Justice* in the course of arguing that the extent to which government should seek to regulate the internal arrangements of firms to protect employees should vary with how vulnerable the external environment makes them.[27] A robust social wage diminishes employees' vulnerability by reducing their exit costs; a minimal one increases it by increasing them.

[25] Iris Marion Young, "Ian Shapiro's *Democratic Justice*," *The Good Society* 11, no. 2 (2002): 76–77.

[26] Ibid., p. 77.

[27] *Democratic Justice*, pp. 182–95.

Young's substantive suggestion, that employers should be required to embrace "family friendly" policies, is best evaluated within this framework. She does not specify which family-friendly policies she has in mind, saying only that government should require "workplace policies that assume that all workers have considerable domestic responsibilities." Let us assume that the responsibilities have to do with child rearing and caring for infirm family members, and that the policies might include paid time off, special consideration concerning promotions (such as delayed tenure clocks in universities), and other kinds of flexibility.

Any blanket imposition of such requirements on employers comes with three potential costs: it reduces the autonomy of firms; it fails to help those working outside the money economy, or the unemployed, with their domestic responsibilities; and it might well give windfall benefits to workers who do lack significant domestic responsibilities.[28] Such considerations suggest that, ceteris paribus, it might arguably be better not to burden the employment relationship with the costs of the family-friendly policies, but from the perspective of democratic justice this is legitimate only if exit costs from employment are low. As those costs increase, the blunt instrument of such a requirement becomes easier to justify in order to prevent employers from taking advantage of employee vulnerability. But I argue that it would be better to incorporate the family-friendly policies into the social wage by means of public subsidies for child rearing (whether in the form of refundable tax credits or in some other form of payment to parents).[29] As for time off for caring for infirm family members, this, too, could be built into the social wage indirectly: by state compensation to employers who grant workers paid time off for family emergencies.

Pressuring employers (in wage negotiations or arbitration settings, or even by pressing for regulations) to provide family-friendly policies is a second-best solution that should be supported in the contemporary United States partly for the reason already noted: that the relative dearth of compensation for such domestic work has adverse affects on power relations within firms. Such pressure is desirable also because it supplies firms with incentives to support moves toward the more desirable expanded social wage approach. In contexts where it can be institutionalized, my sliding quantum rule (which links mandatory protections for workers within the

---

[28] Perhaps the family-friendly policies could be tailored to avoid this last difficulty, as in the Family and Medical Leave Act of 1993. See http://www.dol.gov/dol/esa/public/regs/statutes/whd/fmla.htm [06-07-2002]. But that is not the kind of universal benefit Young calls for, perhaps out of the worry that eligibility requirements themselves constitute an exercise of what she thinks of as "structural" power.

[29] See *Democratic Justice*, pp. 107–8.

firm to the exit costs they face) makes this incentive explicit.[30] With these caveats I agree with Young's substantive suggestion about family-friendly employment policies, but I remain unpersuaded that this stance reflects a different understanding of power relationships from that deployed in *Democratic Justice*.

ECONOMIC INEQUALITY

In "Enough Justice? Enough Democracy?"[31] James Fishkin contends that I should have had more to say about inequality. According to him, by insisting only on a fairly rudimentary minimum with respect to the economic dimension of basic interests, my argument could legitimate substantial inequalities. He expresses concern that "the apparently democratic resolution of . . . non-basic interests either seems to pose a severe injustice or to constitute a seriously defective democratic process."[32]

These issues will be taken up more fully in *Democracy and Distribution*, but two responses are in order here. The first is that inequalities of income and wealth are not necessarily objectionable in and of themselves, but rather because of the ways in which they play into power relationships. Thus I argued in chapters 4 and 6 of *Democratic Justice* that the state should be less concerned to regulate the structure of inequality in domestic and working life when there is a robust social wage than when there is not. Inequalities matter more when there is no social wage because its absence enables those with resources to exert power over those lacking resources, to take advantage of their necessity, as Locke would have put it. As the social wage grows, our concern with economic inequality on this score reasonably diminishes—though there remain many other reasons to be concerned about it. One that I mentioned concerns the role of money in producing differences in influence over the political process. Inequality fosters domination if some interests—those of the

---

[30] The sliding quantum rule links the intrusiveness of regulation of firms to the location of the employment relationship on a continuum from a Dickensian nightmare, where there is no social wage, to a surfer's paradise—where it is robust. (The term *surfer's paradise* is adopted in deference to Philippe van Parijs's argument that the highest sustainable social wage should be paid to everyone—even full-time surfers.) See *Democratic Justice*, pp. 184–87.

[31] James Fishkin, "Enough Justice? Enough Democracy? A Comment on Shapiro's *Democratic Justice*," *The Good Society* 11, no. 2 (2002): 65–69.

[32] Ibid., p. 71. Fishkin contends that democratic justice can legitimize major economic inequalities by requiring that only basic interests need to be secured for all, while allowing the relevant demos to decide how to adjudicate nonbasic interests. He also questions democratic justice's capacity to avoid major inequalities in opportunity, given that collective decisions can perpetuate systematic inequalities, for example by impeding social mobility.

relatively wealthy, for instance—undermine the meaningful participation of others. Fishkin and I are agreed that this "outer constraint"[33] needs supplementing (even though it is flagrantly violated by the *Buckley v. Valeo* regime we currently live under).[34] In many other areas of social life ranging from education, to the provision of health insurance, to resources for the elderly, my argument in *Democratic Justice* made it clear that substantial redistribution from the present status quo in the contemporary United States is needed if the basic interests of the population are to be adequately secured.[35]

A second answer to Fishkin is this. One motivating conviction behind my approach in *Democratic Justice* is that, rather than develop general defenses of egalitarian redistribution, it makes better intellectual and political sense to take on particular inequalities at the point of their impact on the power dimensions of human interaction. It makes better intellectual sense because some inequalities are legitimate, to wit, those that do not foster unjustified exclusion or domination yet promote other desirable outcomes. It makes better political sense because, however many theorists of distributive justice might agree with one another that all inequalities are morally arbitrary, much of the rest of the world persists in maintaining a decidedly deaf ear to this proposition.

When a view that seems intellectually unassailable fails to move people, then it stands in need of rethinking. Opposing demonstrable domination and unjustified exclusion in particular seems to me a better bet than hurling all-encompassing egalitarian arguments into the political void. Among their other defects, these arguments have the demerit of turning the best into the enemy of the good. More than fifty million people in the United States, and some four billion in the rest of the world, live in conditions in which the economic dimensions of their basic interests are either violated or in serious jeopardy of being violated. Were we to approach a state of affairs in which this was no longer true, then I might

[33] Ibid., p. 74. Fishkin questions whether this constraint for inequalities in political power that stem from economic inequalities is too loose. He argues that "there are many forms of distorted political communication that fall short of the extreme result of 'obliterating the participation of others.'" I agree that these are serious problems, but, for reasons elaborated in the text below, am not persuaded that he offers better solutions to them than those described in *Democratic Justice*.

[34] *Buckley v. Valeo*, 424 U.S. 1 (1976), was the decision in which the Supreme Court equated money with speech, rendering the regulation of political expenditures for all practical purposes impossible.

[35] Indeed on the health front, much recent research suggests that reductions in relative inequalities may be important from the standpoint of securing the basic health interests of the poor. There is now considerable evidence suggesting that the level of inequality within societies has a greater impact on their health prospects and longevity than does per capita income or even the availability of medical treatment. See Richard Wilkinson, *Mind The Gap: Hierarchies, Health, and Human Evolution* (New Haven: Yale University Press, 2001).

agree with Fishkin that other economic inequalities should be tackled. Given where we actually are, rejecting an approach that argues for securing basic interests calls to mind those white South Africans who greeted calls for apartheid's abolition in the 1970s and 1980s with the question: why aren't you objecting to racism in the United States?

It should also be noted that Fishkin nowhere specifies how much of a reduction in economic inequality, or how much of an increase in equality of opportunity, he himself favors, or how he thinks this should be achieved. I am skeptical of his panacea of deliberative polls, randomly selected groups of citizens who are asked to debate issues after hearing from various experts. Fishkin says that deliberative polls are designed to promote "thoughtful and informed preferences."[36] He alleges their virtue to be that they produce people who are "more public spirited" and less self-interested, and he contends that the process of deliberative polling will "offer promise . . . to uncover a form of democracy that will also promote justice."

Decentralized deliberation of the sort Fishkin advocates offers some advantages, as I noted in Democratic Justice,[37] but it is a stretch, to put it mildly, to assert that this will lead to reductions in inequalities in income or opportunities, or to better protection of basic interests. Certainly Fishkin supplies no evidence in support of his assertion that although "deliberative preferences do not, by themselves, ensure justice, they offer more hope of doing so." This strikes me as the kind of wishful thinking that informed Thurgood Marshall's insistence, in Furman v. Georgia, that if only Americans understood what was actually involved in administering the death penalty, they would likely oppose it.[38] Instead of this Pollyannaish commitment to the idea that progressive redistribution would be advanced by the promotion of deliberation, I am inclined to think that the better path is figuring out how to put together coalitions that will have an interest in framing the issue so as to garner public support for progressive redistribution.

DELIBERATIVE DEMOCRACY

Fishkin's claim about inequality and deliberation flows from his larger contention that I give short shrift to the benefits of deliberative democracy. In a critique of my subsequent book, The State of Democratic Theory, Fishkin makes heavy weather of the fact that his defense of deliberation

---

[36] Fishkin, "Enough Justice?" p. 74.

[37] Democratic Justice, pp. 50–51.

[38] See Furman v. Georgia, 408 U.S. 238, at 360–69. See also Marshall's dissent in Gregg v. Georgia, 428 US 153 (1976).

differs from those, like Habermas's, that prize deliberation for its alleged propensity to produce consensus.[39] The implication is that my criticisms of deliberation are irrelevant to Fishkin's case for its desirability. Yet one of Fishkin's principal defenses of deliberation is that it allegedly reduces dissensus enough so as to increase the likelihood of single-peaked preferences, which "makes democracy more collectively consistent and more meaningful."[40] But why should we care whether democracy is collectively consistent or not?

Fishkin seems perplexed by my assessment of the literature on Kenneth Arrow's apparent victory over Rousseau. Arrow's theorem raised the possibility that there might be no such thing as a general will in society— or that, if there is, the standard methods of democratic decision making cannot be relied upon to identify it. My view is straightforward. Some recent literature that I discuss in the first chapter of *The State of Democratic Theory* suggests that the actual likelihood of voting cycles is lower than the early literature by Bill Riker and others had contended, unmasking as overblown—on their own terms—the widely trumpeted claims of early public choice theorists about democracy's alleged irrationality. On my account, this debate, while of some academic interest, is tangential to democracy's legitimacy in the real world. This turns not on whether democracy can operate to produce coherent social welfare functions that reflect majority opinion, but rather on whether it can operate to reduce domination by bringing decision making into better conformity with the interests of those who are vitally affected by it.

Taking Fishkin at his word that consensus is not of any intrinsic importance, what is the underlying purpose of democracy on his account? He answers this indirectly, with a series of rhetorical questions. "Do we want to listen to the public when they are confused, uninformed, inattentive? Or when they have a chance to think about the issues, weigh competing sides and become more informed?" The "basic" choice, he tells us, is between deliberative democracy and *"unthinking"* (his emphasis) democracy.[41] Fishkin supplies no reasons for his thoughtfulness requirement, prompting the query by what authority he thinks himself qualified to declare when people are sufficiently well-informed that "we" should be obliged to listen to them. "We" in the United States do have requirements like compulsory education to age sixteen whose partial justification is that voters here should be literate and informed up to some

---

[39] *The State of Democratic Theory*; James Fishkin, "Defending Deliberation: A Comment on Ian Shapiro's The State of Democratic Theory," *Critical Review of International Social and Political Philosophy* 8, no. 1 (March 2005): 71–78.

[40] Fishkin, "Defending Deliberation." A person's preferences are single-peaked when she prefers points that are closer to her ideal point over those that are more distant from it.

[41] Ibid., pp. 71–78.

threshold. Fishkin's rhetorical questions might suggest a case for beefing up these requirements, or perhaps even for an educational qualification for the franchise. However, the staying power of William F. Buckley's forty-year-old aphorism to the effect that he would rather be governed by the first two thousand names in the Boston phone book than by the Harvard faculty is salutary in this regard. Despite the pleadings of Mill and others since the possibility of universal franchise became real in the mid-nineteenth century, proposals for educational qualifications and for weighting the role of the educated (Mill wanted to give additional votes to university graduates) have been stillborn. Indeed, the near-universal legitimacy of the secret ballot in democracies is testimony to the widespread acceptance of the notion that ill-informed opinions count equally with well-informed ones. In democratic politics voters are not obliged to justify their opinions to others.

There is, indeed, literature that dates at least back to Rousseau suggesting that people make better decisions when they do not deliberate. Judges at many sporting events are prohibited from conferring lest they contaminate one another's assessments. The dangers of "groupthink" were eloquently explored in the 9/11 commission report.[42] The apparently ignorant masses often make better judgments than the "informed" few. This is famously the case with markets for predicting election outcomes, which regularly outperform pundits and sophisticated pollsters. The same appears to be true in a host of other settings that have recently been discussed by James Surowiecki.[43] There is considerable evidence that when people deemed by someone (leaving aside, for now, who does the deeming) to be experts "inform" mass opinion, they can influence it. Whether they improve it is quite another matter.

Part of the reason for this is the great difficulty of distinguishing mechanisms that produce better-informed opinions from those that produce differently informed ones. As the social psychology literature on framing effects suggests, full information is available to no one—even in principle. People can keep only a comparatively small number of ideas in mind at any time, with the result that which these are becomes critically important in shaping their attitudes toward political choices. The decisions people make are definitively shaped by the contexts within which they are presented, including the relevant alternatives.[44] Widespread American public support for abolishing estate taxes, which Fishkin mentions, is a

[42] See *The 9/11 Commission Report: Final Report of the National Commission on Terrorist Attacks upon the United States* (New York: Norton, 2004).

[43] James Surowiecki, *The Wisdom of Crowds: Why the Many Are Smarter than the Few and How Collective Wisdom Shapes Business, Economics, Societies, and Nations* (New York: Doubleday, 2004).

[44] For extensive discussion, see *The State of Democratic Theory*, pp. 128–33.

case in point. Close study reveals that there is less mystery about this subject than meets the eye, as was noted in chapter 6 of this volume. The contours of public opinion about the estate taxes are well understood by pollsters and political consultants. When the tax is polled as a stand-alone issue, around two-thirds of Americans think it is an unfair tax that should be abolished. The number goes up slightly if it is described as the "death tax," and it goes down somewhat (to about half the population) once it is explained to people how unlikely it is that they will be among the 2 percent of the taxpayers who actually pay it. However, once the intensity of people's preferences is factored in, abolishing estate taxes turns out to be an important priority for a tiny percentage of voters. When the estate tax is polled as a comparative issue (i.e., compared with possible cuts in income taxes, social security taxes, or capital gains taxes, or with getting rid of the "marriage penalty"), support for it quickly evaporates. Support also disappears if abolishing the estate tax is paired with specific cuts in popular expenditures (such as prescription drug benefits) that would accompany it.

The political groups seeking to abolish the estate tax took brilliant advantage of the running room created by these realities in order to sustain support for abolishing the estate tax as part of President Bush's 2001 tax cut. As described in chapter 6, they flooded the media with the results of stand-alone polls on the desirability of abolishing the estate tax, while the opposition, lacking resources and in any case asleep at the switch, failed to counter this with results reflecting the low relative and comparative support. The pro-repeal forces were successful because they dominated the way in which the issue was framed by the media. The problem was not lack of deliberation. It was lack of effective organization and resources on the antirepeal side, aided and abetted by a gullible media. The press uncritically reported polling by the pro-repeal forces and even mimicked their stand-alone polls rather than conduct independent polls that would have more fully exhibited the true contours of public opinion on this subject. The same was true of nonpartisan pollsters like Zogby.

Fishkin tries to reassure us that agenda-setters in his orchestrated "deliberative polls," in which randomly selected groups debate issues after being informed by "experts" who have been chosen to ensure "balance," will not bias the results. He speaks about "advisory groups including all the major stakeholder groups" who must "agree on the briefing materials, the questionnaire, the agenda of experts" to be put in front of the voters who then engage in the orchestrated deliberative poll. But this just shifts the dilemma one step further back. Who gets to decide, by what criteria, who the major stakeholders are? There is surely as much potential to load the dice—whether consciously or inadvertently—in deciding who counts as a relevant stakeholder as there is in deciding which experts can present sufficiently balanced views to the assembled deliberators.

If by stakeholders Fishkin means those who have a significant stake in the outcome of a decision, in today's world these are often neither citizens nor even residents of a country in which a decision is being made. If Fishkin wants American voters who are deliberating about, say, pharmaceutical, environmental, or labor regulations in the United States to hear from all the relevant stakeholders, will he ensure that they hear from sub-Saharan AIDS sufferers, residents of Bhopal, or Malaysian workers? If so, how will they be selected, and by whom? These examples need only be mentioned to make it evident that an enormous amount of what affects the outcome of a deliberative process is embedded in prior decisions about who is a relevant stakeholder. Fishkin might be inclined to respond that I do not offer an account of who a relevant stakeholder is either. But that is a non sequitur in the present context. (It is, in any case untrue. A good deal of my discussion and defense of the principle of affected interest in recent writings is devoted to how affected interests should be determined in particular settings, and, given that this will always be controversial, what mechanisms should exist to challenge prevailing determinations of them.)[45] The question presently at issue is whether Fishkin's method of determining who is a stakeholder confers legitimacy on the process. Like the programmers of the Fox cable channel, Fishkin might be passionately convinced that he can construct a "fair and balanced" deliberative process. Others are bound to remain skeptical.

The deliberative ideal garners its appeal from a reciprocal model of political discussion—which is why such advocates of deliberation as Amy Gutmann and Dennis Thompson define deliberation by reference to reciprocity.[46] The animating impulse seems to be that well-informed citizens who deliberate in good faith will converge on better policies, so that the institutional design challenge for democratic theorists is to come up with appropriately orchestrated settings to encourage this. Bruce Ackerman and Fishkin's "deliberation day"—a national day of deliberating modeled on his deliberative polls, where citizens would be paid $150 to show up at their local school to deliberate the week before presidential elections—is one such device.

My skepticism of orchestrated processes of this kind leads me to prefer competition to deliberation as a mechanism for keeping democracy honest. Its core ideal is argument, not discussion. Its animating impulse is the robust conflict of ideas about which Mill wrote so eloquently in the sec-

---

[45] See *Democratic Justice*, chaps. 3–7, and *The State of Democratic Theory*, pp. 52–55.

[46] Amy Gutmann and Dennis Thompson, *Democracy and Disagreement* (Cambridge, MA: Harvard University Press, 1996). For extended discussion of their theory of deliberation, see *The State of Democratic Theory*, pp. 22–32.

ond chapter of *On Liberty*. In *The State of Democratic Theory* I made the case that the competition Mill advocated is poorly institutionalized in most democratic systems, and particularly so in the United States, and I proposed a variety of reforms geared to strengthening opposition so as to facilitate more meaningful political argument than we actually see. These reforms have to do with breaking up the two-party duopoly, public financing of elections, diminishing the costs to entry of third parties, and strengthening the hand of weaker groups in democratic systems. If we were going to spend $15 billion a year on improving the quality of American democracy (the cost to the treasury Ackerman and Fishkin estimate for their own proposal), these all strike me as better ways to go than to organize an afternoon of deliberation once candidates have been selected, platforms chosen, interest groups deployed, and campaign funds expended in our current electoral process. Perhaps there are ultimately some imponderables of judgment here, but for me the Ackerman-Fishkin proposal fails the smell test as an appropriately proportionate response to the problem.

In chapter 2 of *The State of Democratic Theory* I explored the conditions under which fostering deliberation is, and is not, desirable from the standpoint of reducing domination—my yardstick for democratic legitimacy. It would be indulgent to repeat those arguments here. In a nutshell, my account involves empowering those who are at risk for domination in any situation to insist on various types of deliberative processes. But I argue that it is unwise to put deliberative processes into the hands of those who can use them to engage in or perpetuate domination. "What we need is a committee to examine this" is a tried-and-true measure for dissipating organized opposition and stalling change. My worry about Fishkin's embrace of deliberation is its indiscriminate character. It calls to mind the George W. Bush administration's approach to fiscal policy. No matter what the problem—a surplus, a deficit, a strong dollar, a weak dollar, a recession—the solution was always said to be a tax cut. At some point one was bound to wonder whether the proffered solution had anything to do with the problem at hand.

PUBLIC INSTITUTIONS

In her critique, Rosenblum also faults me for my relative inattention to public institutions.[47] In particular, she complains that I underplay government's capacity for domination. It is true that I did not engage in the kind of systematic analysis of American public institutions that I did of the civil institutions structuring the human life cycle in *Democratic Justice*. I have

---

[47] Rosenblum, "*Democratic Justice* 'all the way down.'"

begun remedying that deficiency in this book and will take the task up more systematically in volume 3 of *Democratic Justice*. However, I did have a good deal to say in volume 1 about public institutions—both in developing the general argument for democratic justice and in the course of my application of it through the life cycle. Rosenblum's and my differences seem to come down to my skepticism of her impulse to focus on governments as the primary, if not exclusive, source of domination in the world. Governments were the most consequential agents of domination in the totalitarian states that prevailed in Europe during the middle third of the twentieth century, in Saddam Hussein's Iraq, and in Burma and North Korea today. But in nontotalitarian systems of the kind explored in *Democratic Justice* (and especially in the United States where conservatives rail reflexively and endlessly against the state), governments are not typically the main source of domination in people's lives, and often governments can be instrumental in its amelioration. This is all the more notable in view of the massively interventionist role played by Western governments in propping up financial markets during the 2008–9 financial meltdown.

This is not to deny that governments can foster domination in capitalist democracies. Indeed, many of my particular arguments about institutional redesign in *Democratic Justice* are intended to forestall, or at least limit, that possibility. For instance, in my discussion of population policy I argued that, although governments may legitimately aspire to limit population growth to numbers whose basic interests they can reasonably expect to be able to underwrite, they may not legitimately adopt policies in pursuit of this goal that involve state domination over women—such as forced sterilization or abortion.[48] Other examples include the limits on governmental power built into the divided authority regime over children that I propose (particularly with respect to power asymmetries between parents and public officials),[49] and my discussion of the logic of "ratcheting up" in the development of life-extending technologies, which makes it a good deal easier for government to extend human life than to limit it.[50] In sum, it is fair to say that I do not offer a full-blown analysis of

[48] Fortunately there are noncoercive measures such as reducing poverty, increasing women's education, and otherwise enhancing women's opportunities for participation in the labor force—all of which predictably reduce fertility rates. See *Democratic Justice*, pp. 94–96.

[49] I argue that the best way to protect children's basic interests is via a regime that divides authority between parents and the state, where parents have ultimate fiduciary responsibility for children's best interests and the state has ultimate fiduciary authority for their basic interests. I defend institutional safeguards through which parents and the state can check one another's authority, safeguards that take account of, and compensate for, their relative power disparities. See *Democratic Justice*, pp. 81–84.

[50] My contention is that although governments are not obliged to seek policies that may extend human life, once such policies are adopted they should be difficult to reverse because

governmental institutions here, but it is misleading to imply that I ignore their limitations from the standpoint of promoting democratic justice within civil institutions.

It should be noted, in conclusion, that although my discussion of public institutions will be more fully elaborated in volume 3 of *Democratic Justice*, I no more aspire to offer a general theory of governmental institutions than I aspired to develop general theories of child rearing, adult domestic life, work, or arrangements concerning the final phases of life in volume 1. My general argument is that we should promote inclusive participation in decision making and avenues for effective opposition wherever power is exercised in human affairs, but always in ways that involve as little interference as possible with the rest of human activity. What this means for particular walks of life depends on how the path dependencies of inherited institutions shape present and future possibilities. The emphasis is on institutional redesign, not tabula rasa design, on rebuilding the ship at sea. Hence the description of democratic justice as involving a tempered Burkean outlook—tempered not as Rosenblum thinks it should be, but rather to promote the democratization of power relations as they are reproduced into the future.[51] Naturally this means that the institutional reforms democratic justice recommends for the contemporary United States will likely differ from those that make sense for the United Kingdom, South Africa, or India—given their varying inherited institutions and prevailing political possibilities.

---

the threat of such reversal creates a variety of moral hazards and possibilities for domination. See *Democratic Justice*, pp. 209–10.

[51] Ibid., pp. 36–40.

Surveys of Israeli Business Elites

In December 2003–February 2004, we conducted a survey of 25 Israeli business elites. A Jewish Israeli citizen administered the survey through face-to-face interviews with top executives. They were chosen in a stratified sample to include large enterprises in a range of economic sectors: investment banking and holdings, venture capital, insurance, advertising, media and communications, energy, airlines, industrial manufacturing, and technology. The businesses varied in labor insensitivity: 12 had fewer than 50 employees; 5 had 50–100 employees; 3 had 101–500 employees; and 5 had more than 500 employees, with the largest business employing 15,000 workers. Few of the companies (only 2 of 17 respondents answering this question) had employed Palestinian workers in the past decade, with only one of these enterprises continuing to do so today. The enterprises varied as well in the nature of production, with 14 respondents targeting the domestic market and 7 engaged in export production.

A range of executives were interviewed. All had deep knowledge of and vested interests in their company, with respondents including business owners, CEOs, vice presidents, and directors of sales and marketing. They came from a range of political backgrounds: 3 defined their political affiliations as right-wing; 4 were from the middle/center, 9 from the left, 1 from the midleft, and 1 self-described as "Democrat neutral"; 6 failed to identify themselves.

The data from questions reported here:

3. (When you first learned of the Oslo negotiations), would you say that your attitude toward the proposed settlement was

a. Very favorable	b. Somewhat favorable	c. Neutral	d. Somewhat unfavorable	e. Very unfavorable
10	8	4	1	1

4. At that time, how optimistic were you that the settlement would be achieved?

a. Very optimistic	b. Somewhat optimistic	c. Neutral	d. Somewhat pessimistic	e. Very pessimistic
5	9	4	3	3

5. Do you think the Rabin assassination made the peace process

a. More likely to succeed	b. More likely to fail	c. Did not have an affect on the process
1	20	4

6. Was this immediately apparent to you when he was assassinated?

a. Yes	b. No
13	11

9. In particular, do you think that Peres made a strategic error in not calling for immediate elections after Rabin's assassination?

a. Yes	b. No	c. Don't know
15	3	7

10. Was it clear to you that Peres's strategy before the May 1996 elections made peace

a. More likely	b. Less likely	c. Did not have an affect on the process
2	9	12

16. At what point over the past two decades do you think a settlement could most easily have been reached and implemented?

a. Before the Oslo Agreement	b. When Rabin was prime minister	c. When Peres was acting prime	d. When Netanyahu was prime minister	e. When Barak was prime minister	f. When Sharon was prime minister	g. Other (please specify)
12	1		2	2		3

19. How important do you think that concluding the peace process is to your own business prospects?

a. Of major importance	b. Somewhat important	c. Not important at all
20	4	

20. Specifically, how would concluding the process affect your business?

a. Have a positive effect	b. Have a negative effect	c. No effect
22	1	1

26. Do you think that the peace process is a major concern for other business elites as well?

a. No	b. Yes
2	20

Polls on the Repeal or the Fairness of the Estate Tax

The following polls are the basis for figures 6.2 and 6.4. These poll sponsors released national polling data, from 1997 through the end of 2003, in which respondents were asked to evaluate the repeal or the fairness of the estate tax. Data sources include the publications and press releases of the polling organizations and the Roper Center for Public Opinion Research at the University of Connecticut.

Pollster / Poll Sponsor	Poll Completion Dates
Poll Sponsor Is Politically Neutral	
Bloomberg	Mar-01
CBS News & New York Times	Mar-01, Nov-02
Gallup / CNN & USA Today	Jun-00, Feb-01, Nov-02
International Communications Research / NPR & Kaiser & Kennedy School	Mar-03
Opinion Dynamics / Fox News	Jan-03
Pew Research Center for the People & the Press	Sep-98, Sep-00
Rasmussen Research Portrait of America Poll	Jul-00
Zogby International	Feb-98, Aug-99, Oct-00, Dec-00
Poll Sponsor Is Democratic or Opposed to Estate Tax Repeal	
Emily's List	Dec-99
Greenberg Quinlan Rosner Research / OMB Watch	May-02
Penn Schoen Berland / Democratic Leadership Council	Feb-01
Poll Sponsor Is Republican or Advocates Estate Tax Repeal	
Luntz Research Companies	Aug-98, Jan-03
Market Strategies / Republican National Committee	Sep-99
McLaughlin & Assoc / Americans Against Unfair Family Taxation	Jun-99, Jul-99, Jan-00, Sep-00, Jan-01, May-01
Tarrance Group with Lake, Snell Perry / Food Marketing Institute	Nov-00
Wirthlin Worldwide	Aug-99

Index